SPORT SKILL ACQUISITION

Integrating Theory and Practice

Dave Collins, PhD

Jamie Taylor, PhD

Editors

Library of Congress Cataloging-in-Publication Data

Names: Collins, Dave (Sports psychologist), editor. | Taylor, Jamie, 1987- editor.

Title: Sport skill acquisition : integrating theory and practice / Dave Collins, Jamie Taylor, editors.

Description: Champaign, IL : Human Kinetics, 2026. | Includes bibliographical references and index.

Identifiers: LCCN 2024036502 (print) | LCCN 2024036503 (ebook) | ISBN 9781718225794 (paperback) | ISBN 9781718225800 (epub) | ISBN 9781718225817 (pdf)

Subjects: LCSH: Athletic ability. | Sports--Psychological aspects.

Classification: LCC GV436 .S667 2026 (print) | LCC GV436 (ebook) | DDC 613.7/1--dc23/eng/20241022

LC record available at https://lccn.loc.gov/2024036502

LC ebook record available at https://lccn.loc.gov/2024036503

ISBN: 978-1-7182-2579-4 (print)

Copyright © 2026 by Dave Collins and L&A Performance Ltd.

Human Kinetics supports copyright. Copyright fuels scientific and artistic endeavor, encourages authors to create new works, and promotes free speech. Thank you for buying an authorized edition of this work and for complying with copyright laws by not reproducing, scanning, or distributing any part of it in any form without written permission from the publisher. You are supporting authors and allowing Human Kinetics to continue to publish works that increase the knowledge, enhance the performance, and improve the lives of people all over the world.

To report suspected copyright infringement of content published by Human Kinetics, contact us at **permissions@hkusa.com**. To request permission to legally reuse content published by Human Kinetics, please refer to the information at **https://US.HumanKinetics.com/pages/permissions-translations-faqs**.

The web addresses cited in this text were current as of July 2024, unless otherwise noted.

Acquisitions Editor: Diana Vincer; **Developmental Editor:** Melissa Feld; **Managing Editor:** Melissa J. Zavala; **Copyeditor:** Marissa Wold Uhrina; **Proofreader:** Deborah A. Ring; **Indexer:** Andrea J. Hepner; **Permissions Manager:** Laurel Mitchell; **Graphic Designer:** Joe Buck; **Cover Designer:** Keri Evans; **Cover Design Specialist:** Susan Rothermel Allen; **Photograph (cover):** CHARLY TRIBALLEAU/AFP via Getty Images; **Photographs (interior):** © Human Kinetics, unless otherwise noted; **Photo Asset Manager:** Laura Fitch; **Photo Production Manager:** Jason Allen; **Senior Art Manager:** Kelly Hendren; **Illustrations:** © Human Kinetics, unless otherwise noted; **Printer:** Color House Graphics, Inc.

Printed in the United States of America

10 9 8 7 6 5 4 3 2 1

The paper in this book is certified under a sustainable forestry program.

Human Kinetics
1607 N. Market Street
Champaign, IL 61820
USA

United States and International
Website: **US.HumanKinetics.com**
Email: info@hkusa.com
Phone: 1-800-747-4457

Canada
Website: **Canada.HumanKinetics.com**
Email: info@hkcanada.com

E9296

For Joe, Judy, Rosie, Ruby, and Lily, my growing team of performance scientists, and Helen, my live-in nutritionist!

—Dave Collins

For Amy, Annabelle, and Lydia. Thank you for putting up with me. I love you all.

—Jamie Taylor

CONTENTS

Preface ix

Introduction 1

The *It Depends* Approach: Informed Decision Making Based on
Contextual Needs 1

Professional Judgment and Decision Making: Explaining the Why in
It Depends 2

It Depends in Practice: A Well-Founded Example 3

What to Expect From This Book and How to Use It 4

The Conditionality of Coaching 4

Pedagogic Applications 6

Part I Controlling Movement

1 Underpinning Theories and Consequent Approaches: What Do We Want and Need From a Model? 15

Dave Collins and Jamie Taylor

A Historical Approach 17

Approach 1: The Cognitive or Information-Processing Approach 17

Approach 2: The Ecological Dynamics Approach 21

Approach 3: The Predictive Processing Approach 25

2 Challenges of Cognitive, Ecological, and Predictive Processing Approaches 31

Howie J. Carson and Jamie Taylor

Evaluating Approaches: Considering Limitations 31

Common Differences Among Approaches and Practice 39

Potential Solutions: A Multifaceted Approach 40

v

vi Contents

3 Sifting the Useful From the Useless: A Case for Criticality in Coaching 43
Loel Collins and Ray Bobrownicki

The Performance Environment 44

The Nature of Expertise as Adaptive Expertise 45

Being a Critical Consumer: Responding to Environmental and Situational Demands 47

Practical Implications: A Micro, Meso, and Macro Challenge 52

Part II Learning Movement

4 An Either-Or Perspective on Applying the Theoretical Approaches: Where Have They Come From, and How Valid Are They? 59
Howie J. Carson

Understanding the Origins of the Either-Or Debate Between Skill-Acquisition Approaches 60

Solving the Either-Or Problem 61

Which Approach Applies Where and Why? 69

Applying Single Approaches 69

5 Blending Approaches 73
Michael Ashford and Jamie Taylor

A Pragmatic Take on Performer Centeredness 74

Blending Approaches: The Conditionality of Coaching Approach 75

What We Mean by Coaching Methods 76

6 Performer Experience: Challenge and Fidelity 87
Jamie Taylor and Michael Ashford

Performer Curriculum 88

Backward and Forward Planning 88

Explore-Test Continuum 90

The Role of Challenge for Performers 92

Performance Safety 94

Challenge at the Meso Level 94

Fidelity of Practice: How Is the Performer Being Challenged? 95

7 The Special Case of High-Level and Experienced Performers 101

Dave Collins

Particular Aspects of Skill for Elites 102

Execution Under Pressure 107

Optimizing Support for High-Level Performers 108

Part III Performing Movement

8 Mental Skills 115

Rosie Collins

The Evolution of Mental Skills for Sport and Physical Activity 115

Application of Mental Skills 117

Exemplar Mental Skills 118

Mental Skills in Action: Combining Mental Skills for Optimal Impact 126

9 Athlete Management 129

Andrew Cruickshank

Executing Movement During Performance: A MAP Perspective 130

Why Managing Athletes in the Preperformance Phase Is Different and Difficult 131

Athlete Management in the Preperformance Phase: Key Principles and Considerations 133

10 Planning and Leadership Systems 143

Michael Ashford and Dave Collins

Nested Planning for Key Outcomes: Type 2 and Type 1 144

Components of Leadership 146

Group Dynamics 149

Part IV Team Movement

11 Psychosocial Dimensions: Integrating Movement and Psychological Considerations to Optimize Team Performance ... 157

Urvi Khasnis and Amy Price

Importance of Psychosocial Considerations in Team Performance ... 158

A Shared Understanding: Getting Performers and Coaches on the Same Page ... 161

The Essential Role of Metacognition for Team Performance ... 163

Methods for Developing SMMs ... 164

12 Team Management ... 171

Andrew Cruickshank

The Relevance of Team or Squad Culture and Its Management ... 172

Optimizing the Value of Specific Movement Outcomes and Processes ... 174

Manipulating Value: Coaching Tools ... 176

Epilogue ... 183

Underpinning Your Future Development: Next Steps, How to Take Them, and What to Look Out For ... 183

Jamie Taylor and Dave Collins

What to Focus On ... 184

How to Develop Yourself ... 184

And What Should Happen? ... 187

So What Are We Saying? ... 187

Glossary 189
References 193
Index 223
About the Editors 231
About the Contributors 233

PREFACE

Since the 1990s, sport science has seen an explosion in the volume of knowledge generation in skill acquisition and motor control. For the main consumers of this knowledge—sport and other physical activity coaches—this brings mixed blessings. More knowledge brings benefit but only if the knowledge is accurate and helpful (e.g., if it contributes to applied practice). From our perspective of pedagogy and andragogy (the sciences of how people learn, focused on children and adults, respectively) as the central pillars of coaching, more knowledge is a positive development. The same goes for parallel consumers of this knowledge, including teachers of physical education, students of sport science, strength and conditioning coaches, physiotherapy and athletic training professionals, and other domains based on the development and refinement of effective movement. In this text, we will use the blanket terms *coaches* and *coaching* to cover this broad spectrum. Basically, anyone who works to improve the physical performance of an individual or team or who is studying these topics as part of an academic endeavor may find this book useful.

There are downsides to this explosion as well, perhaps inevitably so, which relate to the lack of quality assurance and criticality in application. The point, as made throughout this text, however, is that much of this knowledge is conditional. That is, practical application is often at odds, or at least is tangential, with the epistemological basis of its generation. Or, in other words, it works well but often better in some contexts than others. As a simple example, methods developed and tested with adults may not work so well with children. In this regard, the educator Dylan Wiliam (2013, 16) pithily suggests, "Everything works somewhere, but nothing works everywhere" (2013, p. 16).

As such, a text that carefully and critically considers the burgeoning knowledge through a practical lens would seem both timely and appropriate. As we will emphasize throughout this book, practitioners need to know what should be done to best address the contexts in which they must work, as well as how and why (or why not). This type of approach walks straight into some of the debates that have characterized the field of education in recent years (e.g., differential perspectives on the extent to which more direct teaching methods and reproduction of teacher knowledge should be the primary modality of learning). The consequence is a long-standing debate between those pointing to the relative evidence bases for more direct and less direct pedagogic approaches (e.g., de Jong et al. 2023). This shows where an appropriate balance of both may be best.

> *Intelligent and educated people are less likely to learn from their mistakes or take advice from others. And when they do err, they are better able to build elaborate arguments to justify their reasoning, meaning that they become more and more dogmatic in their views. (Robson 2019, p. 12)*

Of course, this rather provocative quote precedes a carefully evidenced argument for us to improve our rationality quotient—in short, to carefully apply our baloney detection kit (Sagan 1995; see also Stoszkowski et al. 2020) when feeding from what is an unfortunately rather mixed menu, at least in terms of quality and application.

Other developments, or perhaps RE-developments, add to this call for consideration of critical conditionality. A returning focus to the diversity of individuals is also apparent—for example, Anderson and colleagues (2021) examined individual differences and offered an academic rendering of the old saying "different strokes for different folks." Such considerations implicitly require the practitioner to carefully consider the choice of approach they apply. We consider this in more detail within the early chapters, but for the moment, consider the double-whammy challenge of context and character, which just adds to the complications for the coach's decision making!

Reflecting these debates, this text offers a uniquely "pracademic" treatment, linking academic research to its application—that is, what works best in practice. This linkage of research and application can be seen in the form of a professional who straddles both academia and practical application and in the deliberate combination of theoretical knowledge and research skills with practical experience. It is this dual role that allows pracademics to bridge the gap between theory and practice, contributing to academic scholarship and practical implementation. A means of navigating research in practice is termed *professional judgment and decision making* (PJDM), which stresses the need to carefully consider the best approach for that particular context. Considering theoretical knowledge against the practical context as a balanced judgment makes optimal outcomes much more likely.

The knowledge presented in this book is carefully researched and critically considered, drawing from the three major theoretical perspectives that dominate the field: cognitive and information processing, ecological dynamics, and active inference and predictive processing. As such, it offers readers of every persuasion and purpose a useful resource; indeed, our text begins to discuss the practical implications of predictive processing, very much the new kid on the block that has, to date, largely only been available in theoretical treatments. In tandem, we offer you a considered insight into how the knowledge applies to practice—the pracademic treatment mentioned earlier. Whether you are a student of the area or a practitioner looking to improve work with performers, the content should help you make well-informed decisions on what applies where and which selections can be employed for optimal benefit.

As we hope to demonstrate through this text, these informed selections should be a nonbinary choice (Collins et al. 2022), a feature that has become rare as texts have increasingly nailed their colors to a specific theoretical mast. Our position is that this is a mistake that inevitably limits impact. In short, and as revisited throughout the book, careful blending of approaches offers the best way forward in most circumstances. As a more populist version of PJDM, we often refer to this as an *it depends* approach (Collins et al. 2022). A core feature of our argument is that these blends should be both methodological (perhaps less controversial) but also theoretical (more controversial). In both cases, though, we remain consistent in drawing a distinction between methodology and underpinning theory. We make a strong case that, in practice, one should not *dictate* the other. This does not mean that blends are used at every stage, however. Rather, as per the examples later in the book, it may well be that different theoretical perspectives offer different advantages at specific stages or for certain purposes.

In fact, this blended approach seems to reflect current practice. For example, an examination of the underpinning theoretical stances of high-level team sport coaches showed that coaches used theory depending on circumstance and flexibly based on the needs of their context and athletes (Moran, Taylor, and MacNamara 2024). Similarly, Brackley and colleagues' (2020) examination of high-level Australian swim coaches suggested the use of both, in their words, traditional and contemporary approaches (also called *cognitive* and *ecological approaches*). Of relevance to the precepts of the different theories (see chapters 1 and 2 for a more detailed consideration), the coaches seemed to be driven by the aim of developing a perfect technique. Brackley and associates speculated that their participants may have been encouraged toward new ideas by skill-acquisition specialists but that their traditional epistemology of perfect technique had remained untouched. Of particular interest, these authors felt comfortable with the application of new ideas but notably remained at odds with the idea of perfect technique. As stated earlier, it may be challenging, or even a false assumption, to accept practice while rejecting theory or vice versa. In short, trying to use techniques that are epistemologically opposed to targeted outcomes seems a rather odd choice.

The book is presented in four parts, distinct but, unsurprisingly, interlocking to offer a picture of integrated knowledge and skills. After an introduction to the essential *conditional* knowledge that underpins the book, part I, Controlling Movement, considers the three different theoretical approaches to skill acquisition. We present the three in chapter 1 before examining the disadvantages of each in chapter 2. Concluding this part, chapter 3 examines the essential, critical, and comprehensive approach that this variety of knowledge and skills necessitates.

Part II, Learning Movement, covers how these different approaches can be used separately (chapter 4) or in a blended form (chapter 5) before considering the wider ramifications of such an integrated approach. Part III, Performing Movement, and part IV, Team Movement, consider the wider elements of how the approaches are best applied. We examine the mental, organizational, planning and social aspects of skill, offering practical guidance on how skill can best be planned for, developed, executed, and integrated.

Whatever the genesis of this mixed picture, our text explores the rights and wrongs of this blended approach—in short, whether a blended approach is absurd or, as we will demonstrate, a logical decision, even if some practitioners do not yet know it. Finally, we take the opportunity to explore parallel considerations from other disciplines and subdisciplines that carry significant implications for the primary foci of coaching, skill acquisition, and refinement. Thus, chapters on mental skills, organizational structures, and systemic designs are used to offer support while we also consider the macro approaches of criticality, which readers can use to make sure that they stay current through further future study. We hope you enjoy this integrated but diverse offering.

INTRODUCTION

THE *IT DEPENDS* APPROACH: INFORMED DECISION MAKING BASED ON CONTEXTUAL NEEDS

Chapter Objectives

After studying this chapter, you should be able to do the following:

- Understand the advantages of the *it depends* approach to planning and execution in coaching and other skill development settings
- Briefly explain the professional judgment and decision making (PJDM) approach
- Describe the spectrum theory of teaching styles as an early example of the *it depends* approach
- Understand the basics of the cognitive, ecological, and four Es approaches
- Understand the aspects of conditionality: how apparently clear and explicit principles often only apply *some* of the time

As introduced in the preface, the *it depends* approach is built on the premise that each of the different theoretical approaches, which we explore in chapter 1, can make an important and unique contribution to learners' optimal development of skills and more experienced performers' refinement of skills. Following the introduction to the current big-three approaches of **cognitive**, **ecological dynamics (EcoD)**, and **predictive processing** in chapter 1, each chapter follows the same premise of optimizing experience through careful selection and

application. Our approach is usually to employ a blend of techniques drawn from this theory-based menu. Alternatively, one approach may confer specific advantages and be best at a particular age, stage of development, or type of skill challenge. For the moment, consider whether one would coach the same way in the following scenarios: a 14-year-old versus a 34-year-old, a three-week novice versus a three-year experienced athlete, or golf (a comparatively consistent skill, or *closed skill*) versus boxing (a more open skill because the number of possibilities for action, including the opponent, is much greater). These contrasting settings may push a coach toward one theoretical approach over another as offering the most suitable methods or, when the decision between options is closer, toward a blend of tools to best cater to the context.

This makes the selection between choices of theoretical underpinning or coaching tools, or design of blend, a primary concern for any user of skill-acquisition methodologies, whether a coach, student, or performer. Coach decision making is a topic acknowledged to be of growing importance. Indeed, models that break down the what, how, when, and to whom of the decision chain are now a common feature in educational and training courses (e.g., Abraham, Muir, and Morgan 2013). For us, however, although all are important, they miss the most crucial consideration: why (and why not) each particular approach or blend may be most appropriate.

PROFESSIONAL JUDGMENT AND DECISION MAKING: EXPLAINING THE WHY IN *IT DEPENDS*

In the preface, we started to build a case for research-informed practice that is built around the *it depends* approach. **Professional judgment and decision making (PJDM)** is an approach to applied practice promoting informed decision making based on contextual needs—in short, the conditional nature of knowledge and application. This is an idea that several authors, ourselves included, have recommended through various outlets, both peer-reviewed publications and on social media (even though the latter is a far from reliable source). Unfortunately, a few misunderstandings of this approach are apparent: First, PJDM unproblematically models coaching as being as simple as a series of deliberate decisions. This critique is mistaken in that rather than offering a model *of* coaching, PJDM instead aims to provide an approach *for* the coach or practitioner. In essence, rather than trying to represent the significant complexity of the coaching process, PJDM suggests a means by which coaches navigate this complexity. A second critique is that it presents an anything-goes approach. In contrast, and for clarity, PJDM requires deliberate, careful consideration: planning, deploying, then evaluating and refining the approach, along with the ability to deliberately adopt different theoretical frames to make sense of situations and mentally project outcomes. Notably, however, experience would suggest this to be the case for *all* informed and reflective practitioners since people started to question authority. In short, *it depends* is nothing new.

Importantly, the mere gainsaying of PJDM as "anything goes" is an unfair representation of the position. PJDM has the pragmatic notion of fallibility at its core, that no belief is immune to doubt. For the informed practitioner (and our aim for readers of this book), this doubt should extend to a consideration of why different theoretical framings are more or less suitable to the needs of a specific problem. Additionally, and reflecting our universal application of critical evaluation (see chapter 3), this also applies to posing the same questions about the PJDM approach that we suggest. After all, critical methods need to be applied both ways.

We explore more of this criticality in part II of the book. For the moment, note that this careful reasoning process is best made overt and expressed through the approach of PJDM. This is not always the case, however, because paralysis by analysis is a real and present danger for the overthinking practitioner (e.g., Wilding 2021), even if this tendency can be suppressed by all sorts of methods, including electrically. (Research by Luft and colleagues [2017] found that electrical current could temporarily inhibit a person's dorsolateral prefrontal cortex in order to allow creative solutions to problems.)

As later parts and chapters will demonstrate, the basis of PJDM is to explore what approach might best fit the context. As a direct result, practitioners are encouraged to think through how they adapt knowledge and experience, along with changing theoretical frames to optimally cater to their contexts. This idea has gained impact, with applications exploring its role in adaptive expertise in high-performance sport coaching (Taylor et al. 2023) as well as in a wide variety of fields, including coaching in adventure sports (e.g., Mees et al. 2020) and business (e.g., Berry 2021). Chapter 3 discusses these ideas of criticality and conditionality. A starting point for this book is that the practical application of knowledge needs to be both conditional and adaptive. This lies at the heart of our theory-based text and applied approach.

In tandem with the idea of conditional knowledge (*it depends*), we also promote the careful consideration of what might follow from a particular series of decisions. This necessitates another conditional term, the need for consequential consideration. If, as we will demonstrate, coaching decision making represents a chain of choice and actions, the well-informed practitioner must also work their way down the **epistemological chain** (cf. Grecic, MacNamara, and Collins 2013) of decisions, seeking to understand the outcome that may accrue from a particular choice on process or processes (e.g., Crowther et al. 2022). As described in the literature, stemming from their views on how people learn (their epistemology), coaches will make a series of choices on the design and execution of coaching practice. This should not be a linear and recipe-driven process, however, because good coaching (and good coach decision making) is based on a consideration of what each choice means for the eventual experience—in other words, the consequences for the learner.

IT DEPENDS IN PRACTICE: A WELL-FOUNDED EXAMPLE

Even at this early stage, it is important to state clearly, and demonstrate, that an *it depends* approach is not new at all. As one great example, consider Mosston and Ashworth's (2008) spectrum theory of teaching styles, which considers what style or approach the teacher (and coach) should select given the outcomes they want for the session. Figure I.1 shows how the choice of style from the spectrum is applied to the planning, execution, and evaluation of the session or coaching episode.

Originally developed in the 1960s, the idea has received much consideration and application in physical education. It has been revisited in a wider integration by SueSee, Hewitt, and Pill (2020), applying the same principles to coaching. The idea is elegant in its simplicity. Consider two contrasting activities with very different goals and outcomes: rappelling (abseiling) and creative dance. The first requires careful planning by the teacher to ensure safety (and avoid consequent paperwork if things go awry). Student decision making is at a minimum because there are relatively few safe options involved. In short, the teacher sets up an environment in which techniques are demonstrated and students follow, preferably as faithfully as possible. The creative dance class is almost the complete opposite. The teacher designs challenges to encourage creative and novel solutions, but after initiating the work, they mostly stand back and shape the outcomes. The level of decision making in the session is high

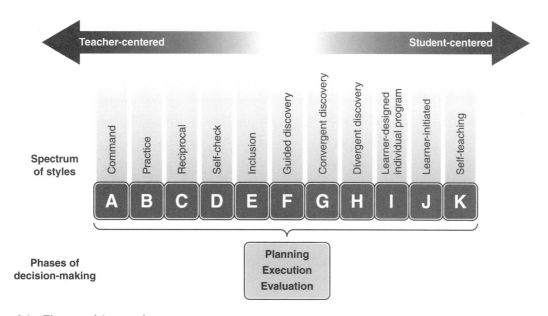

Figure I.1 The teaching styles spectrum.
Based on Mosston, Muska, and Ashworth (2008).

for the students and low for the teacher or coach, although the preplanning demands for the teacher are greater. The spectrum represents "a framework of options in the relationships between teacher and learner" (Mosston 1992, p. 56), requiring decision making as to what is the most appropriate approach.

We might consider the spectrum theory of teaching styles as a meso approach in that it is applied to the design of a session rather than an individual activity (micro) or series of sessions (macro). As we work through ideas in this book, it will become apparent that most, if not all, of the ideas can be applied at all levels: across planning, execution, *and* evaluation. Indeed, this more macro, meso, and micro application is reflected in the more recent reconceptualization of the approach for coaching by SueSee, Hewitt, and Pill (2020). In simple terms, as per example 1 later in this chapter, applications of different theoretical approaches tend to vary across the macro level but, importantly, not always.

WHAT TO EXPECT FROM THIS BOOK AND HOW TO USE IT

So far in this introductory chapter, we have stressed the conditionality of both knowledge and application. Additionally, however, the vital parallel is the need to explore and be able to present the formal justification for the options taken—in other words, the *why*. After all, gaining buy-in from an athlete is a big part of designing training for even the most physiologically driven coaches (Stone, Stone, and Sands 2007). As we will explore later in the book, athlete understanding (and the fullest exploitation of expectancy effects) is a relatively unexplored and underexploited facet of training design, although it offers significant potential (e.g., Lindberg et al. 2023). This principle of promoting and ensuring understanding will clearly apply across every aspect of the program.

Accordingly, each chapter presents a reasoned and balanced argument for the suggestions made. Furthermore, and reflecting the principles espoused previously, the nuances expressed should be exploited to optimize the design of any practice or program in the contexts faced. An almost inevitable consequence is that each context will be associated with several possible solutions and consequential chains of decision making. Note that as a part of this dynamic chain, the

practitioner's own personal characteristics will also play a part in the PJDM process. Part II of the book will explore these ideas, while parts III and IV will present some parallel concerns and issues for deploying them.

Our point here is that aspects of the coach or support provider will clearly influence the environmental dynamic, both directly through what they can effectively offer and indirectly based on the athlete's perceptions of them. Accordingly, effective **case conceptualization**, as psychologists refer to it (cf. Martindale and Collins 2013), which is simply what the practitioner plans to do and why, will fit with a careful consideration as to how all the moving parts (the many and varied factors that must be dynamically integrated) mesh together.

THE CONDITIONALITY OF COACHING

In this section we offer some examples of conditionality. To do this, we will quickly introduce two of the major theories of skill acquisition so that we can offer some contrasts. More careful and considered coverage is offered in the next chapter, and even more detail is offered throughout the book.

For the moment, it is worth reflecting on conditionality across scientific disciplines. For example, consider the wave-particle duality in physics, which sees both electrons and light as being both of these but differentially in certain contexts. Sometimes it is best to think of light as a wave, but sometimes it can be considered a set of particles called *photons*. The research suggesting this was conducted by the father-and-son team of J.J. and George Thompson, who both won the Nobel Prize but for these separate (and contrasting) discoveries. *It depends* is a feature of even the most apparently objective of studies.

An Example of Contrast: Cognitive Versus Ecological Approaches

Let us see how this conditionality may apply in two of the major theoretical perspectives in sport science. Both have been around for several decades now but also, and notably, both have their proponents as well as various (and varying) nuances. Both are supported by research but, as the next chapter discusses, there is a general lack of investigation that is genuinely comparative. This would enable clearer understanding of where each works best. Unfortunately, however, genuinely comparative work is lacking, and what exists is often somewhat flawed. Next we will briefly review the two approaches and what they suggest for practice.

Cognitive Systems Approach

The cognitive systems approach (see Thon [2015] for a brief overview) is often referred to pejoratively by some authors as the *traditional approach*. As the name suggests, it focuses on the development of a central representation of the skill to be learned. The brain is seen as both sorting hat and storage facility, with inputs from the different sensory systems sorted to create an accurate set of reproducible instructions, termed a *motor program*. In seminal work by Schmidt and colleagues (2018), this program also included a prediction of expected sensory consequences, against which the actual movement impacts can be compared. One pillar of the approach is the need to develop an optimally effective program (there is disagreement about whether this efficacy is due to or associated with the form or outcome) that can be consistently executed. Another is the idea of a generalized motor program (GMP) (see Schmidt et al. 2018), which can be used as the basis for transferring ideas from one technique to aid the development of another, or the adaptation of a movement to meet different challenges. This transfer is generally positive, although some aspects of one movement may impede another, especially if they are close but with differences. Think of a golf swing and a slap shot in hockey. General similarities will help, especially in the early stages of learning. Later on, however, the influences of one may be more negative. This is one example of where the applications of a theory can be conditional—it works here but not there. The cognitive systems approach emphasizes the importance of attention, memory, and reasoning, with understanding the movement cognitively seen as important for effective storage of the movements in memory.

Ecological Dynamics Approach

The ecological dynamics (EcoD) approach (Button et al. 2020) has historically been presented as methodologically contrasting with the cognitive approach, although more recent work in these two approaches shows an increasing tendency to overlap, especially in practical application, even if different terminology is used and contrasting processes are inferred. For example, in practical application, the group of methods falling under the label of direct instruction (which includes demonstration) are central to the cognitive approach but have often been questioned by EcoD practitioners as being overly constraining and limiting the learner's (essentially self-driven although often coach facilitated) search for their own optimal solution. Of late, these teaching and coaching tools have been internally accommodated somewhat, being termed *internal constraints*, albeit with much less emphasis than for cognitive approaches. More detail on these differences and other newer approaches appear in subsequent chapters. For the moment, however, the EcoD approach is best exemplified through the use of a constraints-led approach and the famous triangle diagram presented in figure I.2.

This sums up nicely the interaction between the individual, environment, and task that underpins the approach. As stated, learning in this model is a self-driven but coach-facilitated search for personal solutions to the challenge. Key pillars include that no one single perfect technical model exists since both people and contexts are inherently variable, both between each other but also as individuals and contexts whose states will change. Consequently, why show an ideal (through demonstration) and then coach toward

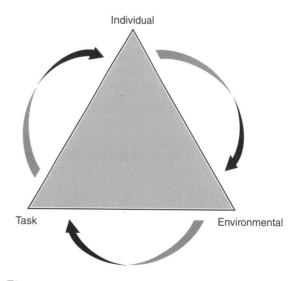

Figure I.2 The constraints triangle model of EcoD.

this through detailed attention to aspects of movement? It is much better to stimulate the learner toward self-organized discovery of the affordances (the opportunities for various actions) available in the environment. Another is the related notion that practice should involve repetition without repetition (Bernstein 1996), the idea that practice should involve an ongoing search process and interaction with one's environment to explore functional movement solutions so that an adaptable technique can be promoted. Finally, the ecological approach emphasizes representative design, in that practices should be realistic to the sport setting on which they are focused. As such, dribbling around cones or hitting a ball against a wall is seen as anathema, both because it is not representative and it is too repetitious. Importantly, however, as we will suggest later, these approaches may have a part to play, albeit that their primary purpose is perhaps not entirely focused on developing technique.

But Even Here It Might Still Depend

We acknowledge that the previously discussed coverage is far too short; indeed, the debate between theoretical approaches and their consequences make up the bulk of the rest of this book. It was important, however, to provide a base against which we can make an early start to our main purpose—that there are positives to be taken from most approaches, especially when they have been developed to offer strong predictive validity to what can be observed in performers as they progress from novice to expert.

Indeed, even at this early stage, we should stress that the differences in implications for coaching practice are much less black and white than many authors (and even more social media gurus) suggest. For the moment, and as an excellent example of scholarly debate, consider the different perspectives on the internal representation idea mentioned earlier. To consider this, we turn to the four Es idea, which is where the neurological research (and sporting research, e.g., Raab and Araújo 2019) has taken arguments regarding representations. The four Es are embodied, embedded, enactive, and extended. As a simple overview, the explanations and consequent implications for practice vary depending on how moderate or

radical one's commitment is to the theoretical perspective (cf. Seifert et al. 2020). The approaches also offer a structure for consideration of balance across these same perspectives—for example, how the different approaches address "questions about the nature of the mind, the mind's relation to the brain, perceptual experience, mental representation, sensemaking, the role of the environment, and social cognition" (Gallagher 2023, p. 1). In keeping with our approach, this text considers the strengths and weaknesses of the different perspectives and, as such, is to be recommended for those in search of further reading. For our purpose, an overview of the four Es is presented in table I.1.

One implication is that not all human behaviors rely on mental representations during execution. Some may be, such as in planning as a prediction of a movement outcome: "If I do this, it should feel like this." Notably, however, some performance states might do without them yet still involve cognition. This enacted cognition seems to be a halfway house with an ecological stance but is more philosophical compared to emerging ideas such as predictive processing, which we consider in greater detail throughout the next two chapters.

PEDAGOGIC APPLICATIONS

Reflecting our contentions for conditionality explored earlier, as the final part of this introductory chapter, we offer a few examples of where we see the practical necessity for overlap. This consideration suggests the need for the deliberate use of theories as frames for sensemaking rather than parameterizing reality—in other words, as an explanation of what may be happening rather than a prescriptive and totally accurate mechanism with direct and inevitable consequences. Ultimately, this involves drawing from the most appropriate theoretical perspective to optimize coaching and skill development based on contextual appropriateness rather than using a philosophical starting point—in short, a PJDM-driven process of planning and execution for coaches. In each example, we offer some simple contrasts that demonstrate how a combination of theoretical perspectives can provide the best solutions, where "best" relates to the outcome benefits to the learner-performer rather than the academic.

Table I.1 Definitions and Examples From the Four Es Paradigm of Embodied Cognition

Four Es	Definition*	Example
Embedded cognition	Cognition emerges through an athlete's exploitation of information in the environment.	A rugby player's decision to carry the ball into a gap between two defenders will be driven by their perception of whether the gap between two defenders emerges as an option when they catch the ball.
Extended cognition	Cognition extends further than the movement of the body alone, to the use of the equipment.	In cricket, the batter's cricket bat becomes an extension of their body before, during, and following the arrival of a delivery. Batters will often discuss the timing of a shot based on how it felt or where it hit on the bat (without visual feedback).
Enactive cognition	Athletes are autonomous in acting, and enacting, on their environment in a local to global and global to local fashion.	In climbing, the athlete closes their eyes and enacts three difficult pitches in their mind. They think through the possibilities of which movement patterns are afforded, based on their strength and comfort within their hold. Then, as they climb, they begin to self-organize as they interact with those affordances.
Embodied cognition	An athlete's mind and body work as one to self-organize while interacting with information being received (reducing the need for computations).	In cycling, the athlete who is in the center of the peloton feels a rider collide with them. The body's sensory capacity organizes the limbs to respond, with neither the time nor capacity to consciously compute what options are available to them. The autonomous change in direction and balance saves the cyclist from crashing.

Definitions adapted from Francesconi and Gallagher (2019).

Example 1: How Learning Takes Place

One big contrast that should have emerged from our whistle-stop coverage is the style of coaching. As methodological generalizations (perhaps overly so, cf. Taylor et al. 2023), cognitive practices stress early use of direct instruction and demonstration, while EcoD pushes discovery and experimentation (albeit often guided or structured) as the best start point. It is also important to stress how different approaches have moved closer to each other although, importantly, often with less than needed recourse to the mechanisms.

Pending more detailed consideration in later chapters, for our present purpose (and indeed, for the author team on this book, all current or recently retired coaches), this represents a first conundrum and a first push in the direction of *it depends*. To put it in simple terms, it is hard to start experimenting and discovering without a basic knowledge, a movement-based vocabulary, with which to attempt this. Furthermore, and bluntly, sport skills carry inherent safety and mechanical

constraints that must be catered to before any voyage of discovery and understanding.

As with other chapters in this book, we suggest that coaches can learn a great deal from studies in more academic styles of learning, with the caveat that it is undertaken with critical care because the challenges are subtly different, both mechanistically and in process. Importantly, however, the learner brains involved in both academic and motoric tasks and many of the learning methods show lots of similarity. As such, the work of de Jong and colleagues (2023) provides a great example. While arguing strongly in support of inquiry-based learning, they show how direct instructional methods can offer an important base from which such inquiry can develop:

Inquiry-based and direct instruction each have their supporters and their uses.

Indeed. it is important to check if there are actually any neuronal differences in the virtues and disadvantages. Indeed, as de Jong et al., state "the effectiveness of each approach depends on moderating factors such as the learning goal, the domain involved, and students' prior knowledge and other student characteristics. Furthermore, inquiry-based instruction is most effective when supplemented with guidance that can be personalized based on these moderating factors and can even involve providing direct instruction. Therefore, we posit that a combination of inquiry and direct instruction may often be the best approach to support student learning" (2023, p. 1).

In this regard we direct the interested reader toward an excellent discussion piece by Bakker (2018) in which he criticizes the polarized either-or arguments leveled against discovery learning. He pushes for a greater degree of sublation, a more nuanced consideration that is wholly representative of the *it depends* approach this book suggests. These points have been made in a sport setting where the absolute support for discovery learning as *the* method for learning (in this case freeskiing and snowboarding) was countered by evidence-grounded calls for a more mixed economy (Ojala and Thorpe 2015; Collins, Willmott, and Collins 2016, respectively). To summarize this example, different approaches seem better suited to different stages in the learning process or used in a complementary fashion in others.

Example 2: Biopsychosocial Impacts of Effective Coaching

This second example is based on the fact that skill acquisition, as with so many other facets of human behavior, is a biopsychosocial phenomenon. First, however, it is important to understand what this impressive but complicated term actually means.

The biopsychosocial model (BPS) (Engel 1977) is a useful and meaningful structure for examining elements that influence behavior, both positively and negatively. Developed in medical settings, the BPS approach can offer considerable explicative power and clear implications. Figure I.3 presents an example of how this might work in determining participation in exercise. An individual's choice of exercise modality, including whether they choose not to, depends on a combination of factors. Biological elements such as body shape, size, and age interact with perceptions of self (psychology) and social group. No single element alone drives behavior; rather, it almost always is influenced by a combination of factors and their interplay.

The approach has even wider applications than exercise. Consider the example of a youth athlete who is biologically maturing earlier than their peers. The biological aspects such as physical size likely will be positive in the short term, because larger children often are more successful (building their personal self-confidence—a psychological construct) and receive more attention from both teachers and coaches (a social situation) (Wattie, Schorer, and Baker 2015). Relative advantages of this sort may confer an early competitive advantage but appear to dissipate later in the development pathway (Niklasson et al. 2024).

Later changes notwithstanding, this initial advantage has received considerable research attention through a construct known as relative age effect (RAE). The idea is that children can be within the same age band as others but, if born early in the qualification year (e.g., September in the United States and England), will almost inevitably carry size and other maturation advantages. Thus, RAE relates to both the physical and psychological advantages achieved by early-born or early-maturing youth. These advantages lead to psychosocial advantage that, in turn, affects achievement and self-concept and is a powerful influence at the time. Interestingly, such RAE effects also can apply to academic work (e.g., Hauck and Finch 1993).

In contrast, however, working through the disadvantages of a late developer is likely to bring its reward later, for both sport (Gibbs, Jarvis, and

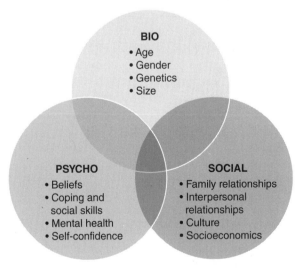

Figure I.3 The biopsychosocial approach.

Dufur 2012) and other areas. Drawing on both biopsychosocial and child development models, these reversed advantages are traced in the literature and attributed to the influence of both sole and interactive factors. In simple terms, the late maturer will face greater levels of challenge. Accordingly, coaching styles (including communication, setting challenges, expectations, and feedback) will need to be tailored to fit the advantaged early born as contrasted with a less mature, later-in-the-year performer. If coached appropriately, however, with a sensitivity to these disadvantages, the performer can catch up and surpass their earlier maturing peers. This brings a confidence boost to the late maturer who has caught up but can be rather problematic for the early maturer who was finding it easy but is now back in the pack.

In short, the importance of psychosocial interactions explain how disadvantages from one influence can be mitigated, countered, or even reversed by influences from others—the linked impacts and effects coact between psychological and social components and, as such, are a focus of the psychosocial element of the BPS (McCarthy et al. 2022).

This same balance of pros and cons applies to most circumstances for humans, including learning skills. In a skill-learning and development process, the coach is concerned with offering the learner a process that results in the most effective psychomotor development, even though some may see this as predominantly or even solely bio-based process of generating changes in movement. In simple terms, good coaches allow for differentiation so that quick or more mature learners are encouraged to make the most of their superior learning equipment. Slower or less mature performers can be supported by different approaches but can often catch up if they do not get disheartened and give up. As such, the coach is making plans to coach differently, emphasizing psychosocial encouragement for some but pushing on motorically for others.

Notice that this process will need to account for other factors as well—for example, embedding the skill, making it pressure proof against the anxieties that characterize many performance environments (Carson and Collins 2015). We will cover this more in later chapters, but we hope that example 1 has already proffered the suggestion that optimal skill acquisition may be best approached through a mixed-mode style, exploiting ideas from different theoretical positions.

Thus, while both cognitive and EcoD underpinnings and their implications have much to offer skill learning, especially through more direct (for the former) or more inquiry-based (for the latter) approaches to developing control, there is clearly more involved. From a psychological perspective, the learner's confidence in their ability to execute effectively under pressure is a distinct, if parallel, concern. Encouraging learners to experiment, an approach that some historical cognitive purists might question, is an excellent approach but perhaps only under certain circumstances. Simpler technical practices (e.g., passing back and forth in an unopposed setting) can be effective in this regard, even when the athlete lacks the principles of representative design stressed by the EcoD approach. This confidence angle also often underpins practice of emergency procedures (e.g., running through emergency drills before parachute jumps or technical scuba dives). In short, whether one considers the implications of a cognitive or an EcoD approach to skill learning, additional goals need to be considered, perhaps achieved most effectively by using a conscious but considered mix and match of tools from different theoretical standpoints.

From the social perspective, demonstrating skill level to others in the team or squad is another distinct but parallel outcome target for the technical development process. Elements of team confidence, termed *collective efficacy* (Shearer, Holmes, and Mellalieu 2009), and shared mental models, the thinking used by members of the same team to plan actions (covered in more detail in chapter 6), can be facilitated effectively by group practices where others can observe and are confronted (and hopefully convinced) by one's technical prowess as a player (cf. Bruton, Mellalieu, and Shearer 2016).

The first and perhaps most important modification to existing theoretical perspectives is placing the learner at the center of the process, with all the foibles that this involves. As we will explore later (e.g., in chapter 1), the three-part interaction of constraints is a sensible and often practical approach to the design of acquisition practices. In parallel, the use of structured progressions is seen as an important feature of the cognitive standpoint. As we hope the mentions throughout this chapter have demonstrated, however, simply acquiring the movement or movements is only one facet of the process, one that, we suggest, is not covered by considering the learning of technique as the sole target of a coaching episode. The multiplicity of outcomes that need to be targeted is further emphasized by the overall inclusion of biopsychosocial concerns. In short, the learner will bring a plethora of individual needs to the process, coupled with the three-part biopsychosocial agenda.

One such means of putting the individual at the heart of the coaching process is the role of understanding, clearly a cognitive or metacognitive construct but one that remains underexplored and typically underexploited. Research has demonstrated the important differences in types of understanding that accrue from watching as opposed to playing a game. For example, an elegant study contrasted the ability to read a deceptive dribble in soccer across players as opposed to lifelong wheelchair-using (and therefore unable to play) soccer fans (cf. Williams and Davids 1998). Unsurprisingly, perhaps, players were far more able to perceive and react to disguises and deceptions presented in deciding and then reacting to the eventual direction of the approaching player and ball.

As will be stressed throughout this book, however, this reflects a perception-action approach to a simple task, which is extremely appropriate within its sphere but does not cater to the role that higher-order cognition may play in facilitating the process. Indeed, as we will show later, emerging alternatives to this approach might be even more effective. Taking a wider view, work on metacognition (Price at al. 2020, 2021) has suggested the importance of understanding in developing tactical decision making. We will return to this in subsequent chapters, looking carefully at the role understanding can play, both directly and indirectly, in driving sport performance. For the moment, however, this is another important adjunct to the skill-acquisition process: the practical skill-acquisition process needs to consider more than just acquiring the skill, especially under laboratory conditions.

Example 3: Internal and External Focus When Learning Skills

Some authors are adamant that an external focus is essential for movement execution (Wulf 2016). However, we believe that even when a large volume of research favors one particular approach, evi-

dence of the contrary position in certain contexts must be considered. Consequently, we would again suggest the need for greater nuance, with significant work suggesting uses for both internal and external foci in particular contexts and desirable ends. Instructions will exert an influence in several directions, such as directing the performers' attention to what they should focus on. Once again, this is covered more coverage in chapter 4.

This differential is well demonstrated by Werner and Federolf (2023). In a "scrutinized review of review studies," these authors suggested that an internal focus was an important factor in changing movement patterns. As we will cover later in chapter 2, we see internal foci as central when refining movement (cf. Carson and Collins 2011). In contrast, an external focus seems more beneficial for whole body coordination, which can, in turn, lead to better overall performance.

In summary, this example presents another situation where apparently straightforward "do this" advice is flawed. The contextually based differentials exposed are supportive of an *it depends* approach. Indeed, the overwhelming support for an external approach seems now to be severely questioned (McKay et al. in press), As later chapters will explore, deciding between approaches can often usefully be based on consideration of the mechanisms through which they might operate, as well as critical consideration of the evidence and whether it was skewed (cf. Bobrownicki et al. 2021, 2023).

Example 4: Desirable Difficulties

Our fourth and final example relates to the idea of desirable difficulties, often viewed as an oxymoron. This well-researched approach stresses the utility of making things harder for the learner (i.e., increasing the levels of mental effort they are required to expend). The leaders in this work are the husband-and-wife team of Bob and Elizabeth Bjork, whose ideas we will explore in more detail later. Readers are directed to their summary paper (Bjork and Bjork 2020), which offers several applied examples, both within and outside of sport.

The approach is situated within the cognitive approach but carries important implications for practice conditions across the approaches. In simple terms, manipulation of difficulties through practice sequencing drives the level of challenge and the way the information is stored for later retrieval and use. As one of several outcomes, the level of difficulty has direct implications for how quickly, or perhaps in what way, the learning takes place. This idea, although recently challenged, has a long history, with a direct contrast between rapid learning and consequent (although perhaps illusionary) progress, against longer and slower but more strongly established learning that results in better retention and transfer.

A recent parallel but unrelated idea has emerged that merits consideration in an *it depends* approach. Termed the *derring effect*, this shows how deliberately making and then correcting errors can enhance performance, even when the error is known to be so. This lies in direct contrast to ideas of errorless learning, which have been popular in certain coaching circles (cf. Masters, van Duijn, and Uliga 2019). Interestingly, at least for cognitive tasks, the effects seem to apply even when the learners are unaware of the process (Wong and Wee Hun-Lim 2022). Similar approaches have already been used in motor tasks, where emphasizing an error to distinguish right from wrong (desired vs. dysfunctional or new vs. old) techniques has been used to support skill refinement (Collins, Morriss, and Trower 1999; Hanin et al. 2013).

Even though these approaches are underpinned by cognitive theory, at least in presumed mechanism, they represent another example of how different methods generate different outcomes. Once again, PJDM is indicated where decisions on how to coach are built on what outcomes are being targeted and the why and why not of the methods emerge as key.

CHAPTER SUMMARY

This chapter provided a quick overview of two key theories and introduced the book and its epistemological underpinnings while also offering some applied examples to demonstrate the importance of a conditional knowledge approach. Readers should know and be able to articulate the reasons why or why not a certain approach or blend of tools is being used. Interestingly, it is good to see theoretical researchers catching up with this idea—for example, the importance for cognitive psychology of considering when things do not work as a means to greater understanding of how they do (e.g., Smaldino, Pietraszewski, and Wertz 2023)—in other words, learning from failures by thinking through why they happened.

Throughout the book, keep the principles of our approach in mind, especially because the practical focus of these principles might read differently from other publications in the area of skill acquisition and refinement—specifically, that holding a debate to clarify the use of certain approaches is an important and professional approach to coaching and therefore an essential component of knowledge. This might sound rather intimidating, however, so some clarifications follow.

It Depends

The main point to emerge from this introductory chapter is that coaches should engage in debate at regular intervals, checking that the procedures they are using are optimal for the context and the individual foibles of the athletes with whom they work. Such critical reflection on methods will characterize effective coaches but even more so those who are upwardly mobile.

However, the debate is not necessary or even particularly useful when done all the time. Paralysis by analysis is a real threat to active coaches, support staff, and students, so it is helpful to get comfortable with a reflective debate *some* of the time such as when planning an important session for example.

This debate does not have to take place in public; it can be a mostly internal one, though it is helpful have someone else weigh in every so often. As later chapters will show, chapter 3 in particular, developing reflective routines is a useful adjunct to professional practice and a feature of adaptive expertise.

But Remember . . .

What we are suggesting in this book is a call for coaches, support staff, and students to know *why* they are doing what they are doing, to critically reflect on theory and data, and to tweak the approach in order to optimize outcome. Importantly, however, the *it depends* approach is not a free-for-all to use anything that has not been shown to work or that has no logical base.

As with many suggestions in innovative environments (e.g., elite sport) approaches may often not be evidence based because research has not had a chance to catch up yet. However, suggestions to raise performance through innovation are usually best conducted as an evidence-*grounded* presentation. Once again, we should be expected to explain why we are suggesting something, usually through a mechanisms-based argument. Notably, however, this won't always be underpinned by direct data collected evidence, especially when seeking genuinely advantage-gaining steps for world-class performers. Given the centrality of context in application, it is highly unlikely that the application of evidence in skill-acquisition spheres will ever be straightforward. What we are proposing is more of a challenge-focused environment where points are made with rational argument. What we are suggesting is *not* a license to dismiss careful planning and consideration in PJDM.

Coaching Has Been Dealing With This Issue for a Long Time

In conclusion, we do not see the *it depends* approach as particularly new or novel, although it does seem to contrast with the perspective that coaches need to adopt a single metatheoretical framework and stick to it, regardless of philosophical and evidential issues. Interestingly, an early development across the cognitive and EcoD perspectives occurred at a conference held to explore the differences. Termed the *motor-action controversy*, the results were assembled and presented as a book (Meijer and Roth 1988), which offers an early perspective on the either-or situation often encountered today. A more balanced consideration may also be a particularly useful adjunct to many of the single-method approaches that characterize some current practice (but not necessarily theory). What we *are* suggesting is a wide-ranging critical consideration of what we can learn from our own and other fields—namely, transferability of what we do to other contexts and a focus toward independent performance in hyperdynamic environments. We hope you will enjoy the journey with us.

REVIEW AND PRACTICAL QUESTIONS

1. What are the principles underlying Mosston and Ashworth's (2008) spectrum theory of teaching styles?
2. Why is the *why* question important in coach PJDM?
3. What are the advantages that result from Schmidt's idea of a generalized motor program?
4. Why is representative design seen as important in the EcoD approach?
5. How does the biopsychosocial approach explain the interactions that take place for more mature children in sport settings?
6. What is one major advantage that is conferred by desirable difficulties?

KEY TERMS

case conceptualization

cognitive approach

ecological dynamics approach (EcoD)

epistemological chain

predictive processing approach

professional judgment and decision making (PJDM)

PART I

Controlling Movement

CHAPTER 1

UNDERPINNING THEORIES AND CONSEQUENT APPROACHES: WHAT DO WE WANT AND NEED FROM A MODEL?

Dave Collins and Jamie Taylor

Chapter Objectives

After studying this chapter, you should be able to do the following:

- Understand what you need from a theoretical approach
- Explain the main principles and operation of the three major approaches: cognitive, EcoD, and predictive processing
- Recognize the different stages of learning within the three approaches and how the learner's performance progresses under each approach
- Consider the relative differences and overlap between cognitive, EcoD, and predictive processing
- Understand the different views of perception that are presented by each approach

Having introduced and exemplified the idea of conditional knowledge in the introduction, our focus now turns to the detail of the different theoretical approaches, their origins, their strengths, and implications for practice. The field of skill acquisition has tended to position individual theories against others. A consequence of that is that different theoretical underpinnings have moved into distinct communities of practice, lacking the cross-pollination that encourages innovation. This lack of innovation may be felt most strongly by the practitioner, which is surely the reason we are all here. As such, this chapter will focus more on theoretical origins than practical implications.

Before we get into these details, however, it is worth considering several aspects of theory—specifically, what practitioners would like or need it to do for them. After this, we offer some general suggestions as to how to discriminate between the approaches, ahead of the active experimentation that we and well-informed authors like Schön (1983) suggest. In short, it is always a good idea to experiment and to revisit tests at regular intervals with respect to the methods. As will be echoed throughout this book, knowing why and why not to apply a particular method or blend is important, with experience a crucial, though not the only, part of this conditional knowledge. In any case, this first section will offer some ideas for a series of litmus tests that can be applied when exploring the text and selecting a preferred model or a blend of approaches.

Consider the straightforward definition of psychology offered on page 1 of a famous fundamental text by Atkinson and Hilgard (first edition in 1953, now in its 16th in 2014!): the science of psychology was designed to "explain, predict and modify behavior." That is probably the best explanation of what a consumer of psychological knowledge (e.g., coach, support staff, researcher) should look for. So what does that mean for theorizing and how it should be evaluated?

A good theory or model will help to explain behavior. What is observed when watching everyone from learners to elite performers should be neatly explained by the theoretical approaches. Once this condition is met, the theory should also offer some predictive power. That is, if these sorts of things are performed in practice, this sort of outcome should be expected, individual differences and particular contexts notwithstanding. Of particular interest to our context here, a good theory should offer knowledge and methods through which to modify what is seen. In other words, the knowledge and methods from a good theory should be used to help one athlete learn a technique quickly and effectively (although these might be separate concerns) or to support another athlete to refine their skill to be more effective in their chosen context.

We suggest two other criteria. First, the effective theory will offer functionality—what is being suggested can be effectively employed in a practical

sense. Second, we offer simplicity. In other words, the explanation or advice offered is simple enough to be understood and applied. Richard Feynman, the famous Nobel laureate scientist, reportedly insisted that a theory (in his case physics) was not good enough unless it could be understood by an undergraduate student. Similarly, Einstein suggested that a theory had to be simple enough to explain to a child. When considering the different theoretical approaches offered, keep in mind these five criteria: Do the ideas help to (1) explain, (2) predict, and (3) modify what you see, while also offering (4) simple and (5) functional advice on how to help athletes? All the models discussed here hold something for the user or researcher. The reader simply needs to probe what is involved.

One other idea to test and apply to theoretical papers, models, and the like is to reflect on the ideas on simplicity. Importantly, these ideas have been endorsed by some scientific heavyweights; it also is important to consider the explanations offered on how the theoretical constructs work—in other words, the mechanisms. This is an increasingly exciting area and has emerged as an important philosophical thrust since the start of the twenty-first century. We will refer to this **mechanistic** approach throughout this text, which is also **pracademic**.

Across the research spectrum, the idea of promoting or even requiring simplicity in explanation is gaining ground. For example, neuroscience is making great strides and developing tools and techniques to examine what and how the nervous system (including, but not limited to the brain) is working. You might compare this "brain plus" (i.e., considering brain and body as inseparable in the planning and execution of action as opposed to the brain alone) idea to the four Es, presented in the introduction and table I.1. Reflecting this progress, theorists should also increasingly offer mechanistic explanations as underpinnings to their presentations. Their consequential advice should include what the practitioner could be doing. Furthermore, as a theory reaches maturity, this mechanistic drive should become an increasingly common feature.

The informed consumer could apply the five criteria (explain, predict, and modify behavior through simple and functional methods), increasingly seeking explanations as to how a particular theoretical approach might work. Indeed, the open-minded author should be showing where their ideas do not work, as much as stressing where they do. We hope readers enthusiastically apply these litmus tests while critically reflecting on the approaches that follow and accept where the test results may lead.

A HISTORICAL APPROACH

In the following sections of this chapter, we offer a description of the three major theoretical approaches that currently, and likely will for some time, dominate the literature. At least to date, they have received a rather differential consideration within the motor control and skill acquisition domain. We then explore these approaches in subsequent chapters to consider the degrees of overlap between them as well as their distinct features and what each offers. All have earlier origins in the literature (see chapter 4 for a more detailed consideration) but following some evolution have become more prominent. For convenience, we will present the three in a semichronological order; this order does not carry any meaning, however. Note that the coverage presented here is targeted at the practitioner, whether coach, support staff member, or researcher.

While reading this book and implicitly starting to compare and contrast the different approaches, it is worth considering how things have evolved, both within and between the three. In simple terms, and what we see as a positive feature of science, new ideas have emerged to address shortcomings in older theories. Good scientific development would best be based on showing how the new theory is better than the old, offering more complete or perhaps even simpler and more elegant explanations for what is observed, thus driving clearer advice on how things can be modified. Such reconciliations have already been attempted, as highlighted in the introduction (e.g., Meijer and Roth 1988). This evolution should be apparent through the historical approach we employ.

APPROACH 1: THE COGNITIVE OR INFORMATION-PROCESSING APPROACH

Theories are often a product of their historical environment, and the cognitive or information-processing approach is no different. While far from being a single theory, as the second title would indicate, the approach originated in a computer-like model of the human brain. Think of the photo in figure 1.1.

Figure 1.1 Human movement control as a computer analogy.
Nicolas Economou/NurPhoto via Getty Images

Built on the idea of distinct subprograms, the information-processing approach divided the control of movement into three distinct stages. First, in the **perception** or input stage, the performer scans the environment, deciding what to focus on and what it means. These data, clearly a selected subset of everything going on (because no one or nothing can compute completely), are then passed to the **decision-making** stage, in which options are weighed and decided on. Finally, at the **effector** or output stage, the decided-on actions are encoded or changed into commands to the motor systems for execution. The computer analogy is clear, although considering these as orthogonal or discrete stages has been one of the biggest points of criticism for the approach. What is thought to happen in this final stage? In short, how are movements encoded and executed?

Open- and Closed-Loop Control

This computer analogy was a key part of the work of Adams (1971), which described open-loop and closed-loop control. In open loop, a set of instructions, termed a *motor program* (MP), are sent from the central computer (i.e., the brain) to the working units (the muscles). One important distinction with closed loop is the extent to which sensory inputs are employed or not considered.

In open loop, the MP is made up of subroutines, which are centrally stored in the brain, then retrieved and assembled to meet the needs of each particular challenge. Storage of all this information presents a capacity problem, which is addressed by the use of the subroutine components for different purposes. For example, anything that involves hitting a moving ball could draw on several subroutines common to that task but assembled in different ways depending on whether the performer is playing baseball, cricket, field hockey, or tennis. Of course, each action carries similarities but is also subtly different, so getting the tweaking done quickly and accurately is another issue. In short, open loop is great for quick and consistent movements that were well learned (e.g., golf swing, sprint start, or Olympic lift), but its explicative power starts to suffer as more complex or novel challenges are faced.

The answer that emerged at the time was the closed-loop approach. The MP is still assembled centrally and sent to the muscles. In this case, however, the loop is closed by feedback coming back from the muscles and movement sensors on how things are progressing. As a consequence, corrections could be calculated and sent before another closed-loop sequence to make further refinements and so on. Depending on the complexity of the movement, more or less closed loops might be needed. This adjustment helps the theory because, by combining open- and closed-loop control, it could now account for movements requiring small adjustments (e.g., balancing on skis) or very complex or novel movements requiring several to's and fro's between brain, muscle, movement sensor (e.g., muscle tension or joint position) and back to the brain (such as playing a racket sport). The terms are still in common usage for mechanical or electrical systems, in which they can work within preset conditions. For humans, however, the approach has been increasingly challenged on the basis of storage requirements, time (assembling subroutines and reacting to closed-loop feedback), and flexibility—for example, how *did* a learner pick up a new technique?

Schema Theory

The solution to these issues came in the shape of the schema theory, developed by Schmidt (1975). A schema can be thought of as a rough outline or overall structure. This approach offered several useful modifications—for example, the generalized motor program (GMP). This solved the storage capacity problems by speculating that subroutines are stored as a cluster of similar movement components, which could be summoned up and then adjusted to meet the needs of a particular situation. Returning to the racket sports example, a player would draw on a GMP of forehands (or a separate one for backhands) then make up and internally try out the instructions before sending them to the muscles. The cognitive approach also introduced the importance of variable practice. If a player had practiced lots of different tennis shots, their GMP would be richer and better able to generate accurate answers to the challenges posed.

Another important component was the generation of two related but distinct schema instances, known as the *recall and recognition schema*. In simple terms, the recall schema generates the instructions to do the job based on the initial conditions, such as where the opponent was standing or how fast the ball was approaching. The recognition schema proactively works out a set of sensory consequences ("If I do this, what should it feel like?") or outcomes ("If I do this, where will the ball go?"). This offers a template against which the actual sensory feedback could be compared so that error information could be generated and adjustments made more quickly. Consequently (and another positive for the theory), athletes could benefit from both effective *and* ineffective performances. This implicitly places an emphasis on the learning impact of ineffective executions. Working out what went wrong and why was as useful, perhaps even more useful, than the positive experiences of success.

The theory has endured, although more recent work has led to challenges, only some of which can be accounted for by adjustments to the theory (Schmidt 2003). Perhaps its biggest contribution has been the drive for variability in practice, applied in theories such as **contextual interference** (Battig 1972). This describes how learners progress most quickly when practice repetitions are similar or blocked (e.g., doing the same movement repetitively). In contrast, more varied practice (e.g., mixing up practice of different shots) generates slower progress, although the same standards are attained eventually. In this varied (or high contextual interference) condition, however, better learning emerges as the task is both more effectively retained (remembered) and can be transferred to address similar but different tasks. Contextual interference has been part of the skill-acquisition literature for many years and is still considered important, even though some reviews have questioned it as overly simplistic (e.g., Ammar et al. 2023).

Another idea to emerge is the impact of specific practice on a particular technique. This idea of **especial skills** (Keetch, Lee, and Schmidt 2009) was seen in basketball, where, for a variety of reasons, players got a lot more practice shooting from the free throw line. This specificity stood in contrast to the benefits of more general or varied practice. It seemed like the repetition of this especial skill led to a stronger MP, which, in turn, resulted in better performance and lower movement variability than shots taken from elsewhere on the court. Of course, the free shot is also more closed in that the number of variables (e.g., position or lack of opponent) is smaller, while shooting from elsewhere in game play is more open with a much greater number of variables. We

will return to this idea of repetition later. For the moment, note that the cognitive approach offers support for both specific and varied practice. Especial skills may emerge in other sports (e.g., use of a seven iron in golf) or for individuals who like to practice certain moves.

Finally, it is important to recognize that the cognitive approach has long since ditched the computer metaphor (the idea that the brain *works* like a computer), instead placing ever-greater emphasis on the idea of internal representation of movement. The importance of knowledge (e.g., "Why would you do it *that* way?") has received increasing support (e.g., Stanley and Krakauer 2013). Research has also highlighted that when **automaticity** (in this context, the ability to do the movement consistently and with little thought) is challenged by emotions such as anxiety and by the increasing importance of conscious control, although differentially based on individual characteristics. The internal planning inferred by studies from the cognitive approach facilitates design of an effective movement solution while also anticipating what feedback *should* be expected, so enabling more rapid adjustment through the comparison of what was expected with what actually occurred.

How Do People Learn?

The cognitive approach's evolution away from any notion that the brain and nervous system operate like a computer (if indeed it was ever anything more than a metaphor) has emphasized the role of mental representations in learning. This has led to greater focus on tools used to develop and strengthen internal representations of movements through understanding and active mental engagement. The major theory of learning in the cognitive approach is the three-stage process of Fitts and Posner (1967).

Stage 1: The Cognitive Stage

In the first—cognitive—stage the emphasis is on the learner developing an idea of how a technique works, looks, and is put together. As mentioned in the introduction, the use of instruction, with subcategories emerging more recently, is particularly stressed here. This tool has a long, rich history in the more cognitive area of academic teaching (Stockard, Wood, and Khoury 2018) and has more recently received attention following a period of dismissal (Cope and Cushion 2020). As part of instruction, demonstrations are used to offer a correct model to the learner. Using a demonstrator who is similar to the learner (e.g., sex, size, age, skill level) has long been suggested as making this process even more effective, although the complexities of interaction between these different categories makes this another *it depends* challenge. Reflecting some of the ideas in schema theory, using a coping model (a demonstration that contains faults as well as positives) has also been shown to be effective but as a longer-term rather than a fast-action tool (cf. low and high contextual interference). Even more thought provoking is what the learner may be picking up from the demonstration. Use of video versus stick figure versus point light (i.e., a series of dots representing joint centers) demonstrations were equally effective in developing the technique being shown (e.g., Ghorbani and Bund 2016). Reflecting this, there has been considerable debate on exactly what is being acquired during a demonstration (e.g., Hodges et al. 2007). These debates notwithstanding, demonstrations generally are seen as a positive tool, at least in the cognitive approach.

Similar debates take place over the use of mental imagery to, perhaps, strengthen internal representation. Imagery is a commonly used tool in learning (e.g., Collins and Carson 2017), and its application in conjunction with observation seems to suggest a combined impact on both motivation and movement, even in learners with particular difficulties (e.g., Scott et al. 2023). Once again, the logic underpinning its use, at least from a motoric approach, is to strengthen the internal representation of the movement schema.

The important things to note here are the **cognitive load**, which is clearly high, against the automaticity and consistency of the execution, both of which will typically be low. The learner is working hard mentally, but this effort is clearly bodily as well, as which muscles to use and which to relax is far from established. As a result, muscular activity is often high and usually inappropriate, adding to the stiff and jerky performance typical of this stage. It is implicit within this stage that some sort of ideal movement is the goal, hence the focus on providing a correct model (see chapter 5) and explicit instruction. For example, observing a model is effective in moving movement execution toward that model, and this impact seems both positive and quick (Friedman and Korman 2019). The point here is what might

actually be acquired—the *exact* movement or overall elements, such as within a template or overall idea of the movement. Once again, as we will see later, this has been another point of contention with other approaches, even though the literature and history of its use is significant. It is also an issue as to what aspect of usage might be best at different stages—for example, developing a template early for novices but allowing a more experimental approach later.

Stage 2: The Associative Stage

As the learner starts to get the hang of things, they start to fit things together. Subroutines (or bits of movement) get strung together (associated), which means a lower mental workload and a more consistent execution. This is good for progress, *but not* if the wrong bits get associated. As such, some coach input to monitor and correct is important. Indeed, incorrect association is seen as a key reason for early-stage learners to be monitored so that fundamentals are well established to provide a sound base for later.

Stage 3: The Autonomous Stage

As the name implies, by this stage all the bits of movement are assembled together in a consistent MP. Performance is consistent while mental load is low due to increased automaticity. This enables the learner to execute the techniques under pressure or in situations of higher cognitive load such as in a competition. It is also worth noting that physical loads at this stage seem more settled, because what muscles fire when and how much has been firmly established. This is further facilitated by stronger and more accurate internal representations, resulting in a reduced need for monitoring or correction. In short, performing skills at this stage requires less effort because the muscle activity is only what is needed.

Summary

The cognitive approach is well established, and, even though features have evolved over the years, it retains some of the more computer-like input-output feel, despite the rejection of this metaphor. Key aspects are the importance of central control, the schema and GMP, early emphasis on a correct model, and the gradual build of autonomy and automaticity in the control of movement.

APPROACH 2: THE ECOLOGICAL DYNAMICS APPROACH

While reading about the cognitive approach, several problems might have become apparent. How did the subroutines or basic component building blocks of movement get learned in the first place? How (or even where) does the learner store all these components? How can they put together movement plans, especially under time pressure or when cognitively loaded by anxiety? And finally, which was not addressed in the previous section, how *does* perception work?

Components of EcoD: Perception and Action

Attempts to address the last question were one of the main drivers in the evolution of ecological dynamics (EcoD). In the cognitive approach, perception was seen through a computer-like lens. Accordingly, perception was indirect, with the system taking snapshots of what was happening, then comparing these internally to compute outcomes ahead of time. A particularly challenging aspect of this was the time-to-event judgment. Simply put, how can the learner best calculate how long until the tennis ball or, even worse, the boxer's fist arrives? The solution is to consider perception as direct. Instead of a series of snapshots and associated (and slow) calculations, performers were seen as looking at and making judgments based on the whole thing. This is shown diagrammatically in figure 1.2.

The idea was suggested by James Gibson, seen by many as the father of ecological psychology (at least in sport), one of the two main theoretical inputs to EcoD. Gibson reportedly got to grips with the approach to explain how pilots could land planes on the deck of an aircraft carrier with so many things happening at the same time. In such circumstances the calculations via indirect (i.e., computed) perception simply could not cope (figure 1.3). Gibson eventually published these ideas in a seminal book in 1966.

An important feature of Gibson's approach is that perceptual processes are seen as innate. That is, rather than perception being something that is acquired, athletes can, even from a young age, react accurately with no need for internal repre-

sentations as a point of comparison. One excellent example of this is an aspect of behavior called *looming*, the automatic response to something approaching someone and their coupled tendency to avoid it. This behavior has been shown experimentally in animals (e.g., crabs; Oliva and Tomsic 2014) and human infants (Van der Weel and Van der Meer 2009). Such studies are important because they offer a mechanism for the processes proposed by Gibson.

Another important feature of the EcoD approach is the idea of **perception-action coupling (P-A coupling)**. Based on this revolutionary idea, rather than the sequential ordering of perception and action as discrete processes, as suggested by early information processing, perception and action are suggested to be integrated and continuous. Once again, this represents a significant advantage because it accounts for rapid reaction techniques such as a block-counter in boxing. Building on earlier work, Gibson (1979) commented on the inseparable nature of perception and action, stressing that working on both in parallel represents the best match for the mechanisms involved. This work was paralleled by Bernstein (1967), who wrote that "the central effectors achieve co-ordination of movements only by plastically reacting to the totality of signals from the afferent field" (p. 107). So in tandem but separately, these researchers saw perception and action as inseparable.

One particularly cogent sporting example involves stepping on and off a moving walkway or escalator. As someone steps on, their perceptual system recognizes this challenge through peripheral vision. P-A coupling and **self-organization** (both core principles of EcoD) make them take a longer step so that they can catch up with the moving steps. At the other end, they once again automatically perceive the finish of the moving walkway and take a shorter step to slow their body down (figure 1.4). Importantly, all of this is automatic.

How do we know? When stepping onto one that is not working, take note. Unless the person walking consciously overrules the coupling, they will still take a longer step on and a shorter step off, even though there is no need to do it.

One important qualifier is that for the P-A coupling to work effectively, the perceptual stimulus must carry all the informational data. In other

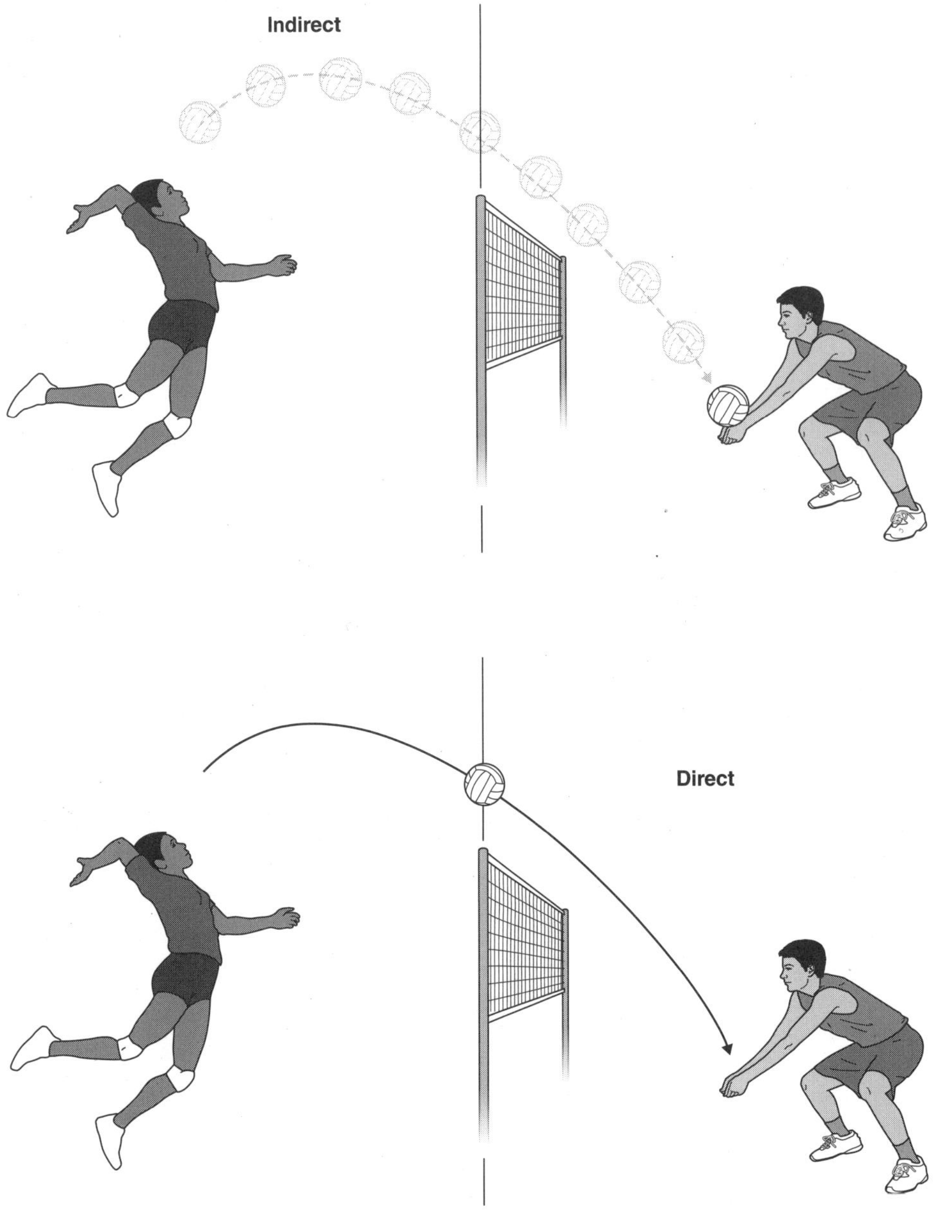

22 Sport Skill Acquisition

Figure 1.2 Direct versus indirect perception. Part (*a*) offers a pictorial representation of indirect perception, where the line and arrival of the ball are worked out from a series of discrete snapshots of the ball position. Part (*b*) represents direct perception, where the arrival point and timing of the ball is directly perceived from the ball's flight path.

words, practice must use a largely identical environment to that being trained for. A good example of this was offered by Pinder, Renshaw, and Davids (2009). Their study showed differences in action when cricket batter faced a bowling machine than when the ball was delivered at identical speeds but by a live bowler. It is important to note that, to ensure effective outcomes, the actions must be coupled to the correct perceptions! Notably,

recent research shows that P-A coupling extends across different modes, not just vision (Bosco et al. 2023). This is even more reason to keep the stimulus environment as representative as possible. In other words, practice environments need to match performance environments as closely as possible, including audio and haptic (sound and feel) stimuli as well. Multisensory environment is the name of the game.

Figure 1.3 The aircraft carrier landing challenge.
U.S. Navy photo by Mass Communication Specialist Seaman Peter McHaddad

Wider Components of the EcoD Approach

EcoD is underpinned by a theoretical blending of ecological psychology, dynamical systems theory, complex systems theory, and the evolutionary sciences. Pedagogic outputs from the EcoD approach include the **constraints-led approach (CLA)** and **nonlinear pedagogy (NLP)**. Both are central to but also, and importantly, driven by the wider approach of EcoD, We will address the wider implications of this approach throughout the book. For the moment, however, and as with our earlier treatment of the cognitive approach, we will consider the direct implications for motor control and skill acquisition.

The first thing to understand about the EcoD approach is the central role played by the performer-environment-task interaction as shown in figure I.2. The perceptual data that are perceived through this triangle (cf. figure I.2) are both direct (see figure 1.1) and meaningful. The information carries implicit meaning to the performer, which forms the relational properties of **affordances**, or opportunities for action. These affordances are framed by constraints that then provide the performer with the affordances as options. In turn, the human (or animal) system engages with the constraints to develop and apply actions as an exploration of what is available. Affordances are therefore not only perceived opportunities seen in the display but also driven by social constructs. For example, in team sports, an attack-focused coach will constrain, and therefore afford, tendencies toward attacking options in their players (Gray 2022). Under CLA, actions are based on what affordances emerge from the triangle, with the three factors contributing differentially to what is eventually actioned.

The way in which this operates is another important distinction. The affordances, which are often perceived unconsciously, act as attractors or rejectors toward certain actions on a continuous basis. EcoD emphasizes the role played by knowledge *of* an environment, as opposed to knowledge *about*; in simple terms, information is directly gained through perception without the need for extra processing through internalized representations (Davids and Araújo 2010). This means that, over time, more stable movement patterns emerge, because of the ways in which the performer-task-environment dynamic can be optimized, rather than by changes toward some ideal movement pattern that is externally applied and consciously driven. This is reflected in the concept of self-organization; in short, the system searches for an optimal solution for itself.

A third feature is the concept of **representative design** (Chow et al. 2011). We have already

Figure 1.4 The moving walkway example of P-A coupling.
Ge JiaJun/Moment/Getty Images

stressed the importance of providing an accurate and realistic picture if learning is to form appropriate and effective coupling. The idea of representative design is based on the importance of practicing with realistic displays and demands. As one often-debated example, tennis players would be discouraged from hitting a ball against a wall. In similar fashion, team-game coaches are encouraged to use game-like practices rather than drills.

The importance of adaptability is also stressed with EcoD (cf. Adolph 2019). Drilling a technique is seen as largely counterproductive, because that specific movement or set of movements is unlikely or even impossible to occur again. Accordingly, repetition without repetition (Ranganathan, Lee, and Newell 2020) is a central pillar, with coaches encouraged to build in variability to any practice. As the approach emphasizes, if we are trying to develop a highly adaptable set of movements, practice needs to reproduce this. This has meant that for some EcoD practitioners, kicking a ball between cones or hitting a ball against a wall is anathema. Interestingly, however, this is not necessarily the case across the literature (e.g., Ribeiro et al. 2021).

Finally, we must address the extension of the philosophical approach defined by EcoD, started perhaps, or at least articulated, by a paper presentation at the first Complex Systems World Congress (Seifert and Davids 2017), with EcoD being applied to performance, physical activity, and physical education. This is an interesting expansion of what started as a perceptually based theory. These wider applications are considered later in the book. For the moment, we return to EcoD as a basis for technique and skill acquisition.

So How Do People Learn?

In the simplest terms, learning in EcoD is a rearrangement of the performer-environment relationship (cf. Baggs et al. 2009). An important feature is the idea of NLP (Chow et al. 2011). Unlike the stable progressions suggested by Fitts and Posner (1967), the key difference that NLP emphasizes is that learning is inevitably lumpy, with progress made in idiosyncratic jumps rather than a smooth process as the system self-organizes through the differential impact of attractors and rejectors—in simple terms, what works and what doesn't.

Reflecting the ideas presented earlier, acquiring a skill or technique is seen as a problem-solving process (Myszka, Yearby, and Davids 2023). As such, the role of the coach is to place the learner in an environment that presents a landscape of options or affordances, often through the manipulation of constraints (a CLA). The idea is that through a largely intentional *but implicit* process of experimentation, the learner will develop their own, personal, and unique solution to the challenge. Ideas of demonstrating or instructing the learner toward a correct template are seen as inappropriate. Indeed, since the movement solution is person-task-environment specific, such encouragement is seen as negative. In short, the coach's role is to facilitate the learner's search for adaptive movement solutions.

The literature lays bare some interesting conundrums, however. For example, how open should this search process be? Some research suggests that challenges can usefully be structured under certain circumstances (e.g., Orth, Davids, and Seifert 2018), especially for younger or less able learners. Furthermore, some (but only some) consider the importance of providing input a priori to facilitate the search. In other words, demonstrations and instruction can be seen as internal constraints, helping to direct the learner's attention toward a search for solutions in certain areas (e.g., Ranganathan and Newell 2010). In simple terms, the practical outputs of the cognitive and EcoD approaches seem to be moving closer together on advice, despite big theoretical differences; albeit what that advice does (i.e., how it works) is still a ways apart.

Summary

The EcoD approach is building support and receives an increasing emphasis in the sport literature and, most notably, on social media. Key aspects are the perception and constraints triangle, P-A coupling, constraints and affordances, and NLP. It is important to note how the two different theories are moving closer together, although there are still clear differences, perhaps implicit rather than explicit, with the mechanisms that underpin how things work.

APPROACH 3: THE PREDICTIVE PROCESSING APPROACH

Our third approach, although not designed for this purpose, perhaps offers a means of navigating some of the theoretical intractability between the cognitive and EcoD approaches. Predictive processing (PP) has a long history in psychology, often first attributed to Helmholtz (e.g., Friston 2010) and the idea that the brain acts to infer,

rather than *always* directly detect, the external states of the world. Theoretically, it has evolved from notions of perceptual inference alone to more embodied notions of predictive processing.

In recent years, PP has become a dominant theory in cognitive neuroscience, though it has yet to take hold in the sport literature. As with the other approaches outlined, it is not a single theory but instead represents a family of theories that consider the brain to actively predict sensory data. Building from the influences of the cognitive and ecological approaches outlined earlier, PP offers a grouping of radical views on human functioning. These theories—predictive processing, predictive coding, and active inference—while subtly different with a tendency to be applied in different domains, all suggest that humans exert adaptive control over their action-perception loops with the aim of minimizing the surprise of sensory input (Parr, Pezzulo, and Friston 2022). Recognizing specific differences between predictive coding as being based more in perception and the extension of active inference to action, our use of *PP* will be used as a blanket term to refer to the family of theories that use prediction to explain human behavior. The careful reader will also notice the predominant use of the jargon used in active inference rather than other formations of PP. Bearing in mind the purpose of this text and in keeping with the rest of this chapter, we hope that brevity means that simplifications are neither overdone nor confusing.

The Free Energy Principle

Underpinning active inference is the notion of the **free energy principle**, which suggests that the prerogative of living organisms (including but beyond humans) is to minimize entropy in the form of free energy (Friston 2010). *Free energy* refers to the difference between the system's current state and a future desired state. As a result, humans will act predictively to maintain their internal states and interact with their environment. This minimization of free energy is where PP helps us accurately predict the environment through internal modeling and take actions that minimize discrepancies between predictions and sensory input.

The free energy principle explains how adaptive self-organizing systems function, as described in the EcoD section. It suggests that humans explain the causes of sense data through the generation of internal models (see the cognitive approach). Over time, the updating of these models help to minimize the difference between prior expectations and unexpected sense data, otherwise known as *surprise* (Sims and Pezzulo 2021). Through the active search for information (referred to as *epistemic foraging*) and the adjustment of internal states (allostasis) and behaviors, we minimize the discrepancy between expectations and incoming sensory data.

The focus of recent PP models has been to tackle specific critiques of reductive approaches that arbitrarily separate mind and body. Thus, much like EcoD, PP can be contrasted with the historical cognitive theories that see perception, cognition, and action acting sequentially and separately. PP also rejects a one-way flow of perception. In the case of the cognitive approach, this is an indirect but passive view of perception where sense data is processed by neurons waiting to be engaged. Therefore, PP continues the criticisms of early cognitive models such as the passivity of perception (Gibson 1979) while also addressing weaknesses in ecological accounts such as an input-output model of perception. PP instead suggests an enactive (cf. table I.1) view of situated perception and action, based on different forms of sense data interoception (internal states), exteroception (external states), and proprioceptive (movement) sense data, rather than the exteroceptive-centric input-output models suggested earlier in the chapter (Linson et al. 2018). In other words, PP stresses the importance of the external picture *and* an internal model.

To do this, PP capitalizes on the strengths of theories underpinned by both the ecological and cognitive approaches. In PP the brain is highly active in predicting the world and proactively shaping our sensory experience (Clark 2023). It offers a top-down *and* bottom-up process whereby the brain actively constructs the expected sensory consequences of actions in the world (top-down) and sensory feedback is used to confirm or disconfirm (prediction error) these predictions (Friston 2018). In short, the brain continuously and actively constructs our worlds. From the top down, PP suggests that we draw on an internal **generative model**, a resource that generates novel data and images based on existing features and properties. The brain's ability to learn about the regularities that characterize its environment allows it to function adaptively. Failure to generate effective representations for action and perception is a significant issue for human functioning. Importantly, these internal models are a long way from the notion of passive mirrors of nature as suggested by Rorty (1979). It is also a significant distance from the view that movement is controlled by representations and knowledge about the environment. These models may be richly developed and detailed, but they can also be fast and frugal, purposed for action, rather than needing to be an accurate representation of the external world.

The generative model can be split into our prior beliefs (often referred to as **priors**) about the hidden states of the world (those not directly sensed) and the relative likelihood of these hidden states (Constant, Clark, and Friston 2021). The combination of priors and likelihood or certainty make up the generative model. The notion of priors represents both explicit knowledge and implicit features of prior experience, hence the use of the term *prior*. In this sense, we can understand priors in a particular domain or context enhancing our ability to make predictions and therefore control actions. Expertise therefore can be seen as holding a highly developed generative model of the relationship between oneself and a particular environment. An example, one of the strongest findings in expertise studies, is that experts are better able to engage in pattern recognition. In essence, someone's priors determine what they see, and the best predictor of future learning is prior learning. The implication is that coaches need to pay attention to an athlete's priors or, in lay terms, what somebody knows and can do. Expert movement therefore can be seen as the brain's ability to use higher-level predictions to drive action and fluidly adjust based on the sensory consequences of this movement.

While the majority of PP approaches refer to internal representations in some form, there are exceptions (Kirchhoff and Robertson 2018). Acknowledging this theoretical diversity, we will proceed on the basis that PP theory generally involves representation of some sort (Sims and Pezzulo 2021). In addition, PP accounts present the opportunity to dissolve old debates about the nature and role of representation in human function (Clark 2015).

The purpose of the generative model is to make predictions, which are then compared to incoming sense data. Where sense data from exteroceptive, interoceptive, and proprioceptive sources contradict the brain's predictions, this is referred to as *prediction error,* or *surprise.* Importantly, this is different from the typical use of the term *surprise,* instead referring to the extent to which a person's expectations differ from their sensory input. Prediction error is the difference between what one expects (their generative model) and their sensory observations of the world. Prediction error can be understood by a process of either updating the generative model (changing prior expectations) or shaping the world in a manner that explains this sensory input. In this sense, perception and action are tightly coupled (as per EcoD), and PP would suggest that humans exercise adaptive control over these perception-action loops. In this case, however, both perception and action are directed toward the minimization of prediction error through a process of either changing one's mind (updating priors) or acting in a manner that brings the world closer to one's prior sensory expectations. This means that perception and learning are the same process but occur on different timescales and lead to ongoing transformation of neuronal networks (Linson et al. 2018).

The reduction of prediction error can, in essence, be seen as the process of learning, with the individual's generative model changing to meet the dynamics of a particular environment. The extent to which predictions, or prediction errors, are weighted by the brain is based on the brain's weighting of reliability and significance through precision weighting or attention. This allows the brain to increase or decrease the weighting of information, estimating the value of predictions and sense data in a specific context. As shown in figure 1.5, only *unpredicted* elements of sensory data are passed further up the cortical hierarchy from lower levels (closer to proximal sensory input) to higher levels (Kiefer and Hohwy 2018).

Attention allows us to pay greater attention to elements of error responses and is therefore central to learning and performance. Those predictions that we estimate to be the most significant sensory consequence likely will be pushed upward to higher levels of abstraction, and in turn, higher levels of neuronal populations that predict those at lower levels (Clark 2023). In short, these situations will lead to an individual becoming more aware of their actions. It follows that PP is informing a growing body of literature on placebo effects (i.e., our beliefs about expected outcomes of an intervention or treatment can have significant consequences for effectiveness). This in part informs the importance of understanding and belief in the coaching process and should do away with the notion that athletes just need to get on with it and follow the program; this an important factor for coaches to consider when thinking

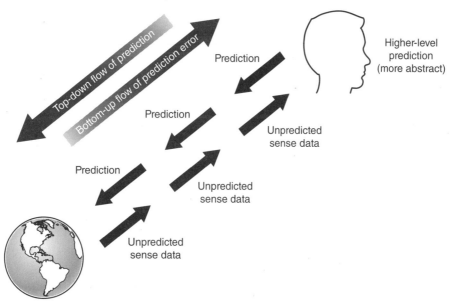

Figure 1.5 The basic predictive processing schema.

Adapted by permission from A. Clark, *Surfing Uncertainty: Prediction, Action, and the Embodied Mind* (Oxford: Oxford University Press, 2016), reproduced with permission of the Licensor through PLSclear.

about the social and cultural arrangements of the coaching environment. We will return to this in chapters 10 through 12.

The Core Importance of Motor Predictions

When it comes to motor control, PP provides an account of movement that navigates critiques of the cognitive approach to motor commands and the challenge of model-less movement in EcoD. Rather than motor representations, PP suggests that the generative model uses prior beliefs about the sensory consequences of actions in the form of motor predictions, highlighting the coupling of action and perception (Adams, Shipp, and Friston 2013). A key difference is that, rather than motor commands, motor predictions are related to the consequences of proprioceptive sense data. Action is then proactively controlled through the fulfillment of these proprioceptive predictions. It also means that actions elicit further perceptions and perceptions lead to further actions, hence the tight coupling of perception and action. Motor control therefore acts in a similar fashion to perception, with the brain using action to achieve a best fit between prediction and sensory consequences. Motor predictions are followed by a cascade of prediction errors that provide online feedback to deliver an action fluently and, in doing so, minimizing the difference between prediction and sense data. Importantly, proprioceptive prediction error can be generated at the level of the spinal cord by the comparison of proprioceptive predictions and proprioceptive input. Thus, the sensory response minimization of prediction error is analogous to reflexive behavior (Adams, Shipp, and Friston 2013).

Based on the notion of a generative hierarchy, active inference draws distinctions between types of action, labeled *habitual*, *perseverative*, and *deliberative* (Parr, Pezzulo, and Friston 2022). Habitual and perseverative behaviors are initiated by lower levels of the generative model, occurring without significant deliberate thought but resulting from goal-directed repetition and a high-precision weighting. Deliberate behavior is conscious and provided by expected prediction error. All three can be combined in sequences of action, the specific balance depending on the experience of the athlete, the ability of the individual to apply attentional resources (e.g., knowing where to look), and the extent to which behavior is habitual.

Through attention, we can modulate the nature of the error signaling to influence both predictions and prediction error. Thus, attention is critical for the execution and learning of motor skill (Harris, Wilkinson, and Ellmers 2023). In this sense, learning in PP is not necessarily seeking reward but the sampling of our environments to reduce prediction error over time (Kiverstein, Miller, and Rietveld 2019). It should be noted that PP theoretically suggests that humans act in a manner that increases the efficiency of action. Fluent movement requires a well-developed inner model through learning the sensory consequences of successful action (Clark 2023), and perhaps, the more these sensory consequences are learned, the harder it is to change movement.

So How Do People Learn?

Under PP, learning is a process of building more accurate predictive models, thereby decreasing predictive error and, as another consequence, increasing the automaticity or efficiency of execution and, core to the approach, minimizing entropy. For example, a judoka might be in randori (sparring) with lower-level partners. As a result of the low challenge experienced, few unexpected circumstances occur and therefore prediction errors are resolved without the need for errors to be pushed to higher levels of the generative model.

This is a process reportedly used by elite athletes. In his autobiography, Frank Shamrock, a former MMA athlete and coach, suggested that in all training situations people need a +1 (someone better), a 0 (someone at the same level), and a -1 (someone less capable than themselves) (Shamrock and Fleming 2012). All of these provide a different level of challenge and open a useful range of possibilities for movement. In a PP sense, the extent of variational free energy is higher when exposed to a higher-level opponent. This exposure likely will lead to more prediction errors being pushed up the neural hierarchy. Notably, however, this does not necessarily mean greater learning, something we will return to later in the book.

Implications for coaching can be found here, based on the notion of error dynamics, with our brains tracking the relative fluency of our actions in the world relative to expectation. Learning environments will present individuals with opportunities that are neither too predictable nor unpredictable. It also might suggest a theoretical underpinning for the importance of challenge and error in learning, both at the micro level (movement by movement) and at the macro level, with the need for athletes to be challenged as they develop and to be exposed to negative error dynamics. A number of papers have considered the role of play in the human experience, defined in a PP sense as a "behaviour in which the agent . . . deliberately seeks out or creates surprising situations that gravitate toward sweet-spots of relative complexity with the goal of resolving surprise . . . play is experientially associated with a feel-good quality because the agent is reducing predictive error faster than expected" (Andersen et al. 2023, p. 463). The search strategies of novices and children might be characterized by a lower weighting or precision attached to prior belief, thus the need to adjust when encountering novel environmental demands. In contrast, more expert or adult cognition may be characterized by a more conservative search pattern, one that is more exploitative based on higher precision of prior belief.

This **explore-exploit continuum** is the choice between exploiting a familiar movement based on higher precision and exploring unfamiliar options, or environments. Thus, it is the expected prediction error that determines the extent to which behavior can be classified as being exploitative or exploratory (see this idea developed in chapter 6). In coaching, this requires a delicate balance, one where novel environmental demands and movement problems are presented in a manner that is neither too complex or chaotic nor is too simplistic. Yet at the highest levels of performance, people need to be exposed to environmental demands that can impose prediction error. For example, a boxer's opponent will always be looking to provide them with an exteroceptive and proprioceptive prediction error in the form of a left hook. The business of the coach or skill-acquisition practitioner is to help the athlete generate predictions about the sensory consequences of movement in a specific environment. Notably, from the approach of this book, PP does not aim to override previous work in psychology. Instead, it attempts to embrace theories from other fields, recognizing the value of empirical work but providing an explanatory framework (Parr, Pezzulo, and Friston 2022).

CHAPTER SUMMARY

This chapter has presented a broad overview of the cognitive, EcoD, and PP approaches. It would seem self-evident that each approach has a great deal to offer the practitioner (e.g., Ashford, Abraham, and Poolton 2021). Yet a bad habit of the skill-acquisition field is straw-personing of alternative approaches, whereby other ideas are presented in the worst possible light. In practice, this fails to move us forward and leads to significant misunderstandings that are only reinforced by additional references. This seems to have had the effect of driving different approaches to entirely distinct communities of practice and away from the needs of practice. The next chapter critically considers the key contrasts and overlaps of the three approaches offered here, providing a basis for more detailed consideration of what bits might work best in given contexts.

REVIEW AND PRACTICAL QUESTIONS

1. We suggest five criteria as the characteristics of a good theory. How does each one apply?
2. What are some advantages of schema theory?
3. What is the role of a demonstration under the cognitive or EcoD approach?
4. What do predictive processing theories suggest about the direction of perception?
5. Explain the explore-exploit continuum.

KEY TERMS

affordance
automaticity
cognitive load
constraints-led approach (CLA)
contextual interference
decision making
effector
especial skills
explore-exploit continuum
free energy principle

generative model
mechanistic
nonlinear pedagogy (NLP)
perception
perception-action coupling (P-A coupling)
pracademic
priors
representative design
self-organization

CHAPTER 2

CHALLENGES OF COGNITIVE, ECOLOGICAL, AND PREDICTIVE PROCESSING APPROACHES

Howie J. Carson and Jamie Taylor

Chapter Objectives

After studying this chapter, you should be able to do the following:

- Understand the limitations of each underpinning approach
- Consider where each approach applies for different movement control problems
- Recognize the need for balance across approaches for different coaching contexts
- Critically consider the value of adopting a single underpinning approach

Chapter 1 presented the underpinnings of three motor learning and control theoretical approaches that are common within the literature. Having delineated these, an important step in developing the necessary criticality as a coach or practitioner is to understand not only what is being proposed but also what is *not* addressed by these approaches. Accordingly, this chapter highlights the various challenges of each approach and how they might limit practice. Our main argument is that no *single* approach, at least not yet, offers the coach or practitioner *all* that they need from either a practical or theoretical perspective. Consequently, we suggest that adopting a single approach inherently limits one's coaching practice and will always be suboptimal

for learners and performers. As we critically explore each approach, consider the points made earlier—that is, what we should expect from an effective approach, what the mechanistic explanations offered are, and the extent to which these are supported by personal experience.

EVALUATING APPROACHES: CONSIDERING LIMITATIONS

To inform critical decision making among the approaches, the coach or practitioner needs to carefully consider the scope of each. Consequently, this will be a feature of several chapters as the three are weighed carefully against the points offered earlier regarding the expectation

31

Cognitive Approach

The cognitive approach is traditionally introduced to coaches or practitioners at the very beginning of their formal education. Yet there is a surprising lack of advanced training available or continued consideration of cognitive mechanisms following a coach's or practitioner's development in experience and knowledge of an athlete's performance demands (i.e., beyond initial accreditation). In this section, we outline several limitations of the research in this area that may account for such occurrences.

Lacking a Unified Explanation

Perhaps because cognitive approaches are the most adopted within skill-acquisition research, many different hypotheses and theories are presented and investigated. Consequently, research from a cognitive approach in sport is extremely broad, drawing inspiration from many domains but also, perhaps inevitably, lacking a unified explanation. Therefore, issues of relatedness between studies can be problematic or confusing. One example of this problem within the skill-acquisition literature is found in literature pertaining to reinvestment theory (Masters and Maxwell 2008), which proposes that possessing and processing explicit knowledge about one's movement is a source of choking under pressure. Now consider the similarity with literature regarding the constrained action hypothesis (Wulf, McNevin, and Shea 2001), which proposes that an internal focus of attention on bodily movements disrupts the automatic self-organizing motor processes during skill acquisition and performance. Studies from both lines of inquiry aim to address optimal cognitive strategies for skill acquisition and subsequent execution, suggesting that the learner should not apply conscious attention to their body movements. This advice is proposed either to prevent the accrual of explicit knowledge and subsequent hypothesis testing during performance (reinvestment) *or* to avoid disrupting automatic and fluent execution processes (constrained action).

Notably, however, this advice contradicts longstanding views within motor imagery research. For example, a recent review by Frank and colleagues (2023) proposed that mental imagery provides a perceptual-cognitive scaffold to inform the action execution process by simulating the expected action effect, sensations, or experience of performing the upcoming movement—that is, an intentional focus on bodily sensations. Despite a substantial and well-established line of research inquiry in motor imagery, however, together with some significant employment by elites and lower-level participants alike, it is not referred to within either reinvestment theory or constrained action hypothesis research. Therefore, it would be reasonable to suggest that specific concepts within the cognitive approach can often appear and progress in silos. In many cases, this occurs with the added confusion of new terminology that is inconsistent yet similar (or even identical) to existing factors, processes, and functions *or* by introducing apparently new knowledge that was actually generated some years before. For example, consider the similar but differently labeled ideas on imagery training: respectively, progressively adding information in the form of image *stimuli* (e.g., environmental or task detail), *response* (e.g., how one feels or their physiological reaction), and *meaning* (e.g., interpreting the situation as being a challenge or threat) propositions in layers to help the performer generate and control their imagery process. These propositions were originally suggested by Lang and colleagues (1980) as a form of *layered stimulus and response training* and then represented within the five Ws (who, where, when, why, and what) framework by Williams and colleagues (2013). As such, these developments can result in rather disjointed communication between researchers and readers, generating confusion and lacking applied impact.

Theory-Driven Versus Practical Application

A second limitation of the cognitive approach is that despite historical calls (Christina 1987) and more recent attempts (Collins and Kamin 2012) to emphasize the important distinctions between different research purposes, skill-acquisition research in sport still tends to test theories with athletes (i.e., to conduct research *through* sport). In contrast, comparatively less attention is focused on research aiming to identify and address pertinent real-world challenges experienced by coaches or practitioners and athletes by providing solutions *for* sport (see chapter 8 for a more detailed consideration of these ideas). Because of this epistemological focus on theory, research often lacks transferability and relevance for practical application. Moreover, laboratory-derived findings are often claimed to have definitive practical implications for coaches and athletes (including elite athletes) when the research had been conducted with novices (e.g., Masters 1992). In simple terms, research in what would seem to be an obviously applied science seems to fail on, or sometimes even seems to avoid, application.

Against this backdrop, the literature is filled with key limitations in study design when it comes to practical application. These include the environmental conditions employed (Moffat, Collins, and Carson 2017), use of comparison groups to determine the effect of any intervention (Bobrownicki et al. 2022), (in)appropriateness of participants (Collins and Carson 2022), and inclusion of different sport science disciplines (i.e., multi- or interdisciplinarity) within interventions being investigated (Carson and Collins 2017). Using this final factor as an example, consider the robust **contextual interference** effect on learning, which suggests that organizing practice into blocks of repeated trials of a single skill before moving on to the next skill results in better immediate performance compared with practicing the same number of trials of each skill but in a randomized order (e.g., Wrisberg and Liu 1991; see chapter 1). However, when tested at a later stage to assess what is retained and how the learner can use their experience to complete a different unpracticed task, the random scheduling seems to promote better retention and transfer. Thus, while immediate performance gains might be desirable in some situations, better long-term retention and transfer to novel conditions are recognized as rigorous criteria for learning to have occurred (Salmoni, Schmidt, and Walter 1984). Figure 2.1 demonstrates this effect using an example of learning three different skills from a single sport: short, long, and drive serves in badminton. Performance, or the number of errors made in this case, is much better for those practicing 50 trials of the same serve type in each block; in other words, it is easier and quicker to get into a groove when using a blocked schedule compared to a random schedule. In contrast, practicing the three serves in a random order (e.g., short, short, drive, long, long, drive, short) results in more errors and apparently slower progress. After a period of no practice, however, those practicing in the blocked condition got worse compared to their performance at the end of the practice period (see also chapter 4). Interestingly, those in the random condition seem to have better embedded what they were practicing, such that they actually *improved* their performance and ability to cope with different task demands in the transfer test, thus demonstrating a crossover effect whereby the better performance observed from those practicing using the blocked schedule is diminished during retention and transfer tests (Goode and Magill 1986).

Explanations of contextual interference differ subtly, but most suggest that greater information-processing demands underpin more robust memory coding processes and the delayed benefits of the effect (see Lee 2012); in short, working harder to store the movements within memory develops a more permanent and effective movement execution. Yet evidence shows that while the effect is robust in controlled laboratory conditions, it is considerably weaker when used within applied settings (Ammar et al. 2023). Several variables have been proposed as mediating the

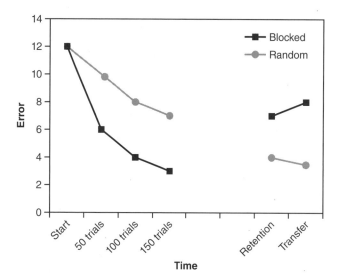

Figure 2.1 An example of the typical performance and learning trends when practicing different skills using either blocked or random practice schedules. Performance during this practice period is better (lower errors made) for the blocked condition. Following a break from practice, performance error is much lower in retention and transfer tests for those practicing with a random schedule.

contextual interference effect, such as skill level, age, task complexity, duration of task acquisition, self-efficacy, and motivation (Barreiros, Figueiredo, and Godinho 2007; Brady 1998; Landin and Hebert 1997). Notably, however, there is surprisingly scarce acknowledgment of the actual cognitive strategy (or strategies) employed by learners when undertaking the prescribed practice regimen. Since it is common for coaches to provide instruction to inform a player's processing of the movement to be performed (e.g., technical cues or primes; Orr, Cruickshank, and Carson 2021; Schempp et al. 2004), it is possible that this may serve to counter or negate the weak contextual interference effect within applied settings for complex, whole-body movements. Reflecting the current approach, much of the research from a cognitive perspective has tended toward the monodisciplinary design by focusing on the practice schedule alone, not always appreciating the interdisciplinary contributions that can be afforded by attending to applied practice demands and good coaching practice that would seek to inform the performer's cognitive processes. By implication, *if* applied research investigated the practice schedules in combination with relevant cognitive strategies, the evidence for a similarly strong effect as seen in the laboratory *might* be more likely.

Extending the previous point, cognitive research in skill acquisition therefore has generally progressed at a slower rate compared to applied practice in terms of integrating real-world performance demands within study designs. More positively, however, this trend may be changing, with indicators that experimental research is beginning to recognize important idiosyncrasies to reflect the reality of sport participation and coaching practice. An example of this progress is exemplified in the study by Meier and colleagues (2020), who investigated different types of instruction when coaching the tennis serve among competitive junior players. Rather than providing consistent instructions across all players in either the analogy or explicit instruction groups (the two conditions being compared), these authors employed an individualized approach by providing analogy or explicit instructions that targeted specific technical errors that had been demonstrated during a preassessment phase. In this way, the intervention was closer to current coaching practice, with players more likely to

relate to why the instruction was being provided as opposed to being confused by unfamiliar instructions, a feature that has been shown to disrupt performance (Maurer and Munzert 2013). Thus, for fairer comparisons between training approaches, more research needs to address the interaction with participants' previous experience within a sport (including previous coaching) and their specific training needs.

Information Processing Versus Interactive, Bottom-Up Perspective

Finally, research from the cognitive approach primarily focuses on the information-processing demands and commands based on an athlete's ability to represent the situation and their upcoming actions. In contrast, much less has been investigated over the past century regarding the nature of cognition as an interactive and immersive phenomenon with sensory processes from a bottom-up perspective.

Indeed, while still acknowledging the existence and role of representations in most tasks, an enactive view of cognition (see table I.1) seeks to address high-level cognition in rare contexts such as flow states when focus, awareness, creativity, and intention are integrated, but the action execution occurs without representations involved (Krein and Ilundáin-Agurruza 2017). Another state is a Japanese state called *mushin* (無心), signifying an empty mind or mindless state, a condition stressed by traditional martial arts. Both states emphasize being in the moment, having mindfully fluid awareness, and not getting caught up or distracted. **Embodiment** is the key underlying feature within this approach to action execution and to how the world is experienced; action constitutes cognition *and* perception (see also table I.1). Therefore, cognition is not limited to or located within the brain; rather, it is found as a result of the continuous activities and environments in which we engage. Performers in these types of states function with a clear purpose compared to when needing a more adaptive control style (Christensen, Sutton, and McIlwain 2016) but one that is more efficient due to less computational processing required when performing the skill. In other words, the utility and reliance on mental representations during motor planning and subsequent motor execution phases of a performance are temporally dynamic. While enacted and embodied cognition is gaining more traction within the sport literature (e.g., Raab and Araújo 2019), further exploration is needed on how this approach to the mind and body extends beyond the phenomenological account and to show the entire picture using methods that capture movement dynamics and more fundamental sensorimotor processes.

The EcoD Approach

Proposed as a direct alternative to the cognitive approach, the EcoD approach has gained more traction with coaches or practitioners and in research interest over the past 20 years. However, the following limitations highlight several critical concerns regarding its applicability to the coaching process and its mechanistic development within research.

Too Limited Across the Whole Coaching Process

Reflecting a change in research focus to address the need for a contextually situated understanding of action execution (i.e., not laboratory based), the EcoD approach has been criticized for being too limited in its ability to account for the positive contribution that many common coaching practices have on skill acquisition and performance. For example, Bobrownicki and colleagues (2023) challenge the expressed principle of representative design, that practice *always* needs to simulate the representative demands of performance. Rather than optimal preparation requiring athletes to realize and act directly on affordances, performance can also be informed by a series of progressions in both planning and execution during the months, weeks, and days leading up to competition. In team games, especially those with a greater element of collision (e.g., American football), such practices include the utility of performance reviews, opponent evaluations, formation of team identity, and decision making about strategy that help direct coaches when designing and supervising specific plays. This review-then-apply cycle reflects work by Richards and colleagues (2017) as a process of "thinking slow to think fast." The idea is that fast responses across a team evolve through a combination of off-field review and activity (including play board presentations and watching game film), then applied in specifically designed drills and practices, then reviewed and refined off field, and so on.

Practice, especially those with a greater element of collision (e.g., American football), can be informed by the progression of off-field activity including performance review, opposition analysis, and equivalent strategies.

David Rosenblum/Icon Sportswire via Getty Images

From an EcoD perspective, such activities that serve to construct representations of play and their technical requirements would be viewed not only as suboptimal but as impossible since the mechanistic underpinnings do not include the cognitive architecture to justify their inclusion. Indeed, even within the competitive performance itself, Bobrownicki and colleagues (2023) acknowledge at least *some* role of cognitive planning when deciding on the tactics to employ as opposed to relying *only* on EcoD mechanisms (e.g., direct perception, self-organization, movement emergence). This perspective, therefore, appreciates the need for additional approaches over and above an EcoD one alone to more parsimoniously explain the long-term processes that result in skilled action in context.

Lack of Conceptual Clarity

A second limitation of the EcoD approach is that both between and even within published articles there is a lack of conceptual clarity and consistency. This presents an obvious challenge for the researcher aiming to set hypotheses and evaluate relative advantages. We contend that it also presents an even greater challenge for the practitioner when considering the differences between approaches and being sure about what they offer as a guide for practice (see Alali, Collins, and Carson 2024). Given that elite-level athletes report their coaching as a source of confidence (Hays et al. 2007), it would be interesting to better understand how this factor might affect an athlete's learning or performance journey. As an example of this inconsistency, at a theoretical level, the key concept that differentiates between the cognitive and EcoD approaches is the notion of internal representation. Both Handford and colleagues (1997) and Seifert and colleagues (2017) dismiss any centralized structures as a means to interpret information or to control movements. However, a more recent article by Araújo and colleagues (2019) says that behaviors can be controlled in a way *not necessarily* requiring mental representations, even though these same authors state that "in ecological dynamics, there is no internal knowledge structure or central pattern generator inside the organism responsible for controlling action" (p. 10). Equally confusing, Correia and colleagues (2019) explain "little focus" (p. 121) on strengthening mental representations, which seems to not dismiss them entirely. These appeals to a weaker sense of representationalism might enable EcoD theorists to navigate the challenge of how to coordinate team behavior, the role

of knowledge in the perception of affordances, and the inherent conflict between planning for future action and how one directly perceives the future (Linson et al. 2018). However, in doing so, they also seem to move outside the theoretical boundaries of ecological psychology, toward a more pragmatic perspective similar to enacted cognition described earlier. Accordingly—in the sporting literature, at least—some inconsistencies exist between what was originally proposed as an alternative to the cognitive perspective. While some adhere to the original foundations of Gibson (1979), others appear to be moving closer to a middle ground, seemingly less committed to a fully antirepresentational view.

It is this lack of need for representations, or prior knowledge, that would seem to present the most significant practical challenges for the EcoD approach. While some have made a strong case that, regardless of underpinning theory, there may be little difference in what an athlete's training *looks* like, we would suggest that the presence or absence of internal representations, and the consequent allowances made, has significant implications for the nature of coaching practice. While an observer might not notice significant differences between the activity design of the coach who decided to adhere strongly to theoretical boundaries (perhaps with the exception of the use of more drill-like activities) or be more permissive in how they exploited the precepts, we argue that the relative importance placed on the representations involved in a given activity might fundamentally change the direction and application of their practice. For example, while an elite golfer may undertake a practice round on the day before a tournament irrespective of the approach adopted by a coach, the cognitive perspective may engage in tournament-specific planning behaviors such as noting which clubs to hit, putting to expected hole locations on greens, and assessing the conditions of key areas on the course to know where might represent a safer miss—notably, all unrepresentative in their design. On the other hand, an EcoD coach may encourage a more simulation-like approach to playing the course as if it were a competition round itself. In short, theoretical perspective does matter, a point we return to at the end of this chapter.

Do Internal Representations Exist?

It is here that the EcoD approach is subject to another significant challenge. If internal representations or priors (see chapter 1) do *not* exist, it becomes very difficult to explain empirical evidence showing that prior beliefs and understanding impact on learning (e.g., Bobrownicki et al. 2019). Indeed, if one were to dismiss the existence of an internal representation, the implication would be *not* to develop an athlete's understanding of why they are doing what they are doing (e.g., Abraham and Collins 2011). In doing so, this again makes it difficult to explain significant empirical evidence showing the positive impact resulting from a *change* of belief during the process of skill acquisition and learning (Lindberg et al. 2023).

As an example of the issues that arise when disregarding the existence of internal representations, consider the process of **perceptual attunement** (i.e., becoming highly sensitized to attend to relevant sources of information) proposed by ecological psychology and seen as a means through which performers on the same team come to view things in a similar fashion. This challenge is considered later in chapter 12. For the moment, and as an explanation, Araújo and colleagues (2019) refer to the same self-organizing mechanisms of the motor system to describe neuronal patterns of behavior experienced during attunement. Accordingly, neuronal organization is explained to reflect a temporary resonance of the perceptual system to environmental information; Gibson (1966) called the brain "a self-tuning resonator" (p. 146). When the brain resonates it means that the learner has become tuned to specific environmental energy patterns. This resonance is achieved through the embedded and embodied brain-body-environment system. There are several issues arising from this explanation, not least concerning what neural resonance is intended to achieve, how to develop it, and what this means from the learner's perspective. In other words, it lacks mechanistic explanation as well as evidence of how it works.

Predictive Processing Approach

At the time of writing, predictive processing (PP) approaches have become the dominant explanation for general human functioning and behavior in the broader literature. Yet this does not mean that its application for skill acquisition is without challenges. These will be discussed in terms

of theory and practice, first by addressing some common theoretical critiques of PP.

Philosophical Challenge

A common philosophical challenge of the free energy principle (see chapter 1) is the so-called dark room problem. This questions the underlying principle of PP that the prerogative of human functioning is the reduction of prediction error, or surprise. The essence of this critique is that, if all human behavior aims to result in a reduction of surprise, why do humans not seek out states of minimal sensory change by sitting in dark rooms? This poses a broader challenge related to the capacity of individual theories to provide a unified theory of everything. Can PP really offer a catchall explanation for the mental lives of all humans and their behavior, attention, learning, affect, and memory? Some have suggested not (e.g., Sun and Firestone 2020). This problem has been debated at length, with proponents of PP suggesting that the dark room problem represents a misunderstanding of prediction error and the notion of surprise. The counterargument is that if humans are to respond to biological needs—they need to stay warm, nourished, and otherwise healthy—the dark room does not allow this (Friston, Thornton, and Clark 2012).

The same critical reasoning could be applied to a particular problem in sport. Indeed, it seems difficult to explain through the prerogative of surprise reduction why people are driven to push themselves outside of their comfort zone to become truly elite sporting performers. Theoretically, PP would tackle this by suggesting that humans not only act based on their current perception of prediction error, but also to minimize future, expected prediction error. Humans can generate action policies to engage in a mixture of exploratory and exploitative behavior, allowing them to progress to the states they would like to experience (Kiverstein, Miller, and Rietveld 2019).

Lack of Neurophysiological Evidence

PP has also been criticized based on a lack of neurophysiological evidence to support assumptions and a lack of empirical testability (Kogo and Trengove 2015).* In other words, and returning

---

*This criticism can apply for much work across the three approaches. Indeed, explanations are often proposed as alternatives with insufficient recognition of, or recourse to, applied settings. As suggested, good theories should explain how things work in practice, thereby offering some clear implications for application.

to the mechanisms mentioned in the introduction, how *does* PP work and which structures are involved in achieving it? Acknowledging these concerns, an increasing body of research is investigating some of the core predictions of the theory; however, this also remains in its relative infancy. For example, the strength of evidence supporting the entwinement of perception and cognition has been questioned (Firestone and Scholl 2016). Thus, some would suggest that PP's attempt to unify historically separate functions is overly simplistic, especially since evidence for how movements work is also lacking across the functions it aims to unite. Taking a broader view, it is reasonable to suggest that PP can be used to explain a significant body of neurophysiological evidence. This doesn't mean however that there is irrefutable evidence *for* the theoretical presuppositions of PP, including the existence of expectation and error units in neural processing (Walsh et al. 2020). Yet in comparison, it would be wholly unfair to suggest that the alternative approaches are fully evidence based. Indeed, all theories presented in this chapter should be taken as being entirely fallible and we should expect that they will be improved or refuted over time.

Lack of Practical Application

Given our practical focus, for the moment, the key challenges for PP seem to be in practical application rather than theoretical grounding. PP offers a theoretically robust account of human functioning, even though the fine details are debated. A particular challenge is the extent to which PP has been applied in the motor skill acquisition literature. This contrasts with both the cognitive and EcoD approaches, which, despite mechanistic issues, are embedded in practical application by coaches and, with variable quality, in educational programs. Even in the fields where PP has been applied, it is difficult to point to broad practical differences. This may lead some to question the ecological validity of PP and application to human learning, because much of the empirical literature has come from developmental robotics (Kiverstein, Miller, and Rietveld 2019). Taken at face value, this leaves PP open to arguments of oversimplification and liable to attract a "nice in theory" attitude from practitioners.

When it comes to application, this is a familiar critique directed at work emanating from

neuroscience, with the suggestion that findings at the neuronal level have little to do with the biopsychosocial complexity of human beings and skill-acquisition practice. The findings of neuroscientific study and their application in education is another good example, with an argument to suggest that the two fields are based on different levels of analysis and that neuroscientific findings therefore cannot lead directly to coaching or teaching application (Willingham 2009). The same critique may be applied to the existing relevance of PP in that its use requires extensive bridging between research and practice and between practice and research. This is beginning to change since Harris and colleagues (2022), for example, used active inference to account for findings across the anticipation literature in sport.

Such positive evolutions notwithstanding, we suggest that if these challenges become critiques, they are ill founded unless we begin to see a generation of oversimplifications and assumptions toward the application of PP in practice. To this end, we strongly discourage coaches from moving toward identifying themselves as something akin to a "predictive coach." Indeed, we would suggest that this would be incoherent with the approach in the literature thus far (e.g., Parr, Pezzulo, and Friston 2022), which has been to understand existing empirical findings, something that PP may have the capacity to do across the literature. As such, PP should be used as a means for coaches and practitioners to reflect on the mechanisms that underpin, rather than prescribe, practice. We certainly see no pedagogic revolution on the horizon as a result of recognizing top-down and bottom-up processing (Taylor et al. 2023). As an example, while major theoretical differences exist between the cognitive notion of motor commands and the PP notion of motor predictions, it is wholly unclear what the pragmatic differences are between the theories. If motor commands are considered to be signals that drive motor units without contextual specificity, in contrast, motor predictions encode the predicted consequences of movement (Adams, Shipp, and Friston 2013; Frank et al. 2023). In both cases, depending on the level of learning and the type of desired outcome, the point of reference for the coach seems to be the enhancement of representation, though perhaps at different levels or for use at different times (Friston, Mattout, and Kilner 2011).

Lack of Implication for Team Coordination

Another area of concern regarding application is the current status of the PP approach in relation to the coordinated skilled actions of groups. PP, and particularly active inference, *can* be applied to social systems as a means of describing a system's function, such as in the business organizational setting (Khezri 2022). Notably, however, while the free energy principle provides a useful framing and descriptor for the conceptualization of an organization (or team) as a complex system, the extension of a generative model beyond an individual seems a point of contention. Theoretically, it may be interesting to consider a novel descriptive framing of a social system, but for the moment it is unclear what the different practical recommendations are. If this means that a team or organization functions as if its collective priors (team members) form a generative model, or similar to the literature on shared mental models (see chapters 10-12), this represents overlapping knowledge structures (or indeed priors) (Van den Bossche et al. 2011) and we end up in much the same place—practically, at least.

COMMON DIFFERENCES AMONG APPROACHES AND PRACTICE

Thus far, we hope that we have been able to offer a fair and grounded critique of each approach; however, a simple summary might help here:

1. Cognitive theories have been criticized for lacking the ability to explain how abstract processes are linked to in-action control and the extent to which research has been able to capture realistic performance demands in sport in order to reveal more complex cognitive processes.

2. EcoD, conversely, while perhaps being better able to explain in-action control, does not explain how knowledge or priors affect individually skilled action and how teams coordinate action.

3. PP approaches (particularly active inference) present the opportunity for a unification of sorts, with generative models internalizing environmental interactions and being used to support action control. However, much like any theory, it lacks empirical verification for *all* tenets of the approach and has received little practical application.

This leaves coaches and practitioners with questions as to where, indeed whether, they should invest their thinking and professional development in a single theory. Is there a difference between theory and practice that needs to be acknowledged, especially if the fundamental motivation is practical change rather than testing of theories? We would argue that if a coach feels pressured to choose one single approach and unable to step outside its boundaries, this inherently limits their practice.

Another important consideration is the depth of understanding required to meaningfully comprehend the ideas presented within academic literature. Practically speaking, it is undoubtedly challenging to differentiate between, for example, the various interpretations of PP and the different philosophical positions on the nature of representations. From the EcoD approach, the potential for confusion is high since some authors hold tightly to the notion of direct perception, whereas others hold a weaker notion of representation as per recent theories concerning enacted or embodied cognition. When using the cognitive approach, equally, a range of theoretical presuppositions are proposed. It is here that the real danger of extrapolating from approaches to practice is revealed. This is the difference between the PJDM orientation for professional practice and a theoretically based paradigm. For some researchers, taking an evidence-informed position is anathema to standard scientific research practice (i.e., the idea that only factual knowledge gained through observation and measurement is trustworthy). From a researcher's perspective, this is not necessarily wrong, especially because their working remit is typically tighter and narrower than for those working within real-world applied settings. As practitioner-researchers, however, the use of theory *needs* to be broader than rigidly applying one single approach.

In the introduction we referred to the need to explain, predict, and modify behavior (Atkinson and Hilgard 1953). Each approach presented here offers different strengths and weaknesses in this regard (see also the case study in chapter 4 for practical examples). In addition, these are far from the only theories informing human functioning, and some will rightly question our categorization. A full overview of human functioning might be a little beyond the scope of this book. Our purpose is to outline the relationship between theory and practice. If nothing else, we would suggest at this point that the coach or skill-acquisition practitioner cannot act in the best interests of their athletes by being solely theoretically driven. To do so may result in advice that is more evangelical than practical and performer focused. In this sense, we agree with the suggestion of Chow and colleagues (2023) that "theory therefore may be viewed as a companion or co-coach supporting our own decision making and development" (p. 6). Where we may diverge from the view of Chow and colleagues is that, given the weaknesses of the different approaches and indeed the lack of any tight boundaries around each, practice requires multiple approaches to be used in order to support coach decision making with all of its biopsychosocial complexity. Using the maxim of Kurt Lewin (1943), "there is nothing as practical as a good theory" (p. 118). We just need more than one.

POTENTIAL SOLUTIONS: A MULTIFACETED APPROACH

With this in mind, the coach has a choice: Specifically, should they choose to pick a side from the various approaches that have been advocated in the sporting literature, even if the mainstream neuroscientific and philosophy of mind literature has progressed beyond that which is used in the sporting domain? To what depth are coaches required to understand and use this literature? Do coaches need to be aware of the various implications of types of representations that are argued for among different PP perspectives or of the vagaries of more or less representational views of active inference? Given that careers in the philosophy of mind have been spent arguing such things, we would argue not. While PP may offer a way forward in the so-called representation wars between those with a representational underpinning (cognitivists) and dynamists (in the sport literature, EcoD) (Clark 2015), it is yet to resolve any conflict within the domain of skill acquisition. For all the reasons that we suggest, we would argue that there is instead a need for coaches to see the relative strengths and weaknesses of each approach and deploy theory to inform practices against the intended training outcomes. This means that rather than being overly theoretically driven, theory needs to form a part of **evidence-informed practice** (figure 2.2) (Taylor et al. 2023).

Accordingly, a coach needs to understand the relative strengths, weaknesses, and applicability of various approaches, but not the deep philosophical nuances. Perhaps most importantly, a critical ability needs to be applied to the quality of evidence generated and how this might transfer to a particular context (see chapter 4 for detailed critique of evidence). The implications of this are for an inclusive and diverse use of theory, evidence, contextual demands, and personal experience for the coach to examine their practice. The evidence-informed coach, therefore, will aim to operate at the nexus of the needs of the context (e.g., what is expected by the athlete and the time of season), the coach's personal experience (e.g., taking account of their individual capacities, what might work with an individual athlete), and the best available evidence. As an example, the context of a swim coach will be very different from that of an American football coach (see case study). These differences will be reflected not just in terms of differences between

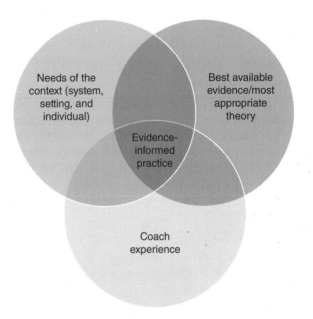

Figure 2.2 Evidence-informed practice components.

Chapter 2 Challenges of Cognitive, Ecological, and Predictive Processing Approaches **41**

CASE STUDY

COMPARISON OF CONTRASTING SPORT CHALLENGES

For the American football coach, there will be different facets of the coaching role that are better suited to the various approaches outlined. For example, in terms of content, a coach could sensibly draw on the tight coupling of perception and action, as per EcoD and PP, to provide ample opportunities for a running back to perceive opportunities and affordances once they have been handed off the ball and are aiming to avoid defenders on their way to the end zone (Yearby et al. 2022). They will surely not, however, underpin their team blocking schemes using direct perception of shared affordances, that theoretically would not use the perceiver's expectations or mental representations of performance solutions (cf. Silva Pedro et al. 2013). If using a single theory, it is difficult to see how a coach might account for the need for this shared understanding, the absence of which would surely lead to a breakdown in an offensive play. Indeed, this is in no small part because the blockers cannot see the running back or directly perceive where they will run in the future, a significant issue if an athlete is much slower and up to 110 lb (50 kg) heavier. Contextually, these challenges are a long way from the needs of a swimmer who does not require tightly coordinated team actions for competitive success. Similarly, in swimming, injury risk in practice is far less of a concern. Based on practical experience, swim coaches also might not value skill acquisition as highly as physiological improvements.

the levels of athlete (see chapter 7), the individual and team focus (see chapter 11), the context of day-to-day management (see chapter 9), and the nature of group dynamics (see chapter 12), but on a host of other biopsychosocial factors suggested throughout this book.

The example in the case study is not an edge case, but rather represents prominent challenges in nearly every coaching situation. Depending on one's background, coaches may be drawn to a particular approach. But it is important to consider the capability of that approach to address pertinent contextual demands within the performance domain as a major factor for underpinning the practice.

We explicitly shy away from the need to make specific choices concerning theoretical framing because skill acquisition in sport exists at the edge of all theories outlined. Consequently, our aim here is to consider what applied skill acquisition really *depends on*, thus moving the field beyond debates about the best theoretical approach and toward enhancing practice (Ashford, Abraham, and Poolton 2021). Notably, if the coach takes this step, they may risk the paralysis-by-analysis problem referenced in the introduction. To be clear, this multidimensional assessment of *all* elements of practice is not something recommended on a day-to-day basis. What we are clear in suggesting is that coaches need to take the time to reflect on and evaluate their positioning, their use of theory, and the quality of evidence they use with some regularity. It is this consideration of why that underpins a PJDM approach.

CHAPTER SUMMARY

This chapter has highlighted the various challenges of each approach and how they might limit our practice. Our main argument is that no single approach, at least yet, offers the coach or practitioner *all* that they need from either a practical or theoretical perspective. Consequently, adopting a single approach was argued as inherently limiting one's coaching practice and always being suboptimal for learners and performers. As we critically explored each approach, we addressed what should be expected from an effective approach, what the mechanistic explanations are, and the extent to which these can and should be supported by coaching experience.

REVIEW AND PRACTICAL QUESTIONS

1. On what does motor learning research from a cognitive perspective focus?
2. What are the weaknesses of the cognitive perspective?
3. What are the weaknesses of the EcoD perspective?
4. What are the weaknesses of a predictive processing perspective?
5. What are the representation wars?
6. On what basis do we suggest that coaches should look to a multi-theoretical perspective?

KEY TERMS

contextual interference

embodiment

evidence-informed practice

perceptual attunement

CHAPTER 3

SIFTING THE USEFUL FROM THE USELESS: A CASE FOR CRITICALITY IN COACHING

Loel Collins and Ray Bobrownicki

Chapter Objectives

After studying this chapter, you should be able to do the following:

- Understand the complexity of sport and performance environments and identify variables that constitute and affect these
- Appreciate the adaptable and flexible nature of expertise
- Recognize the need for critical thinking when operating in sport and performance contexts
- Explain the practical implications of *it depends* coaching

The earlier chapters of this book have explored relevant skill-acquisition theories. It is important to note, however, that effective athlete and performer support involves far more than simply understanding skill acquisition. Indeed, skill-acquisition theory and practice by themselves will be insufficient to guide real-world athlete support, which typically requires deployment of a diverse range of skills and knowledge in the face of competing needs and demands (Bobrownicki et al. 2023). For instance, coaches, who represent the principal users of skill-acquisition literature, must balance the available theories of skill acquisition with and against equally complex theories of organizational psychology, sociology, talent development, teaching (pedagogy, andragogy, and heutagogy), and more when working with performers. As such, it is critical for those involved with or interested in skill acquisition to understand learning and performance environments, the wider coaching and performer-support processes, and how theories of skill acquisition are then applied within these.

In addition to these considerations, it is also important to recognize and appreciate the hyperdynamic environments in which learning and performance take place and the adaptability and flexibility that coaches, skill-acquisition specialists, and other support staff must demonstrate to operate successfully within these. To generate the requisite adaptability and flexibility, however, coaches and practitioners must develop not only **declarative knowledge** and practical skills but also their capabilities as thinkers and decision makers (Collins et al. 2022). In this regard, coaches, skill-acquisition specialists, and support staff need to become pedagogically agile (Mees et al. 2021; Barry et al. 2023), continually developing their knowledge of why, how, and under what conditions approaches may apply if they are to respond to the demands of dynamic sport and performance environments effectively.

Putting all of these elements together is a difficult task, however, and fraught with challenges (e.g., recognizing that performer support is a complex, adaptable, and future-focused process; learning effectively from previous experiences). Quality coaching and performer support are cognitively demanding, characterized by complexity and nonlinearity with pre-scripted routines and off-the-shelf solutions more prone to failure than success. In other words, coaching and performer support require the consumption, evaluation, integration, and application of diverse sources of knowledge—alongside preparation and nested decision making—to develop bespoke and tailored solutions. Therefore, to navigate the demands and apply the theory from the introduction and chapters 1 and 2, it is critical to comprehend learning and performance environments; select, appraise, and make sense of a range of knowledge sources; evaluate these against previous experiences; and, crucially, consider how these relevant skills and knowledge may inform present and future decision making (Collins and Eastabrook 2023; Collins et al. 2022). With this in mind, this chapter starts by laying out and examining the performance environment before exploring the nature of expertise, its development, and the importance of criticality in responding to the demands of these environments. We conclude by considering the practical implications for the performer-support process more generally and for skill acquisition more specifically.

THE PERFORMANCE ENVIRONMENT

Learning and performance contexts are complicated, dynamic, and highly contextual, typically occurring in ill-structured and fast-changing environments (Nash et al. 2024). Learning contexts typically emphasize development through practice and experience (e.g., of physical, technical, tactical, or cognitive components), while performance environments aim to facilitate high performance and fulfillment of potential through a range of tools and resources, such as evidence-informed coaching, sport science support, and high-quality training facilities.

Across these contexts, coaching and performance-support practices extend beyond the traditional views of the observant coach with whistle, stopwatch, and clipboard at the ready. Not only is performer support highly dynamic because it responds to a set of complex contextual demands, but also because change (e.g., through learning or in performance) is commonly what coaches, skill-acquisition specialists, and support staff aim to enact, achieve, and manage. Indeed, constant change is a core feature within these contexts, generated by the unique characteristics of every performer's interaction with support activities, and demands ongoing decision making and review from the coach (Collins et al. 2018).

One way that interested parties may enhance their comprehension and understanding of their wider performance context is to consider the contribution and interaction of biological (e.g., height, weight, or musculature), psychological (e.g., confidence or motivation), and social aspects (e.g., leadership or team cohesion). Despite its origins in the medical domain (see Engel 1977), this biopsychosocial model has been adapted and increasingly applied to a range of developmental settings, including sport and performance (Collins et al. 2022), on the premise that behavior (and, in turn, learning and performance) cannot be explained by biological, psychological, or social factors in isolation (figure 3.1; see also discussion in the introduction). As such, these three components represent critical aspects of the performance environment that should be reflected throughout decision-making processes.

In addition to these considerations, a range of further factors may ostensibly be external to the immediate performer-supporter interaction but nevertheless affect strategy and decision making. For instance, factors such as culture, sporting policy, and immigration laws can present significant implications for the support process and, consequently, athlete development or per-

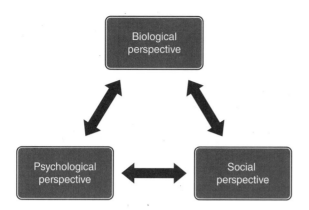

Figure 3.1 The biopsychosocial model.

formance (see Bobrownicki and Valentin 2022). Helpful frameworks and diagnostic tools for understanding such factors include PESTLE (see table 3.1, adapted from Argyris 1996), a model of six overlapping and interactive components that evolved from Aguilar's (1967) original framework.

Within the performance environment, further consideration may also be given to the activity being performed or skill being developed or refined. To help better understand associated demands and constraints for sport and related activities, for instance, Collins and Carson (2021) proposed that sport (in this case, the action and adventure variety) comprises an environmental dimension—ranging from natural (e.g., traditional mountain climbing) to wholly manufactured (e.g., indoor climbing)—and a regulatory dimension—ranging from personally regulated (e.g., sea kayaking) to externally regulated (e.g., slalom kayaking). Their resulting model integrating these factors presents the environmental dimension on the horizontal axis and the regulatory dimension on the vertical axis. As shown in figure 3.2, using a skiing example, different forms of a sport can be considered and plotted against these two axes. This model can aid in identifying the constraints and, therefore, the demands for performers and their supporters that should be acknowledged alongside other considerations within diverse and dynamic performance contexts.

THE NATURE OF EXPERTISE AS ADAPTIVE EXPERTISE

Given the many variables that compose and affect the skill-acquisition and performance landscape, there are significant implications for skill and knowledge and how these are applied. For instance, coaches must apply their skills and knowledge within a range of appropriate options that reflects the interactions between the performers, the environment, and the coaches themselves toward identified aims. Based on this, the nature of expertise becomes particularly salient for those working in sport and performance environments.

On one hand, coaches, skill-acquisition specialists, and other supporters may demonstrate **routine expertise** (Hatano and Inagaki 1986; Hatano and Oura 2003), which relates to the performance of standard tasks (e.g., free throw shooting or fast-break drills in basketball) involv-

Table 3.1 PESTLE Model

P = Political	Take into account government policies, the stability of that government, the potential for changes in policy
E = Economic	Funding, economic growth or decline, globalization, inflation, interest rates and the cost of living, labor and consumer spending
S = Social	Lifestyle factors, cultural norms and performance expectations
T = Technology	GPS tracking, video, data recording and analysis, artificial intelligence (AI)
L = Legal	The constantly changing legal landscape—employment law and employment tribunal decisions, working practices, safeguarding, and health and safety regulations
E = Environmental/Ethics	The impact of coaching decisions on the environment, carbon emissions associated with travel to a venue, social responsibility and ethical sourcing of goods and services that may affect procurement
	The principles, morals, or ethical problems in a coaching relationship, issues such as power imbalance and its exploitation in the coaching relationship, and safeguarding may be evident; aspects of social responsibility are also at play

Adapted from J. Law, *A Dictionary of Business and Management*, 5th ed. (Oxford: Oxford University Press, 2009).

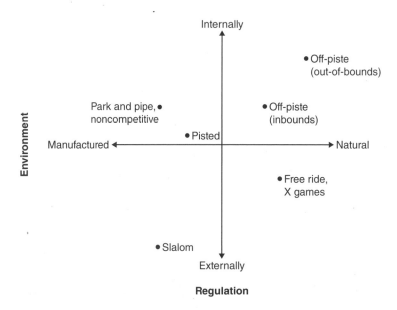

Figure 3.2 Conceptualization of modern sport.

Adapted from Collins and Carson (2022).

ing small, functional units or few variables with minimal error (Simon, Collins, and Collins 2017). The structure of sessions informed by routine expertise is typically characterized by consistent or standardized routines, recipes, and practices (e.g., administering basketball camps with the same predetermined activities year after year) that only *could* match the situational demands (Collins and Collins 2016). These routinized practices focus on the development of competence in a finite set of circumstances with minimal cognitive loading or without higher-level decision making (Collins and Carson 2021).

Sport and performance contexts, however, will ordinarily require creativity and flexibility in order to provide functional and prompt responses to unexpected and novel needs (Collins et al. 2022), which routine expertise alone will typically be insufficient to address. For this reason, as a useful and important development, coaches and practitioners can evolve toward and demonstrate **adaptive expertise** (Hatano and Inagaki 1986; Hatano and Oura 2003). For adaptive expertise, decision makers must use and build on many of the same skills and knowledge that constitute routine expertise, but such skill and knowledge must be deployed flexibly and adaptively in response to unique needs and challenges as they arise (Trotter et al. 2018). In other words, the components that relate to routine expertise (e.g., the order and structure of drills and practices within a session) must be taken, reconfigured in response to athlete and environmental needs, and then applied adaptively, resulting in effectively unlimited possibilities when appropriately tailored (Collins et al. 2022). For example, if critical equipment or facilities are unavailable, adaptive experts can modify, rearrange, or replace tasks as appropriate to ensure that key aims or needs are still addressed. Such adaptive expertise reflects the conditionality necessary to assess the interaction of variables inherent in sport and performance environments needed to arrive at practice and decision making that are contextually specific. Importantly, as the unpredictability and messiness of the environment and practice increase, so do the demands for adaptability for coaches, skill-acquisition specialists, and other support staff within these contexts (Mees and Collins 2022).

In the literature, three key dimensions have been proposed to contribute to adaptive expertise (e.g., Hatano and Inagaki 1986; Hatano and Oura 2003):

1. *Domain-specific skills.* For domain-specific skills, which are particular to a certain area or discipline, adaptive experts conceive these as "dynamic and evolving" (Carbonell et al. 2016, p. 169) rather than fixed (which is more reflective of routine expertise; Crawford et

al. 2005). Based on this, adaptive expertise is associated with continuous engagement with and the development of more diverse sources of knowledge in order to learn not only what works (along with how, when, and why) but also what does *not* work, which represents a critical consideration for coaches and those working in performance environments (Collins et al. 2023). In effect, adaptive experts will actively "enrich and refine" their skills and knowledge in order to maintain and enhance their standing (Crawford et al. 2005, p. 5).

2. *Innovation skills.* The progressive engagement and learning of domain-specific skills both underlie and are supported by the second dimension for adaptive expertise: innovation skills. Innovation skills relate to the transfer of existing skills, knowledge, or practices in novel and unique ways (Schwartz, Bransford, and Sears 2005). Although routine expertise may also use domain-specific skills, adaptive experts are uniquely able to recognize when existing approaches will not work and demonstrate innovation through the reshaping, refining, or repurposing of those existing tools or strategies. These novel and often proactive approaches are typically driven by the interaction of the environment and performers alongside the availability of resources such as equipment, facilities, staff, or time (Collins et al. 2022). Importantly, empirical work also supports the contribution of both domain-specific skills and innovation skills to adaptive expertise (e.g., Carbonell et al. 2016).

3. *Metacognitive skills.* For metacognitive skills, the third proposed dimension of adaptive expertise, the empirical evidence has been more equivocal, but research nevertheless indicates that experienced practitioners (e.g., coaches and skill-acquisition specialists) are metacognitively active by reflecting on their own thinking, decision making, and learning, even if they may experience difficulties in articulating or conveying this (see Mees et al. 2020).

Along with **metacognition**, however (see also chapter 11), findings from Mees and colleagues (2020) have suggested that situational comprehension also underpins planning and reflection and further characterizes adaptive expertise.

Such **situational comprehension** comprises two components:

4. **Situational awareness** (Endsley 1995), which refers to the ability to perceive and understand one surroundings, including the people, objects, and events happening in the immediate environment. Endsley proposed that situational awareness includes three levels relating to the perception, comprehension, and anticipation of the situation.

5. **Situational demands** (Mees and Collins 2022), which relate to the requirements of the environment, the people, and the session objectives.

Situational awareness in basketball, for instance, could be exemplified by perceiving relevant elements (e.g., positioning of teammates and defense, time remaining, ball placement, and number of player and team fouls), understanding the significance or meaning of these various elements or events (e.g., positioning of defenders may indicate their overarching strategy), and then anticipating or projecting future status or actions (e.g., understanding defensive strategy indicates where defenders might move and therefore which offensive strategies may exploit this). According to Mees and colleagues (2022), situational comprehension involves projections of how situations may subsequently evolve *and* how performers may develop in response to taken decisions and interventions.

BEING A CRITICAL CONSUMER: RESPONDING TO ENVIRONMENTAL AND SITUATIONAL DEMANDS

To facilitate or enable their capacity for adaptation, alongside their capability for innovation and metacognitive practice, coaches, skill-acquisition specialists, and associated support staff need to be critical consumers of knowledge. **Critical thinking** enables practitioners to be adaptable experts by focusing on the most appropriate sources of information and the highest quality of evidence to develop knowledge and inform practice. To be well educated, well informed, and professional, as advocated by Culver and colleagues (2019), practitioners should scrutinize their environment, their knowledge, and the underpinning sources used to inform their practice (Stoszkowski et al. 2020; Tiller et al. 2022; Collins and Eastabrook 2023). Even if we accept this, however, what does it mean to be critical?

What Is Criticality?

Conceptions of critical thinking vary. For instance, Dewey (1938) limited criticality to thinking about one's observations, experiences, and experiments. Others, such as Bailin and colleagues (1999) and Ennis (1962, 2015), included the products of that consideration, thinking about, and appraisal of the products of critical thought. Critical thinking has also been conceived as a judgment (e.g., Dewey 1938; Lipman 1987). Differences in interpretations notwithstanding, it is nonetheless evident that critical thinking links with the judgment and decision-making processes at the heart of the *it depends* approach and reflects the positions of Ennis (2015) and Bailin and colleagues (1999) that actions *and* beliefs are the logical endpoints of critical-thinking processes. In conceptualizing critical thinking, Bailin and colleagues (1999) proposed three features that characterize the critical-thinking process in learning and performance contexts, on which Eastabrook and Collins (2023) further elaborated. In this regard, critical thinking

1. is aimed at making a decision on what to think or do,
2. involves intention and striving to meet standards for accuracy and appropriateness with regard to the thinking,
3. meets the aspired standards to at least a threshold level (the quality of critical thinking will operate on a continuum), and
4. has an intention and outcome that can be actioned (Eastabrook and Collins 2023).

Regarding the basis of critical thinking, Stanovich and Stanovich (2010) grounded the practice in the thinker's rationality, fitting the thinker's beliefs with their world to optimize goal fulfillment while also highlighting the "propensity" to override the suboptimal with an "autonomous mind" (p. 227). Such skills and abilities would logically appear to be the ability to recognize ineffective aspects of performance, theorize as to possible solutions with the tools at hand, apply those new or adapted tools, and then evaluate their application. In so doing, critical thinking becomes an aspect of the adaptive

expertise highlighted earlier, with coaches using and questioning information rather than simply accepting, absorbing, or replicating it. According to Eastabrook and Collins (2023), such criticality encompasses a set of five interlinked components that underpin effective practice and scaffold critical thinking for practitioners:

1. A set of values and beliefs that offer a lens through which practice can be reviewed
2. An understanding of the sources of knowledge that could inform practice
3. The capability to make sense of practice experiences
4. Curiosity and inquisitiveness
5. An ability and willingness to add to the conversation

Values and Beliefs

Because values and beliefs about practice and learning shape real-world practice (Perry 2014), understanding of these interlinked concepts is vital. For instance, values and beliefs can be used to compare or evaluate outcomes from critical thinking and, in turn, can form the basis of how knowledge is integrated into practice. According to Perry (2014) and Schommer (1994), values and beliefs range on a continuum from naive to sophisticated. A naive perspective accepts knowledge as clear, distinct, fixed, and grounded in prescribed models; reinforced by authority sources; and associated with rapid learning. This contrasts with a sophisticated perspective, which holds knowledge as complex, changing, dynamic, and gradually acquired via cognitive processes (Howard et al. 2000; Schommer 1994), with learning constructed through reasoning and reflection (Howard et al. 2000). Practitioners whose beliefs and values reflect the naive portion of the spectrum may possess tendencies toward didactic, routine-based, and prescribed approaches. Practitioners whose beliefs lie on the other end of this continuum may entertain and employ a range of different practice approaches, depending on the situational demands, including prescriptive or routinized practices if they are appropriate. In this respect, criticality links to adaptive expertise. Coaches' beliefs and values manifest in their coaching practice through a relationship described as an **epistemological chain** (Grecic and Collins 2013; Christian et al. 2020).

This metaphorical chain is a consistent, logical relationship with a rationale and justification, demonstrating beliefs in action (Grecic and Collins 2013; Christian et al. 2020). Several authors have also suggested that these metaphorical chains connect practitioners to the values and developmental philosophies of the certifying or employing bodies (e.g., the Football Association way, the Royal Yachting Association way, the British Association of Ski Instructors way, or even *my* way). Although Nelson and colleagues (2006) suggested that this could be little more than indoctrination and at the whims of fashion and opinion, Mees and colleagues (2020) have identified links between employers' and awarding bodies' educational philosophies and the development and evaluation of their coaches, with the chain representing more of a framework that may become pertinent in areas such a career success and qualification.

Interestingly, differences between practitioners' beliefs and their actions may indicate meaningful development of their own beliefs but limitations in the pedagogic skills necessary to enact their newly forming values (Collins, Collins, and Grecic 2015). Indeed, such a disconnect may be required and desirable as an aspect of development for coaches and skill-acquisition specialists and emblematic of the necessary criticality for adaptive expertise. Once established, however, those beliefs and values may represent biases that affect judgments on new sources of information. As such, coaches, skill-acquisition specialists, and support staff must be aware of the potential of their own biases by exercising their metacognition (see table 3.2).

Understanding Potential Sources of Knowledge: Not All Sources Are Created Equal

Literature is a clear source of potential knowledge with peer-reviewed research—alongside more accessible and digestible "gray" sources (Benzies et al. 2006) of information such as magazine articles, some books, blogs, social media, case studies, and reports—offering a range of potential influences. Understanding the quality of these sources involves both critical thought about and comprehension of these knowledge sources, and with the wide availability of resources, it is essential to know where information is coming from, because some sources are more credible than others. With this in mind, Eaton (2018) presented a hierarchy of source quality, which is presented with examples in table 3.3, that can guide coaches on how to evaluate information from such sources.

Research in applied practice (e.g., coaching) rarely answers the big questions or provides *the* answer; instead, it frequently generates more questions, proposes multiple interpretations, and points to other avenues of investigation. Although this may suit scholars, this can challenge those who may be seeking clear answers to current real-world demands, such as coaches and other practitioners. Nevertheless, research findings rarely exist as absolutes and, consequently, any claims—implied or otherwise—must be viewed with high degrees of suspicion and require judicious application of criticality. In this way, values and beliefs play a role in what practitioners can expect from research and how fixed the findings are. In essence, it is essential to exercise criticality of any claims, implied or otherwise, made by the research because real-world contexts are unique and, as such, any findings must be contextualized by coaches.

Making Sense of Real-World Experiences

The ability to learn by understanding practitioners' experiences can facilitate insight into their own and others' practices (Nelson, Cushion, and Potrac 2006). This reflection on experiences—a fundamental aspect of adaptable practice in response to situational demands—enables practitioners to link one experience to the next and learn. Lamentably, but perhaps not surprisingly, Nash and colleagues (2022) reported that many practitioners do not perceive themselves to reflect on their practice. Although such a position is conceivable, with many practitioners focused on "in-action" thinking and addressing the problem at hand, it contrasts with the "on-action" (Schön 1983) reflective models offered in coach education (Collins and Collins 2019) that may often be undervalued. At the heart of critical thinking is an assumption that practice can constantly be improved and an acknowledgment that fixed

Table 3.2 Examples of Potential Bias

Bias	What it looks like
Dunning Kruger effect	Two parts: (1) the less the coach knows, the more confident they are likely to be, and (2) the more straightforward they find an activity, the less likely they are to understand the difficulty of that activity for other people
Declinism	Remembering the past as better than it actually was and expecting the future to be worse than evidence suggests
Groupthink	Allowing the social dynamics of a group situation to override the logical outcomes
Placebo	Believing in an ineffective action, behavior, strategy, or treatment, which then makes it effective
The bystander effect	Presuming someone else is going to do something
A framing effect	Being unduly influenced by context and delivery
Anchoring	Letting initial judgments influence those that follow
Optimism	Overestimating the likelihood of positive outcomes
Pessimism	Overestimating the likelihood of adverse outcomes
The fair world hypothesis	Assuming there is universal moral balance or fairness where good deeds are rewarded and bad deeds punished
Attribution error	Judging others on their character but personally on the situation
The halo effect	Fondness for or attraction to someone influences consequent judgment or evaluation
In-group	Unfairly favoring those who belong to one's group
Confirmation	Favoring things that confirm existing beliefs
The knowledge curse	Understanding something and then presuming it to be obvious to everyone else
Self-serving	Believing failures are due to external factors but successes are personal responsibilities
Sunk-cost fallacy	Irrationally clinging to things that have already incurred significant cost
The backfire	When core beliefs are challenged, it can cause them to believe those beliefs more strongly
Negativity	Allowing negative things to influence thinking disproportionately
Availability	Judgments are influenced by what most easily comes to mind or is most readily available
The Barnum/Buncam effect	Seeing personal specifics in vague statements by filling in the gaps
Reactant	Doing the opposite of what someone is trying to make you do
Belief	Where a conclusion supports existing beliefs, rationalizing anything that supports it

Table 3.3 Hierarchy of Source Credibility

Credibility	Description	Example
Most credible	Scientific sources that have gone through peer-review processes. Peer reviews assess the quality of the investigation, its interpretation, and any findings. Peer review is typically anonymous and involves multiple experts evaluating manuscripts in a cycle until the quality and rigor required for publication are met.	Journal papers, conference presentations, and proceedings
Credible	Scholarly articles found in books from experts are frequently collections of invited articles checked and collated by coordinating editors.	Academic books typically published by academic publishing houses (e.g., Sage, Routledge, university presses)
Acceptable	It contains accurate information that is supported by evidence or can be verified from trusted sources. Good materials in this category frequently cite their sources (typically from journal articles or books).	Publications from academic presses, professional and trade magazines, encyclopedias, government websites (.gov), and educational websites (.edu)
Less acceptable	There are few or no references, limited supporting evidence, resources with outdated information, or ambiguity regarding author intentions.	Newspapers, journalism, magazine articles, books from nonacademic sources or that are self-published, websites, and podcasts
Untrustworthy	These sources have intentions other than the presentation of nonbiased knowledge.	Social media, commercial websites (.com), organization websites (.org), and Wikipedia

Based on Eaton (2018).

approaches will be insufficient because performers and contexts will always vary. In essence, practitioners aim to question and challenge their assumptions and those around them. This questioning enables practitioners to problem solve by recognizing the need for new solutions, to internally justify and rationalize their decisions, and, in turn, become more agile and coherent with their beliefs and values. These practices facilitate the epistemological chain cited earlier. In doing this, practitioners can become more creative, imaginative, resourceful, and prepared to adapt to new ways and methods of thinking and practice, flexibly applying the resources they have at hand.

To aid in developing the requisite criticality, Eastabrook and Collins (2023) proposed five key requirements for effective critical appraisal of practice sessions:

1. A clear purpose for the appraisal
2. An experience to appraise that has relevance to that purpose and has the potential to elicit learning
3. A way of capturing that experience so it can be described in sufficient richness, depth, and detail
4. An appraiser with sufficient, high-level comprehension of the experience that can understand the relationships of the different parts
5. An appraiser with sufficient comprehension to also distill the learning into essential actionable parts

In addition to understanding the experiences of coaches and skill-acquisition specialists, learners' perspectives may also yield insight into how performances are understood, how practice might be framed, or how future learning objectives are created. Despite recognition that performer support is a collaborative affair between practitioners and learners (Jowett and Slade 2021), learners' perspectives have traditionally been underrepresented (Becker 2009). Learners' perspectives should be about something other than whether the coaching was good; they should be more nuanced, investigating the impact and perceptions of different practices at different times and contexts. After receiving learner feedback, practitioners can either act on it (the intention to act differently next time), store the information, or gather more feedback (figure out what to do with it or choose to ignore it if it is ill informed, contradictory, overplayed, or just nonsense)

The Curious Practitioner: An Inquiring Mind

Hattie and colleagues (2015) highlighted that coaches (teachers) are not researchers, but they do have the power to be evaluators of their impact. As such, critical minds would consider the effect of new information on the processes and outcomes of their practice. In this process, practitioners formulate hypotheses on the impact of the new knowledge in a similar fashion to anticipating the impact of interventions (Eastabrook and Collins 2020). For example, observing an athlete's performance can lead coaches to propose an intervention based on what is required to improve that performance, consider the potential outcome of that intervention against their experiences, observe the resulting outcome, and then reformulate subsequent interventions. Coaches observe intervention effects and measure the impact against anticipated changes in performance, beliefs, and values before creating subsequent interventions—a cycle of hypothesizing, theory generation, and testing. Any new information can be treated similarly as practitioners seek to understand what has and has not worked in their practice. Once changes are identified, suitable methods can be used to test their impact in practice. The goal is to test any new information and its suitability for the individual, the practitioner, and the specific context.

Adding to the Conversation

Practitioners typically aim to encourage professional development and a way to achieve this is through engagement with their community of practice (CoP). This engagement limits the risk that, for instance, all coaches individually figure out the same things or just repeatedly "rediscover" the same things. Indeed, there is value in critically sharing experiences, information, and considerations while being open to new sources and experiences. The SECI spiral model (figure 3.3; Nonaka and Toyama 2003) offers one approach in which experiences and information are socialized (S) through practice, guidance, observation, and dialogue with other practitioners. That knowledge is subsequently externalized (E), converted from uncodified, **tacit knowledge** into **explicit knowledge** that can be codified, articulated, and thus shared by the CoP. Once codified, that knowledge is combined (C) and converted into accessible sources such as books, documents, manuals, papers, podcasts, and social media clips. Finally, that knowledge is then internalized (I), converted into tacit knowledge, and individualized to use. If it is unshared, the knowledge base is restricted in moving forward. Sharing knowledge and engaging in the zone of uncomfortable debate (ZOUD) have inherent value to coaches, skill-acquisition specialists, and other practitioners. This helps to challenge assumptions and practices and should be encouraged as common practice (Bailey 2011). Moreover, without such critical discourse and sharing, new ideas, practices, and concepts can become unduly overhyped and prone to confirmation, cognitive, or blind-spot bias.

On this basis, such professional conversations should be open and shared, including (1) sources of new information; (2) thoughts and notes on how that information might be applied; (3) details of any application—whether practitioner or academic, including variables and anticipated changes, rationales, and explanations of the methods used—and (4) outcomes of application including what did not work.

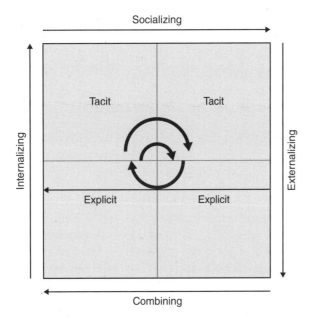

Figure 3.3 The SECI knowledge-sharing model.

PRACTICAL IMPLICATIONS: A MICRO, MESO, AND MACRO CHALLENGE

An important impetus for this book is that applied practice involves not only the understanding and application of motor learning principles but also the necessity to pull together further, diverse strands of knowledge (e.g., team dynamics, sport psychology, physiology, coaching science) alongside these to address the needs and circumstances of performers (see Bobrownicki et al. 2023). In addition to this diversity of knowledge and understanding, however, the conditionality of that knowledge also represents a key component for practice. In this regard, a key premise is that relevant skills and knowledge will apply and work well in real-life settings but only in certain contexts (Collins et al. 2022). Indeed, as discussed in the introduction, given the complexity and messiness of sport, no one approach could provide *the* answer across all contexts and the most functional or appropriate approaches will always depend on multiple interrelated factors, such as the person being coached, the skills being taught, the environment in which the learning is taking place, and the intended outcomes.

One way this complexity may be managed is through planning. Planning has long been recognized as the "link between aspirations, intentions, and activity" (Lyle 2002, p. 125). Building on early conceptualizations, Abraham and Collins (2011a) suggested nestedness to optimize coaches' planning and thinking processes, whereby coaches can formulate their intention for impact and pull together diverse bodies of knowledge to chart the steps necessary to achieve desired outcomes (see Martindale and Collins 2005). Such nested planning involves first accounting for the "macro" (i.e., performers' long-term needs and overarching goals) before considering meso-level concerns (component socio-motivational and tactical factors that enable attainment of macro-level goals; Abraham and Collins 2011b). Finally, there is the micro level, which relates to session-by-session activities addressing situational matters. Nested planning allows coaches to be responsive to the shorter-term needs of performers without losing bigger-picture coherence (Jones and Wallace 2006). This nestedness facilitates a cycle of planning, reflection, and replanning (Hoffman et al. 2014) while acknowledging the inherent complexity and dynamism of performers and their environments (Klein 2007).

With this in mind, PJDM (Abraham and Collins 2011; Collins and Collins 2015, 2016; Martindale and Collins 2005) represents an essential concept for practice and, as such, across the chapters of this text. Indeed, PJDM informs nested decision making (see chapters 5 and 11) and helps promote an effective blend and integration of tools and approaches toward a host of goals and targets

CASE STUDY

NESTED PLANNING IN SEA KAYAK COACHING

Ali is a sea kayaking coach who works on the island of Anglesey in North Wales. Ali is employed to work with a group of four unknown sea kayakers for a five-day program in the early spring that aims to refine their technical, tactical, and cognitive skills.

Ali's macro plan starts five weeks before the program. Conditions around the island of Anglesey are predicted based on long-range weather forecasts, tidal information, seasonal data, and Ali's previous experiences in Anglesey in early spring (top-down process). Ali also anticipates the logistical constraints for the week: availability of resources, transport, and equipment (bottom-up process).

Three weeks before the course, Ali emails the sea kayakers to start building rapport and to understand their aims and objectives at a macro level (i.e., their overarching objective) and meso level (i.e., for the five-day program), which represents top-down and bottom-up processes, respectively. Ali gets to understand their experiences and perceived skill levels. At this point, Ali also draws on recent experience around Anglesey and mid-range forecasts for the likely conditions for the five-day program to facilitate updating of the top-down plan.

On the first day of the program, Ali further updates the conditions and weather forecasts for the coming five days, double-checks the logistics (updated top-down), and then meets the clients in person for the first time. Ali summarizes and confirms the clients' aims and objectives for the week to provide a coherent set of goals for the five days to follow (bottom-up). Ali then selects a venue (intention to act) for the first day on the water; the venue provides a range of environments and conditions in which the sea kayakers are observed. While on the water, Ali confirms ability levels, the anticipated conditions at the venue, *and* the appropriateness of each kayaker's aims and objectives (ensuring the bottom-up). Over a late lunch on the beach, Ali presents an initial plan for the subsequent day and possibilities for the final three days.

Each day, Ali reconfirms and updates the condition reports, reviews the kayakers' progress, and makes appropriate adjustments to respond to the situational requirements (the micro plan). On a session-by-session basis, Ali has an overall aim or objective that has been agreed on with each kayaker. Depending on ability levels in each session, Ali identifies appropriate starting points for each kayaker for that part of the coaching process and then implements tailored activities and goals based on the conditions at each venue and matched to each kayaker's step-by-step development. Anticipating each kayaker's most likely performance of a task before resetting the goal, Ali observes the actual performance and then selects an approach that is most likely to achieve the desired development for each client. This is either by adapting a well-practiced approach or creating a new strategy if the situation is unique.

Ali always has comprehension of the conditions, checks and rechecks the accuracy of the information that informs taken decisions, and retains the flexibility to adapt the plans in response to the meso and micro aspects (nested planning).

Coaches of adventure sports, such as sea kayaking, face many contrasting macro factors with the seasons and environment (e.g., the tides, winds, and sea swells), all of which are outside the control of coaches.
Charlie Munsey/Corbis/Getty Images

(e.g., short-term and long-term team aims). For instance, coaching staff for a professional American football team in the National Football League (NFL) may need to balance a range of aims and goals, such as preparation for upcoming games, managing player health or injuries, qualifying for the postseason, enhancing draft positioning, and developing players. In managing these complex and, at times, competing needs, PJDM assists coaches in balancing the contributions of classical and naturalistic decision making (CDM and NDM, respectively; introduced in chapter 10), which typically work in synergy—the exact proportions of each dependent on the conditions at hand—and rarely in isolation. In practice, key tenets within PJDM are that both CDM and NDM will apply, but their suitability or appropriate blend must be matched to the circumstances, while the planning process must be as conditional as practice itself. Hence, effective practice involves both bottom-up and top-down processes in which clear links between micro, meso, and macro levels can be maintained.

The dynamism of sport and the resulting conditionality of decision making will require skills and practices that often apply or have implications across multiple levels of this decision-making process. For instance, coaches will need to be able to assess performer needs, identify problems, and determine how these can be addressed (i.e., problem solve). In addressing performer needs across these levels, however, there will often be contextual trade-offs (Collins, Carson, and Collins 2016). For example, when weighing available options (e.g., availability of particular conditions, such as off-piste skiing condition), coaches may need to deviate from long-term, macro-level aims (e.g., individual player skill development) to address short-term needs (e.g., due to injury in the team, a player may need to play out of position). Effective reflection, in addition to composing a key component of adaptive expertise, also represents an important practice and skill across the levels of nested decision making. For instance, coaches may reflect on action (i.e., after coaching); in action (i.e., during coaching); or on action, in context (reflecting within the coaching session; Collins and Collins 2015). This can involve decisions regarding specific practices within matches or training sessions or broader activities or interventions. Notably, in-action reflection affords coaches the capability to make actionable changes because they are still in the moment, but this form of reflection is also more demanding and more characteristic of experienced practitioners (Mees et al. 2020).

For different sports and activities, the nature and composition of the levels can vary considerably. For instance, Collins and Collins (2016) identified contrasting macro factors for adventure sports coaches, such as sea kayaking, with the seasons and environment (e.g., the tides, winds, and sea swells)—which are outside the control of coaches—comprising macro aspects of their planning. For the meso level, the conditions on the day, which coaches can manage with careful venue selection, can differentiate the coaching and planning process from sports such as basketball or American football. At the micro level, coaches and practitioners will consider the technical and pedagogical demands for a given sea kayaker within groups of kayakers as part of individualizing the coaching process.

Regardless of the sport or activity, however, with this nested approach to decision making, the contributions of theory and practice for relevant domains (e.g., physiology, biomechanics, and organizational psychology) will vary based on the micro, meso, and macro levels. For skill acquisition more specifically, scholars have debated the potential and relative contributions of available approaches within PJDM. According to Bobrownicki and colleagues (2023), in American football, which involves significant decision-making and planning elements (e.g., macro-level offensive and defensive multiseason coaching philosophies, meso-level weekly opponent preparation), alongside dynamic and fast-moving play (micro-level in-game play execution that better reflects perception-coupled action), there is scope for pragmatic integration of skill-acquisition approaches (see figure 3.4 for potential contribution). Such pragmatic integration can, in part, reflect or correspond to levels of nested planning within PJDM. In doing this, however, it is also important to consider and balance other needs, aims, and objectives that coaches, skill-acquisition specialists, or performers may want to develop or emphasize (e.g., developing confidence, motivation, team cohesion), which may sometimes conflict (e.g., the best short-term method for enhancing confidence may conflict with preferred skill-acquisition practices). Deployment of PJDM process can help in balancing competing aims and practices to find the best pathway forward for performers.

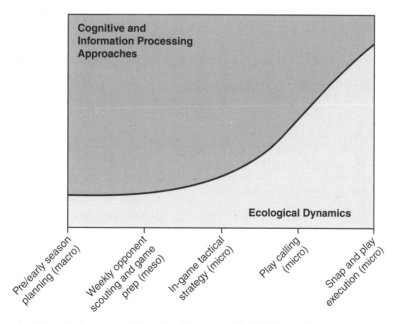

Figure 3.4 Inspired by Bobrownicki and colleagues (2023), the figure proposes potential contribution of skill-acquisition approaches across planning and execution stages in American football and illustrates how conditionality might apply in real-world settings.

Adapted from Bobrownicki et al. (2023).

CHAPTER SUMMARY

In this chapter, we have demonstrated the complexity of sport and performance environments and examined key concepts, skills, knowledge, and associated frameworks for operating and making decisions within these environments. For coaches, skill-acquisition specialists, support staff, and performers, it is important to recognize the dynamic, ever-changing contexts in which learning and performance take place and the resulting demands on, and for, expertise, flexibility, criticality, decision making, and practice. Successful learning and performance require coaches, practitioners, support staff, and performers to pull together, scrutinize, and integrate diverse strands of knowledge and practice to work toward nested goals developed through informed decision making and planning. Against this backdrop, it is important for coaches and skill-acquisition specialists to recognize that skill acquisition represents just one cog in the complex learning and performance machine, operating alongside other aims and objectives (e.g., developing confidence, motivation, team cohesion). Determining where and how skill acquisition best fits requires adaptive expertise, critical thinking, and PJDM processes to facilitate vertical and horizonal coherence. Understanding and applying the principles in this chapter can help in selecting the most appropriate courses of action to suit the needs of performers.

REVIEW AND PRACTICAL QUESTIONS

1. Thinking about the PESTLE model, what are the legal factors for your sport that may influence the environment in which you practice?
2. Thinking about the biopsychosocial model, what social factors may influence participation in sport?
3. Which sources of information are most credible for informing decision making, and which require the most scrutiny?
4. What is the micro level in nested planning and how does it relate to the other nested levels?
5. For a nested plan, describe how the planning process works.

KEY TERMS

adaptive expertise

critical thinking

declarative knowledge

epistemological chain

explicit knowledge

metacognition

routine expertise

situational awareness

situational comprehension

situational demands

tacit knowledge

PART II

Learning Movement

CHAPTER 4

AN EITHER-OR PERSPECTIVE ON APPLYING THE THEORETICAL APPROACHES: WHERE HAVE THEY COME FROM, AND HOW VALID ARE THEY?

Howie J. Carson

Chapter Objectives

After studying this chapter, you should be able to do the following:

- Understand the sources and underpinnings of either-or explanations presented within skill-acquisition research
- Recognize how study design may bias outcomes of apparently valid research
- Appreciate the different contextual factors, or conditions, that influence the degree of relevance provided by different skill-acquisition approaches
- Plan coaching practices that are optimally aligned to different skill-acquisition approaches
- Recognize how different approaches may be appropriate based on individual differences such as age, stage, and prior experience

Chapters 1 and 2 addressed several skill-acquisition approaches, with a clear suggestion that taking a multi-theoretical view offers advantages to meeting performers' different needs. Chapter 3 explored the applied implications—such as a coach implementing an evidence-informed approach—stressing the fundamental importance of critical decision making to the training design and execution process. Reflecting this, developing decision-making skill should be considered crucial within national governing body education and development systems (e.g., coaching awards, British Psychological Society chartership, and British Association of Sport and Exercise Sciences accreditation; Li, Carson, and Collins 2023). In extending the idea that different approaches can apply in different contexts, for different performer needs, and to address different purposes, the present chapter builds on this understanding by exemplifying the consequences for decision making and technique execution when taking one or another of these approaches.

UNDERSTANDING THE ORIGINS OF THE EITHER-OR DEBATE BETWEEN SKILL-ACQUISITION APPROACHES

By design, this book critically examines skill-acquisition theories and literature from a unique applied perspective. Some understanding, therefore, of the discipline's evolution might reveal the significance of the current transitory and exciting stage. More pertinently to our purpose, however, such understanding should affect decision making when practically employing an evidence-informed approach.

Without providing a complete history of the discipline (see Christina 2017; Summers 2004), it is important to understand that skill-acquisition research during the mid-20th century was notably quite broad in scope and outcome focused (e.g., research intended to solve practical problems for industry workers and those requiring specialist skills, similar to this book). Studies spanned multiple contexts, including the learning of electrical trade skills (Woodward 1943) or upskilling marksmen in the armed forces (English 1942). Obviously, at that time there was no wearable technology or sophisticated computer software to probe motor control processes, but researchers

recognized the need to improve societal systems through a behavioral perspective—that is, understanding what people *did*. One disadvantage, however, was the lack of mechanistic understanding that underpinned skill improvements. Consequently, research became more theoretically driven by adopting controlled laboratory study designs, employing simplified tasks *but* measuring movement characteristics in order to probe aspects of cognitive architecture and function (e.g., Fitts and Radford 1966; Higgins and Angle 1970). Thus, researchers became more focused on understanding what was happening in key processes—for example, between information being provided (e.g., presentation of feedback) and the movement execution. Notably, Christina (1987) acknowledged the level of theoretical insight gained by taking this more process-focused approach but warned that these information-processing, or cognitive, theories were limited when applied within real-world practice due to the limitations of research design characteristics.

By the 1990s, the constraints-led approach (a concomitant of ecological dynamics [EcoD]) offered an alternative process-focused theory by combining the study of complex natural systems, movement coordination, and ecological psychology (Handford et al. 1997). Incorporating ecological factors meant that explanations needed to account for movements being situated in meaningful contexts. Ironically, while many studies remained laboratory based (e.g., Al-Abood et al. 2002; Button et al. 2002; Williams and Davids 1998), theoretical underpinnings shifted from focusing on cognitive processes toward ongoing and emergent characteristics during the action itself, with a primary emphasis on **direct perception-action coupling** (i.e., action control without need for internal information processing or retrieval of movement from memory). In summary, skill-acquisition research in the last century witnessed a changing landscape, initially from an understanding of behavioral outcomes to mainstream cognitive processes and then concurrently to real-time, in-action control.

With better technological advancement, greater accessibility to university postgraduate degrees (e.g., professional doctorates), and the increasingly professionalized and competitive sporting domain, the 2010s saw an upsurge in practitioner-led research and the rise of the **pracademic** in sport (Collins and Collins 2019). In this regard, pracademics uniquely fulfill the role of practitioner, researcher, *and* educator such that they can effectively bridge the gap between understanding, conducting, and explaining research relative to professional demands on practitioners. Not only has this evolution afforded better and more long-term access to representative participants (e.g., genuinely high-level athletes) in their training and performance contexts, the conceptualization of new problems to be solved, but also an acknowledgment of how off-field coaching practices integrate with on-field movement control (e.g., Collins, Collins, and Carson 2022). As we continue into this outcome- *and* process-focused era, models of performance have become necessarily more complex (e.g., Christensen, Sutton, and McIlwain 2016). Additionally, societal pressure has increased to provide meaningful and bespoke solutions for applied stakeholders, especially when publicly financed (e.g., the requirement for impact case studies within the UK government's Research Excellence Framework assessment). While theory-driven research of the past 100 years arguably has been challenged in its ability to apply across different and diverse contexts, practitioner-led research has recognized the value of *both* cognitive and EcoD approaches within sport (Bobrownicki et al. 2023). However, with theorists often unable or unwilling to reconcile these differences between approaches, the debate has largely remained stagnant and been presented as an either-or reality.

Recognizing the Social Context of the Discipline

Although sport scientists are well established as members of support teams, personnel have typically catered to the core disciplines of psychology, physiology, and biomechanics. Indeed, despite Williams and Ford (2009) calling for skill-acquisition specialists to assist in supporting Olympic athlete development, Steel and colleagues (2014) found 17 times more physiologists, 8.6 times more biomechanists, and 5.6 times more psychologists working in Australian sport institutes. Reflecting a unique challenge for skill-acquisition specialists, given the either-or situation, was the perceived understanding and knowledge that coaches and athletes thought a skill-acquisition specialist should possess. Specifically, this spanned biomechanics, psychological skills, performance analy-

sis, and strength and conditioning. Furthermore, participants viewed the role of a skill-acquisition specialist to be most closely aligned to that of a coach, with 61% not using a skill-acquisition specialist within practice. Indeed, this suggests that coaches and athletes are unsure about where exactly skill-acquisition specialists fit within the support sciences.

It is plausible, depending on the skill-acquisition specialist's theoretical approach, knowledge, and skills, that their input could center on biomechanical analyses and encourage a more hands-off intervention approach *or* practices more closely aligned to performance psychology that could be more hands-on and advocate a proactive mental skills-based agenda. Such diversity challenges the discipline to sell a consistent message to stakeholders. For those fluent across the different approaches, and as put forward in chapter 3, there needs to be a comprehensive case conceptualization process to formulate an appropriate intention for impact. Notably, this thoroughly **pantheoretical** process is uncommon for most sport scientists and therefore increases the challenge for skill-acquisition specialists when attempting to apply innovations in the field.

SOLVING THE EITHER-OR PROBLEM

Now that the origin of the either-or situation has been explained, the important focus needs to be on *how* to make effective judgments. Ideally, research will have undertaken fair comparisons between the approaches so that the rationale for employing one over another may be truly evidence grounded. Unfortunately, no large resource exists to draw on in this regard, and consequently, coaches, applied researchers, and all consumers of skill-acquisition research (including interested athletes) need critical ability to effectively interpret and use the evidence available.

Lack of Comparison Studies

Unfortunately, only a few empirical studies have tested the approaches to skill learning, and of these, results are mixed. Studies have shown the principles of the EcoD approach to enable more diverse technical solutions in novice youth tennis players when manipulating equipment and rule constraints (i.e., net height, target area, court size, the use of different balls and rackets, and specific task goal) in addition to outcome-focused instructions versus a cognitively oriented intervention consisting of being provided with prescriptive and repetitive drills, with instructions reflecting an ideal movement pattern across the different tennis stroke phases (Lee et al. 2014). Interestingly, while the former EcoD-oriented intervention resulted in more diverse movement solutions, no difference was observed in the accuracy scores after intervention. Similarly, Orangi and colleagues (2021) assessed the development of adaptive action control in novice adult soccer players who were also tested for transfer in a match following the 12-week intervention. A cognitively informed intervention group received an explanation of the skill and practiced an ideal technique template; they also received technical instructions, performed repetitious practice but with adjustment of the difficulty, and received augmented coach feedback. The EcoD-informed group did not receive coach instructions or augmented feedback. Instead, general instructions explained the task purpose with the implementation of varied task constraints (e.g., changing shooting distances and angles or using different sized targets) to encourage different motor solutions and adaptation. Findings revealed that those in the latter intervention, which promoted practice variability, demonstrated increased creativity and varied their actions. (See also Gray 2018, 2020, for examples in baseball batting resulting in more hits and superior swing parameters resulting from EcoD-informed interventions.)

Notably, however, other studies have found no differences in skill-based interventions. For instance, Lindsay and colleagues (2023) found no difference for novice adult weightlifters receiving an intervention informed by the cognitive approach that consisted of explicit motor instructions, repetitive drills, and error-correction feedback toward an ideal technique, when compared with an EcoD-informed intervention of short analogy-based instructions in addition to applying chalk on the barbell and poles in front of the participant to guide the movement trajectory. Likewise, Deuker and colleagues (2023) compared a cognitively informed soccer skills intervention for skilled youths consisting of repeated or similar drills, explicit instruction, performance and formative feedback following each

trial (including immediately after a performance error), verbal support, and coach-led decisions regarding task complexity, with an ecologically informed approach consisting of small-sided games with specifically manipulated constraints to the environment (e.g., size of the pitch) and task (e.g., number of goal posts increased to four, rules governing player roles, rule changes to associate outcomes with specific execution plays) over five weeks. Findings revealed no difference between the groups for dribbling or change-of-direction sprinting skills. For passing skills, however, the cognitively informed intervention group improved between the pretest and posttest and between the pretest to retention test but decreased significantly between posttest and retention test, whereas a comparable improvement was found in the ecologically informed intervention group that was also maintained between the posttest and retention test. In all studies, caution must be exercised when interpreting the findings since it is questionable whether a comprehensive consideration of each approach was truly applied and, therefore, a *fair* comparison provided. Even when studies have not compared across approaches, significant sources of bias, which may favor one approach over another, must be acknowledged.

How Investigative Design Can Bias the Outcomes of Research

In progressing our understanding of where the either-or situation originated, we must look more deeply when interpreting research findings to understand *how* this has persisted across the main EcoD and cognitive approaches. Remember that predictive processing is a relatively new approach that has not received much empirical investigation within sport. In doing so, this enables a critical examination of both research findings and the underpinning methodology when assessing the relevance that evidence may have for any given context, athlete need, and intended outcome. While one might be forgiven for thinking that *all* published and peer-reviewed scientific evidence is unbiased, rigorous, and valid in its conduct, it is questionable whether this is the case when making recommendations for applied practice. Table 4.1 presents several methodological components within research designs (subsequently examined in greater detail), accompanied by questions that are intended to interrogate research through a critically evaluative and applied lens. Goginsky and Collins (1996) used a similar approach to explain inconsistent findings within mental practice research.

Control or Comparison Group

Control or comparison groups are vital to interpret study findings, ensure credibility and validity of research, and promote applied impact. In short, such groups provide a reference to assess the difference or impact that a certain manipulation (e.g., practice schedule, feedback strategy, demonstration format) can generate. If, however, an inappropriate control or comparison group is selected, this can influence the suggested impact, leading to misinterpretation and suboptimal recommendations for applied practice (see Bobrownicki et al. 2022 for a critical review of control groups). Recognizing and replicating *current* recommended best practice within a control or comparison group should represent a desirable alternative of **active treatment** (i.e., a condition that replicates a known, usual, or good practice approach). Accordingly, evaluating a study's control or comparison condition can inform the decision-making process regarding whether to adopt the intervention, in whole or part, with a learner.

Initially, consider whether a control or comparison group has been used at all. In case-study research, for instance, the athlete typically acts as their own control reference with before, during,

and after data demonstrating any change in process pertaining to the movement planning and execution, and, usually, performance outcome (although this is not always the aim). In doing so, case studies enable rich and detailed reporting of interventions, thorough and specific justification, as well as direct implications for applied practice. Consequently, these serve as good ways to develop and exemplify ideas. Crucially, case studies require regular athlete monitoring to ensure **internal validity**; that is, the longer and more often changes are observed, the greater certainty there is that differences are a result of the intervention and not an unaccounted-for external event or factor. Notably, Barker and colleagues (2020) found that case studies with fewer (i.e., < 8) baseline observations of "normal" and well-established performance or process(es) tended to inflate the effect of psychological skills and behavioral interventions when compared to studies reporting higher numbers of baseline data points. Since individual case-study research is most common within cognitive psychology (e.g., Jackson and Baker 2001; di Fronso et al. 2016), this indicates the potential for greater risk of bias among case studies when compared to the EcoD approach.

When an independent control group *has* been included, however, the proposed active treatment has not always been critically considered in relation to best coaching practice (Bobrownicki et al. 2018; Collins, Carson, and Toner 2016).

Table 4.1 Methodological Components Within Research Designs

Methodological component	Critical questions from an applied *it depends* perspective
Control or comparison group	• Have control or comparison groups been included? If not, why not? • What type of control or comparison groups were included? • What criteria were used to balance the groups (e.g., skill level, previous sporting experience)?
Task	• Why was this task chosen? • What is its applicability to applied situations? • Is this task familiar to participants?
Measures	• What data are collected? • Do the measures reflect the theoretical perspective? • How are skill-acquisition effects measured?
Participant instructions	• Are the instructions relevant to the task? • What modality are participants instructed to use, and is this appropriate? • Are the instructions balanced for length between groups? • Are manipulation checks used to ensure compliance *and* gain feedback from participants?

From a cognitive perspective, Bobrownicki and colleagues (2018) highlight fundamental flaws in this design regarding implicit motor learning research. Here, studies have consistently biased the implicit group by reducing their cognitive demand when compared to an unrealistic, unhelpful, and unrepresentative list of instructions provided to the traditional explicit group (see more detail later when discussing participant instructions). This is important because the study intention was to compare different types of information processing, yet the use of an *imbalanced* control or comparison group limits its ability to meet this aim and thus warrants critical consideration of claims made to *not* provide explicit technical instruction.

Likewise, for studies that have compared theoretical approaches, comparison groups have not always represented current best practice. Gray's (2018) baseball study compared a constraints-led method with internal and external focus of attention groups (see table 4.2) to change experienced batters' already well-established and long-practiced technique. However, as explained later in chapter 7, the current recommended process for changing such skills involves five stages—analysis, awareness, adjustment (re)automation, and assurance—with specified practice regimens in order to apply an initial internal focus of attention to destabilize the existing automated control and modify the movement representation (i.e., the awareness and adjustment stages), *then* to remove conscious attention away from that technical aspect targeted for change and build confidence in the newly refined whole-skill execution (i.e., [re]automation and assurance stages)—that is, an interdisciplinary and progressive process (Carson

and Collins 2011). Thus, at least based on existing literature, the internal focus condition used by Gray was considerably misrepresentative and incomplete.

In summary and across either approach, it is challenging to evaluate the effectiveness of proposed interventions due to poor and biased comparisons drawn.

Task

To assess a skill-acquisition intervention, researchers must design a task that can be measured using **dependent variables** (i.e., what changes as a result of the manipulation made) such as performance, self-confidence, or movement variability. For theory-driven research *through* sport (Collins and Kamin 2012), researchers are very selective in deciding on the nature of the task in order to clearly understand a narrow phenomenon of interest (e.g., anxiety, visual scanning, or anticipation). Accordingly, tasks have typically been used for their compatibility with the theoretical approach from which they are being researched. Therefore, it is important to be aware of these when evaluating the implication of such biases.

From a cognitive perspective, tasks have tended to be simplistic, especially in recent years when technology has been employed to understand neural and visuomotor mechanisms underpinning execution, for instance. For example, Gallicchio, Cooke, and Ring (2016) used a golf-putting task with skilled ($M_{handicap}$ = 1.5) and novice golfers requiring 60 straight putts on a flat indoor artificial putting surface 2.4 m away under low-pressure and high-pressure conditions (see also Beilock et al. 2002). Even under pressure and distracting conditions, the task is so unquestionably easy

Table 4.2 Experimental Manipulations Administered by Gray (2018) Across Constraints-Led, External, and Internal Focus of Attention Conditions

Condition	Manipulation
Constraints-led	Participants had to hit over a virtual barrier that was manipulated in distance and height such that a launch angle of >19 degrees was required.
External focus of attention	Three instructions provided, one per block of trials: • "Get the bat on the same plane as the incoming pitch" • "Drive the ball over the infield" • "Contact the bottom half of the ball"
Internal focus of attention	Three instructions provided, one per block of trials: • "Get your hands under the ball" • "Move your arms at an upward angle" • "Drive up, off your back foot"

for skilled golfers that they would not have to think about their movements. Thus, while these studies do elicit differences between expert and novice levels of automaticity, this only provides part of the performance picture due to the relative task ease and repetition (i.e., overfamiliarity) for skilled participants. Indeed, Christensen, Sutton, and McIlwain (2016) distinguish between "smooth," "adaptive," and "problem solving" control styles adopted by skilled performers, suggesting that there is an imbalance toward tasks requiring smooth or automatic control when, in reality, the applied demands also necessitate transitions across other control styles to achieve success (further consideration of this concept is covered in chapters 5 and 6; Swann et al. 2016). In the putting example, this might include having to negotiate different ground slopes (usually multiple and in different directions) and environmental conditions (e.g., wind or shadows on the ground). As a result, these task designs have promoted a somewhat biased view that experts are perhaps *more* automatic and efficient in their control than real-world performance can demand.

Concerning the EcoD approach, tasks, both empirically and discursively, have generally addressed open and interceptive skills such as batting, catching, or kicking a ball (e.g., Bennett et al. 1999; Fitzpatrick, Davids, and Stone 2017). Reflecting the self-organizing and emergent mechanisms explained in chapter 1, research has focused on these in-action coordination adaptations and interactions with environmental and task constraints. Consequently, performance of these tasks often necessitates a relatively high degree of movement variability and has illuminated the complexity of movement solutions as an interaction between dynamic factors. Arguably, however, this overfocus on self-organizing processes has weakened the overall understanding of professional practice contributions that enable such functional control to emerge (Bobrownicki et al. 2023). In other words, the tasks employed within this approach do not comprehensively account for situations in sport where training and support seek to develop player understanding and conscious self-regulatory processes to actively take control over performance outcomes. Therefore, one must question what *other* processes might contribute to the study, or even enhance execution, that are not necessarily addressed by the researchers.

Measures

Within skill-acquisition research, many variables can be measured, with researchers employing a variety of tools to assess neural and muscular

The performance picture of a task is dependent on the skill level of a performer.
Blend Images-Roberto Westbrook/Tetra Images/Getty Images

activity (e.g., electroencephalography and electromyography), movement (e.g., kinematics, joint forces, and player position within a game), self-report protocols (e.g., think aloud), and performance outcome data. When deciding on the relevance of research to inform practice, a critically applied perspective should consider whether the measures employed comprehensively or appropriately explain a practical problem to generate meaningful implications. In this regard, different theoretical approaches typically employ measurements that underpin the processes relevant to *their* specific explanation. So EcoD might employ behavioral analyses of team dynamics and inter- and intraindividual movement variability (e.g., Araújo and Davids 2016; Seifert et al. 2014), cognitive approaches might probe participants' knowledge of skills or neural activation associated with motor planning and execution (e.g., Beilock and Carr 2001; di Fronso et al. 2018), and predictive processing approaches might employ visual search and response time measures (e.g., Warren-Westgate et al. 2021). Consequently, the generally limited and selective use of measures to date simply perpetuates a narrow ability to conceptualize real-world skill-acquisition practices, thus avoiding findings that could suggest alternative, potentially more complex, solutions and further reinforcing the either-or situation.

In addition, measures of skill-acquisition effects may also demonstrate different levels of relevance to applied settings depending on *how* they are operationalized. Take the well-used condition of **retention**, which assesses performance following an interval without practice. Figure 4.1 shows an example of data comparing performance during acquisition and retention phases when practicing three tasks 50 times each using either blocked (i.e., consecutive trials of the same task before moving onto the next task) or random (i.e., an unstructured order but equal number of task executions) schedules. Indeed, most studies compare the performance level for the same task practiced during the acquisition phase (e.g., Souissi et al. 2021).

From an applied perspective, we can consider whether the design is appropriate based on at least two factors. First, are these interval periods realistic when compared to typical training schedules that might be influenced by training culture, accessibility, or participant age? For instance, some learners might only practice on a weekly

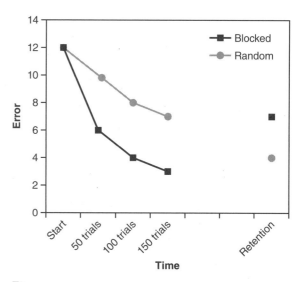

Figure 4.1 A representative example showing performance retention following a practice delay after practicing with either blocked or random practice.

basis. Therefore, differences found between practice conditions after a 24-hour retention period may become meaningless. Second, we can ask whether the retention measurement is particularly helpful for coaches. In many sports there is opportunity to improve performance during play (e.g., when substitutes come on in team sports or when plays are structured in multiple blocks such as tennis or cricket). An alternative retention measure might be to report the amount of time or number of trials needed to return to a criterion standard obtained following the practice period (Leavitt and Schlosberg 1944). This is, after all, what coaches typically assess in practice following a warm-up and reflects the demand for players to respond quickly within play. Whether it is the measurement being employed or its implementation, research can seem rigorous and valid but in fact may be limited in its explanatory power and impact within practice, thus, serving to overestimate the impact of an approach and promote one approach over another.

Participant Instructions

Adopting a critical perspective also applies when evaluating communication with participants. Indeed, communication relates to research specifically investigating verbal instruction effects on learning and performance, but equally when researchers explain how participants should complete a task during the experiment. Within skill-acquisition research, much debate and concern regarding this aspect of methodological design has occurred and for several reasons (e.g., Herrebrøden 2023; Toner and Moran 2014), all of which threaten the **external validity** (i.e., extent to which it relates to *actual* coaching practice) of findings and, consequently, bias the implementation of one practice over another.

These external validity issues have mainly been directed toward the cognitive approach, in which most research focuses on verbal instruction and **augmented feedback** (i.e., feedback provided by a source external to the body, such as a coach). Accordingly, two substantial bodies of evidence that exemplify this concern address a performer's attentional focus (Wulf 2013) and the accrual of rule-based knowledge (Masters and Maxwell 2008) during skill acquisition. In the former, research compares an internal focus on bodily movements to an external focus on the movements' effect. Of this, authors have stated that an internal focus represents instructions underpinned by "practitioner wisdom" (Wulf 2016, p. 1294). On close inspection, however, internal foci employed in empirical research are typically irrelevant to achieving task success, unfamiliar to skilled participants, assumed to operate exclusively from an external focus, and insufficiently tailored to participants' specific technical needs. For example, Abdollahipour and colleagues (2015) required national-level gymnasts to execute a simple jump and 180-degree turn while positioning the hands inward across the chest. Whereas the internal focus instruction was "while airborne, focus on the direction in which your hands are pointing after the half turn" (p. 1809), the external focus instruction was "while airborne, focus on the direction in which the tape marker [fixed to the gymnast's chest] is pointing after the half turn" (p. 1809). By contrast, Bernier and colleagues' (2016) study in elite-level figure skating revealed one skater reported that "during the approach to the jump, actually, I'm doing the jump in my head: I have the same sensations in my body, and I feel like I'm doing it in my upper body and hips [i.e., a whole body/holistic internal focus]" (p. 261). As such, comparing these studies regarding the timing and content of attentional foci employed is problematic. Specifically, in the study by Abdol-

lahipour and colleagues, the internal focus was directed toward a feature of the movement that is irrelevant to generating body or hip rotation, which *is* more central to achieving a half-turn in the air (as suggested in the study by Bernier et al. 2016). Furthermore, Loze, Collins, and Holmes (2001) and Collins, Moffat, and colleagues (2023) found evidence that the visual cortex becomes *less* engaged in the moments preceding a pistol shot and golf putt for skilled participants, suggesting a switch from external visual control to a state of inward intention. Therefore, it is unsurprising that an external focus is typically superior for performance and learning within these studies, since the comparison biases disrupt control processes on several bases compared to an outcome-relevant instruction.

In extending these concerns, imbalances in cognitive load when comparing different information-processing characteristics have also been identified. Specifically, Bobrownicki and colleagues (2018) highlighted biases when investigating the effect of reducing rule-based knowledge through **implicit motor learning** (i.e., subconscious and without relying on verbal rules) versus the accrual of knowledge through verbal instructions as a process of **explicit motor learning** (i.e., conscious use of rule-based knowledge). Over 30 years, explicit learning has been purportedly based on "traditional coaching" by implementing 6 to 14 step-by-step instructions versus an implicit or analogy method comprised of 0 to 2 instructions (see Bobrownicki, Carson, and Collins 2022). An example of this contrast in seated basketball shooting is shown in table 4.3 (Lam, Maxwell, and Masters 2009). Based on these studies, recommendations are that learners should practice implicitly to avoid paralysis by analysis when experiencing symptoms of high anxiety. Again, however, the explicit group had a disproportionate amount of information to remember when compared to the analogy group, as shown in table 4.3. In fact, expert golf coaching practice typically only employs one or two explicit instructions (Schempp et al. 2004), which has subsequently been shown not to differ when using the analogy method (Bobrownicki et al. 2015). As such, study of implicit learning methods has been criticized on the basis that it is no more effective than explicit learning, does not offer anything new to current coaching practice, is questionable as to whether it is even longitudinally possible, and is therefore irrelevant within sport coaching (Collins, MacPherson, et al. 2023).

Finally, regarding the delivery of verbal instructions, it is necessary to consider *how* movement information is processed by performers. Building on contemporary mental imagery research, Frank and colleagues (2023) explained that imagery affects function at a perceptual level to create an expectation of the upcoming movement experience (i.e., what it will be like during the execution), akin to the predictive processing approach (cf. chapters 1 and 8). In this way, motor imagery is not considered functionally equivalent to motor processes (despite evidence of imagery activating motor areas in the cortex) but instead serves to inform the motor execution, as reflected in the quote offered by a figure skater earlier in the study by Bernier et al. (2016). However, research has not always been congruent with this concept when optimally preparing athletes to control their movements. For example, Giblin and colleagues (2015) asked skilled tennis players to adjust their knee bend and on-court position during the serve technique by different extents using verbal instructions relating to joint angles and centimeter distances. Moreover, even when manipulation checks are used to question whether a participant followed the instructions, this alone may not be entirely valid. For example, Orr, Cruickshank, and Carson (2021) found that some elite-level golfers individually adjusted their focus *despite* instructions provided by their coach during a lesson. In addition to checking during experimental trials, obtaining more detailed participant feedback

in terms of what and *how* they were thinking is also necessary to fully comprehend instructional effects.

While it might appear that critique in this regard can only be directed to research using the cognitive approach, a case also needs to be made for EcoD studies, in which the exact verbal instructions provided are often vague or nonexistent. For example, according to a study by Hristovski and colleagues (2006) examining the emergent and nonlinear nature of punching in boxers:

> *The boxers also complied with a number of other instructional constraints including the requirement to perform sequences of strikes in a parallel stance with their toes aligned with different distance markers from the target. Before starting the activity, performers were stringently reminded not to overbalance which is a prerequisite for a successful punch. . . . The choice of distance between the lower limbs in the parallel stance was left to the boxers. Also, there were no specific instructions on the movements of performers' feet except to maintain a constant distance from the target. (p. 64)*

On the other hand, in a study by Pinder, Renshaw, and Davids (2009) examining information-movement coupling in cricket batting, there was no mention of instructions provided.

Taking these two examples, other than questioning the coherence between rationales to offer or withhold instructions, the issue of external validity applies with regards to whether this truly represents an authentic coach–athlete interaction

Table 4.3 Condition Comparison From a Sample Explicit Versus Implicit Learning Study in Basketball

Explicit instructions	Analogy (implicit) instruction
• "Support the ball with the hand of your non-shooting arm." • "Keep the forearm vertical before shooting." • "The shoulder, elbow, and wrist should be in line with the rim before shooting." • "During shooting, the ball should move from below the chin upward and forward in the direction of the basket." • "Extend the elbow fully at ball release." • "Follow through by snapping the wrist forward so that the palm of the shooting hand is facing downward." • "Release the ball with your fingertips." • "Hold follow-through (keep wrist firm) until the ball hits the rim."	"Shoot as if you are trying to put cookies into a cookie jar on a high shelf."

or even the individualized motor preparation strategy that an athlete might employ.

WHICH APPROACH APPLIES WHERE AND WHY?

Despite these biases within research, aspects of all three approaches can be identified within good coaching practice. Therefore, this section considers the range of explanations as to why some learning factors might be a better fit for one perspective than another.

Cognitive Principles

Key features emphasized by the coach will be underpinned by the view that a performer must become independent in understanding and applying associative connections between the task and movement requirements, the perceived experience, and the outcome within memory through active thinking processes. With practice, these associations should become increasingly, even if not absolutely, subconscious (Christensen, Sutton, and McIlwain 2016; cf. Fitts and Posner 1967). Indeed, this may incorporate the active involvement of learning to learn (or *learnacy*; Claxton 2002) as part of the performer's pathway and both on- and off-field training. For this cognitive development to best support learning, practice design will engage processes involved in generating, storing, and retrieving movements from memory. As such, the coach will consider aspects and properties of attention, decision making, pattern recognition, memory, problem solving, and anticipation.

Ecological Dynamics Principles

When applying the EcoD approach, learning is less concerned with acquiring movement but instead functional adaptability and transformation by perceiving environmental and task properties. Directly perceiving meaningful information means that quality practice necessitates consideration of task and environmental characteristics in relation to the performer's individual constraints (e.g., physical flexibility or balance). The representativeness of training to the performance context supports the affordance (i.e., opportunity for action), emergence, and self-organization of different movement patterns to arise and adapt through exploration. Therefore, variability plays a crucial role in transitioning between movement patterns and expanding one's functional movement repertoire because this stimulates search processes within the **perceptual-motor landscape** (i.e., the tendencies in perceiving and moving). An important concept is that progress is expected to be nonlinear, so proportionate change in one variable (e.g., time or number of executions) does not result in a proportionate change in performance. As such, coaches will design more hands-off activities, focusing on the relationship between the individual's capabilities, the task requirements, and the environmental conditions.

Predictive Processing Principles

Predictive processing emphasizes the interaction between a learner's experience and expectation of events and the **active inference** requirements to functionally adapt when these expectations are not met. Learning in this regard is related to more quickly and accurately anticipating future outcomes within the sporting context. In this way, performance is characterized by different information-processing demands as opposed to one uniform state. Thus, this necessitates an exploration of multiple sources of probabilistic information pertaining to the task, environment, and sensory information. Through experience, the generation of an accurate predictive model becomes more reliable due to the enhanced integration of information picked up and the ability to reconstruct new models when they do not best fit the presenting challenges.

APPLYING SINGLE APPROACHES

Earlier sections have offered insights into how the three major approaches might be understood, suggesting that a this-versus-that consideration may sometimes be erroneous or based on biased data. With these principles in mind, the following case study exemplifies how each approach might contribute to a coach's decision making when designing and evaluating practice.

CASE STUDY

TEACHING BEGINNERS GOLF: THE THREE APPROACHES APPLIED

Cognitive Application

For beginner golfers, one of the most prominent issues is not knowing what to do, how to do it, and *why*. Therefore, the golfer and coach will work to coconstruct an understanding of the task and how it can be achieved without overwhelming attentional resources. Through both mental and physical practice, the aim is to generate a personally meaningful representation for storage within long-term memory that acts as a scaffold for future executions. Therefore, communication, mental aspects of rehearsal and reflection, as well as providing a movement template needs to relate to the golfer's existing understanding based on previous experiences and perceptions. In practice, two or three associated fundamental techniques—typically linking the setup and in-swing phases—may be explained and demonstrated as appropriate for the learner's physique, age, and sex, for example. The coach will encourage preperformance routines consisting of mental (e.g., imagery) and physical (e.g., a practice swing) rehearsal cues to prime execution. Feedback will be both *to* (e.g., video of what a model technique looks like) and *from* (e.g., questioning to stimulate intrinsic feedback processes) the player to check for understanding. Task difficulty will be set to challenge movement reproducibility under different execution demands (e.g., shot length, curvature, or direction), if the movement itself does not present too much of a challenge alone. Overall, there must be balance between practicing quality repetitions (i.e., achieving and knowing what effective technique looks and feels like) without disengaging due to too easy or too difficult demand.

EcoD Application

In applying an EcoD approach to teaching golf, emphasis is on the exploration of movement possibilities in relation to task and environmental demands. Accordingly, the coach will not prescribe technical solutions to the player but instead will facilitate the perception of information to inform the golfer's search for an effective motor solution. This might include the manipulation of task constraints such as varying the distance and size of marked-out target zones or using barriers to hit over in order to promote the emergence of functional solutions within a specific golfing scenario (e.g., a pitch shot over a bunker toward the green). In this regard, the coach will offer feedback (considered an informational constraint), but not regarding the movement form. Instead, this may relate to clubhead kinematics (e.g., "consider how steeply the club is moving when it hits the ball") as a stimulus for promoting different search behaviors. In addition to manipulating task constraints, environmental constraints such as different grass lengths and conditions (e.g., wet and dry), as well as hitting from different elevations (e.g., high up on a hill, which alters the playing distance due to extra ball carry) can be implemented to guide learners to new **affordances** (i.e., an opportunity for action resulting from the interaction with crucial environmental and task information). Finally, goals may be set that represent scenarios within the game for the player to problem solve based on shot type and club used (e.g., using different clubs to achieve the same outcome). Overall, the emphasis is on providing rich interactions and exploration of movement solutions.

Predictive Processing Application

While the predictive processing approach has been discussed for time-constrained interceptive sporting tasks requiring anticipation, the principles may still apply in closed and self-paced contexts. However, it must be stressed that its general application within sport remains at a nebulous stage. For the coach, it is important to understand the beginner player's prior knowledge resulting from their experience in both golf and another sports (if appropriate), which informs the player's internal model and expectation of the challenge involved. Given a relatively limited experience of the game, active inference processes will be significant and potentially inaccurate or inefficient. The coach will work proactively with the player to identify and prioritize the most valuable sources of information for them to attend to, thus pre-sensitizing the representations and assisting cognition and perception during engagement with the task and environment. Watching golf on the television (e.g., within the golf clubhouse) and purposefully directing the golfer's attention to key task demands might offer an informative problem for them to solve before watching an expert perform their evaluation (e.g., reading different slopes on the green) and physically attempt the challenge. Indeed, faster recognition and interpretation of these sources will be determined by their relevance *and* the player's ability to resolve any unexpected stimuli. Therefore, structured progression across technical, task, and environmental characteristics might facilitate this process in a meaningful way, through a backward chaining method and reviews of representative performances on video, for instance. Here, the task and naive expectation will be increasingly generalized from simple to complex skills (e.g., putting to chipping to pitching to full swing) in order to promote understanding of accurate execution parameters while implementing manageable surprises, such as a tee shot that is more exposed to a cross wind, to embed both movement and outcome experience.

CHAPTER SUMMARY

This chapter has reinforced, exemplified, and extended the need for critical decision making when applying an evidence-informed approach. First, the either-or origins within skill-acquisition research were presented to demonstrate the parallel relationship of approaches over many decades but also its lack of integration. Crucially, the recent increase in practitioner-led research was identified as highlighting the approaches' distinctiveness and incompatibility when presented as alternative explanations to the same problem. In other words, effective practical solutions are not understood as either-or options as presented by cognitive and EcoD approaches. Indeed, this confusion or lack of clarity was suggested to have created a barrier to skill-acquisition specialists making significant applied inroads when compared to less divisive sport science support disciplines. Examining the implications of taking a research-informed perspective to practice, a review of studies that had compared different approaches showed only few examples, with mixed results and methodological limitations. Methodological characteristics were explored to exemplify how criticality might be used to identify important biases when seeking to understand research evidence. Finally, a case study illustrated where knowledge derived from the cognitive, EcoD, and predictive processing approaches might apply within a skill-acquisition context. This case study demonstrated that each approach has its merits when addressing different aims and aspects of the performance and learning challenge.

REVIEW AND PRACTICAL QUESTIONS

1. What are the four evident transitions within skill-acquisition research since the early 20th century?
2. Why might skill-acquisition specialists face difficulties when integrating with applied sport science teams?
3. What are some of the methodological components that should be critically reviewed when seeking to employ evidence-informed practice?
4. In which phases of performance do each of the cognitive, EcoD, and predictive processing perspectives most predominantly apply?

KEY TERMS

active inference
active treatment
affordance
augmented feedback
dependent variable
direct perception-action coupling
explicit motor learning

external validity
implicit motor learning
internal validity
pan-theoretical
perceptual-motor landscape
pracademic
retention

CHAPTER 5

BLENDING APPROACHES

Michael Ashford and Jamie Taylor

Chapter Objectives

After studying this chapter, you should be able to do the following:

- Appreciate a suggested split of coaching methods into two broad categories: activity design and coaching style
- Recognize how coaching styles and activity design can be blended to shape effective skill-acquisition
- Understand the conditional nature of knowledge and evidence within skill learning
- Explain the pros and cons of applying different coaching methods for different purposes
- Recognize the breadth of methods available to coaches and where these may be blended to support skill learning
- Critically reflect on the difference between functional variability and optimal skill templates and how these ideas can be effectively applied

Theories offer insight into how things work but, over time, are often disproven or enhanced. It is logical and unsurprising that in skill-acquisition and coaching, approaches have developed based on theoretical beliefs about "the way things are." For instance, the foundational theories discussed in the introduction offer contrasting theoretical approaches to human movement control (e.g., cognitive or ecological theories). If all human behavior is initiated through the need to reduce uncertainty (cf. Parr, Pezzulo, and Friston 2022), it is perhaps logical for researchers to bias their assumptions toward their starting position rather than aim to test the efficacy of a particular theory, especially one

new to them and their mental structure of the skill world. This is interesting for two reasons. First, it increases the likelihood that a person's assumptions might override or ignore contrary evidence, and second, the tail is often wagging the dog, because skill-acquisition principles become stuck as a result of strict adherence to theoretical boundaries.

Chapter 4 demonstrated the tendency of researchers to offer a metaphorical chain flowing from their approach to their methods to their findings and inferences. This has often resulted in authors suggesting a single, contemporary way of skill-acquisition (Taylor et al. 2023), albeit with some notable exceptions (e.g., Renshaw et al. 2019a). Put simply, advocates of foundational theories of skill learning have often sought to drive the coaching methods being used by coaches. In contrast, a growing body of work suggests that an absolute conception of knowledge or shaping coaching practice from within theoretical boundaries is unhelpful (e.g., Collins et al. 2022; Bobrownicki et al. 2023). In other words, "do it this way because that is what that theory says" might be a less than helpful, or even a harmful, approach.

Across domains, even within the most evidence-based professions, there is often a void between research and practice (cf. Tomkins and Bristow 2023). Measures of skill learning have frequently explored the realities of performers and coaches by proxy, and any concerns regarding validity, reliability, and trustworthiness within analysis procedures are often mitigated but never quashed completely (cf. Ferguson, Carson, and Collins 2023). For example, we understand that neural activity is at the heart of a performer's skill learning, yet measurement of neural activity is mostly conducted in static circumstances (Wittenburg et al. 2017) rather than real-life learning and performing environments. Thus, within the field of skill acquisition, more should be done to recognize the fallibility of research findings and implications where that research needs to be consumed with an open and skeptical lens (cf. Collins et al. 2022).

Taking a pragmatic view, skill-acquisition knowledge should not be treated as a perfect representation of truth (Giacobbi et al. 2005). Pragmatists suggest that research provides a useful map of the world rather than a correct one, using methods that are practically meaningful. Shier (2017) nicely summarized the key features that pragmatists should adopt, including

- being open and skeptical to theories and their practical use,
- rejection of ideas that stand on beliefs,
- acceptance that all knowledge is questionable,
- being driven by practical problems, and
- recognizing key social and contextual factors (see also the advice offered in chapter 2).

For the purpose of this chapter, we consider a blending of theoretical approaches focused on practical application and use rather than adher-ence to theoretical foundations and beliefs. To put it simply, methods before methodologies.

A PRAGMATIC TAKE ON PERFORMER CENTEREDNESS

The idea of learner centeredness has grown from the educational domain (e.g., Rymarz 2012), which posits that teachers can use different styles to either increase or decrease generative activity. In this sense, **performer centeredness** is presented as methods used by the coach to ask the learner or performer to produce movement in a learning episode (Mosston 1966). Unfortunately, the notion of being athlete or performer centered has drifted away from the relative weighting of coach or performer generative activity on a continuum of practice, instead adopting a false dichotomy between performer and coach centeredness. This dichotomy is grounded in coaching methods considered best practice rather than the generative nature of the performer's experience. This has led to discovery-based and implicit approaches being promoted as wholly better, while instructional and more explicit methods are considered always worse. This type of false dichotomy does an injustice to coaches, moving practice away from using an appropriate blend of styles based on the needs of the performer.

Practitioners might choose instead to look to recommendations that are couched in more flexible language such as "find the right balance" and "consider individual difference" when seeking an optimal blend (Williams and Hodges 2023). The quality of a coach's decision to employ a particular coaching method, instruction, question, drill, or small-sided game should be measured by its impact on the learner, not by the method itself. Rather, some approaches might work better or worse than others, but in practice, a blend is likely most appropriate.

So how can we better understand performer centeredness in skill-acquisition? Rather than being a way of coaching within set parameters based on discovery learning, being performer centered should focus on a holistic understanding of the performer, what they want, and what they need (cf. Penney and Kidman 2014). Consider if a young gymnast wants to develop the movement pattern to execute a somersault within their floor routine. Each time they project up and forward, they bail out of the movement sideways, because they have developed neither a feel nor an understanding for the tucking of their knees into their body to generate speed and momentum through the movement. The coach who continues to ask the performer to figure it out by adopting discovery-based, implicit learning approaches may generate reduced confidence, increased anxiety, and uncertainty. Even if the gymnast eventually does get it, they might subsequently be limited by the experience. In contrast, the coach can scaffold this problem by filming and slowing down the movement, presenting video footage, and then incrementally supporting a feeling of what the tuck should feel like. Here, the decomposition of the whole skill may support increased understanding, perceived competence, and self-efficacy in the movement pattern. As an additional benefit, the performer learns to apply an approach that is useful for them in the longer term. Consequently, performer centeredness has nothing at all to do with specific methods to the acquisition of skill; it is more about the wants and needs of the person being supported and the quality of the coaching methods used to support acquisition. In other words, and as highlighted in the introduction of this book, making decisions based on psychosocial rather than only bio considerations.

Applying well-established methods from the literature, Abraham and Collins (2011a) suggested that there are broadly two ways in which coaches think when supporting skill-acquisition. Fast and intuitive thinking is a less deliberate course of cognition (Klein 2008). In contrast, classical decision making (CDM)—slow, thoughtful thinking—is much more deliberate (cf. Abraham and Collins 2011a). Deliberate decisions capture mental projections and predictions about the way the performer experience should be shaped for skill learning, both immediate and in the longer term. When coaches plan deliberately, in a slow thoughtful way, to support skill learning (cf. Carson and Collins 2015), a critical consideration of the evidence, the methods, the context in which that evidence has been produced, and the practical implications should take place.

Notably, some suggest that skill-acquisition should be an evidence-based endeavor (cf. Bergmann et al. 2021), yet this is a near impossibility. To be evidence based in skill-acquisition, practices would need to offer a prescribed dose of activities and interactions that have an already established

and probable outcome of learning and acquisition. Skill learning is a complex biopsychosocial endeavor and cannot work this way if we are to take account of individual and contextual differences (cf. Bobrownicki et al. 2022). We would suggest instead that evidence should be considered pragmatically and carefully blended with other ideas. Evidence should inform skill learning and development but not blindly drive it. It is this careful consideration of evidence, context, and professional judgment that makes up evidence-*informed*, rather than evidence-*based*, practice.

BLENDING APPROACHES: THE CONDITIONALITY OF COACHING APPROACH

Reflecting these considerations, rather than adopting a single approach, skill-acquisition methods should be conditional on context and the performer's wants and needs (Collins et al. 2022). Understanding where to start requires mental projection toward a desired end and deliberate formulation of intended impacts (cf. Martindale and Collins 2005). But how does the well-intended coach consider additional elements (i.e., the wants and needs of their performers)? Addressing these issues, Taylor and colleagues (2023) shared the prevalence of cognitive load theory (CLT), which refers to the assessment of a performer's prior knowledge (what do they already know?), the nature of new knowledge being introduced (what do they want and need to know for skill learning purposes?), and the difference between them (the amount of cognitive load). From here, coaches can assess prior knowledge and make a judgment on an acceptable amount of new knowledge that can be introduced without overloading the performer (Taylor et al. 2023).

Yet it is important to realize that reference to knowledge does not only mean explicit, declarative knowledge; it also includes procedural knowledge (the whats and whys) and tacit knowledge (that which is locked in). Alternatively, ecological perspectives would describe these types of knowledge as building performers' knowledge about sport-specific skills (cf. Woods et al. 2020). Instead, the ecological perspectives prioritizes a performer's wants and needs as being focused on their prior experience of movement patterns under valid situations (cf. Gray 2020). Indeed, Silva and colleagues

(2013, p. 768) suggest that "successful coordination, whether at a team or individual level, was supported by perception of relevant information that provides affordances, or, in Gibson's (1960) words, knowledge of the environment."

Some of this debate may be difficult to unpack given the different starting conceptions of some cognitive and ecological approaches. Importantly, this is not to suggest that either is correct, but instead that coaches need to take account of explicit, implicit, and tacit knowledge as the residue of experience. This is especially the case if we are to acknowledge that changes to a human's state and behavior regarded as learning will always be a result of their experience (Schunk 2012). To navigate these linguistic issues, rather than practical difficulties, we suggest there is value in drawing on the notion of priors (cf. Taylor et al. 2023) to consider all knowledge and previous experience of performers rather than prioritize either explicit or implicit knowledge. Therefore, we will now refer to *priors* for the remainder of this chapter, with the following examples promoting the conditionality of supporting skill learning in performers.

WHAT WE MEAN BY COACHING METHODS

Previous work has suggested that coaches have two broad categories of **coaching methods** making up their approach to shape performers' skill learning (e.g., Muir and North 2023). These can be categorized as (1) activity design and (2) coaching style. Activity design refers to the performer experience, which is shaped by activities introduced by a coach. Coaching styles capture two-way interactions between a performer and coach across a coaching episode rather than a distinct moment in time (Pill et al. 2021). How these categories of methods might be considered as part of a coach's planning is exemplified in figure 5.1, with intentions for impact flowing from the bigger picture nested plan (see chapter 3) and followed by planning of activity design and coaching style.

In tables 5.1 and 5.2 we draw on a pragmatic blending of approaches where coaching methods are perceived as options to select from in practice, with conditional evidence informing their selection in some places but not in others. Table 5.2 is shown in the coaching styles section.

Activity Design

The broad coaching method of activity design captures how coaches can design activities to support a player's experience to progress toward a desired intention. Figure 5.2 captures key considerations in the effective design of activities for skill learning, which we will now explore in detail. Williams and Hodges (2005) studied the structure of activities focusing on two main features: the variability of practice and contextual interference. These work from constant to **variable** and from **blocked** to random. Previous research suggests that constant practice of repeated attempts of a single skill or technique leads to short-term success (Breslin et al. 2012). In such cases, however, a lack of performer understanding and deliberate

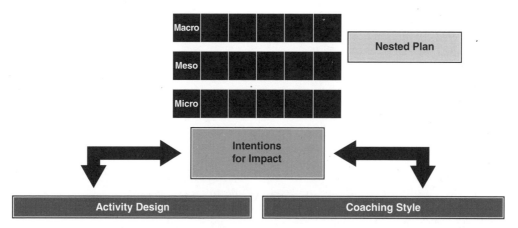

Figure 5.1 A diagram of desired intentions for impact and planned coaching styles and activity design.

Adapted from Abraham et al. (2009); Till et al. (2019).

Table 5.1 A Blending of Concepts Across Theories in Activity Design

TASK CONSTRAINTS	
Manipulation of constraints	The boundaries placed on an activity (task), the individual, or through surroundings (environmental) that shape the skill behavior of performers (Chow 2013)
Implicit (action)	Skill learning in the absence of conscious or explicit knowledge about how (Powell et al. 2021)
Explicit (epistemic)	Skill learning through conscious understanding of the facts and rules of the movement (Powell et al. 2021)
FOCUS OF ACTIVITIES	
Information-movement coupling	Opportunities to perceive information coupled with skillful actions through the activity (Chow 2013)
Functional variability	Functional solutions to a specific task, where no movement is repeated (Chow 2013)
Attentional focus	Focus can either be external (outcome driven) or internal (body movement driven) (Chow 2013, p. 472)
Optimal skill templates	A movement pattern, broken up into components, that is optimal when performed appropriately (Carson and Collins 2016)
THE NATURE OF THE ACTIVITY	
Whole	Activities that challenge performers to produce the whole skill (McMorris 2014)
Part	The decomposition of skills into component parts (Powell et al. 2021)
Part-progressive	Activities require the layering of parts, which build toward the whole skill (McMorris 2014)
Blocked	Practice of a single skill for a block of time (Williams and Hodges 2005)
Variable	A single skill produced in a variety of ways (Davids et al. 2003; Schmidt 1975)
Random	Several skills practiced in a random order (Shea and Morgan 1979)
Exaggeration	The overstatement or emphasis of task information that requires specific skill responses (Tan et al. 2012)
Tactical complexity	The difficulty associated with the problems posed by the activity (Tan et al. 2012)
Massed or constant	Single skills practiced over extended periods with minimal breaks (Abraham and Collins 2011a; McMorris 2014)
Distributed or interleaved	Short durations of skill practice that facilitate comparisons between movements (Chen et al. 2023)
Individual	Skills being learned by the performer alone (O'Connor, Larkin, and Williams 2017)
Paired	Skill learning in pairs (O'Connor, Larkin, and Williams 2017)
Drills	Predetermined movements in a set routine (O'Connor, Larkin, and Williams 2017)
Small-sided games	Games that reduce the number of opponents on each team (Cushion et al. 2012)
Possession games	Performers must retain possession of the ball (Cushion et al. 2012)
Conditioned games	Games that alter conditions to exaggerate actions (Wade 1967)
Representativeness	Activities that represent the true nature of the skill being performed in its competitive form (Chow 2013)
Contextual interference	The *contextual interference effect* refers to activities that offer interference through multiple skills, or increased variations of the skill being learned (Powell et al. 2021)

involvement might lead to boredom and a lack of transfer (Taylor et al. 2023). Instead, variable practice can result in limited success initially but, if applied appropriately, might yield long-term learning and transfer (Williams and Hodges 2005). Blocked practice has been found to be useful for short-term success and in early stages of skill-acquisition (Li and Wright 2000), where it can increase the self-efficacy of performers (Abraham and Collins 2011b), but sole use is often found to limit transfer to performance (Williams and Hodges 2005). Random practice is often detrimental to short-term performance as contextual interference increases (cf. Magill 2011), but it enhances long-term retention and learning.

The same conditionality of coaching methods also has been suggested by advocates of methods of skill development (Renshaw et al. 2019b), though perhaps more tightly parameterized by the two main frameworks used to inform skill-acquisition using the ecological approach: (1) nonlinear pedagogy (NLP; for more detail, see Chow 2013; Correia et al. 2019) and (2) the constraints-led approach (CLA; for more detail, see Renshaw et al. 2019a). Authors advocating for these frameworks have offered alternative conceptions of activity design to move away from part-progressive methods of coaching, instead suggesting that coaching methods should in turn be less linear in nature. Table 5.1 demonstrates the definitions of each of the five pedagogical principles of NLP: information-movement coupling, manipulation of constraints, attentional focus, representativeness, and functional variability. Authors have built on this work to offer four distinct environment design principles making up the CLA, including the *session intention*, *constrain to afford*, *representative learning design*, and *repetition without repetition*. Session intention should drive the performer's experience and be aligned with the performer's intentions and needs (Renshaw et al. 2019). Constrain to afford makes use of practice conditions that invite engagement with specific affordances; for example, by providing a target zone on a fairway for a golfer driving off the tee, the coach might facilitate implicit skill development through information-movement coupling. For both ideas, representativeness of the competitive environment is essential. In this example, the fairway cannot be too narrow (or too broad). Finally, repetition without repetition captures the idea of functional variability, that no movement is absolutely identical or repeatable. Under this thought process, the golfer should explore multiple swings, something that might be encouraged using task constraints.

A few empirical articles have begun to test the efficacy of CLA interventions versus other approaches to skill learning. These studies have shown the four principles of CLA enabling tennis players to develop a larger variety of technical solutions (Lee et al. 2014); baseball players to develop greater technical execution, movement variability, and comparatively better performance outcomes (Gray 2018); soccer players to have more creative actions (Orangi et al. 2021); and

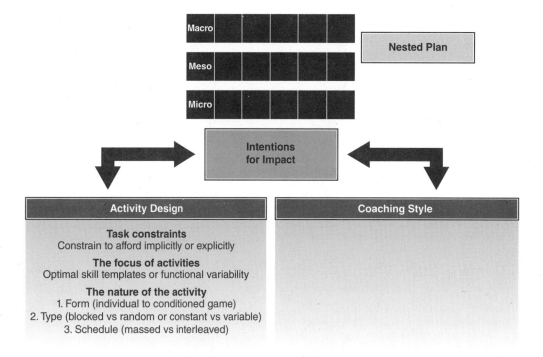

Figure 5.2 *A worked example of intentions for impact and activity design.*

baseball players to get more hits (Gray 2020). Notably, however, comparative studies also found no differences in skill-based interventions in weightlifting (Lindsay et al. 2022) or drill-based and small-sided game intervention groups in soccer (Deuker et al. 2023) and no performance differences in tennis (Lee et al. 2014). In all cases, caution should be exercised in interpreting these research findings given critique of the validity of control conditions and the challenge of comparing one entire approach to another. So far, too few studies have been conducted to allow us to reach conclusive standpoints. In short, our focus should be less on theoretical boundaries and more on the appropriate blending of coaching methods.

Historically, the activities that performers take part in have been framed in multiple ways, such as practice structure (cf. Gray 2018), learning activities (Muir and North 2023), training activities (Till et al. 2019), or practice design (Hodges and Lohse 2022). Here we adopt the label *activity design* to reflect that the acquisition of skill does not just happen on the pitch, court, grass, or arena. It can also happen off field during meetings, debriefs, video sessions (Ashford et al. 2023; Richards et al. 2017), or indeed whenever the performer is reflecting, something very common at high levels (cf. chapter 7). Similarly, activity design may not be set up with the purpose of learning and might be framed toward maintenance or building confidence. The question is whether these experiences happen by design or by chance. Therefore, we identify three key foci to enable effective blending of approaches: task constraints, the focus of the activity, and the nature of the activity.

Task Constraints

In the design of a performer's skill learning and performance, the manipulation of task constraints is common among different research perspectives. Recent reviews from ecological (Araújo et al. 2019) and cognitive (Williams and Jackson 2019) research approaches advocate the manipulation of constraints to support skill learning. Importantly, however, differences arise regarding the explicit (Ashford et al. 2023) or implicit (Renshaw et al. 2019) use of constraints in practice. Advocates of the *constraints-led* approach to skill-acquisition suggest the design principle of constrain to afford as being central to effective activity design (Renshaw et al. 2019). Put simply, this means that the task constraints employed within an activity

should shape an affordance landscape and, in turn, encourage repetition without repetition, whereby participants are asked to repeatedly explore the execution of a skill without a need or desire to repeat the exact same movement twice (Woods et al. 2020). By this definition, constraints are a constant in every activity because an affordance landscape is always available if a performer can perceive it (Wilson et al. 2018). Under this approach, task constraints such as this can create subtle bridges to the skillful movement in an implicit fashion. For example, a rugby coach may set up an activity that challenges four attackers to score versus two defenders in scoring channels, placed at the two touchlines of a very wide pitch. The activity challenges the players to score, while implicitly, it is challenging the players to execute passes over a wider distance than they usually would.

In contrast, activities where skillful solutions are explicitly shared with players may support performers to understand why the constraints of an activity will shape their skill learning, creating motivation and buy-in to skill learning. Thus, the careful blending of task constraints from different research perspectives can support coaches to consider the conditionality in how they may be employed. First, methods of activity design may afford implicit affordances through information-action loops without reference to knowledge (Correia et al. 2012). Second, coaches can create explicit epistemic affordances, where declarative and procedural knowledge sources guide the perceptual strategies of performers and their requisite movement responses (e.g., I know where to look and what I am looking for). In this regard, constraining to afford implicitly may be summarized by suggesting that individuals must *move to perceive or perceive to move*, while explicitly, it may be captured by suggesting that *what we know determines what we see*. In keeping with the rest of the book chapter, however, evidence would suggest there is a time and a place for both (cf. Ashford et al. 2022). Thus, it is the question of whether constraints are applied implicitly or explicitly that forms appropriate blending of approaches through activity design.

The Focus of the Activity

The notion of functional variability in skilled movement is universally accepted in the skill-learning literature (Magill and Hall 1990). No movement is ever identical, even for the most skillful expert in their sport executing a skill that requires a consistent outcome (cf. Portus and Farrow 2011). However, theoretical implications have suggested that this means that working toward optimal technical models is an example of poor practice (Gray 2020). In some cases, especially for more open movements like an open play pass in team sport, a higher bandwidth of variability for effective movement solutions seems logical. For more closed skills, the bandwidth of variability for an effective solution may be tighter. For instance, Green, Tee, and McKinon (2019) conducted a review of studies exploring maximal force production in a scrummaging position in rugby union. Functional variability was a factor, but only from a position of consistent angles at the hip, knee, and ankle joints enabling maximum horizontal force. We suggest that a coach's focus on skill learning, and by extension the performer's focus, should embrace the notion of functional variability. However, skill templates that do not limit performers' movement but perhaps (from an ecological standpoint) shape the search through a set of principles will promote enhanced understanding, learning, and performance over time (e.g., using skill templates with para canoeists; Simon, Collins, and Collins 2017).

The Nature of an Activity

The notion of desirable difficulty is one strongly evidenced in the skill-learning literature (e.g., Yan, Guadagnoli, and Haycocks 2019). Desirable difficulties (Bjork and Bjork 2011) refers to making things just hard enough, but not too hard, to promote learning. This often includes slowing learning down for the performer. However, there is conditionality in how difficulty can be scheduled for performers. On one hand, a massed block of incremental difficulty may be applied progressively, task by task and session by session. Instead, difficulty may be scheduled differently by leaving spaces and distributing challenge between weeks, raising the challenge when a movement is revisited. Therefore, we suggest that coaches should engage in both forward and backward thinking to consider how difficulty is scheduled for a performer with reference to skill-acquisition over time. This can be conducted with a careful, evidence-informed selection of key concepts (see

table 5.1) suitable to frame an appropriate performer experience.

Coaching Style

The broad method of coaching style captures the recognition and interruption of a performer's practice through an interaction, which supports a player's experience to progress toward a desired intention. Figure 5.3 encapsulates our key considerations in the effective employment of coaching styles for skill learning, which we will now explore in detail. Mosston and Ashworth (1994; see also the book introduction) first developed the spectrum of teaching styles to offer a "non-versus" framing for the use of teaching methods in physical education. Different styles were proposed to have different impacts on the performer rather than a recommended way of teaching. The idea of a style was used to capture a reciprocal teaching and learning process rather than a distinct behavior offered by a teacher to a student. More recently, Pill and colleagues (2021) reconceptualized this work for the purpose of sport coaching and skill-acquisition. In a similar approach to Mosston and Ashworth (1994), these authors suggested that a coach's style should be driven by the content to be acquired (e.g., the syllabus), performer's prior learning, their experience, and the needs and wants of the group and individuals. Table 5.2 lists these styles from A to K, defining their purpose.

Table 5.2 also describes Pill and colleagues' (2021) notion of clusters of coaching styles: reproduction and production. In contrast, styles A through E, the reproduction cluster, capture coaching styles that require the reproduction of content drawn from the coach's knowledge and are therefore more instructional and content driven. In contrast, styles F through K, the production cluster, tasks the performers to produce previously developed knowledge and apply it to skill-based problems they are being asked to solve. For instance, when a coach works with a young tennis player to break down and acquire each component of a tennis serve, through understanding, feel, and the development of comfort over time, they are using the reproduction cluster teaching style. When a professional tennis player tweaks their serve technique, making small adjustments to increase power, spin, and accuracy, they are applying the production cluster. At the heart of all these ideas so far has been the needs

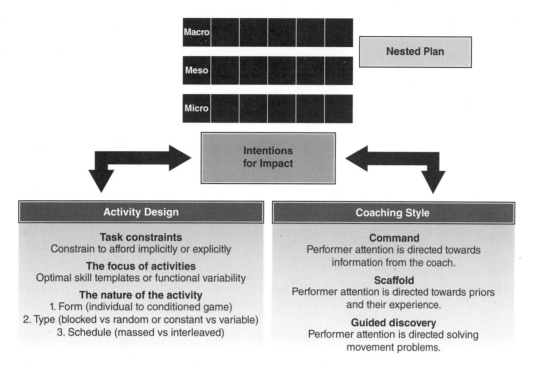

Figure 5.3 A worked example of intentions for impact, planned coaching styles, and activity design.

of the performer regarding what skills are being learned or mastered. This demonstrates common ground across all perspectives, where the design of the experience for the performer should be guided by an understanding of the performer's priors (Taylor et al. 2023; Renshaw et al. 2019). Importantly, however, this guidance should be evidence informed rather than theory driven. Otherwise, there is a risk of a rather limited, suboptimal set of solutions being generated. Our interpretation of theory suggests that the more skill priors a performer has developed (successfully, to be exact), the more coaches should adopt styles that fall later in the alphabet.

Setting and Solving Problems

A similar framing has also been developed in the literature, referring to the conditionality and decision making behind a coach setting or solving problems for performers (Ashford et al. 2022). Some suggest that skill-acquisition and refinement can only take place through *setting* problems for performers, by notions such as repetition without repetition, movement variability, and performer discovery (Myszka, Yearby, and Davids 2023). However, in a situation where a performer lacks the movement capability or understanding to solve a problem through skillful movement, this type of approach may sometimes hinder learning and is unlikely to yield a timely discovery of an effective movement solution (Taylor et al. 2023). Yet a coach who always solves problems is unlikely to enable performers to develop independence or active involvement in their learning. As a result, we suggest that the need for a coach to form a unitary position as always either setting or solving problems for performers is at odds with both logic and evidence (de Jong et al. 2023).

Coach Behavior

An alternative framing of what the coach does to support the performer's learning is the notion of coach behavior. The Coach Analysis Intervention System (CAIS) is a systematic observation tool, designed to capture the use of discrete coaching behaviors. Systematic observation tools have been identified as a method of supporting coaches to better understand themselves and their pedagogical practice (Cope, Partington, and Harvey 2017; Cope et al. 2022). However, following application of these types of tools (Ashford et al. 2022), it appears several issues are associated with their use. For example, Cope and colleagues (2017; 2022) suggest that systematic observation data are only useful when coaches are asked to compare their intended methods of delivery against what

82 Sport Skill Acquisition

Table 5.2 An Adaption of Teaching and Coaching Styles From Mosston and Ashworth (1994) and Pill et al. (2021)

Coaching style	Definition and description	Clusters	Command canopy	Scaffold canopy	Guide discovery canopy
A—Coaching by command	Listen, obey, and execute skill	Reproducing coach knowledge			
B—Coaching by task (practice)	Participants asked to work from A to B of a skillful movement task				
C—Reciprocal coaching (peer coaching)	Partner observation and feedback of skillful movement				
D—Coaching by individual programming (self-check)	Independent practice and decision making regarding execution of skill learning				
E—Small group coaching (inclusion)	Creating role responsibilities with performers in groups				
F—Coaching by guided discovery	Guiding performers to find skillful solutions through setting problems	Performer knowledge to solve problems			
G—Coaching by problem-solving (convergent discovery)	Coach sets a problem, and performers find a single skill to solve it				
H—Coaching for creativity (divergent discovery)	The coach and performer set the problem together, and multiple skillful solutions can be produced				
I—Player designed, coach supported	The coach offers a theme or problem, and the performers design the specific task to create skill learning				
J—Player initiated, coach supported	Players take responsibility for the design of the activity; the coach then offers support where needed				
K—Player self-coaching	The performer now becomes both coach and performer				

Adapted from Mosston and Ashworth (1966); Pill et al. (2021).

was delivered. In some practical instances (despite the literature advising against it; e.g., Cushion 2010) this has led to coaches being told how they should behave, such as that they should question more and instruct less. This wrongly removes the decision-making capacity of a coach to explore what a performer needs at a particular time and, most importantly, why (Collins and Collins 2015). This also ignores the meaning behind a coach's delivery and the notion that "it's not what you do, it's why you do it." There are, of course, limits to any research method and what one can reasonably expect from a single tool, and it is

important to note that behavioral analysis was not developed to consider the impact of coaching behaviors (Cushion 2010). Nonetheless, inappropriate use of behavioral analysis or a sole focus on behaviors carries limitations, something that has been highlighted for a number of years (Abraham and Collins 1998).

Taking account of the need for an understanding of the meaning of coaching behavior, Pill and colleagues (2021) adapted the work of Mosston and Ashworth (1994) by grouping coaching styles under canopies. Canopies of coaching styles allow the coach to consider how discrete behaviors are blended in a particular coaching episode. Deliberately planning for canopies of coaching style allows the coach to be highly intentional and offers a point of reference for intuitive responses to performers. We have created our own interpretation of these canopies to better guide a coach to consider how styles could be applied; we suggest three categories.

1. *Command canopy:* Styles that direct a performer's attention to information from the coach
2. *Scaffold canopy:* Styles that direct a performer's attention to priors
3. *Guide discovery canopy:* Styles that support performers to solve movement problems

In practice, we suggest that planning for canopies prevents the coach from being overloaded with plans for discrete behaviors and encourages adaptive practice. This does not undermine behavioral analysis from a research or analysis perspective; it just allows the coach to consider the meaning of their actions and how they may shape the performer's attention.

Notably, this lack of meaning is a part of a broader problem across the literature in that it has tended not to investigate the affective side of skill learning (Carson and Collins 2016). Given that skill-acquisition is biopsychosocial (cf. Collins et al. 2012), skillful movement, either for the first time as a child or the thousandth time as an adult, is the consequence of the complex interaction of biological, psychological, and social factors (cf. Carson and Collins 2017; dos Santos et al. 2016). The affect of a coaching style can be caring, challenging, conflicting, pressuring, or praising—and perhaps all at once. Evidence suggests that performers can often benefit from both harder (challenging, setting standards, or expectations) and softer approaches (empathic accuracy and openness) (e.g., Taylor et al. 2022). Interestingly, this seems to be a shared perspective across research perspectives (Renshaw et al. 2019a; Carson and Collins 2017). Therefore, a performer understanding why a coaching style is being used is likely to support skill-acquisition.

Deliberately planning for canopies of coaching styles allows the coach to be highly intentional and offers a point of reference for intuitive responses to performers.

Mayur Kakade/Moment/Getty Images

CASE STUDY

CHANGING COACHING STYLE OVER TIME

A young cricketer has been seeking to improve their timing and ball connection in their repertoire of shots over the previous six weeks. While their priors would suggest that some progress is being made, development and improvements have been inconsistent. By observing and video-recording their performance, their coach has identified that their head position is inconsistent and, consequently, so are their timing and ball connection. The coach thinks it would be useful to clearly define and diagnose the issue, share this with the player, and discuss potential changes. The coach and the player agree on the intentions of a 12-week block of time, and the coach prepares the player for the likelihood that performance will likely decrease before it later improves.

The coach begins the block of skill learning, by using a **command style** to draw the player's attention to what an appropriate head position looks and feels like. The coach is in essence aiming to solve the problem for the performer. Over this block of four weeks the player is asked to learn and memorize key principles regarding their head movement. Video footage is used to demonstrate how these principles look, raising the performer's awareness and is followed by a higher volume of different forms of feedback on their progress. The coach designs individual and drill-based activities to exaggerate the problem and make the performer aware, leading the performer to consider, "What does this feel like when I get this wrong versus right?" These activities shift between constant (of one shot being practiced) and variable practice (numerous shots being tested) in a blocked and massed schedule. Explicit awareness of task constraints is also generated. They include (1) the reduced pace of the bowling delivery to reduce the complexity of the movement and (2) the hold position from the point of contact with the ball to exaggerate the relationship between head and bat position.

Over time, the coach aims to lessen their support, enabling the player to become more independent and aware of their performance, which indicates to the coach that the performer's priors have adaptively changed through the method of reproduction. By checking for priors, the coach then moves into the next block of four weeks, in which they use a **scaffold style** through setting problems by questioning, use of verbal challenges, and referencing the retrieval of priors. Here the coach varies between asking the performer to reproduce priors (retrieval) and produce priors to solve problems (transfer). The coach interleaves and distributes two central activity designs. The first is conditioned game scenarios, where task constraints are employed implicitly by creating affordances through fielding positions. The bowlers in these activities are then coached to offer specific deliveries of line and length that exaggerate information and thus the performer's shot that follows. The implicit constraints are used to promote the performer's focus on how many runs they can score in a set number of balls. The second activity design employs a blocked and variable activity, where explicit focus of attention is returned. This is designed to check for understanding (show me, tell me, execute) as to the consistency of the new movement.

CHAPTER SUMMARY

In summary, following a critical evaluation of the skill-acquisition literature, we suggest that the concepts discussed in this chapter offer utility somewhere but, importantly, not everywhere. Splitting a coach's methods into two broad categories—activity design and coaching style—generates conditional, evidence-informed options to optimize skill-acquisition. It is desirable that the coach uses deliberate thinking to mentally project appropriate coaching styles and activity design in pursuit of intentions. However, deliberate thinking is only ever useful to guide more intuitive responses in action (e.g., Ashford et al. 2022). Deliberate thinking should guide a coach's attention by knowing where to look and listen, knowing what to look and listen for, and solving the problems intuitively. This balance of judgment between deliberate and intuitive thinking should shape coaching styles and activity design and, in turn, the performer's experience. This notion of delivery is nicely summarized by Dylan Wiliam (2013),who suggests that a bad curriculum well taught will always provide a more optimal learning experience than a good curriculum badly taught. Flowing from our considerations in this chapter, pedagogy will trump content, because it will shape the performer experience. How the coach might engage in particular activity design or use a given coaching style will be considered in the next chapter.

REVIEW AND PRACTICAL QUESTIONS

1. What are the two broad categories in which a coach's methods can be separated?
2. What is the distinction between coaching behaviors and coaching styles?
3. What are the three canopies of coaching styles, and how might they be used?
4. What are the advantages and disadvantages of a more command-based style?
5. What is meant by constraining to afford in an explicit or implicit fashion?
6. What is the difference between optimal skill templates and functional variability, and how may they be blended practically?

KEY TERMS

activity design

blocked

coaching methods

performer centeredness

ariable

CHAPTER 6

PERFORMER EXPERIENCE: CHALLENGE AND FIDELITY

Jamie Taylor and Michael Ashford

Chapter Objectives

After studying this chapter, you should be able to do the following:

- Understand how to influence performer experience for skill-acquisition
- Recognize how the concept and types of fidelity can enhance skill-acquisition
- Consider the different ways that performers can interact with skill-acquisition activity
- See how using levels of curriculum can enhance coach deliberative and intuitive thinking
- Distinguish between types of errors in skill-acquisition

The previous chapter focused on the evidential base for the three approaches. From this understanding, the coach or practitioner makes decisions through a pragmatic, conditional, and blended consideration of their activity design or coaching style. This chapter will extend these considerations by exploring how a coach's overall approach affects and shapes the performer's experience. Taking this broader focus might help coaches and practitioners navigate and further understand the nuances presented by different bodies of skill-acquisition research. Here, we suggest the need for a consideration of performer experience and how this may influence the practitioner's approach to skill-acquisition. If we are to acknowledge that the performer does the learning (cf. Schunk 2012), coaches should plan

for desirable performer experience. Therefore, as suggested in chapter 4, the route to a desired end should capture the quality of the evidence, the coach's approach, and the desired performer experience.

This orientation is part of the increasing recognition of the centrality of the experience of the performer and what is going on for them. That is, the focus of our work with the performer must extend further than simple notions of their engagement. Instead, we need to consider what is going on for them at any moment in time and whether that actually constitutes learning (cf. Hendrick and Heal 2020). In this regard, Abraham and Collins (2011a) proposed three golden rules for learning that coaches could use to enhance their decision making:

1. Make the content as personally relevant for the performer as possible.
2. Promote performer understanding whenever possible, especially when working toward long-term development.
3. For rapid, short-term results, make the session mentally easy for the performer; for long-term development, make it harder.

Notably, each of the three rules focuses on the experience of the performer rather than what the coach does. This focus on the performer is reflected by a range of theoretical stances—for example, considering concepts like retrieval and intentionality so that, despite different theoretical underpinnings, when combined they might offer useful practical blends. While we claim no novelty in the idea that performers play the central role in the process of skill-acquisition (e.g., Ericsson, Krampe, and Tesch-Römer 1993), what has tended to be ignored is the relationship between a coach's intentions, the coaching style, activity design, and performer experience. Indeed, much existing literature has tended to make assumptions about the nature of performer experience through the observation of behavior alone (cf. Ashford, Abraham, and Poolton 2021), something that has received greater conceptual attention with the concept of curriculum.

PERFORMER CURRICULUM

While emanating from education, the notion of curriculum has been used extensively across sporting contexts, both in practice and in research (Abraham et al. 2022). In practice, curriculum has tended to be used as a list of content to be covered (better seen as the syllabus). For practical purposes, curriculum refers to the totality of experience, lived by the performer (Kelly 2009; Taylor and Collins 2022; Moran, Craig, and Collins 2024). Based on the need to understand curriculum from the perspective of the performer and not just content to be delivered, we can also look at curriculum through different lenses or levels, depending on who is looking (e.g., Clemmons et al. 2022).

These levels of curriculum can act as a reflective tool for the coach or practitioner to consider the differences between what they might intend to do, what they deliver, and what the performer experiences (table 6.1). It is likely that each level is subtly different and may, at times, be wholly incoherent from the others. Indeed, it could be considered a limitation (as far as transferability goes) that much existing research has focused on exploring coaches' enacted curriculum, both in terms of the coach's activity design (e.g., practice scheduling) or what the coach does (e.g., internal and external cueing). Curriculum modeling instead encourages acknowledgment that, while we might put significant time, energy, and thought into the planning and delivery of coaching, what really matters is the lived experience of the performer. Importantly, none of this is to suggest that the coach forms these intentions absent of athlete involvement (compare with the golden rules presented earlier), something more recently referred to as *cocreation* (Renshaw et al. 2019). Instead, it acknowledges that performers will arrive with their own intentions and the aim of the coach should be the coupling of these intentions with the enacted curriculum. It also means that one important indicator of effective practice is comparing the coherence of performer experience against **intentions for impact** (Martindale and Collins 2005) (see figure 6.1).

BACKWARD AND FORWARD PLANNING

We referred to forward and backward thinking on a micro level in chapter 5, and now we will consider it in the bigger picture. A variety of literature in education points to the value of backward thinking, something that might be obvious for

Table 6.1 Levels of Curriculum

Planned curriculum	Coach and performer intentions for performer experience
Enacted curriculum	The coaching approach deployed against these intentions
Experienced curriculum	How the performer experiences the coach's approach
Hidden curriculum	The impact of power dynamics, micropolitics, social norms, and dynamics on the coaching situation (Cushion and Jones 2014)

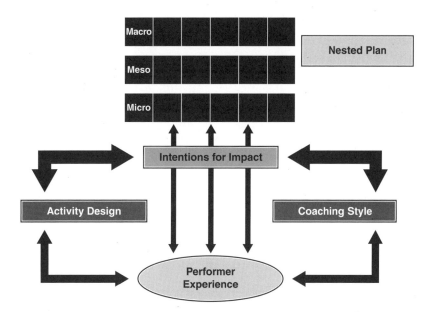

Figure 6.1 The thread of performer experience for coach decision making.
Adapted from Abraham et al. (2009); Till et al. (2019).

many but is a fundamental element of practice if coaches are to effectively reflect on the aims of their practice and make necessary adjustments. This backward thinking "'begins with the end in mind,' involving identifying future performance relative to the participant's current context to allow the formulation of goals over time" (Till et al. 2019, p. 13). This means that coaches use more deliberative thinking to work backward from a desired intention. This allows for a consideration of how various elements of practice might be nested within one another.

A critique of backward planning has been the relative determinacy of objectives—for example, "By the end of this session, all athletes will be able to do ____." By framing objectives in this manner, the typically nonlinear vagaries of human development are ignored, especially because people arrive in the coaching situation from a variety of different start points, or different priors (see chapter 1). These differences will lead to fundamental variation in the way different performers experience the same activities. As a result, there is some debate about the relative value of definitive learning objectives. This indeterminacy is part of the reasoning that a professional judgment and decision making (PJDM) approach uses the notion of intentions for impact (Martindale and Collins 2005) to consider how the performer will be affected rather than just what outcomes they should achieve. For the coach, this can be an especially difficult activity when trying to frame the outcomes of an individual session (micro level).

As is accepted across theoretical paradigms, short-term adaptation within the context of a training session does not necessarily lead to longer-term learning and transfer (Lohse et al. 2019). Indeed, this difference is encapsulated in the third of Abraham and Collins's golden rules, as described earlier. A lack of longer-term thinking might lead coaches to frame their judgment on the speed at which performers adapt to the individual activities. Perhaps the greater danger is a coach's reflection toward performers being focused on how "good" they were today. The risk is that if this style of reflection is repeated, skill-acquisition practice will always be framed by short-term adaptation rather than long-term learning, retention, and transfer.

Consequently, the coach needs to formulate objectives at multiple levels (macro, meso, micro; Abraham and Collins 2011b). Longer-term learning and transfer is not necessarily observable in the short term and requires coaches to consider changes for the performer over time as illustrated by the consistent reference to intentions for impact described in the previous chapter. Perhaps contrary to some views in coaching practice, this deliberative thinking can be used to significantly enhance more intuitive actions taken by the coach in practice (Kahneman and Klein 2009). As a result, we suggest that coaches need to use this more deliberative thinking to focus not solely on engagement but instead to plan and shape performer experience through activity design and coaching style (the planned curriculum). What the coach then does in practice should be subject to flexible replanning (Klein 2007) and more intuitive changes that help move performers toward desired experiences (the enacted curriculum). Ultimately, however, the focus should be on the performer's experience (see figure 6.2) and what might be desirable (the experienced curriculum). This will be considered using a multitude of theories concerning the lived experience of the performer or learner.

EXPLORE-TEST CONTINUUM

A fundamental lens through which to consider a performer's experience is the explore-exploit continuum of human behavior (see chapter 1 and Friston et al. 2015). In a skill-acquisition sense, the continuum relates to the relative novelty or familiarity of an individual with a movement solution or interaction with their environment. Exploration is a state of novelty seeking, whereas exploitation refers to the maximization of previously developed capabilities (Schwartenbeck et al. 2013). Consider the difference in desirable experience for two high jumpers, one who shortly will be competing in an international competition (exploitative) and another who, in the off-season, is going to begin a period of significant technical change (exploratory). While both will be challenging (cf. Abraham and Collins 2011a), the nature of the challenge from both a control and a mental skill perspective will be qualitatively different.

Building on this modeling, a typology of the relative stabilization of skill-acquisition and underpinning neural activity has been suggested. This comprises

1. *expansion*, involving the initial expansion of the ensemble to provide a large pool of neural circuits from which to make an optimal selection;

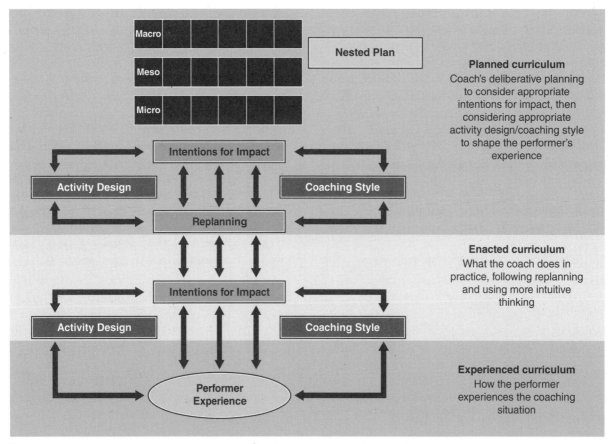

Figure 6.2 The expanded thread of performer experience for coach decision making.

Adapted from Abraham et al. (2009); Till et al. (2019).

2. *exploration*, involving the probing of different motor patterns to achieve a goal through the development of neural structures;

3. *selection*, as in the selection of a movement pattern within certain parameters; and

4. *refinement*, or the ongoing synaptic remodeling over time to the pattern (Lövdén, Garzón, and Lindenberger 2020).

Similarly, practical applications of the ecological dynamics (EcoD) approach have used Newell's (1985) framework of skill level, a progression from coordination stage to control stage involving refinement and stabilization before a skill stage when performance becomes adaptive. It has been suggested that performers can interact with their field of affordances available based on their skill level and constraints imposed, ranging from exploring to exploiting to executing (Renshaw et al. 2019).

Going a step further, we add the label *retrieve*, drawing on notions from educational psychology to describe "an active attempt by a student to recall or recognize, and then reconstruct, their memory of knowledge during initial learning" (Agarwal, Nunes, and Blunt 2021, 1412). In a skill-acquisition context, this involves the active attempt to perform movement patterns previously developed, without coach support, for the purpose of checking for the relative stabilization of skill. Finally, the label *execute* represents various forms of pressure training, with the coach aiming to generate higher levels of pressure relative to competition (or transfer conditions). Pressure training involves the deliberate use of pressure to allow performers to practice coping with pressure and therefore maximize transfer to the competitive arena (Stoker et al. 2016). This is not necessarily to suggest a linear stage-based acquisition of skill, with a gradual progression toward automaticity akin to Fitts and Posner (1967) (see also

chapters 1 and 7 on the desirability and nature of automaticity). Instead, we draw pragmatic links between neurological data related to the stability of neural circuits and the performer's experience. This allows both coach and performer to understand and label the purpose of an activity based on desirable performer experience. The nature of the learning experience has become a much-debated topic, one with a long history in education (Dewey 1938) and in sport (see chapter 5 and discussion of performer centeredness). The typology outlined in table 6.2 offers practitioners a starting point to consider coherence between the nested plan, their intentions for impact, and how they shape performer experience with their activity design and coaching style.

Based on our practical experience, a common frame of reference for many coaches is refinement, with sessional success indicated by a reduction in the number of errors in a manner consistent with deliberate practice (Ericsson 2020). This narrow focus may be a result of early-stage coach education, when planning and reviewing is encouraged on a sessional basis rather than longer term. For this reason, many are drawn to the shorter-term adaptations rather than longer-term learning and transfer (e.g., Lohse et al. 2019). A typical (sometimes referred to as *traditional*) session format across sports often involves a coach selecting a technique, which is subsequently refined over a series of part-progressive drills, building into a more whole-like activity. If these methods are deployed on an ongoing basis, it will be rare for the performer to be invited to engage in training that is outside the bandwidth of refinement. A way to check for this style of thinking is to reflect on, or ask a coach following a session, "How was that?" If the first thing that comes to mind was the improvement in performance over the course of the session, it is worth considering why what was done was done. To be clear, we are

Table 6.2   Desired Interaction of Performer with Activity

Expand and explore	Searching for and probing different motor patterns or team coordination to achieve a goal
Selection and refinement	Selection of a movement or team pattern within certain parameters, followed by gradual, ongoing synaptic remodeling
Retrieve	Performance of previously developed movement patterns, without coach support, to check the relative embeddedness of skill
Execute	Pressurized activity used to maximize transfer to performance

in no way advocating a best way for performers to interact with activities nor that the tenets of deliberate practice are inappropriate. Rather, like the blended approach outlined in chapter 5, considering performer experience encourages us to see that different approaches may or may not be useful and why.

Acquisition requires performers to expand their motor skills through exploring different patterns and options. It also requires the careful refinement of previously selected skills under increasing challenge levels. Regular retrieval of skill development with reducing support and increasing pressure indicates progress and build confidence in the ability to transfer to competition. This requires careful long-term planning on the part of the coach and the ability to engage in ongoing replanning to meet the needs of athletes. Notably, the coach must consider not just the performer's acquisition of a movement pattern but also their capability to meet the demands of the environment shaped by their priors. This is especially important in oppositional sports (e.g., team, combat, or racket sports) in which the movements of one side are related to an opponent (Gréhaigne, Wallian, and Godbout 2005; Gréhaigne and Godbout 1995). As the capabilities of the opponent change, they challenge the movement skills of the other differently. For example, in team sport, it is frequently said that the best way to increase the challenge of decision making in attack is to increase the movement capabilities of the defender.

THE ROLE OF CHALLENGE FOR PERFORMERS

In this section we consider something akin to the desirable difficulties presented in chapter 5, which refer to the scheduling of activities designed to slow but strengthen the acquisition process (Bjork and Bjork 2011). As a subtle contrast, we will consider how the relative difficulty of the task being performed might affect skill-acquisition. The notion of challenge has been explored across the educational and coaching literature at length. Here, we define challenge at the micro level, in line with the work of Mariani (1997), whose original teacher challenge and support framework acted as a catalyst for future versions in the sporting literature: "something that tests

strength, skill or ability especially in a way that is interesting." Mariani elaborated by suggesting, "When we challenge our students we are actually asking them to go beyond a safety zone, so to say, and venture out into possibly dangerous and risky areas" (p. 7). In doing so, we explicitly suggest that providing challenge for performers is a core feature of skill-acquisition practice as well as their psychological development (cf. Moodie, Taylor, and Collins 2023).

Challenge Point at the Micro Level

Challenge point theory explicitly relates to the performer's experience of functional task difficulty (how hard a task is relative to the performer's capabilities), the information available to the performer (Guadagnoli and Lee 2004) and their psycho-emotional state and psychological skill (see chapter 8). That is, a performer is more likely to benefit from a challenging activity when they believe it to be within or just beyond their current capability, when they are well rested, and when they have confidence in the psychological skill to make adaptive sense of their circumstances.

In this sense, it seems accepted that desirable challenge sits in a Goldilocks zone, where too much or too little challenge is inappropriate for learning. Multiple frameworks have aimed to identify the optimal error rate, with suggestions ranging between 10% and 30% (e.g., Wilson et al. 2019). While these types of data might be a reasonable guide, work with individuals requires careful consideration of context and individual response. Returning to the heuristic for performer experience presented in chapter 1, Frank Shamrock, the former MMA fighter and coach, suggested that a fundamental feature of performer progression is exposure to different levels of competition: +1 (more capable), 0 (equal capability), and -1 (less capable) (Shamrock and Fleming 2012). In this sense, he suggests that exploratory interactions are less likely to occur when competing with someone of a higher level. However, it is important to highlight that the level of competition is not equivalent to the way the performer interacts with skill-acquisition activity or the level of experience in competition. Consequently, competing with a lower-level (-1) opponent *could* provide a higher challenge level if the performer's intention is more exploratory to develop less competent movement skills.

Lower-level opponents or activities can provide an invitation for action, one a coach might amplify, encouraging exploratory rather than exploitative interaction and increase the performer's experienced challenge. In this sense, we can probably infer that expansion and exploration is a costly activity (compare with earlier notions of expected free energy in chapter 1).

Types of Error

Building on the heuristic of an optimal error rate, in addition to the volume of errors, coaches must consider both the type of error and what constitutes an error in the first place. Edmondson (2023) suggested a typology of error; we have adapted this typology specifically for application to skill-acquisition (figure 6.3).

Depending on the interaction between the performer, coach, and activity, different types of error are desirable. As a general heuristic, an error resulting from a lack of preparation or effort is far less useful for skill-acquisition than errors resulting from high functional task difficulty or experimentation.

As a result, if performers are to benefit from challenging activities, they need to understand why they are doing what they are doing (Abraham and Collins 2011a). In this sense, desirable inter-

Figure 6.3 A spectrum of error types.

Adapted from Edmondson (2023).

CASE STUDY

MICRO-LEVEL CHALLENGE

A skateboarder aiming to land a new trick might set and exploit different levels of challenge in an exploratory session, exploring and pushing the boundaries to land a new trick (+1 challenge, low success) while also skating around and recovering through playful activity (-1 challenge, moderate success) (cf. Collins, Willmott, and Collins 2018). From a behavioral perspective, both activities could easily be framed as either expansion or exploration; what would define the difference in this case is the meaning making of errors. Desirable errors that occurred during a period of +1 challenge would be the result of experimentation. Less desirable errors could be the result of a lack of forethought or reduced focus owing to fatigue.

Now take the example of a wheelchair basketballer in a conditioned game, focused on transition offence. They are aiming to refine a recently introduced pattern of play (see chapter 11 for team coordination). Here, desirable errors would result from functional task difficulty, because activity design is increasingly variable, rather than experimentation. Similarly, in this context, it is worthwhile to pay attention to what actually constitutes an error, something of which elite performers seem to grow an increasingly refined sense (see chapter 7). For a high-performance player, an error could be the failure to catch the ball on her fingertips, away from the body, which hinders the speed of transition up court. This would be different for a community-level performer for whom an error might simply constitute dropping the ball.

action with activity is not necessarily externally observable by the coach. For impact, it is the performer who needs to experience the error and digest its meaning, not simply the coach acting as fault finder and corrector.

PERFORMANCE SAFETY

If we can establish that the level of challenge and how a performer interacts with activities are core features of skill-acquisition, we need to consider how the affective context might enable or hinder development. A prominent current concept in sport is the notion of psychological safety, initially developed in the organizational setting (Edmondson 1999). Psychological safety is defined by two core characteristics: first, people not being rejected for being themselves, asking for help, or saying what they think, and second, mistakes not leading to negative consequences, allowing individuals to feel safe to experiment (Edmondson 2018). In the organizational context, psychological safety has been strongly associated with enhanced learning and sharing of knowledge (Edmondson and Bransby 2023). Yet issues appear with the transferability of psychological safety into the performance sport domain (Taylor, Collins, and Ashford 2022). In addition, among several empirical studies, exploratory learning interactions appear to have been limited by low psychological safety and high selection pressure (Sweeney, Taylor, and MacNamara, in press; Taylor, Ashford, and Collins 2022). However, this reduced psychological safety also seemed to promote greater focus and attention to detail, in turn enhancing refinement.

In the majority of performance contexts, selection pressures occur, when people are judged based on their performance and their errors. This can be recognized at the same time as seeing tremendous value in seeing the need for performers to engage in exploratory activity and make errors. Some scholars have chosen to redefine psychological safety for use in sport (Vella et al. 2022) and others with more of a mental health emphasis (Walton et al. 2023).

We recognize the value of psychological safety as a concept with significant value in the organizational setting; however, rather than redefining it for use in sport, we instead suggest the notion of **performance safety**. This idea is distinct from the desirability of people voicing concerns and refers to the perceived consequence or judgment from error or poor performance. High performance safety is a temporally bound perception, built through careful contracting and role clarity (cf. chapter 10) that there will be no consequence for mistakes and may encourage expansive or exploratory behavior. For example, a soccer player who is making the transition to from left back to left-sided midfielder is advised that they will have a full preseason's worth of matches and that they are guaranteed selection for the first five weeks of a season before they will be judged based on their performance. In contrast, low performance safety refers to a high perceived consequence from error, akin to the desirable state induced by forms of pressure training, the aim of which is to help athletes experience anxiety and nervousness during training (Kegelaers and Oudejans 2022). As such, in the continuum of experience proposed earlier, "test" refers to the deliberate exposure of athletes to a level of pressure. This could take the form of scenario training in which errors might have perceived social consequences or, as is suggested in the pressure training literature, "consequences can take the form of judgment, such as evaluation by the performance director or a leaderboard that publicly displays each athlete's scores" (Low et al. 2023, p. 2). We do, however, stress the conditionality and care required when using these methods rather than through a barrage of perceived punishment or embarrassment.

CHALLENGE AT THE MESO LEVEL

The previous section considered how performer challenge might be experienced during specific activities at the micro level (session by session). Now we will consider meso-level challenges that act over a period of time, potentially disrupting a performer's broader development (Savage, Collins, and Cruickshank 2017). Meso-level challenge is more likely to elicit significant **emotional disturbance** (Taylor and Collins 2020). While negative emotional states are often seen as an impediment to learning and longer-term adaptation (Anyadike-Danes, Donath, and Kiely 2023), they can also offer significant benefit if appropriately exploited by the performer. This is because negative emotion in response to events often

High performance safety can mean there will be no consequence for mistakes, and it may encourage expansive or exploratory behavior by a player.

Hagen Hopkins/Getty Images for the New Zealand Paralympic Committee

leads to periods of detailed reflection and can act as a catalyst for change (e.g., Taylor and Collins 2021). Clearly, this also poses risks; prolonged and undirected rumination can have a significant impact on performance and well-being (McEwen 2019). Yet if properly harnessed, there is also the potential for significant long-term performance benefit. As a result, it appears that the performer and coach's ability to forecast (Williams and MacNamara 2023) and make sense of emotional states after challenge are critical for subsequent adaptation (Taylor and Collins 2021).

FIDELITY OF PRACTICE: HOW IS THE PERFORMER BEING CHALLENGED?

The final feature to consider is understanding *how* the performer is being challenged. A lengthy history of work points to specificity of practice as a principle of skill-acquisition (e.g., Henry and Smith 1961). Specificity is a notion derived from exercise physiology suggesting that "a major characteristic of motor learning seems to be its relative specificity to the feedback sources available when it occurred" (Proteau 1992, p. 90). Specificity in skill-acquisition suggests that what a performer learns depends on what they practice and the conditions of that practice (Schmidt and Lee 2019).

Perhaps the most important output from the specificity of practice principle was the prediction that performance of two different skills would have little overlap (e.g., swimming and running). A contemporary model developed by Hodges and Lohse (2022) offers a two-dimensional framework for practice design, drawing on the notion of challenge point and based on functional task difficulty. Here, functional task difficulty refers to the difficulty of a task, relative to the capability of the performer, a combination that, when coupled with high specificity, is suggested to be optimal for the transfer of learning.

A related but distinct concept emanating from ecological dynamics is the notion of representative design (as discussed in chapters 1, 4, 5, and 7). Representative design "emphasises the need to ensure that experimental task constraints represent the task constraints of the performance" (Pinder et al. 2011, p. 148). Further, representative learning design depends on coach activity design staying as close to the game as possible (Gray and Sullivan 2023). One acknowledged weakness of the way representative design has been used is to focus on the manipulation of task constraints and ignore the experience of the performer, something beginning to be addressed by the concept of affective learning design (Headrick et al. 2015). Similarly, some literature using an EcoD approach

CASE STUDY

INTENTIONS FOR IMPACT TO PERFORMER EXPERIENCE

During the off-season and early season, a high-performance basketball coach has invested significant time in their team scoring more 3-point shots. This aim is nested within a macro-level agenda of preparing players for tactical changes in game (see figure 6.4). These efforts have included the on- and off-court development of shared mental models to allow key players to get open more often against organized defense. A sub-focus would be subtle technical refinements to three players (see chapter 7). The coach now plans to use two weeks of training to test the embedding of these offensive tactics and build confidence in skill execution. For this specific session, the coach's intentions for impact are aimed toward testing this embedding under pressure. Using this intention, the coach takes an explicit success criteria into the session based on a high success rate (two out of three 3-point shots scored). Where identified, the coach plans to use errors to focus the attention of players on key elements of their process, either tactically or technically (see figure 6.5).

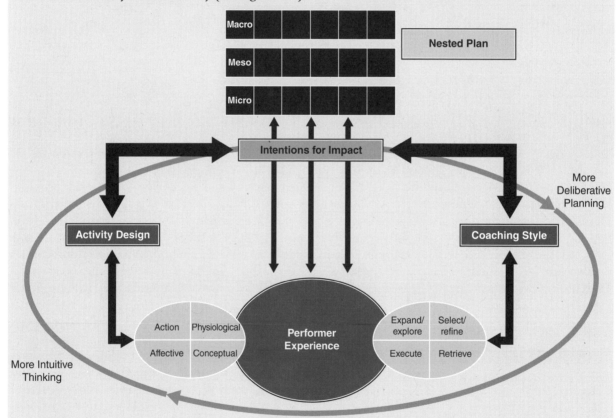

Figure 6.4 A fully developed thread of performer experience for coach decision making.

Adapted from Abraham et al. (2009); Till et al. (2019).

Performer Experience

Ideally, the coach is aiming for players to interact with the activity with an execute approach, where they should feel pressurized and a level of affective fidelity. Similarly, using a full-sided game, the players should experience high-action fidelity. Given the explicit awareness of the scenario, tactics to be used on both sides, and the stop-start nature of the activity, players will only experience moderate physical and conceptual fidelity. That is, the session will not replicate game demands physically or in the problems to be solved.

Chapter 6 Performer Experience 97

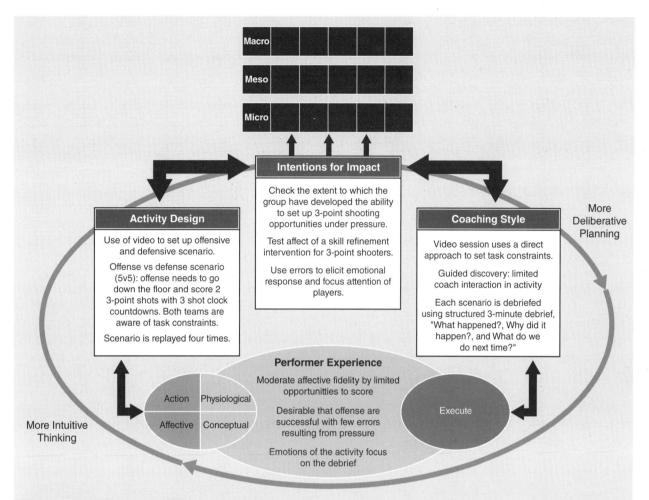

Figure 6.5 A case study example of deliberative planning

Adapted from Abraham et al. (2009); Till et al. (2019).

Activity Design and Coaching Style

To achieve these intentions, the coach plans for a video session prior to training that sets up the game scenario using examples from the highest level and positive demonstrations from previous training. On court, the coach plans to use a 5v5 scenario starting from a baseline pass and using a 30-second shot clock. The coach also plans for their off-court coaching style to be command style, using video to prime offensive movement with previous examples and direct the specific defensive tactics to be used. In session, the coach plans for a more guided discovery approach, limiting coaching interaction until a more formal debrief can be held on court, using the questions "What happened?," "Why did it happen?," and "What do we do next time?" at the end of each set of three plays.

By adopting an intentional stance, the coach makes "if-then" plans to support their more intuitive thinking in action, not "sticking to a plan." If performance is significantly lower than expected (two or three attempts scored), the coach plans to reduce pressure by removing a defender and playing 5v4. Similarly, the coach can move to a scaffold coaching style if players resort to an outcome focus in the debriefs.

has advocated for a conditional spectrum of representation of the learning environment (Renshaw et al. 2019).

Building on these useful concepts, we suggest a pragmatic framing to consider *how* the performer is being challenged. To do this, we draw on the notion of **fidelity** (see also chapter 7). Fidelity refers to the extent to which a real-world system is re-created, not only in terms of how it looks but also the affective states, cognitions, and behaviors of those engaging with it (Harris et al. 2020). That is, fidelity focuses attention on not only what activity design might look like (e.g., use of task constraints) but also how performers experience and interact with the activity in question. Thus, it is an excellent example of a concept that bridges different theoretical approaches. While it is typical to see reference to high- or low-fidelity activities, this is too simplistic a view to be useful for coaches, especially because the same activities might be experienced entirely differently by various performers (Hamstra et al. 2014). As a consequence, different types of fidelity can be applied in a pragmatic fashion to consider how performers are being challenged. Across different fields, these types of fidelity have been defined in different ways, most typically pertaining to the context of simulation or the manner in which simulations were used (e.g., Paige and Morin 2013).

Using table 6.3, we can consider the notion of whole and part practice outlined in the previous chapter and decide what parts of the whole are appropriate to challenge the performer in a particular activity. This in no way suggests any sort of mind-body dualism; instead, a pragmatic framing for the coach to consider is which dimensions of fidelity are most appropriate to emphasize in their activity design. We can then shape the constraints of activity design and adapt coaching style accordingly. For some, this might sound a little "back to the future," with equivalent ideas being discussed for a long time. For example, a 1967 English Football Association coaching manual suggested that "all coaching should begin with some form of realistic competitive situation," with lower levels of realism only being used when "working for a clear understanding of ideas" (Wade 1967, p. 186). We aim to extend these early ideas by suggesting a continuity of practice for coaching and skill-acquisition that goes beyond the pitch, court, track, dojo, or studio and encourages innovative use of simulation, performance analysis (Richards, Collins, and Mascarenhas 2017) and the increasing use of tools such as virtual reality (e.g., Gray 2019). By considering the types and relative fidelity of practice, we can consider how we are challenging performers and what this might mean for their ability to transfer skill-acquisition to performance.

Table 6.3   Types of Fidelity

Action fidelity	Skills acquired in practice and those acquired in the performance should be similar (adapted from Riccio 1995)
Physiological fidelity	The extent to which the physiological demands of the practice replicate those of competition
Affective fidelity	Similar emotional responses elicited by activity (e.g., stress or fear) as those in performance
Conceptual fidelity	The extent to which the perceptual-cognitive demands, or types of problems faced in performance, are represented

CHAPTER SUMMARY

Previous chapters have examined the principles of different theoretical ideas, where these might apply in practice, and their weaknesses. Chapters 5 and 6 have deliberately blended concepts from these theories, applying them where most contextually appropriate. This has not been to generate testable hypotheses but instead to offer a pragmatic framing for coaches to enhance skill-acquisition—in other words, a consideration of how theory translates into day-to-day coaching. We suggest that, by using performer experience as a focal point for skill-acquisition, while adding to the complexity and difficulty of measurement, it inevitably leads to the dissolution of binary methodological debates. The framework we have suggested builds on an extensive body of previous work (e.g., Abraham et al. 2009; Muir et al. 2011; Till et al. 2019), with a focus on helping the coach deliberately plan for performer experience, their coaching style, and activities, then to use this planning to adaptively and intuitively progress to overall intentions (Ashford et al. 2024). This focus on the performer experience allows for consideration of desirable practice at different points in development. In practice, we hope this allows for the adaptive use of existing heuristics, such as the golden rules of learning (Abraham and Collins 2011a) and the SAFE framework (Williams and Hodges 2023).

REVIEW AND PRACTICAL QUESTIONS

1. What is meant by the idea of intentions for impact?
2. Explain the differences in performer interaction with activities and when they might be desirable.
3. Why is challenge important in skill-acquisition?
4. What is the hidden curriculum?

KEY TERMS

challenge point theory

emotional disturbance

fidelity

intentions for impact

performance safety

CHAPTER 7

THE SPECIAL CASE OF HIGH-LEVEL AND EXPERIENCED PERFORMERS

Dave Collins

Chapter Objectives

After studying this chapter, you should be able to do the following:

- Critically reflect on what differences exist for high-level or experienced performers and how these differences can best be accounted for
- Understand the application and mechanisms of the five A model for skill refinement
- Understand the commonalities and key differences between shaping and switching for skill refinement
- Recognize the differential impacts of high- and low-fidelity environments on learning and performance
- Understand the use of emotional and psychological periodization as tools for balancing high-intensity training demands
- Understand the mechanisms through which higher-level performers can function better from alternative perspectives
- Critically reflect on the nature, targets, and methods of optimal skill support for high-level performers

The main focus of this book is on skill acquisition and execution for "normal" people. Given that this will reflect most performers and therefore will pique the interest of coaches and students, such a focus is both considered and appropriate. When it comes to high-level performers, however, things are different, sometimes subtly but often quite drastically. High-level performers are, almost by definition, not normal but special in a number of ways. As one of several examples considered in this chapter, their skills were usually both acquired and automated

101

long ago, suggesting that their technical training requirements are different. Defining someone as *high level* carries complexities—only slightly fewer than the even more contentious term *elite* (cf. McCauley et al. 2022). Both terms have often been used somewhat liberally, with studies describing everyone from medalists at world and Olympic levels to Division III collegiate athletes as elite or high level. Throughout this chapter, consider the level of competition (football involves more competition than Ultimate Frisbee), the number of people involved (there are more competitive runners than skeet shooters), and the complexities for the performer (F1 as opposed to karting)

Experienced performers (i.e., those with several years of sports involvement under their belt) may not be high level but will often display many of the same characteristics—or at least think that they do. Such assumptions, both grounded and groundless, also often affect coaches and support providers. Many of the same issues identified in the previous paragraph will also apply. As a simple consideration, however, think how committed the experienced performer is. Do training and performing play a significant role in their identity? If so, they are likely to display greater investment and interest.

Whatever the definitions used to distinguish high level and/or experienced athletes, such individuals show several variations from grassroots performers, younger children and people just starting in a sport. Accordingly, a critical consideration of differences is called for, especially since many methods also can be useful earlier in the performance pathway. Finally, since most skill developers are at least keeping an eye on those performers at the top of the tree and what their latest trends are, it is good to inform the view, albeit that as many myths are debunked as factual insights provided.

As a first step, it is important to acknowledge and make evident the level of assumption apparent around skill development. Several meta-analyses and reviews (e.g., Richardson et al. 2023) report the central role played by assumptions in coaches' interpretations of theory (e.g., how views on learning and pedagogical knowledge affect evaluation and application of ideas). It is important to acknowledge that, to be optimally effective, methods should be evidence based or at least evidence grounded. The second qualification

becomes particularly important with higher-level performers because generally, support providers will be seeking new and unproven methods in their search for the next edge. In a parallel characteristic, albeit with a different genesis, the experienced coaches and performers often base their beliefs on experience. Unfortunately, this is often ill considered or not revisited with the sort of critical consideration needed in this fast-developing and guru-rich area (see MacNamara and Collins 2015; chapter 3 in this book), and the simplified notions are often presented in early-stage coach education courses. In both cases, albeit for somewhat different reasons, a careful sieve must be applied to decision making on how to plan, what approaches to use, and how practice is designed and applied.

Even though much of the literature purports to address the full spectrum of performance, the differences apparent in high-level and experienced performers are often not considered. Complete change is not always necessary, but, reflecting individual subtleties that good coaches acknowledge and account for, similar tweaks are often of benefit. For example, prolific authors in this area developed a skill-acquisition framework for excellence (Hodges and Lohse 2022). In an otherwise excellent and comprehensive review, they did not consider the different objectives of practice (e.g., refinement versus acquisition, embedding versus learning, psychosocial versus psychomotor) that are more common in high-level environments. Of course, such omissions often are down to terminology and language (cf. Blasi et al. 2022). Nonetheless, we suggest through this chapter that high-level performers are sufficiently different and hold sufficiently different needs, such that a more direct consideration of their needs is appropriate. Many of the same concerns will apply to experienced performers so, for brevity, we will use the blanket term *high level*, unless clear distinctions between these categories are necessary.

PARTICULAR ASPECTS OF SKILL FOR ELITES

If the case for differences in high-level and experienced performers is accepted, how are these differences addressed? This first section considers the psychomotor factors that characterize these groups and how their special needs can be met.

Skill Refinement

Having made the case for different treatments, we start with a method that is applicable across the spectrum of performance levels, used to change well-embedded movements. Research has increasingly recognized both the importance of but also the key differences in skill refinement as opposed to acquisition. **Skill refinement** is best thought of as adjusting already developed skills and eliminating mistakes, something performers of all types will need at one time or another.

The major work in this area, the five A model (Carson and Collins 2011), is firmly rooted in the cognitive perspective. With its emphasis on the manipulation and exploitation of attention and the use of error, it also resonates with more recent work in predictive processing. The basic idea is to reestablish conscious access to movement, make changes, then reautomate and protect the new version. The stages are shown in table 7.1.

The first stage, analysis, is an important selling job, convincing all concerned that the change is worth the cost. Changing a skill can take a while, especially if all five steps are completed, ensuring that the skill is restabilized and pressure proofed. For example, in applied work, changing the take-off leg in an international long jumper took four months, while our work in judo with Andrew Cruickshank showed that it can take almost six months to go from analysis to pressure-proofing execution at world-class tournament level. In some cases, such as with a senior athlete nearing retirement, the analysis must include an even more careful cost-benefit consideration. In short, how long will it take against how much improvement will accrue?

Stage 2, awareness, should aim to de-automate the old, less desirable pattern of movement. In almost every case, the old movement will have been practiced through many repetitions and be well established. Accordingly, the performer will be less likely to be attending to what the movement feels like, having long ago moved to an external focus on the outcome. Even when awareness of the new movement *is* attained, the old style will almost always feel comfortable.

The adjustment stage makes use of a shaping or sudden approach, focusing on contrast between the old style and the new, or at least the best approximation of the new. The case studies in this chapter offer applied demonstration of the switching (a return to an earlier style; Collins, Morriss, and Trower 1999) or the shaping approach (a change to a completely new movement; Carson, Collins, and Jones 2014). In either case, contrasts are used to highlight the differences between the old (well established and comfortable) and the new (feels odd). This contrast is often best encouraged by augmented cues (cf. Case Study: Switching Back to an Earlier Version) or video feedback (cf. Case Study: Shaping a New Skill). In either case, however, the old is phased out and an increasing number of repetitions of the new target move is required. The fading out of the old skill often beneficially includes an occasional return, since now the old way feels odd. The bottom line is that the contrast between the old way and the new way (see also Hanin et al. 2013) serves to stress the focus that the performer must consciously adopt.

Stage 4, reautomation, is often neglected or shortchanged because both coach and athlete want to get on with it. This is, to say the least, unfortunate since failure to re-automate the skill can result in sudden, spontaneous, and uncontrolled switching between the two or a complete failure of the change process in which the old movement returns to dominance (Toner et al.

Table 7.1 The Five A Model of Skill Refinement

Stage	Description
Analysis	The reasons for and nature of change are carefully scoped, then sold to the performer. Understanding the change and the reasons for it provides motivation for what is usually a challenging process while also facilitating the mechanism of the change.
Awareness	The current technique is called into consciousness, and the changes aimed for are identified.
Adjustment	The technique is modified, usually (but not always) through a staged process.
Reautomation	The new movement is internalized so that it is no longer within conscious awareness.
Assurance	The performer (and often their coach) develop confidence that the change has been made, so avoiding any further tinkering.

2020). When used well in combination with the planning and goal setting established in stage 1, this is where the coach does their stuff to good effect. The athlete must be offered a variety of challenges throughout which they must maintain a strong and consistent execution of the new skill. This is covered in both case studies, but for the moment, consider the use of physical fatigue as an excellent way to parallel the pressures of competition. Known as *combination training* (combining physical fatigue with high pressure demands for skill execution), this approach is a useful tool in its own right as a means of testing the performer's ability to focus correctly—that is, on the right things at the right level of concentration and at the right time (see Collins, Doherty, and Talbot 1993; chapter 8 of this text).

Finally, the assurance stage cements the changes and helps prevent either the performer or coach attempting more tweaks. After analysis, this stage is also one that is often neglected. This stage relies on high-quality planning by the coach and support professionals, using a progression of increasingly challenging competitions and outcome measures (e.g., results) coupled with process feedback through video to build the performer's confidence in the changes made.

Embedding Skills

The idea of embedding skills through repetitious **drilling**-style training has been criticized by several authors, most strongly by those using an ecological perspective to underpin their practice. In contrast, Carson and Collins (2015, 2020) suggested that the strengthened technique, plus enhanced confidence in it for both the performer and their team, could serve as an effective biopsychosocial tool to counter performance anxieties. Given that the use of repetitious drilling is common practice across sports, cultures, and contexts, especially for high-level performers, we pursued the mechanisms as to why or why not this may be effective, applying the principles and methods espoused in this book (see chapter 3).

CASE STUDY

SWITCHING BACK TO AN EARLIER VERSION

Jon was a world-class field athlete who had suffered a comparative slump in the last few years. Biomechanical analysis had been a part of his support team for a number of years, and this enabled us to search for what had changed in his execution. This analysis, completed with his involvement, showed that his body position at the point of javelin release had changed, due perhaps to several injuries and surgical intervention. The change needed was a return to a more sideways position just prior to release.

The position was cued by his front nonthrowing hand. Jon seeing the back of his hand generated a more sideways, "shut-off" position—how his action had been a few years earlier. In contrast, Jon seeing his palm generated a more open, front-on stance, which was how he was throwing now. To make this more obvious, we used a bright two-color disc on his front hand, then started the awareness and adjustment stages using his front hand position as the cue. As he progressed, the old method cue was phased out with more repetitions of the target version. Occasional returns to the old version generated a stronger contrast, as Jon quickly grasped the target movement. Indeed, not only did he recognize and move quickly to this target shut-off version, his stance was even more sideways than it had been in the past. In short, it was even better than what we were all working toward.

Reautomation was completed by use of fatigue in association with throwing drills, with form carefully monitored to ensure compliance. Assurance was promoted by the use of biomechanical analysis, results in lower-level and then high-level events, and thorough debriefs with the athlete and coach. Finally, the new action was tested with 2D and 3D videoing throughout a season, culminating with the Olympic Games.

CASE STUDY

SHAPING A NEW SKILL

Briana was an Olympic weightlifter who had a fault in her snatch technique. She would receive the bar too far behind her head, necessitating a recovery forward. This was a consistent problem, but, in a major competition, Briana attempted a close to maximum weight, resulting in a valgus strain (functional abduction) of the right elbow joint. This movement is normally inhibited by the ulna collateral ligament. The athlete had been aware of this problem for some time; however, the combination of the weight attempted plus flawed technique resulted in a partial rupture of the ligament. As such, the analysis stage and buy-in from the performer were made easier. Without a significant change in technique, Briana would have to retire from the sport.

The awareness and adjustment stages were completed through a series of careful and progressive steps. Briana completed light lifts and training drills with an emphasis on the bar being received above her head. Especially at first, this felt extremely uncomfortable and often resulted in her losing the bar forward. Video of sessions was scanned to find the best version of the day, which was then used as the basis for Briana's mental rehearsal. As a result, what was an exception became the rule as her technique was shaped toward the new target version. The process was then repeated with a new, even closer approximation, and so on.

Reautomation was completed by executing a number of repetitions at a high percentage of one-repetition maximum, all with careful monitoring to maintain the new technique. Finally, assurance was promoted through a number of progressively challenging competitions, culminating with a performance at the Commonwealth Games. All five stages were needed to make the change to an acceptable and functional technique. Follow-up analysis three years later showed that the change had been maintained.

A Lower Need for Representative Design?

The strongest argument presented by opponents of drilling is the lack of fidelity through representative design—that is, low levels of perceptual-cognitive realism and hence the limitations of learning that might accrue. Yet, as presented in chapter 6, the principles of representative design, and practice fidelity more broadly, are well established, and there is little doubt that they play an important role in transfer to performance. Interestingly, however, a well-designed systematic test of the representative design methods by Krause and colleagues (2019) suggested that the impacts were nonlinear, particularly that different levels of representative accuracy affected different features of skill execution. As they summarized, "Coaches and/or practitioners can apply the findings from this study to improve the design of practice and/ or experimental tasks as it relates to their athletes' priorities, i.e., higher task representativeness is not always more effective nor is low representative practice always less effective" (p. 2567).

Such complexities notwithstanding (another case of *it depends*), significant support exists for using the embedding approach, especially as a learning tool. In a seminal paper, Dhami, Hertwig, and Hoffrage (2004) built on the earlier work of Brunswick (e.g., 1956) to emphasize how research on environmental decision making needed to consider a more accurate and complete representation of the environment—in short, performer-environment interrelationships. This has since been extended to stress the importance of what people see, or elements of conceptual fidelity have been prioritized ahead of other elements of practice. In short, "practice how you want to play" (a commonsense principle) has been extended to decry alternatives such as kicking or hitting a ball against a wall. Never mind that this approach represented (no pun intended) a common early method reported by many eventual elites, including Johan Cruyff and Roger Federer.

As defined by Pinder and colleagues (2011), for a practice task to be representative it should

- maintain the perception-action coupling apparent in the actual event,
- use many of the same informational variables from the actual event,
- reflect the same movement constraints, and
- generate similar emotions to those experienced in the actual event.

Importantly, we suggest that very few, if any, of these conditions are apparent in certain practice and preparatory behaviors of high-level performers. As examples, consider the common use of unopposed practices (especially as a feature of final preparation—the captain's run) or passing drills in team sports, the use of dry drilling in action sports and adventure activities such as freefall parachuting or technical diving (very common practice of emergency actions, hopefully not to be used), and the almost ubiquitous use of mental rehearsal. However, it is important to consider that some features mentioned by Pinder and colleagues are often created by the high-level performer in the visualized scenario.

Why might these differences be a feature of higher-level performers? Are there compelling underpinning reasons, or are they just ignorant of, or even ignoring, what is suggested? One reason may be the idea presented in the introduction of this book, that skill practice often serves a variety of purposes across the biopsychosocial spectrum, not just psychomotor development. In short, many of these higher-level performers may be using a type of enactive cognition as an important part of their training (see table I.1). Alternatively, from a cognitive or predictive processing perspective, performers are exploiting their strong internal models of skills, based on predictions of what will, or might, be needed. In essence, performers prepare by executing a kind of embodied mental rehearsal.

Returning to the example used earlier, the captain's run or walk-through will use an unopposed practice style to check for and strengthen shared mental models and collective efficacy, a social impact across the team so that they all know what they are going to do. Similarly, dry drilling ahead of a risky activity is psychologically reassuring because the performer reaffirms their capacity to handle any possible challenge. Finally, the use of imagery has been shown to serve a wide variety of purposes, with mental rehearsal before execu-

tion serving as an effective promoter of aspiration, self-efficacy, and feelings of preparedness (Simonsmeier et al. 2021).

Of course, many of these ideas apply to less-able performers. So why are they so applicable (and commonly observed) in high-level performers too? Part of the answer may be found in the literature on fidelity—in the present context, how genuinely representative a practice condition actually is. The point is that all high-level and many experienced performers have spent a great deal of time thinking about their sport and how things are executed. As a consequence, their internal models (the model they use to understand what is happening) will be well developed. If this model is appropriate, they will be able to rapidly build an accurate picture of consequences on what a particular move will feel like and where it will fit. As an example of this, imagine a soccer coach showing the team a set of movements on an Xs and Os board. The players can take in the information rapidly from this low-representation display, translate it into actions to be taken, and effectively recognize the situations portrayed, then react accordingly. As parallel examples, racing drivers can still benefit from use of low-fidelity driving games with little representative design (a long way from a high-quality simulator), even though the best testing will result from the high-tech, high-fidelity version.

In summary, high-level and many experienced performers make use of a variety of low-representative design options in their training. Transfer from these low-fidelity models being facilitated by their rich internal models which enable them to abstract knowledge and actions rapidly and accurately, leading to more accurate and effective practice and, finally, performance outcomes.

A Quick Sidestep Look at Fidelity

The level of fidelity also plays an important role when deciding on what is most applicable to the learning process (see also chapter 6). Alessi (1988) suggested that different levels are optimal for different abilities, with those who are less able benefiting from lower levels of fidelity. In contrast, Massoth and colleagues (2019) suggested that those who are less able can actually suffer from too high a level of fidelity when learning surgical skills on simulated patients. As with so much in this field (and this book), things are more complex and nuanced, as the review offered by Hancock and colleagues (2019) shows well. In short, different types and levels of fidelity can affect the quality of learning for different stages of expertise. More consideration of this aspect is offered in other chapters.

Emotional and Psychological Periodization

A final difference apparent in high-level performers is how they might use periodization as a tool for activity design, both the execution of and recovery from it. Given how much more serious practice is for those at this level (after all, it is generally their profession as well as a passionate love), training will often be more intense than for lower-level participants—or at least it should be. This intensity will be exacerbated when the performer is under selection pressures, the upcoming event is highly significant, or the training itself carries some risk (physical, psychological, or both). Freeskiing and motorsport are two examples of this latter category.

In all these cases, the use of emotional and psychological periodization is an important tool to control for the impacts of intensity in training, both real and perceived. Thus, in a similar fashion to the ideas of physical periodization and recovery (e.g., warm downs, also known as cooldowns), intense sessions are followed by relaxation to promote recovery and consolidation. Indeed, sleep learning (improved performance following a period of sleep) may play a big part in this process (Ruch, Valiadis, and Gharabaghi 2021). In the longer meso and macro terms (see also chapters 10 and 11), training is arranged to allow for variability in the challenge across sessions. As Collins, Willmott, and Collins (2018) reported for freeskiing and snowboarding, a pattern across days of push-drill-play enabled variation across intense days practicing new and dangerous moves, mixed practice of established tricks, and days on the hill to remind everyone what they enjoyed about the sport in the first place.

EXECUTION UNDER PRESSURE

Another big difference—and therefore area for consideration—relates to how high-level or experienced performers execute under pressure. Skills pertaining to this are covered thoroughly in other chapters, so in this next section, we will simply consider what differences might be apparent for high-level or experienced athletes. The big thing to remember here is that high-level performers usually will possess and be able to deploy a good level and range of mental skills (see chapter 8).

Days of push-drill-play enabled variation across intense days practicing new and dangerous moves, mixed practice of established tricks, and days on the hill remind a snowboarder what they enjoyed about the sport in the first place.

Hoptocopter/iStock/Getty Images

All will have individual patterns of strengths and weaknesses but certainly sufficient to function effectively under pressure. The same is true for experienced performers, although to a lesser extent. Importantly, however, they may well function more effectively merely because they have been there before. So what specific differences can be seen, and accounted for, in these groups?

Multi-Action Planning (MAP)

As will be mentioned in chapter 9, **multi-action planning (MAP)** offers a new perspective on emotional regulation under pressure. As that chapter specifies, MAP distinguishes four types of thinking, only two of which (types 1 and 2) are genuinely functional. The main advantages for high-level or experienced performers relate to the frequency of type 1 and type 2 thinking (Bertoli et al. 2012) and some key transitional differences that are emerging in our own research. The original model talks about switching, often uncontrolled, across four types of thinking. Importantly, however, work by Kellerman and colleagues (2024) has demonstrated a more selective and controlled pattern in high-level performers (in this case international medalists in judo) with switching less spontaneous and solely between types 1 and 2. For our present purpose, this is indicative of better and more focused self-regulatory skills.

Meshed Control Theory (Mesh)

This idea is covered in more detail in chapter 8. **Meshed control theory** (Christensen, Sutton, and McIlwain 2016) is a cognitively focused theoretical approach that offers a useful extension to the automaticity idea that previously dominated in descriptions of better performers. As such, it displays links to the cognitive and predictive processing approaches. The big advantage of the theory is how it accounts for the use of lower-level automatic control to free up higher brain functions for tactical decision making—in short, a control advantage. This reflects ideas introduced earlier by cognitive theorists, such as Schmidt and Wrisberg (2008), who suggested that automaticity "frees the best performers to engage in higher-order cognitive activities, such as split-second shifts in strategy during a basketball game or spontaneous adjustments in the form or style of a movement in dance or in figure skating" (p. 202).

Empirical work examining mesh has shown that less experienced performers can also be developed to cope with more complex decisions on the fly (see Christensen and Bicknell [2022] on mountain biking). For the present purpose, however, note that high-level performers experience a double-whammy advantage. First, skills are better automated (cf. ideas on embedding earlier) to a higher level. Second, relating to higher-order tactical thinking, there will be a much more insightful and detailed set of expectations, resulting in less of what predictive processing would refer to as *surprise*. As such, higher-level performers, especially if well primed and considered tactically, will exhibit faster, more accurate reactions and a greater capacity for thinking on the job. Once again, the benefits for experienced athletes follow these same lines but probably to a lesser extent, in terms of both speed-accuracy and in-event processing capacity.

OPTIMIZING SUPPORT FOR HIGH-LEVEL PERFORMERS

As this chapter has shown, several key differences between lower- and high-level performers are observed. Notably, these differences are somewhat nuanced, making it even more important that support is carefully considered. Chapter 4 already covered some of the challenges emerging from the growing interest in skill-acquisition—some positive, such as an increasing emphasis on professional development and qualification for coaches, and some less so, such as the growth of salesperson-style skill acquisition gurus who promote their goods with little or no emphasis on the essential analytic precursor—a case conceptualization of what is needed across the levels, types, goals, and timing of the individual performers. Without this complex evaluation, it is more likely that the skill prescription will draw from one approach rather than the blend, which this book has suggested to be necessary.

In response to this need for clarification of what high-level performers might need, this section covers some considerations of what expertise is needed, how it should operate, and some potential pitfalls that might be encountered and how to avoid them.

Specialist Skill Support for High-Level Performers: Is It Needed and in What Form?

First, we need to consider a bit of history. Skill acquisition used to be seen as a distinct discipline (see comments in chapter 4). Indeed, it formed the entirety of sport psychology. The only other stuff going on was in personality testing. More recently, skill acquisition and motor control has maintained (and even further evolved) a role as a separate domain, often allied with biomechanics, while sport and performance psychology has grown into one of the most dominant disciplines. In parallel, skill-acquisition support has become a favorite service for social media gurus. The problem is that, yet again, it does not give the practitioner the essential opportunity to evaluate where the performer is, what they need, and what approach may be best, which psychologists describe as a case conceptualization (cf. Martindale and Collins 2007). Only then can the support practitioner or coach truly apply the careful and critical processes of professional judgment and decision making (PJDM; cf. chapter 3), which underpins the *it depends* approach espoused in this book. For the present purpose, such an evaluation and bespoke design is likely to be even more important for high-level performers. Given these considerations, what might effective skill development support look like with higher-level athletes?

Operating Skill-Acquisition Support: How Should It Work?

As stated earlier, the process must be based on some form of evaluation, covering more than just asking "What do you want?" A data-informed breakdown of the performer's strengths and weaknesses is an important starting point to inform the coach's decision making. Additionally, however, some other, potentially subjective evaluation of the coach is also needed, especially since skill development will be a big part of their job description. Furthermore, as with so much in sport science and medicine support, work will often be more effective when provided with and through the coach. This will not always be the case, especially when confidentiality is an issue (see the next section), but certainly this should be the norm.

Another consideration is to build skill development into the nested and periodized plan the performer is following. As the five A model shows, changing skills is a long and complex job, especially if the outcomes are to be positive. It also relies heavily on getting the coach and performer on board, involved, and eventually driving the process (Kearney, Carson, and Collins 2018). These time challenges will make it important that skill development and refinement is scheduled appropriately, allowing sufficient time for the reautomation and assurance stages, which can sometimes be neglected. In the case of a high-level performer, new skills must be sorted and embedded well in advance of the major competition for that year, typically a world, an Olympic, or a Paralympic event.

Therefore, and as stressed elsewhere in this chapter and book, all concerned must buy into and commit to the process and outcome. Such processes are usually most effective with an individual focus at any level, but this is all the more important with a high-level performer so that the cost-benefit of skill change and development can be weigh against other factors involved.

Modus Operandi and Balancing Inputs: Staying in Your Lane Versus Team Support

How the skill support practitioner works is another important consideration, albeit one that shares a great deal with the integration of the other support team members. As highlighted by Alfano and Collins (2020, 2021; also Burns and Collins 2023), this is best done through an **interdisciplinary team (IDT)** support structure, where specialists can openly debate and evolve methods up front before presenting and enacting a united-front plan to the athlete. Clearly, several parallel support disciplines must be involved in decision making on the skill development agenda (primarily driven by the coach), some because space must be found by limiting other inputs (e.g., strength and conditioning) and some because of the wider challenges to the athlete's mental profile (e.g., the psychologist). Skill development is a key skill for performance psychology and is often best led in conjunction with the coach (cf. Carson and Collins 2016).

One important factor must be considered regarding the interaction between specialists.

Practitioners are commonly told to stay in their lanes—that is, make sure they attend to their part of the performance pie and leave other domain specialists to do the same for theirs. While possibilities for conflict are inherent, this is staggeringly counterproductive and actually prevents the style of interdisciplinary work that is increasingly seen as the best approach (Alfano and Collins 2020, 2021; Burns and Collins 2023). Since larger support teams are likely to be the norm with high-level performers, consideration of optimal practice while avoiding internecine strife is clearly of relevance in this chapter.

In simple terms, what is needed are working structures that avoid the potential challenges, both across practitioners and in sending multiple and contradictory messages to the athlete (cf. Taylor, Cruickshank, and Collins 2021), while also enabling the IDT and the performer to benefit from critical consideration and subsequent interaction on what are clearly complex and multifaceted challenges. Figure 7.1 offers a solution, in this case framed against another complex challenge: injury recovery.

This model, developed in conjunction with ace medic Bruce Hamilton and world-class physio Neil Black, was used to drive processes in the UK national athletics team. It does both jobs, avoiding different information getting to the athlete while also accounting for the essential interactions and involvement that ensure optimal use of the IDT. The rules are as follows:

- One specialist is the point of contact for the athlete and coach. Only they communicate with the coach-athlete pair, while everyone else can offer suggestions or ask questions of that lead individual but not the athlete or coach.

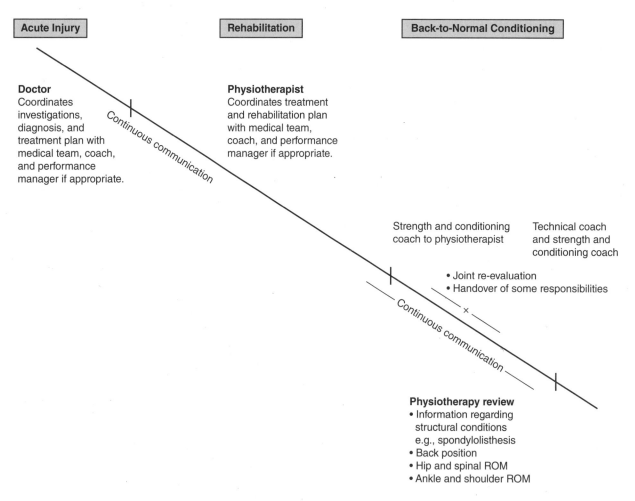

Figure 7.1 Interdisciplinary operation against role clarity in injury.

Chapter 7   The Special Case of High-Level and Experienced Performers   111

- The lead specialist changes as (in this case) the athlete recovers. After something like a 48-hour period, when the medic is focused on diagnosis and intervention design, the lead role passes to the physio. the same rules apply, except that now all communications go through the physio.
- Later, the lead role passes to the strength and conditioning coach (same rules apply) until control is passed back to the technical or sport coach.

- Discussion and debate are encouraged; gainsaying others or implied criticism are not.
- Notably, people are not staying in their lane, but all are involved in offering the best service.

Transferring this process into the IDT for a skill change may be desired. What is needed is to identify and clarify the lead role at any stage (cf. chapter 10), then develop a culture of sharing with appropriate confidentiality (cf. chapter 12).

CHAPTER SUMMARY

In this chapter we have covered several issues associated with skill development specific to high-level (and perhaps experienced) performers. Readers should note the differences involved in skill change and refinement as opposed to skill acquisition. Note that especially in the case of such high-level and committed performers, conscious involvement and understanding of the process are key.

We also talked about the need to pressure proof or embed skills and how this can be accomplished by using a blend of practices. Some will importantly require high levels of representative design, but some elements of low-representation drilling also will be needed. Indeed, these are also common parts of the diet for a high-level performer.

The chapter concluded with some considerations and recommendations for how specialist skill support may best be deployed with these cohorts. Note that many of the ideas presented may also apply lower down the pathway, depending on what support is available for the athletes. Youth academies, especially in professional sports, show similar concerns.

REVIEW AND PRACTICAL QUESTIONS

1. What are the differences in using shaping or switching in the five A model?
2. Name two factors suggested by Pinder and colleagues (2011) to increase the level of representative design in a practice.
3. Explain the ideas behind the push-drill-play approach to periodization in high-risk sports such as freeskiing and snowboarding.
4. Briefly explain the advantages that higher-level performers can display under the MAP and MESH approaches.
5. What concerns and advantages can accrue from an interdisciplinary team when supporting skill change (development or refinement)?

KEY TERMS

drilling
interdisciplinary
meshed control theory

multi-action planning (MAP)
skill refinement

PART III

Performing Movement

CHAPTER 8

MENTAL SKILLS

Rosie Collins

Chapter Objectives

After studying this chapter, you should be able to do the following:

- Understand the importance of case conceptualization in a mental skill intervention to ensure appropriate skills are deployed with appropriate timing against each performer's general and personal needs
- Explore the theoretical underpinnings of selected mental skills, with an understanding of how these could influence and enhance skill-acquisition, refinement, and execution
- Consider the complexity of both learning and performance environments and the need to maintain a flexible approach in the application and deployment of mental skills

Whether a sport psychologist, coach, or athlete, any individual involved in sport has likely experienced or witnessed the power of mental skills. They could be using imagery to unlock a new and complex movement, self-talk to manage some niggling doubts, or expertly deploy breathing techniques designed to achieve the optimal level of focus for skill execution. Unfortunately, however, the popularity of mental skills may well be their biggest weakness. Within this chapter, optimal deployment of these important interventions is discussed, whereby needs are identified through a coherent process and the mechanisms of mental skills are discussed to encourage increased understanding before deployment.

THE EVOLUTION OF MENTAL SKILLS FOR SPORT AND PHYSICAL ACTIVITY

With the professionalization of sport came the professionalization of sport sciences. In recent decades, sport psychology, originally seen as an offshoot from the grandfather discipline of pure psychology, has become a sought-after discipline as performers strive to reach and surpass their potential. Collins and Kamin (2012) proposed a three-stage evolution of the research within this domain (mentioned in other chapters but presented here in full). While applicable to many disciplines currently growing in the sporting arena, Collins and Kamin suggested that *psychology* research appears to have progressed as follows:

1. *Psychology* through *sport:* At this stage, research is focused on the development of the parent discipline by using investigations in a variety of environments. Sport could be one of these, but the main thrust would be to advance psychology—for example, understanding how pressure environments might affect an individual's anxiety response.

2. *Psychology* of *sport:* As a discipline progresses, it starts to develop a distinct body of knowledge, in this case, what we could properly call *sport psychology.* Specific theories pertaining to sport are developed and codified as a separate discipline. For this, consider some of the sport-specific anxiety theories (e.g., catastrophe theory; Hardy 1990).

3. *Psychology* for *sport:* At this stage, ideas, theories, and approaches are being used with sport as the primary focus. Psychology still plays an important role, but the focus is on the performance. In this case the parent discipline is subjugated to the target domain. Still considering anxiety in sport, some models (such as meshed control, explored in more detail later) have attempted to explain the process of skill execution under different performance conditions.

While some research might emerge from one or even two of these value-based positions, it is unlikely to satisfy all three. As a result, the field of sport psychology has been flooded with a great number of constructs (plus the various and sometime spurious suggested interventions to promote them) that are not always fit for purpose within performance sport. This, coupled with the knowledge that many sport psychology practitioners graduate from their foundation studies with a weak grasp of the motor control domain (and therefore a limited understanding of how to affect or promote effective skill-acquisition or execution; Winter and Collins 2015), certainly indicates a worrying expertise gap.

Take, for example, popular psychological constructs such as grit or resilience. Not only could these arguably hail from the psychology *through* sport research position (grit originating in an educational setting, for example; Duckworth et al. 2007); they also offer limited applied implications for how to promote better (more consistent, more proficient, or just downright better) skill execution. An argument for this would be that constructs such as grit or resilience are outcomes, constructs, or characteristics achieved at the end of a development journey. In contrast, however, when practitioners and coaches wish to support their performers, they would do well to consider equipping them with the appropriate skills required—in essence, offering a process to achieve the outcome (cf. Collins, MacNamara, and Cruickshank 2018).

In taking a process view, our understanding of mental skills (not just the what but the crucial how and when) has evolved greatly. This has occurred at a micro level, whereby the research underpinning a single mental skill has improved. Take goal setting, a stalwart of the mental skills approach. While establishing SMART (specific, measurable, attainable, realistic, and time-specific) goals was seen as a great leap forward in the 1980s (Doran 1981), this principle is now seen as oversimplified (Swann et al. 2022). In contrast, throughout this book we have encouraged practitioners to develop nested goals (see especially chapter 3) with their performers, creating a more coherent understanding across support systems of how each objective might best be achieved. However, this has also occurred at a macro level, promoting a more global understanding of the mental skills, or characteristics, performers might acquire and require across their career span and beyond. These skills are then deployable not only in psychosocial incidences but also, and most pertinently for us, in psychomotor ones.

The Psychological Characteristics of Developing Excellence (PCDEs; see figure 8.1; MacNamara, Button, and Collins 2010a, 2010b) are a set of 10 mental skills and characteristics that best embody the mental skills approach to performance support. Honed through extensive research, the PCDEs have been identified as the distinguishable skills possessed by expert performers in a number of performance domains.

The PCDEs offer a coherent framework for practitioners to consider when exploring the use of mental skills. At a singular level, the implementation of the mental skill can be effective in a number of skill-acquisition and execution contexts. However, it is important to consider the interlinked nature of mental skills as well.

Figure 8.1 The Psychological Characteristics of Developing Excellence (PCDEs).

1. Effective and controllable imagery
2. Focus and distraction control
3. Self-regulation
4. Quality practice
5. Realistic performance evaluations
6. Role clarity
7. Commitment
8. Seeking and using social support
9. Goal setting and self-reward
10. Planning and self-organization

Take, for example, self-regulation together with focus and distraction control. A performer's ability to focus on the task at hand, thereby ignoring distractions, would be heavily affected by how well they are able to self-regulate. Likewise, the self-regulation technique may well include a focus strategy. For the context of this chapter, the intention for impact (cf. chapter 5) when prescribing or using mental skills is the most pertinent to consider. What are we expecting to happen by deploying this PCDE or any other mental skill? It is at this stage that a coach's theoretical assumptions are important to consider. For practitioner looking to deploy mental skills with athletes or performers, understanding the theoretical lens through which they are approaching each performance problem will likely be a key driver in the decision-making process.

APPLICATION OF MENTAL SKILLS

When understanding which mental skills are effective in promoting skill-acquisition and execution, it is essential for practitioners to consider further elements such as how and when (and implicitly why and why not) each of the mental skills should be deployed. Applied sport psychology practitioners may wish to follow a number of frameworks (see Keegan [2016] for a useful applied summary). However, mental skills are not, and should not be, under the sole purview of the sport psychologist (Moodie, Taylor, and Collins 2023).

For coaches and skill-acquisition specialists, having a clear grasp of the process of applying mental skills can make a great and complementary contribution to their efforts. For example, a performer proficient at focus and distraction control would be able to enhance their skill-acquisition greatly. Or perhaps a performer with realistic performance evaluations (i.e., better able to understand their development areas) could home in on specific development areas instead of wasting precious training time making generic or cosmetic improvements. The same applies to an athlete with the ability to maximize their time on the grass, court, piste, or ice by supplementing those sessions with effective and controllable imagery. To do this effectively, coaches and practitioners would do well to consider performance as a multifaceted construct or, more simply put, through a biopsychosocial lens (cf. chapter 3). In some performance contexts, this occurs already due to the multi-, or even better, interdisciplinary support teams operating together. However, for those working more independently, it is imperative that they avoid viewing a performance concern or event at face value, instead delving a little deeper into the broader picture and context to identify what might actually be occurring.

In order to do this, as identified, a process of **case conceptualization** should be used. The process of effective case conceptualization is addressed in more detail elsewhere (see chapter 7). In relation to the present context, however, a couple of factors must be considered. When faced with a performance concern, we should be flexible in our thinking, creating a working hypothesis as to what the underlying causes may be. Being a *working* hypothesis, this case conceptualization should be updated when new information becomes available. By sufficiently completing and then refining this case conceptualization process on an ongoing basis, the most appropriate mental skills intervention can be deployed, as opposed to just relying on the first identified possible solution, also known as **satisficing** (Lipshitz and Strauss 1997). Additionally, should multiple performance concerns arise concurrently, case conceptualization would encourage prioritization of these concerns, ensuring the application of interventions are aligned and appropriately timed, avoiding a "kitchen sink" approach to support. This approach is particularly important for challenges of skill-acquisition or refinement, since, as shown by this book, the factors involved are rather complex.

Finally, and perhaps most pertinently for our purpose here, one *might* consider the theoretical position constraining the performer's practice. Not all mental skills align coherently with all theoretical approaches outlined within this text. As such, practitioners who align strongly with any one of these approaches should proceed with caution and careful thought (cf. chapter 3). In summary, when faced with the question of which mental skill to choose, when to use it, and how it is anticipated to work, the answer is, quite frankly, it depends.

EXEMPLAR MENTAL SKILLS

It is outside the scope of this chapter to offer a comprehensive overview of all mental skills (see Collins and Cruickshank 2022). Instead, here we will consider exemplar mental skills with a particular focus on the potential impact of each on the three theoretical approaches.

Effective and Controllable Imagery

One of the best-researched constructs within the field of sport psychology, and perhaps one of the first psychology *for* sport research topics, imagery is broadly defined as the "creation or re-creation of an experience, involving quasi-sensorial, quasi-perceptual and quasi-affective characteristics" (Morris, Spittle, and Watt 2005, p. 19). In essence, imagery, as it is most commonly deployed now, is a full sensory experience, used to produce internal images. The explicit purpose is to aid the learning, development, and performance of complex motor skills and not just applied to the replication of optimal skill templates.

Theoretical Explanations

Several potential theoretical explanations exist for the mechanism of imagery. For ease, these are briefly highlighted here:

1. *Psychoneuromuscular theory (Jacobsen 1931; Carpenter 1984):* This theory postulates that imagery facilitates the learning of motor skills due to the nature of the neuromuscular patterns activated during the imagery process. Theorists argue that by creating the image of a motor skill internally, the relevant muscles innervate similarly (yet reduced in magnitude) to that of physical practice.

2. *Symbolic learning theory (Sackett 1934):* Symbolic learning theorists would argue that imagery supports creation of a motor program, thereby promoting the acquisition of skills through strengthened movement patterns stored internally.

3. *Bio-informational theory (Lang 1977, 1979):* This theory suggests that an image (created through the process of imagery) functions through an organized set of propositions: (a) stimulus propositions, or the skill being imaged; (b) response propositions, or the imager's response to their created image; and (c) meaning propositions, or the significance of the event. These three propositions taken together create a prototype for action, thereby supporting physical practice with enhanced knowledge of the movement.

4. *Functional equivalence theory (Jeannerod 1994):* In a way, this aligns with the underpinning principles of the three prior theories, proposing that mental imagery is effective in skill-acquisition and execution because it promotes the same neural structures in the brain as when the actual movement is executed.

While these four models of imagery have come under scrutiny, there is certainly some consistency between them in that they all suggest that the brain acts as a mediator for motor skills, coding and storing the movement through both physical and mental practice. However, the view of imagery as a cognitive construct has been contested, even from a predictive processing perspective. Instead, some researchers have attempted to explain the function of imagery through an ecological lens. Because imagery is an action that can be completed without external stimulus, individuals have argued this would suggest that the process is decoupled from the environment and therefore seemingly fails to align with the ecological dynamics (EcoD) perspective. In contrast, Sims (2020) suggests that imagery is actually stimulus sensitive and therefore still coupled with the learner's environment, assuming that this learner is producing sensory factors they have experienced before. For example, Fitts's law, which states that movement time increases in proportion to the distance to and width of the target, has been shown to apply in either actual physical or mental simulation (i.e., imagery) environments (cf. Decety and Jeannerod 1995). Notably, this explanation does not extend to movements not yet executed, such as a particular dance sequence before initial execution. It does, however, fit imagery to the EcoD approach, with some seeing it as an internal constraint that can coact with external features to shape the performer's search for solutions.

Our consideration of these theories is also limited in that they only aim to explain imagery from the perspective of skill-acquisition and perhaps skills refinement. That is, these theories explain how imagery supports the learning of a skill but not how imagery might be useful to prepare performers for execution under pressure. To achieve this, more comprehensive models of imagery have been developed to assist performers, coaches, and practitioners in how best to use this important mental skill.

Imagery in Action: Imagery Models

Having explored why imagery is an effective tool for motor skill-acquisition and reflecting the biopsychosocial approach emphasized earlier, it is important to turn to broader imagery models to better understand how imagery can be used. The first attempt came from Paivio's (1985) functions of imagery, in which Paivio divided the functions of imagery to support performers' understanding of how they might use the tool effectively. As shown in table 8.1, with supporting examples, Paivio identified five functions of imagery.

Paivio's functions of imagery require a high degree of knowledge, both of the imagery process and the intention of the performer. As an alternative, Holmes and Collins (2001) developed the PETTLEP model, setting out a number of parameters that an athlete (and coach or support provider) should consider (see figure 8.2). Holmes and Collins suggested that while as many factors of the PETTLEP model should be considered to optimize the impact of imagery on skill-acquisition, different factors might be prioritized or deprioritized depending on the skill stage of the performer. For example, take a golfer looking to use imagery to enhance their short game. Early in this process, they might supplement physical practice

A fencer that performs well against training partners, but struggles to couple their action to novel opponent movements, could use imagery to support this performance.
Jordi Sales/Moment/Getty Images

Table 8.1 Functions of Imagery With Sport Examples

	Function	Explanation	Example
Motivational	Motivational specific (MS)	Visualize the attainment of specific goals to aid adherence to a training regime	A sprinter may have noticed a performance plateau, failing to improve their personal best in several months. In this event, the performer could use MS imagery to visualize improved overall performance, thereby continuing to push at training.
	Motivational general—mastery (MG-M)	Imaging performing well to maintain confidence	A fencer could have experienced a number of losses in a row. Using MG-M could promote generic confidence, helping avoid dwelling on the string of poor performances.
	Motivational general—arousal (MG-A)	Using imagery to either increase (psych up for a performance) or decrease (gain emotional regulation) arousal	A boxer might use imagery to obtain optimal arousal levels having completed their ring walk. This imagery might relate to skill execution as well more contextual factors such as their environment.
Cognitive	Cognitive specific (CS)	Visualize a specific movement pattern to enhance overall motor execution	A tennis player could use CS imagery to enhance the execution of a complex movement such as a tennis serve.
	Cognitive general (CG)	Use scenario-based imagery in order to rehearse set plays or routines	An American football running back could use CG imagery to mentally rehearse their role in various plays.

Based on Paivio (1985).

with imagery with particular consideration of the task, focusing on timing, stage of learning, and perspective. Practically, this would result in an imagery process focusing on the fragmented elements of the task and their temporal (timing) components (e.g., back swing, loft, strike, landing zone) viewed from an **external perspective** (third person). As the performer progresses, becoming more proficient at this skill, the imagery can become more complex, introducing other elements of the PETTLEP model. This is where the purpose of imagery shifts away from being purely a tool to enhance skill-acquisition and becomes more effective for skill execution. This would result in a more neuromuscular imagery process, often moving to a predominantly **internal visual perspective**, including physical movements, with a greater consideration of the appropriate emotional state or performance environment. Referring back to the golfer example, the performer could start to use imagery to prepare for changing weather conditions or performing with the emotional pressure of leading the field.

By and large, until recently, the most parsimonious explanation for the effectiveness of imagery came from the cognitive approach. Work such as that of Schack and Mechsner (2006) has argued that a skill's motor programs (see chapter 1 for an exploration of theories such as Schmidt's schema theory for a more comprehensive explanation of motor programs) are stored internally as mental representations. As such, imagery and other visualization tools have arguably been seen as a means to enhance the depth or strength of these mental representations, allowing them to be deployed in live sporting scenarios. Other work, such as Sims (2020) mentioned earlier, has attempted to explain the mechanism of imagery through an EcoD perspective, but it remains somewhat unclear how perception and action remain coupled. This coupling is seen as directly responsible for producing movement solutions (skill execution). On this basis, however, it seems inconsistent to argue that motor imagery aligns with this perspective. This notwithstanding, other researchers have attempted to explain imagery

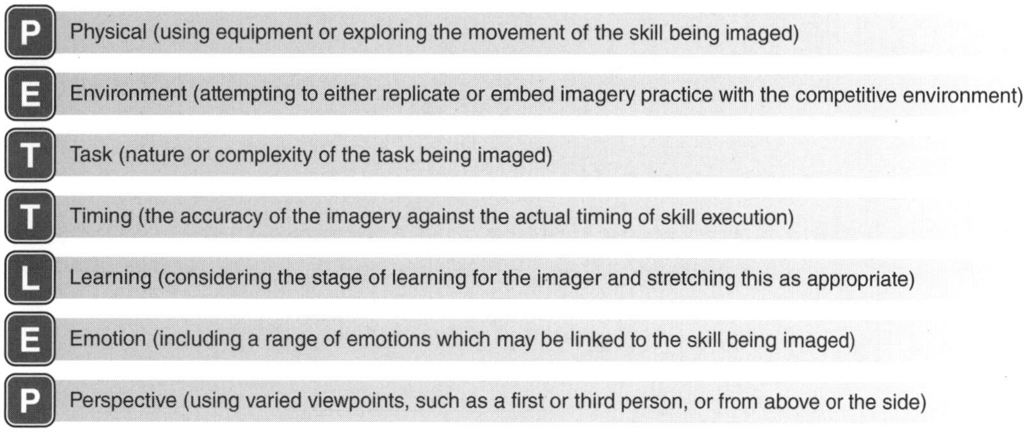

P
Physical (using equipment or exploring the movement of the skill being imaged)
E
Environment (attempting to either replicate or embed imagery practice with the competitive environment)
T
Task (nature or complexity of the task being imaged)
T
Timing (the accuracy of the imagery against the actual timing of skill execution)
L
Learning (considering the stage of learning for the imager and stretching this as appropriate)
E
Emotion (including a range of emotions which may be linked to the skill being imaged)
P
Perspective (using varied viewpoints, such as a first or third person, or from above or the side)

Figure 8.2 **The PETTLEP model, with brief practical explanations.**

Adapted from Holmes and Collins (2001).

through a predictive processing perspective. Indeed, Ridderinkhof and Brass (2015) argued that motor performance is most likely enhanced by imagery due to an overlap of brain activation in regions responsible for both anticipation and motor execution (e.g., the premotor cortex). This is not a quantum leap from explanations offered by original theories such as Jeannerod's functional equivalence theory.

Realistic Performance Evaluations and Critical Reflection

Realistic performance evaluations would be defined as the ability to accurately know what was good and not so good in a performance or training session, but also, more importantly (especially in the context of this book), having the willingness and support to do something about it. However, how these might affect a performer before, during, and following completion of their performance should be considered to best identify which strategies could be most effective.

Reflection on Action

Just like technical skills, reflection is a skill that needs to be developed. Traditionally, the process of reflection was seen as linear, demonstrated by models such as Kolb's reflective cycle (1984; figure 8.3) and Gibbs's cycle (1988; figure 8.4). These cycles encourage the learner to describe an

Concrete Experience
Produce a motor skill
Reflective Observation
Reflect and evaluate the skill execution
Abstract Conceptualization
Identify potential changes needed for skill execution
Active Experimentation
Carry out adjusted motor skill

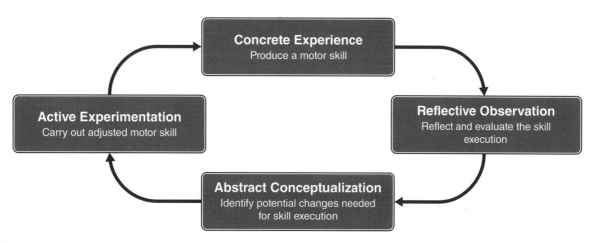

Figure 8.3 **An adaptation of Kolb's reflective cycle (1984).**

Adapted from Kolb (1984).

CASE STUDY

USING IMAGERY

Similar to the example of MG-M imagery in table 8.1, we will look at a case study from a deeply motorically complex sport: fencing. (*Note:* There are three different disciplines of modern fencing, but for the purposes of this case study, we will explore épée due to the increased complexity of counterattacks.) In this case study, Otto is a fencer looking to improve their overall performance, typically progressing well through an event before being knocked out by more experienced fencers, typified by their broader repertoire of skills. Following case conceptualization with Otto, it becomes clear that they have acquired a breadth of movement skills in training but struggle to perform these under pressure, particularly when needing to counterattack. As such, this would indicate a skill transfer and anticipation concern, in which the performer cannot accurately predict what their opponents might do next. That is, Otto is able to perform well against training partners but struggles to couple their action to the movements of novel opponents.

Imagery could be a great mental skill to support this performance concern, but several appropriate approaches could be taken. For example, through a functional equivalence explanation, imagery of the required moves would enhance their specific movement patterns (or internal representations). One argument for poor performance under pressure is that the required skills are not yet well enough learned; therefore this imagery approach would aim to make these skills more robust to performance under pressure. This imagery would complement, as opposed to supplement, any actual technical training.

Alternatively, imagery could be used to support Otto's ability to react to their opponent's move, effective most likely through a predictive processing model. Applying the PETTLEP approach here, Otto could engage in a comprehensive (and ideally immersive) imagery program, in which they re-create live fencing scenarios, exploring the possible strategic solutions that could be deployed.

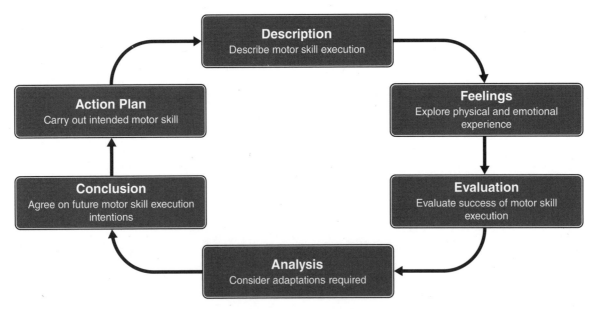

Figure 8.4 An adaptation of Gibbs' reflective cycle (1988).

Adapted from Gibbs (1988).

event, consider how they might have felt about the event, and finally encourage the learner to create an action or solidify the information learned as a result of this process.

While these cycles can be effective tools to maximize learning experiences, they are limited. Cycles of this nature promote reflection *on* action, in essence exploring an event afterward to maximize learning opportunities. This type of reflection would be useful for an athlete following an event that lacked self-regulation. Take, for example, a soccer player sent off following a dangerous foul. Using this linear process would encourage the player to review not only what happened (the difference in execution between a legal tackle and the dangerous movement they produced) but also why (particularly focusing on the intent behind their action and how this might have affected the execution of an otherwise well-learned skill) and how this might have affected them (exploring the emotional reaction to the event). Theoretically, it is most likely that reflection of this nature aligns most strongly with a representational perspective (cognitive or predictive processing), encouraging individuals to deliberately think back to stored information, or memory, to process the experience effectively (Stephens and Tjøstheim 2022). It might also have an impact through ideas such as **contextual priors** (Collins, Collins, and Carson 2022), whereby the performer might be primed to attend to certain elements of the technique or the outcome (cf. predictive processing as described in chapter 1). Finally, the wider construct of priors (what the performer arrives with; see earlier chapters, particular chapter 1) is also a consideration here. But what wider applications can be seen for reflection?

Reflection for Action

Reflection strategies have developed further, expanding beyond reflection *on* action to reflection *for* action (Schön 1983). Reflection for action expands the traditional reflection cycles, which typically focus on understanding the past and planning actions from this, because the main purpose is to process information to better execute and perform moving forward (i.e., priming for action in the future). Of course, this may still include typical methods whereby actions are reviewed. One great way to promote more realistic performance evaluations is encouraging athletes to debrief their performance using the following structure: the good, the bad, and the ugly. Take, for example, a golfer who struggles with realistic performance evaluations (i.e., after every poor performance, they come off the course claiming to have been deeply unlucky), thereby struggling to improve because they do not appropriately focus training on their development areas. By using this reflection for action strategy, the golfer is encouraged to identify three actions they delivered well (the good), two actions that were poor and would require a return to focus in training (the bad), and one silly error in which their execution was particularly poor, perhaps due to an extraneous variable (the ugly). This removes any unhelpful dwelling on factors outside of the performer's control, as well as promoting a more realistic evaluation of their overall performance. In this instance, the numbers suggested (3-2-1) offer a functional weighting to a performer who might be tempted to focus mostly on the negatives. This is not only immediately unpleasant but also restrictive to skilled performance through limiting working memory (Bruning et al. 2023).

From a skills perspective, this enhances the learning experience by encouraging the performer to consider their actual development areas as opposed to viewing all performance negatively and therefore thinking all aspects of performance need to be enhanced. Note that a process like this is not dissimilar to that of the big-five approach, described in the epilogue, which encourages coaches and practitioners to reflect on their decision making to enhance future actions.

However, as elements such as technology have progressed, the tools for reflection for action have greatly improved also. This has opened the possibility to use more analysis options as part of performance debriefs. This might take place during practice; for example, artistic pursuits such as diving can use live-video replay to assess the quality of skill-acquisition movements. In this case, the coach and athlete can review footage in between training blocks, exploring what the performance *felt* like, in comparison to what the movement *looked* like (encouraging an external visual-kinesthetic perspective to associated imagery practice). Alternatively, technology might be used to enhance the reflection for action process after practice. In this case, team sports could use video analysis to review games and training sessions, using the footage as prompts (Ashford, Abraham, and Poolton 2021). In particular, this type of reflection for action would begin to explore skills such as decision making and anticipation, surveying the information garnered by performers to execute the skills and actions chosen.

Theoretically speaking, several approaches could be drawn on to explain the mechanism of reflection for action. Because critical reflection in this way requires information pertaining to skill execution and decision making to be recalled, this indicates this information is being stored in some way, aligning with a cognitive perspective. However, an equally parsimonious explanation could come from a predictive processing perspective. As explained in chapter 1, predictive processing promotes the reduction of surprise via enhanced predictions. Therefore, reflection for action likely affects effective skill execution due to a priming mechanism.

Reflection in Action

Finally, performance evaluations and critical reflection have advanced to produce a much more nuanced process: reflection *in* action. Reflection in action refers to processes that support a performer to make sense of what they are experiencing and then update their knowledge, whether contextual, decision, or related to movement execution, *during* their performance. For example, take a center back in soccer who seems unable to block a cross into the box, because they are always expecting their opponent to take them on in a 1v1 dual. Reflection in action would enable the player to update their knowledge of their opponent's performance patterns and adjust their own strategies accordingly.

Sometimes reflection in action may appear as a more automatic process, whereby performers engage in a live trial-and-error approach to performance (again consider predictive error processes). This would require them to take several different approaches (using a basketball example, perhaps marking their opponent tighter to limit options, or encourage teammates to support them, double marking the opponent player as well) until they find a solution that creates the desired outcome. Ecologically, this likely would be described as a process of perceptual attunement (Gibson 1979), whereby the performer self-organizes based on

information constraints, resulting in various adjustments in skill execution until success is achieved. However, Araújo and colleagues (2019) suggested "there is no internal knowledge structure or central pattern generator inside the organism responsible for controlling action" (p. 10). As such, reflection in action of this nature likely would be better explained through a predictive processing perspective, whereby skill execution is updated through anticipatory coding (Pezzulo 2008) using prediction error information during performances. Alternatively, reflection in action could be explained by the cognitive perspective, considering the role of contextual priors. In this instance, the role of dynamic contextual priors must be considered. A dynamic contextual prior refers to information evolving within an event (e.g., personal performance or coach instruction; Levi and Jackson 2018). Take coach instruction during performance as an example; an athlete's skill execution could be influenced by not only the information they interpret on a court but also from feedback or guidance offered from the courtside.

Focus and Distraction Control

As sport psychology research progressed, understanding and identifying performers' optimal focus levels for performance received extensive research. Focus and distraction control relates to a performer's ability to know what is important, knowing how to stay focused on it, and knowing what to do to both avoid and counter distractions. This is essential for learning or amending a skill as well as executing under a number of performance conditions.

Optimal Focus Levels for Performance

As mentioned, when explaining the concept of psychology *of* sport, a number of sport-specific theories explaining the relationship between anxiety and performance have been proposed. Initially very basic in nature, drive theory (Hull 1943, cited in Weiner 1985) suggested that arousal and performance had a positive linear relationship, meaning that the more physiologically aroused a performer was, the better the performance. This failed to account for the drop-off in performance quite regularly experienced by performers when they experienced overarousal. Enter, the inverted-U theory. Yet still, the inverted-U suggested a positive linear increase followed by a negative linear increase after peak performance, still failing to explain the most instantaneous performance drop-off most often experienced. As such, catastrophe theory (Hardy 1990) was introduced to mitigate this. However, the most consistent criticism of these arousal theories is the lack of consideration for individual differences. Rectifying this, Hanin (2000) explored the individual zone of optimal functioning (IZOF), or, more simply, "the zone."

Interestingly, some popular constructs, such as Csikszentmihalyi's (1990) work on **flow**, could be taken as an indication that optimal performance is something that happens to a performer, not something that is achieved. Alternatively, work from Swann and colleagues (2016) exploring the difference between making-it-happen and letting-it-happen performances or from Bortoli and colleagues (2012) and Robazza and colleagues' (2016) work on multi-action planning (MAP) instead argue for a more mediated approach, requiring performers to curate their successes through carefully managed performances. (Chapter 7 offers a more comprehensive overview of this topic.) In relation to skill execution, the key point we can draw from these theories is that some form of regulation is likely required in order to perform optimally within complex and pressured performance conditions.

Creating the Optimal Performance Focus

While exploring the theories underpinning performance focus demonstrates the need for self-regulation and management of focus to achieve effective skill execution, there are conflicting ideologies surrounding *what* a performer might focus on and the mechanism of *how* this might operate. For example, consider the concept of quiet eye (QE). QE is defined as the final point of fixation within a performer's environment, lasting over 100 ms (Vickers 1996), and has historically been viewed as a key causative mechanism, and therefore expectant feature, of peak performance. As QE training increased in popularity, it was suggested that a quiet eye might also mean a quiet mind. Interestingly research originating from contrasting theoretical perspectives indicates that the location of gaze matters less for performance, seen in ecologically driven research with soccer goalkeepers (Franks, Roberts, and Jakeman 2019) and cognitively within golf putting (Collins et al. 2023). Instead, key determinants of performance are more likely the functionality of information

Achieving optimal levels of focus and distraction control is an essential process during skill execution.
Simonkr/E+/Getty Images

obtained during gaze fixation and the resultant cognitive processes, seen as a switch from external *attention* to an internal *intention* for skill execution (Collins et al. 2023).

Expanding this, if skill execution is affected less by where a performer is looking, or indeed what a performer is looking at, what this individual is cognitively *focusing* on appears the most important feature of performance. Research by Wulf and colleagues (2001) suggested that should a performer focus on internal aspects of motor execution, this skill would likely break down (cf. constrained action hypothesis). To avoid this, Wulf (2016) argued that performers should *always* focus on external stimuli. Importantly, both within a skill-refinement and skill-execution context, this hypothesis has been strongly challenged (Herrebrøden 2023), and the prescribed superiority of an external focus is not always the case (see also comments in chapter 4).

Within a skill-refinement context, for example, Carson and Collins (2011) have demonstrated that an internal focus on skills is paramount to maximize the learning of a newer version of the refined skill, using contrast drills (comparisons of feel) between the new and the old movement (see the five A model explored in chapter 7). However, even within skill-execution contexts, research indicates that sometimes an internal focus of attention is not only effective but also preferred. For example, an internal focus on the whole movement, as opposed to parts of a broken-down skill, can offer performance benefits, with an aim to holistically prime the movement for execution in future (Collins 2011). As such, practitioners might need to be prepared to consider the role of both internal and external foci when appropriate.

At this stage it is pertinent to consider cues as a mechanism for managing focus and distraction control. Benz and colleagues (2016) explored the role of coaching instruction and cues for enhancing sprint performance. Their review suggested that a selection of different instructional tools should be used to support learning, although they suggested that external or neutral (e.g., "heels to the ground" as opposed to "push through the floor") cues are superior. However, Winkelman, Clark, and Ryan (2017) later compared highly experienced sprinters with athletes who use sprinting as part of their sport (e.g., soccer players). These findings indicated no significant dif-

ferences in performance between external focus, internal focus, and control conditions, suggesting that as performers become more skilled, they are not affected by direction of attention. This indicates, as supported by Maurer and Munzert (2013), that an internal or external focus affected performance considerably less than the familiarity of the performance conditions. In essence, if a performer is familiar with an internal focus during motor skill execution, this focus will not have a detrimental effect on their performance, whereas an external focus would be negative because unfamiliarity would be the factor of difference, not the direction of attention. As another contrasting view, Schoenfeld (2016) explored the role of internal and external cues, concluding that an internal cue is far superior to maximize muscular development, meaning that the appropriate focus needs to be deployed based on the goal of the task. All these contrasting positions suggest that focus may be yet another factor that can be manipulated along a continuum, depending on the exact aims of the intervention. In this regard, it is also worth contrasting the use of technical cues with a more holistic **source of information**, which offers an effective reminder of the whole skill, often through the use of movement rhythm (e.g., MacPherson, Collins, and Obhi 2009).

Finally, and expanding on this concept of priming, we return to the construct offered earlier in this chapter relating to contextual priors. With many sports, but perhaps particularly in team events, static contextual priors about opposition may do well to direct a performer's attention during skill execution, thereby avoiding unhelpful or incongruent details that could derail performance. Indeed, this would link well with work explored in chapter 5, in which epistemic affordances are discussed. In this case, what a performer knows will directly affect what they see, observe, and interact with (i.e., a mechanism for directing attention).

MENTAL SKILLS IN ACTION: COMBINING MENTAL SKILLS FOR OPTIMAL IMPACT

So far in this chapter, we have considered the essential processes before intervention (e.g., case conceptualization) as well as explored a select few mental skills (or PCDEs). However, the reality of

CASE STUDY

PROMOTING FOCUS

Within motorsport, drivers are required to execute their skills to minute detail while traveling at high speeds. Distractions can be dangerous, with serious consequences. As such, achieving optimal levels of focus and distraction control is an essential process during skill execution.

Olive is a driver struggling to achieve the required lap times when out on track alone. This can occur in a number of settings, such as during a qualification flying lap or when leading a race. Following the case conceptualization, it becomes apparent that Olive's best lap times come when chasing another competitor on track. Notably, this is not based on the physical advantage gained from slip streaming. Instead, it appears that during Olive's best laps, they are able to execute performance akin to a letting-it-happen state, whereby they have a high level of intensity behind actions but have less to consider in terms what comes next in the circuit. Instead, when more isolated on track, Olive is trying to create a similar flow-like focus. As such, they are failing to be prepared for the upcoming corner combinations of the complex circuit, seeking a more automated performance, resulting in slower lap times.

How best to support Olive would likely depend on the coach's view of their performance context. Taking a purely ecological perspective, it would seem appropriate to maintain the direct coupling between the driver and their environment, encouraging them to instead manage physiological arousal levels during each lap. However, the use of cues could also affect Olive's performance. Segmenting the track and assigning cues relating to their performance intention (i.e., smooth through a chicane) could aid Olive in their anticipation or prediction of what to expect next, a helpful alternative to the traditional way to remember a circuit, which is the names of each corner.

Alternatively, a coach could work with Olive to better understand their performance states. While a flow-like letting-it-happen state may seem optimal, Olive might want to consider the mechanisms of achieving a performance state like this. Using the switch from external attention to internal intention could equip Olive to become more familiar with their performance states and therefore regulate through a performance (achieving the different levels of focus needed during qualification, battles for position, and maintaining consistent lap times to safely complete a race from the lead).

---

skill-acquisition, refinement, and execution is complex, meaning coaches and practitioners need to consider a nuanced approach for intervention. The **meshed control theory** (mentioned as an example of psychology *for* sport; Christensen et al. 2016) offers a useful explanation for this nuanced approach in action.

Christensen and colleagues posited that during the process of skill-acquisition, once a performer becomes proficient in a skill, performance is not fully automatic (i.e., requiring no cognitive contribution), nor does it remain completely conscious (i.e., requiring the same amount of cognitive control as novice execution). Instead, meshed control takes a hybrid view, whereby cognitive control reduces but is ever present. When we are engaging in familiar or unchallenging tasks, cognition

is freed up to consider more complex tasks. (For example, a tennis player who is most comfortable on grass courts will not need as much cognitive contribution to basic skill execution but instead can focus on higher-order tasks such as where to place the ball with their next return.) However, once the performer finds themselves in difficult or unfamiliar situations (perhaps playing on clay), focus would need to be drawn to previously automated skills. This approach fits well with the predictive processing–based notion of hierarchical action representations (Proietti, Pezzulo, and Tessari 2023).

Coaches and practitioners looking to support performers would do well to consider the theory of meshed control when exploring the use of mental skills. This view of scaled cognitive contribution infers that for the most effective impact, multiple mental skills might need to be combined. In essence, throughout a performer's experience of learning, adapting, and then executing motor skills, their needs remain individually complex but will also differ depending on contextual factors. Returning to our tennis player example, and using the mental skills explored within this chapter, each of the three mental skills explored would be relevant *throughout* the performer's journey. As such, practitioners should consider using a process of **combination training**, whereby performers are equipped with bespoke skills packages (Collins and Collins 2011). This would ensure that, regardless of the potential performance challenges they may face, they are prepared to deploy the appropriate mental skill best suited for success.

CHAPTER SUMMARY

The study of mental skills is a vast and complex area and one that is often overlooked in the process of skill-acquisition, refinement, and execution. As such, mental skills are an essential component for all practitioners, not just sport psychologists, to consider. However, to benefit from the performance impact of these constructs, coaches and practitioners must be prepared to engage in their complexity. In the first instance, a case conceptualization is essential in order to correctly diagnose a performance concern, thereby identifying the most appropriate *combination* of mental skill interventions for the performer's context. However, the responsible practitioner also should consider the mechanism responsible for each mental skill's effectiveness in order to align it with their intention for impact.

REVIEW AND PRACTICAL QUESTIONS

1. Outline the importance of effective case conceptualization before offering a mental skills intervention.
2. What are the features of the PETTLEP model, and how might a coach promote each one to enhance a performer's imagery experience?
3. Reflection *for* and *in* action can be promoted by several different tools. Explain two of them.
4. Meshed control theory is a hybrid model. What does this mean?

KEY TERMS

case conceptualization

combination training

contextual priors

external perspective

flow

internal visual perspective

meshed control theory

satisficing

source of information

CHAPTER 9

ATHLETE MANAGEMENT

Andrew Cruickshank

Chapter Objectives

After studying this chapter, you should be able to do the following:

- Outline similarities and differences between the four types of performance within the multi-action plan model
- Understand reasons why managing athletes before a performance episode or event is different from other coaching contexts
- Describe some of the primary intentions that drive effective coaching in the preperformance phase
- Describe important elements of coaching structure and design in the preperformance phase
- Explain how coaching styles might vary across different ages, stages, levels, or expectations in the preperformance phase
- Outline important considerations for coaching feedback in the preperformance phase

Having considered the role of an athlete's mental skills in chapter 8, this chapter focuses on the role played by coaches as they manage factors that contribute to an athlete's ability to perform—or execute—movement. More specifically, emphasis shifts from how an athlete's internal mental resources and skills shape movement outcomes to the **coaching intentions**, **coaching structure and design**, and **coaching style** that an athlete interacts with as they prepare to execute movements in a performance event or episode, as opposed to coaching intentions, structure, and style as an athlete expands, explores, selects, and refines their movement (Lovden, Garzon, and Lindenberger 2020). For further clarity, the specific moment when the

athlete intends to perform can be self-chosen and administered (e.g., undertaking a particular mountain climb on a set date) or scheduled and administered by others (e.g., an organized basketball competition). In addition, the lead-up to performing may last minutes or hours (e.g., as part of an "experience day" or "have a go" event), days (e.g., ahead of next weekend's game), or weeks to months (e.g., a preparation camp for a major event). Regardless of the precise scenario, however, managing athletes so that they can execute movements on the day reflects a parallel but distinct subspecialty of coaching. As such, this chapter aims to highlight some of the key principles and practices that characterize effective preperformance coaching.

129

Recognizing that the best place to start is often the end when it comes to our efforts to overcome, solve, or simply give our best shot to a particular challenge, establishing what intentions, structures, and styles are more appropriate for coaches to deploy in the lead-up to a performance event or episode therefore requires us to be clear on what successful movement execution *in the event or episode* involves. A plethora of factors—spanning the biological, psychological, and social—contribute to the effective execution of movement when it matters. To recognize this complexity, but enable a bottom-line focus, this chapter will use the extended **multi-action plan (MAP)** model (Kellermann et al. 2022) as a biopsychosocial backdrop before considering what effective athlete management requires when movement execution becomes an athlete's primary goal.

EXECUTING MOVEMENT DURING PERFORMANCE: A MAP PERSPECTIVE

Originating in the work of Bortoli and colleagues (2012), MAP is an applied, evidence-based model that can be used to explain and enhance the execution of movement during a performance event or episode. Referring to Kellerman and colleagues' (2022) review and extension, as summarized in table 9.1, MAP is made up of four distinct performance types (PT), with each type characterized by its own set of biological, psychological, and social markers. More specifically, type 1 and type 2 performances are housed in the optimal half of the model, with type 3 and type 4 performances housed in the suboptimal half. As a further split, type 1 and type 4 performances are characterized by the more automatic control of movement, whereas type 2 and type 3 performances are characterized by more conscious control and effortful movement. On this basis, MAP recognizes that optimal performance is not always more automatic (as per type 2) and suboptimal performance is not always more consciously controlled (as per type 4).

Drilling down further, type 1 performances are characterized by a confident execution and light monitoring of the task's core movement components, with physical and mental resources readily available to support a positive appraisal and approach to managing the dynamic aspects of performing (e.g., the distractions of an opponent or an unexpected event). In contrast, type 2 performances are characterized by a greater perception of threat. More specifically, this includes actual or perceived factors that pose a risk to movement execution and outcomes, such as the best players in an opposing team, the out-of-bounds area on a golf tee shot, a common point of error in an ice-skating routine, or a prob-

Table 9.1 Overview of MAP

Performance feature	PERFORMANCE TYPE			
	Type 1	Type 2	Type 3	Type 4
Movement quality	Optimal		Suboptimal	
Control of movement	More automatic	More conscious	More conscious	More automatic
Remaining mental resources	More available	Less available	Less available	More available
General nature of movement-related cognition	Monitoring of core movement components	Promotion; control of core movement components	Excessive control of core; non-core components	Withdrawal; detachment from movement components
Purpose of emotion and action strategies	Maintain PT	Maintain, upregulate PT	Upregulate PT	Upregulate PT
Immediate emotional profile	More pleasant; functional	Less pleasant; functional	Less pleasant; dysfunctional	More pleasant; dysfunctional
Parallel constructs with (a degree of) conceptual overlap	Flow	Clutch; making it happen	Choking	Lack of focus

Based on Kellermann et al. (2022).

lematic section of a wet motorsport track. Type 2 performances are also associated with less pleasant emotions, with mental resources recruited to exert tighter control of task-relevant components to help the athlete achieve their desired outcome in the face of these perceived threats. In the case of type 3 performances, a threat or internal focus also occurs; however, a differentiating factor is that these orientations are either less relevant, irrelevant, or excessive in relation to the task at hand, therefore contributing to suboptimal execution. In other words, mental resources are overallocated to aspects that do not support optimal movement. Finally, type 4 performances are characterized by a withdrawal from or disinterest in aspects that support optimal movement (e.g., feeling like the task has been completed, or giving up). As such, less effort is applied and more mental resources may be available; however, these resources are recruited suboptimally in terms of ultimate movement quality. Although not covered in detail here, it is important to note that MAP has also found differences in physiological markers across the four PTs (e.g., variations in skin conductance and temperature, heart rate, blood lactate, postural adjustments, and cortical activity; Kellermann et al. 2022).

Ultimately, Kellerman and colleagues' (2022) review and progression of MAP states that an athlete will benefit from five primary aspects:

1. Having well-established, core movement components
2. The ability to recognize which PT they are experiencing when performing
3. The ability to maintain or drive an **upregulation** in their PT through effective **action and emotion strategies** (i.e., to proactively move from type 4 and 3 to type 2 and 1)
4. The ability to counter and control any **downregulation** through effective action and emotion strategies (i.e., to proactively prevent a drop from type 1 and 2 to type 3 and 4)
5. Greater levels of perceived control and confidence in all of the above

Achieving such mastery is far from easy—and largely dependent on the extent to which the athlete can deliver or achieve each of these elements under conditions of elevated arousal. Indeed, this difference in arousal is one of the primary reasons why managing athletes toward executing movements on the day reflects a parallel but distinct subspecialty of coaching.

WHY MANAGING ATHLETES IN THE PREPERFORMANCE PHASE IS DIFFERENT AND DIFFICULT

Before considering some specific principles and practices that can help athletes achieve or return to type 1 or type 2 performances during a performance event or episode, it is important to spend more time unpacking why this area of coaching has and will continue to be a particular challenge. In other words, what exactly is different and difficult about the act of performing? Clearly, a wide range of factors come into play here. However, for brevity, this section will maintain a bottom-line perspective.

More specifically, and whether executing movements in a participation, pathway, or senior elite context, the act of performing is typically associated with efforts to take on and hopefully achieve a *meaningful* goal or, to be more exact, a goal that is *personally* meaningful, meaningful to *others*, or often a combination of both. Indeed, to reach the stage of performing movement, an athlete will have inevitably invested not only energy into the process but also emotion and, especially for those pursuing a movement goal over a sustained period, their identity (cf. Timler et al. 2019). In most cases, performing is also a social act in the sense that other people (e.g., peers, coaches, parents, selectors, spectators, media) will be invested in and influencers of the athlete's movement execution, whether that arrives through their involvement before, during, or after performance. In this sense, personal achievements are often collective achievements, and personal disappointments are often collective disappointments. Unfortunately, however, others will often try to take credit while avoiding blame. As such, movement success is often perceived or framed, whether consciously or not, as an "us success," while movement failure is often perceived or framed, whether consciously or not, as a "me failure."

These **attributions** notwithstanding, it is important to recognize that (1) aspiring to perform requires and elicits *emotional investment* and (2) performing therefore will lead to *emotional consequence*. In this respect, many aspects of a performance can be explained by an athlete's perception of challenge and consequence or, more specifically, the extent to which they see the events and experiences of performing as positive and surmountable versus negative and to be avoided (Jones et al. 2009).

It is also important to note that perceptions of consequence can be influenced by both pre- and postperformance thinking or, in the case of the latter, the athlete's attribution style (Rejeski and Brawley 1983). Indeed, how an athlete—and their coaching and support team—explain a performance after the event or episode can do much to shape what's expected to happen next time. In this vein, coaches need to be mindful of striking an appropriate balance between the personal and the collective in post-performance reviews. For example, and reflecting the points made earlier, efforts need to be made to ensure that success is not predominantly framed as a collective outcome (i.e., "*We* achieved what *we* set out to do") and failure predominantly framed as a personal outcome (i.e., "*You*, the athlete, didn't achieve what *you* set out to do").

From a mechanistic perspective, the link between perceptions of consequence and performance can be usefully viewed through the lens of **attentional control theory** (ACT; Eysenck et al. 2007). More specifically, this theory is based on the principle that anxiety is generated when a goal is perceived to be under threat. In the case of athletes performing movement, some typical goals include the desire to be competent, the desire to be looked on favorably by others, or the desire to be better than others; these can all be threatened on the day by both internal factors (e.g., thoughts and feelings) and external factors (e.g., the opposing team, weather, referees).

Consequently, the anxiety generated by these perceived threats diverts attentional resources away from the primary task (e.g., performing movement) to detecting the sources of threat as well as delaying disengagement from these potential threats once found (Eysenck et al. 2007). As such, ACT states that anxiety disrupts the balance between an individual's top-down, goal-directed attentional system (i.e., the system influenced by goals, knowledge, and expectation) and the bottom-up, stimulus-driven attentional system (i.e., the system influenced by behaviorally relevant sensory events), leading to a greater role of the latter. As a result, anxiety impairs the ability to stop attention from being redirected (i.e., inhibition) or to bring attention back to task-relevant stimuli if it has (i.e., shifting), ultimately affecting the processing efficiency of working memory and, by virtue, movement performance. In MAP terms, the implication is that the perception of threat increases levels of anxiety, which leads to working memory being filled with more threat-related or irrelevant stimuli, which leads to the deployment of compensatory strategies, often in the case of physical performance, involving extra effort being put into monitoring or controlling movement (Bortoli et al. 2012). More simply, unmanaged anxiety increases the chances of a type 1 or 2 performance becoming a type 3 or 4 performance. An illustration of attentional control theory and links with MAP is shown in figure 9.1.

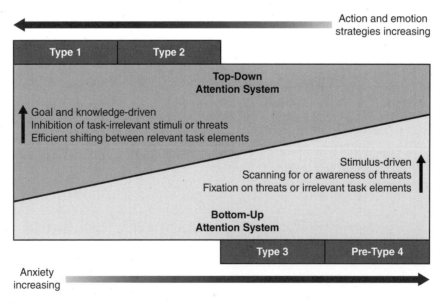

Figure 9.1 A depiction of attentional control theory and links to MAP.

Overall, it is the *consequences* of emotional investment that often prove to be one of the most significant factors for coaches to manage preceding (then during and after) a performance episode or event. Primarily, this is the athlete's excitement at potentially achieving—or the anxiety of potentially not achieving—their goal. The precise nature of these consequences and their interactions with motivation, confidence, and attention are, as with any aspect of human behavior, highly individualized. For example, emotional investment and consequences can lead some athletes to overprepare, seek perfection, and force things in an attempt to limit the chances of mistakes on the day or against a belief that more is always better, as is characteristic of type 3 performances (Kellerman et al. 2022). On the other hand, some athletes do the opposite, easing up on effort or quality in an attempt to conserve energy or save the "good ones" for the performance episode or event or by becoming overly energized and distracted by thoughts of a successful outcome and losing sight of the processes to achieve this, as is characteristic of type 4 performances (Kellerman et al. 2022). It is also common for some athletes to withdraw from certain aspects of preperformance preparation or to perceive more or greater physical, psychological, and social niggles ahead of performing as a self-protection strategy. In other words, and whether done consciously or not, this involves developing reasons for a potential underperformance up front (Török, Szabo, and Orosz 2022). Finally, greater levels of emotional investment and consequence can also lead some athletes to become overly concerned with the movement that others expect or want them to execute on the day. Or, again highlighting the lack of single solutions in coaching, some athletes may become overly closed to the views and feedback of others as they double down on suboptimal movements that they have invested much time and energy into previously.

In summary, the task of managing athletes in the lead-up to executing movement is tightly woven with their emotional investment in the performance, plus the emotional consequences of it going well or not so well. However, it is also important to recognize that this general circumstance can play out in lots of different ways across different athletes. It can also play out in lots of different ways for the same athlete given that, in most cases, each performance situation presents a unique mix of context, challenge, and reward. As such, athlete management heading into a performance clearly needs to work to some guiding principles while recognizing that these principles need to be tailored and blended in different ways at different times (Abraham and Collins 2011). Focus now moves to consider some guiding principles to factor into athlete management processes in the preperformance phase.

ATHLETE MANAGEMENT IN THE PREPERFORMANCE PHASE: KEY PRINCIPLES AND CONSIDERATIONS

Having outlined the nature of the challenge facing those responsible for managing athletes in the lead-up to performing, this section considers some key principles and considerations in three areas of coaching practice emphasized in previous chapters: coaching intentions, coaching structure and design, and coaching style. Returning to the framing outlined earlier, the lead-up to performing covers the phase when athletes are no longer prioritizing the expansion, exploration, selection, or refinement of their movement repertoire and instead preparing to execute this repertoire in an imminent event or episode (whether self-chosen or scheduled by others). As also noted earlier, this preparation phase may last for minutes or hours, days, weeks, or sometimes months (e.g., before the Olympic or Paralympic Games in some sports).

Coaching Intentions in the Preperformance Phase

As discussed in detail within chapter 5, coaching practice is best directed—and best evaluated—against a coach's intentions—in other words, the rationale behind their decision making and actions (Abraham and Collins 2011). With respect to managing athletes in the lead-up to performing, the opening sections in this chapter have outlined some important focuses for the coach from which to build their intentions. Fundamentally, the messages presented so far highlight the need for coaches to adopt a dual approach when preparing athletes to perform, namely the following:

1. Managing their perception of the performance challenge and consequences (to limit the levels of anxiety generated)

2. Maximizing their control of and confidence in their ability to sustain, return to, or work toward a type 1 or type 2 performance in the face of various execution-relevant and execution-irrelevant stimuli.

In other words, a key role of the coach is to manage perceptions of pressure and to optimize the extent to which athlete movements are **pressure proofed** (Carson and Collins 2016; Low et al. 2022) (see also chapter 7). Once again, the balance and blend of these two approaches will vary from athlete to athlete, sport to sport, and level to level.

For instance, with athletes at lower levels of objective performance (e.g., participation sport) or those executing movements that have yet to be sufficiently embedded (see chapter 7), the intention of the coach is generally weighted toward managing the perception of pressure or the actual pressure of suboptimal execution (i.e., the management of risk). In short, deescalating the actual or perceived consequences of things going wrong is an appropriate emphasis in this general situation. In terms of athletes executing movements at higher levels of objective performance (e.g., in elite sport) or movements that have been sufficiently embedded, the intention of the coach is instead generally weighted toward helping athletes feel in control of and confident in their core components and their action- and emotion-based strategies. To reiterate, however, these two agendas do not represent an either-or approach. Instead, coaches in any preperformance context need to work on both pressure perceptions and pressure proofing at the same time if optimal outcomes are to be achieved. By adopting this dual approach, the likelihood of athletes achieving type 1 performances will logically start to increase, as will the value an athlete places on type 2 performances and the ability to upregulate in general (i.e., their strategies lead to better execution and therefore better consequences). Similarly, and as detailed in chapter 8, these outcomes can also feed into more general **expectation effects**, all of which act as significant contributors to long-term commitment and progress (Thom, Cuay, and Trottier 2020).

The Structure and Design of Coaching in the Preperformance Phase

Moving from the coach's intentions to the ways in which these are delivered, the structure and design of coaching interactions once again plays a major role in whether desired movement outcomes are achieved. More specifically, attention here will be placed on the framing, content, and social dynamics of coaching sessions, followed by the volume and sequencing of coaching sessions. For those working in a participation context, emphasis is typically placed on the former (i.e., framing, content, and social dynamics), given the limited time that coaches typically have with athletes. In contrast, those working in a pathway and elite performance context are typically afforded greater time with athletes, therefore holding the potential to address a wider range of structure and design elements, such as the overall volume and sequencing of coaching sessions.

The Framing, Content, and Social Dynamics of Coaching in the Preperformance Phase

Regarding the *framing* of coaching sessions, and in line with the general intentions summarized earlier, it is important for coaches to ensure clarity on what a preperformance coaching session is targeting and what success will look like. As previously covered, the targets will sensibly include the embedding or pressure proofing of core movement components and strategies for reaching, maintaining, or transitioning between different PTs. In terms of clarity on what a successful session might look like, goal setting once again plays a key role in directing attention and effort, as well as providing an important reference point for in- and postsession evaluations. In this respect, and returning to earlier comments on the consequences of emotional investment, imminent performance often pulls athletes toward a state of forcing it or, alternatively, toward a state of avoidance or complacency (Kreiner-Phillips and Orlick 1993). Or, to use a simple framework, some athletes begin to expect or demand their practice to be permanently great, losing sight of the fact that much practice is either okay or good, while others may begin to expect or settle for practice that is okay, losing sight of the merits of pushing for good or great practice in the final preperformance phase. Ensuring that the goals and expectations of practice are clearly framed before the session therefore can do much to promote an appropriate focus and intensity. Returning to these goals and expectations after the session can then also be an effective means to close the loop and reinforce the athlete's control of and confidence in their abilities or to highlight gaps that need to be addressed or worked around.

Considering the *content* of sessions in the preperformance phase, this is informed by the framing of the session. If the session goal is to help athletes identify the difference between execution-relevant and execution-irrelevant stimuli, the coaching session needs to contain a mix of both. Similarly, if the session goal is to help athletes rehearse their strategies for maintaining or transitioning between different PTs, the session needs to include activities that require or promote the use of these strategies. For example, coaches in rugby union might deliver sessions that emphasize the use of huddles during breaks in play for the team to solve problems that have drawn them into a type 3 or type 4 state. Or golf coaches might deliver sessions that emphasize the use of postshot routines during a task that requires them to hit multiple shots within close proximity of a difficult target. As a simple but effective example from the same sport, Luke Donald, captain of the European team at the 2023 Ryder Cup, prepared his players to make a fast start in the event by having team members play three-hole matches (against each other) during practice rounds, a task that required players to play well and push hard from the start, given that these practice matches lasted a fraction of the potential 18-hole duration of a match in the event itself. Ultimately, if athletes are to have optimal control of and confidence in their core components and coping strategies on the day, these need to be explicitly practiced in advance. Or more precisely, they need to be practiced with purpose and intensity.

Digging into this idea of purpose and intensity, and again resonating with earlier points on emotional consequence, these two factors are largely driven by sessions that have personal meaning to the athlete. In addition to seeking to mirror the external conditions and stimuli of a performance event or episode, emphasis also needs to be placed on mirroring the internal conditions of the event or episode—in other words, making the session matter so that athletes prepare under a degree of biological, psychological, or social equivalence. As such, coaches would do well to ensure that personally meaningful challenge and conse-

Coaches in rugby union can use huddles during breaks to help teams solve problems and practice strategies for maintaining or transitioning between different PTs.
Patrick Khachfe/Getty Images

quence are built into preperformance sessions. For example, these might be generated by increasing the difficulty or novelty of the movement task by changing the internal state of the athlete (e.g., undertaking the task under fatigue [see combination training in chapter 8] or after recalling an over- or underperformance) or by changing the context in which the task takes place (e.g., having peers, other coaches, or spectators watch and review the athlete's execution).

In terms of the social dynamics of coaching sessions, one of the main considerations in this area is managing whom athletes practice with, alongside, or in the presence of others. Indeed, this book has stressed the significance of social factors throughout, and coaching in the preperformance phases is no different; in fact, social factors can often be magnified during the heightened state that many athletes find themselves in as they approach a performance challenge. As such, social factors can also be used to both dial up or dial down pressure depending on the needs and goals of the individual (Low et al. 2022). For example, designing sessions in a way that pairs or groups close competitors against each other or in view of each other can do much to elevate emotional intensity and reactivity due to the inherent effects of comparing oneself to others. Similarly, designing sessions in a way that pairs or groups athletes with mutually positive relationships can do much to downregulate emotional intensity and reactivity. If relevant, careful thought also needs to be given to who will be on the coaching team on the day. For example, it is common in elite sport for athletes to be managed and supported by coaches for an international event or game who are different from their club coaches. In these situations, work is thereby needed to ensure that the unfamiliar coach's actions or opinions are not viewed as a threat or an unmanageable threat on the day. For example, coaches may look to design sessions in a way that provides chances to optimize their shared understanding with the athlete and for the athlete to effectively execute movement in the coach's presence.

The Volume and Sequencing of Coaching in the Preperformance Phase

As suggested thus far, preperformance training is, in most sporting pursuits, more mentally demanding than physically demanding, with these mental demands linked to the emotional intensity and reactivity that performance generates. As such, another important feature of athlete management in the lead-up to performing, particularly for those who work with athletes on a regular basis, is **psychological load** (Mellalieu et al. 2021). Indeed, although type 1 states can be energizing, it is important to recognize that these tend to be less frequent and more transient than type 2 and type 3 states, which, because of the mental energy that is usually required to maintain or transition to the next level (i.e., type 3 to type 2; type 2 to type 1), are inherently more fatiguing (Kellerman et al. 2022). Supporting this view, much research has shown that **self-control** (akin to self-regulation in the PCDE list covered in chapter 8) is an energy-consuming process (Hagger et al. 2010), and preperformance practice, in many respects, provides a significant test of self-control. Research has also shown that as self-control resources become depleted, performance generally tends to drop too (Dorris, Power, and Kenefick 2012). As such, a key challenge for coaches is structuring preperformance sessions in a way that generates the required purpose and intensity to prime athletes for the conditions of performing while not depleting their reserves in a way that performance drops to the point where their perceived control of and confidence in their skills to cope take a damaging or irrecoverable hit. In this respect, the volume of mental demands both across and between sessions needs careful planning. Indeed, because self-control is a generic and limited resource, the more an individual draws from their self-control reserves between or before sessions, the less self-control they will have for the session itself. Recognizing and adjusting for the impact of extra-sporting demands, such as educational exams or challenges with personal relationships, therefore can be crucial for striking the best balance between pushing and pressuring an athlete's intended on-the-day movement and protecting and promoting their confidence. Once again, the importance of finding the best blend for the individual is reinforced.

Coaching Style in the Preperformance Phase

Having considered the general intention, structure, and design of coaching in the preexecution phase, attention now turns to the style in which this is delivered. In this regard, a key determinant in adopting a specific coaching style relates to the extent to which an athlete is focused on learning new ways to execute their movement on the day or maximizing confidence in their currently established ways to execute movement on the day. More specifically, this might include the degree to which they are learning or building belief in how they will monitor and manage their core components, plus their strategies for reaching, maintaining, or switching between different biopsychosocial states. With the performance event or episode imminent, most coaching in this phase will be heavily geared toward building the athlete's confidence in and positive expectations of their skills. In this vein, effective coaching is often reflected by a general "remind, reassure, and reinforce" style rather than one that seeks new or better ways to do things when there is insufficient time to fully embed and pressure proof. However, the appropriateness of this approach in specific situations depends, as one example, on the athlete's level of knowledge, skill, and confidence. For example, in cases where an athlete has lost confidence in their existing monitoring, action, and emotion strategies—or feels like these are in urgent need of refinement—switching to a more learning-supportive style to generate a new way of doing things is required. A learning-oriented style also will be more appropriate in other cases where athletes are less able to draw on preexisting knowledge, such as coaches working with younger, less experienced, or less skilled athletes (Mosston and Ashworth 2008).

From a learning perspective, and originating from the work of Mosston (1992) (see introduction), Pill and colleagues' (2021) spectrum of sports coaching details a range relationship and interaction styles that can be deployed by a coach to support athlete learning, spanning from entirely coach led to entirely athlete led. More specifically, and referring to Mosston and Ashworth's (2008) original labeling, the continuum is split into a series of substyles (from the coach-led end to the athlete-led end) known as the (A) command style, (B) practice style, (C) reciprocal style, (D) self-check style, (E) inclusion style, (F) guided discovery style, (G) convergent discovery style, (H) divergent discovery style, (I) learner-designed individual program style, (J) learner-initiated style, and (K) self-teaching style. Resonating with messages across this book, none of these styles is automatically right or wrong or better or worse. Instead, the effectiveness of a coaching style operates relative to the precise context, athlete, and goal in question—in other words, how appropriate the style is to the desired outcome.

Regarding context, one important factor here is time, or by when the coaching intentions or objectives need to be delivered or achieved. As alluded to throughout this chapter, time is a more obviously finite resource in the preexecution phase. In other words, the end point (i.e., the performance episode or event) is usually more concretely fixed, with the start point defined by the conclusion of the preceding expansion, exploration, selection, or refinement phases. In practical terms, and as noted earlier, the preexecution phase typically lasts between minutes and months (depending on the sport, goal, and level of athlete) rather than months to years. As such, the general theme here is that athletes and coaches are generally working on tighter timescales, meaning that the closer the performance event or episode is, the more emphasis is placed on *reproducing* preexisting knowledge and skills than on *producing* new knowledge and skills (Mosston and Ashworth 2008). According to Mosston and Ashworth, coaches working with younger, less experienced, or less skilled athletes will therefore adopt more of an A-to-E approach (i.e., harnessing the command, practice, reciprocal, self-check, or inclusion styles). In contrast, coaches working with older, more experienced, or more skilled athletes will have greater scope to operate at the learner-led end. For example, a young swimmer heading into their first intraclub meet in a week's time will likely benefit from a significantly different coaching style when it comes to learning an emotion-based strategy for use on the day as compared to an experienced professional basketball player who is trying to learn a refined emotion-based strategy for free throws in next week's game.

As a final example of the conditionality of style, take the critical aspect of risk—in other words, the consequences of the performance episode or event not going to plan. Indeed, although much of the work done by coaches in the preexecution phase intends to optimize the athlete's perceived control of and confidence in the execution of movement, a primary responsibility of any coach is to ensure that this is balanced against the management of likely threats to the well-being of the

For a judo player with a history of ankle injuries, the coach must consider physical, psychological, and social risks.

Bojanstory/E+/Getty Images

athlete. It's important to stress that this is not just physical well-being but psychological and social too. Certainly, risks in all three are often present at the same time. For example, take a judo player with a long history of ankle injuries who is planning to execute a recently refined *tachi waza* (standing) technique in their next event. In this case, consideration needs to be given by the coach to potential physical risks (e.g., reinjury if the technique is executed poorly) but also to potential psychological risks (e.g., the impact on confidence if the technique is not effective) and social risks (e.g., losing standing with peers if the technique fails and contributes to another first-round loss). In sum, the decision to work in a more coach-led or athlete-led manner needs to factor in the ability of both coach and athlete to recognize and mitigate against risk.

Coaching Feedback in the Preperformance Phase

As stressed throughout this book, external (or augmented) feedback plays a critical role in attainment of movement outcomes, including that provided by the coach. In this respect, coaching ahead of a performance event or episode is no different. However, rather than providing feedback to support the expansion, exploration, selection, or refinement of an athlete's movement, a coach's point of reference is once again the fundamental intentions of this phase—that is, to optimize the athlete's perceived control of and confidence in their core components and strategies for reaching, maintaining, or transitioning between different PTs. Additionally, what value or judgment is attached to the feedback is also important—in other words, whether the feedback is perceived in positive, neutral, or negative terms.

Generally speaking, practice in the preperformance phase typically benefits from feedback that is perceived to be more positive, acting to reassure or convince the athlete that they have the psychosocial skills to perform on the day. Indeed, because recognition and reward are significant sources of motivation, feedback can be one of the most effective tools that coaches have at their disposal (Mason, Farrow, and Hattie 2020). In the context of preparing athletes to perform, positive feedback on the effort put into their emotion and action strategies, as well as the outcomes they support, can do much to elevate the motivation to keep using these when it matters most. Such feedback can also do much to elevate an athlete's expectation that their strategies will work when it matters most (Kellermann et al. 2022). That said, there are also lots of instances when negatively perceived feedback can be beneficial to an athlete in the preperformance phase, particularly as a method to counter complacency. Once again, the best approach reflects a question of balance. For example, this might mean providing enough negatively perceived feedback to help keep an athlete on their toes but not so much that their overall control of and confidence in their ability to execute takes a significant hit. In contrast, the best approach in another context might involve providing enough positively perceived feedback to optimize control and confidence but not so much that the athlete loses sight of areas that they need to keep on top of or starts to question the coach's honesty over the level they can perform at (Taylor, Collins, and Cruickshank 2021). Similarly, the optimal frequency, timing, and duration of feedback is also heavily athlete dependent, with the coach required to provide a continually bespoke blend that is not too much yet not too little, not too quick yet not too delayed, and not too long yet not too short. Once again, the best frequency, timing, and duration of feedback in the preperformance phase is that which helps the athlete to feel in control of and confident in their core components and strategies for reaching, maintaining, or transitioning between different PTs.

It is also important to note that all feedback will operate relative to whatever baseline is established during expansion, exploration, selection, and refinement phases. Indeed, as increasing levels of anxiety can lead athletes to scan for threats to performance—then engage with these for longer if found—significant differences in feedback valence just before the day can go some way to generating a perception that something threatening is on the horizon. As such, consistency in messaging can do much to maintain goal-driven attention and offset some of the effects that anxiety can generate.

As well as considering *what* feedback is provided in the preperformance phase (see chapter 4), the role of feedback is also largely shaped by *who* provides it and *how* they provide it (cf. Taylor, Collins, and Cruickshank 2021). In terms of *who* provides the feedback, the preperformance context can often place even greater significance on the profile, power, and trust of the provider. Certainly, a positive combination of these factors can do much to reassure and reinforce an emotionally heightened athlete on their ability to meet the challenge of the imminent performance event or episode. Once again, exactly who can fulfill this role will vary across sports, athletes, and ages and stages. For example, younger athletes will typically benefit from the feedback of coaches and parents, whereas some older athletes might benefit most from the feedback of others such as peers or competitors. Indeed, sometimes the best approach a coach can take is to step away and encourage the feedback to come from other channels. The effects can also work the other way, with actual or perceived criticism from those possessing a sufficient degree of profile, power, and trust. For example, a key aspect of athlete management in the lead-up to performing is helping athletes recognize who to listen to or engage with but also who *not* to listen to or engage with. For example, many elite athletes intentionally remove themselves from social media in the lead-up to competitions for this purpose, partly to avoid any irrelevant noise but also to avoid comparison with competitors. Indeed, it is common for athletes in some sports to post videos of their training ahead of competition, typically presenting a positive image of their skills to build their own perceptions of control and confidence but to also distract or promote self-doubt in their opponents.

Regarding *how* feedback is provided, the tone and tempo of delivery are two other important components for coaches to consider (Taylor, Collins, and Cruickshank 2021). Indeed, both can do much to escalate or deescalate the intensity of a session, typically using quicker and louder delivery to escalate and slower and quieter delivery to deescalate. Once again, each situation will require a different blend based on the level of intensity and reactivity that the athlete brings to or experiences during the session. For example, quicker and louder feedback to an athlete in a high-arousal state may push their intensity over the edge, unless the athlete has the skills and confidence to operate with this. The extent to which feedback is presented in an open or closed manner will also influence an athlete's attention and emotion.

As a final consideration, it is important to recognize that coach feedback is invariably one of many sources of information that an athlete receives in the lead-up to a performance event or episode. Indeed, feedback can come from a host of individuals or groups, including other coaches, peers, parents, selectors, fans, or social and broadcast media. This feedback can be solicited and welcomed, but it can also be the opposite. As such, another element of athlete management before a performance event or episode involves helping individuals to improve or consolidate their feedback literacy skill, including their ability to distinguish relevant and useful inputs from irrelevant and unhelpful inputs. In this respect, and while often delivered with good intentions, feedback from others may operate in contrast to the coaching intentions listed earlier. For example, this might include working to elevate levels of perceived consequence and anxiety, draw attention to threats or irrelevant stimuli, place less value on type 2 performance, or generally lower expectations of successful execution.

CASE STUDY

PRINCIPLES OF PREPERFORMANCE COACHING IN ACTION

As an example of what the principles discussed in this chapter might look like and how they might be integrated when preparing an athlete to execute movement on the day, consider this hypothetical case of an early career but strong potential high jumper preparing to compete in their first Olympic Games in six weeks. In terms of their profile, the athlete has enjoyed competing in front of big crowds but tends to downplay their chances of performing at their best when competing in new major events for the first time; they believe that this requires everything before the day, then on the day, to run perfectly, which they feel never really happens to them. They have also underperformed on two occasions in the host city when they were a junior, the latter involving an unexpected early exit from a final after not being able to mentally recover from two failed attempts at a comfortable height during the initial phases. Since this time, however, they have committed a lot of effort to refining their emotion (e.g., breathing and self-talk) and action (e.g., rhythm-based cues and sources of information, imagery) strategies to help with their response to setbacks as well as optimizing performance from the start, which have worked to excellent effect in the last two seasons, because their form has continued to climb.

Against this backdrop, the coach sets an overall intention of helping the athlete strive for a *positive* day rather than a *perfect* day—in effect, managing the perception of both the challenge (i.e., to be positive rather than perfect) and consequences (i.e., "there is a chance I might not be happy with my result, but I can be happy with my performance if I am positive in all that I do). As the other side of their dual approach, the coach also intends to tap into the value that the athlete places on their preexisting emotion and action strategies as well as building expectations that these same strategies can facilitate an optimal performance at the Games. Driven by these intentions, the coach then structures the final training phase around positive performance sessions, sessions in which the content simulates competition and whereby success is framed, first and foremost, in terms of the athlete's positivity in their approach and responses, as supported by their emotion and action strategies. These goals are also explicitly shared with the athlete's training partners, who then play a role in recognizing and rewarding the athlete's commitment during the session (social dynamics). Importantly, the psychological load in the days before and after these sessions are lowered significantly to maximize mental reserves for the session. In the training environment, an image of the host city is placed on the wall behind the landing area, with local music also played during the athlete's warm-up. As part of a collaborative coaching style, the coach also asks the athlete to set positive heights to start and finish their session—in other words, not a more comfortable or easier option. The feedback process is also initiated by the athlete, who reviews the session against a self-developed list of positive performance behaviors, with the coach using these opportunities to reinforce the athlete's ability to deliver these in competition while returning regularly to the message that the performance goal is to be positive, not perfect.

CHAPTER SUMMARY

As highlighted throughout this chapter, coaches can play a significant role when it comes to managing athletes toward the successful execution of movement on the day. To do so effectively, coaches require a strong understanding of the various biopsychosocial states and strategies that underpin optimal performance, with this understanding then being used to drive the intentions, structure, design, and style of their work. From an intentions perspective, coaches are encouraged to help athletes to (1) manage their levels of arousal and anxiety by supporting their perceptions of challenge and consequence and (2) maximize their control of and confidence in their ability to sustain, return to, or work toward a type 1 or type 2 performance (Kellermann et al. 2022). In terms of the structure and design of coaching, this chapter has also presented some ways in which the volume, framing, content, and social dynamics of coaching can all be managed to support the aforementioned coaching intentions. Finally, the role and nature of feedback was also considered, spanning the what, who, and how of effective delivery in the lead-up to a performance event or episode. Ultimately, this chapter has highlighted some general principles and practices for effective preperformance coaching while emphasizing that the best approach for a specific athlete or group requires these principles to be balanced and blended in the best way at the best time.

REVIEW AND PRACTICAL QUESTIONS

1. How do the four performance types detailed in the multi-action plan (MAP) model vary in relation to the quality of movement, levels of conscious control, available mental resources, immediate emotional profile, and the purpose of emotion and action strategies?
2. Why is athlete management in the immediate lead-up to a performance episode or event different from coaching in other contexts?
3. What are the two fundamental coaching intentions in the preperformance phase?
4. Why are time and an athlete's preexisting skills important factors in relation to deciding on a coaching style in the preperformance phase?
5. What are some important factors with regards to *who* provides feedback to athletes in the preperformance phase?

KEY TERMS

action and emotion strategies

attentional control theory (ACT)

attribution

coaching intention

coaching structure and design

coaching style

downregulation

expectation effects

multi-action plan (MAP)

pressure proofed

psychological load

self-control

upregulation

CHAPTER 10

PLANNING AND LEADERSHIP SYSTEMS

Michael Ashford and Dave Collins

Chapter Objectives

After studying this chapter, you should be able to do the following:

- Critically reflect on what might be causative or correlational in improving the quality of skill acquisition, especially when framed against the coach–athlete relationship
- Understand the importance of planning and nested planning
- Explain the uses of multilingual leadership and how ideal styles may change with context
- Recognize the importance of role clarity and how this can be effectively established and embedded
- Understand the importance of shared mental models and perceived equity and how these can be most effectively developed

Readers who started this book with a focus on skill acquisition, as either a consumer (e.g., coach) or early practitioner (e.g., student), may have become increasingly bemused as to why the text would examine so many other, apparently parallel, constructs such as mental skills, planning, leadership, or teamwork. The bottom line is that, anecdotally, these structural constructs can strongly influence a performer's learning, gaining confidence in and executing the key skills discussed earlier in the text. In short, a performer does not just learn skills; they need to execute the right ones at the right time and in the right way, under pressure. That takes planning and well-designed structures and systems. This explains the broader treatment we offer.

Reflecting many of the conditional or contextual knowledge points made in earlier chapters, there is a parallel need to see how well non-sport research in this area actually applies to the performance environments we are discussing. For example, compelling evidence shows that interpersonal factors such as the big five trait characteristics (i.e., openness, neuroticism, conscientiousness, extraversion, and agreeableness) play a huge part in the type and style of leadership a person adopts or adapts (cf. Fiske 1949). Importantly, however, these are not of equal weighting, nor is there complete agreement on which factors predominate. For instance, agreeableness has recently been seen as more influential in leader impact than other personality characteristics such as extraversion

143

(Hunter et al. 2012). For other researchers (e.g., Judge et al. 2002), extraversion is king. Perhaps the picture has changed with time.

In any case, the growing importance of agreeableness supports the idea of servant leaders, whereby employees who are not necessarily in positions of leadership are able to lead, inspire, and generate servant followers, an emerging and influential idea in the mainstream leadership literature. It is paralleled by the work of Jowett and colleagues (e.g., Jowett and Pocwardowski 2007), which stresses the importance of servant leadership. As we will examine in this chapter, it is also important to understand the following factors:

- Context (e.g., for ambitious high-level performers something that is arguably a much more personal and ego-driven agenda than normal life)

- Directionality (e.g., "Do I think the servant leaders are useful?" Is this usefulness sufficient for both to feel a relationship, vice versa, or a bit of both)

- Causality (e.g., "Why might I feel this coach is useful for me"; i.e., interpretation of their motive)

Each of these factors is a fundamental social psychological issue, but an in-depth discussion is outside the scope of this book. We leave the interested reader to search through specifically focused investigations that might shed more light on issues such as directionality. In simple terms, a performer might ask, "Do I have a good relationship because *my* coach helps *me*, or is this working the other way around?" In short, "Do I like them because they help me or are they helpful because I like them?" (e.g., López de Subijana et al. 2021). For our present purpose, and reflecting the ideas we have espoused throughout this book, we will focus on the mechanisms rather than the overall effect (see chapter 2). Consequently, our focus in this chapter will be constructs that might more directly affect skill acquisition and execution.

NESTED PLANNING FOR KEY OUTCOMES: TYPE 2 AND TYPE 1

In performance sport, the desired end in mind may be driven by the internal expectations of those in the upper echelons of an organization, such as a soccer club's short-term desire to qualify for the Champions League. It also can be driven by external expectations, such as the lottery funding structures provided to Olympic programs (e.g., by the Australian Institute of Sport and Sporting Commission), which are often dependent on medals over a four-year cycle. Either way, the end in mind is almost certainly driven by a combination of internal and external expectations that, at least, should flow through the layers of the system and influence the thinking and behavior of all involved (Collins and MacNamara 2022). Consequently, the importance of forward and backward thinking through careful **nested planning** (introduced in chapters 5 and 6) is an essential component in how effective systems, sporting organizations, and teams function (cf. Abraham and Collins 2011).

Abraham and Collins (2011) considered the application of dual systems theory of decision making (e.g., Sloman 1996) to the sport coaching domain. This idea suggests that coaches organize decision making broadly within two frameworks. The first is type 1 decisions, which are largely intuitive, responsive, and rapid (e.g., Collins, Collins, and Carson 2016), working forward to a desired outcome. This is also known as naturalistic decision making (NDM). The second is type 2 decisions—classical decision making (CDM)—which are much more thoughtful, deliberative, and slow (e.g., Ashford et al. 2023), allowing for time and consideration of backward thinking. Some have suggested that the act of supporting a performer's acquisition of skill is an entirely intuitive endeavor, whereby coaches support performers' in-the-moment needs through the application of type 1 decisions (e.g., applying the coaching methods put forward in chapters 5 and 6; Harvey et al. 2015; Lyle 2010). Others (ourselves included) would see this as a balance between the two styles, with type 1 and type 2 (NDM and CDM) used at appropriate times and in an appropriate balance. In this regard, planning, which is an example of type 2 decision making, has also long been recognized as central to the coaching process (Jones, Housner, and Kornspan 1995) and framed as the "link between aspirations, intentions and activity" (Lyle 2002, p. 125).

Two other issues are noted here. First, several other theories refer to "types" of thinking—for example, our focus on multi-action planning (MAP) in chapter 7. Do not get confused about these types. The second issue is that more recent work on NDM has extended it to include deliberative thinking, a process termed *sensemaking*. Indeed, research into more intuitive (type 1) decision making suggests that almost all such decisions can be reviewed after the fact as a check for appropriateness (e.g., Collins, Collins, and Carson 2016). The key here is that types 1 and 2 decisions are not distinct from one another but rather are interlinked and complimentary (Klein 2007).

An age-old cliché says that "no plan survives first contact," and evidence from the coaching domain would be consistent with this idea (cf. Ashford et al. 2022). Despite some lay thinking in coaching practice, this does not mean that planning is useless. Planning offers an essential reference point to help coaches make sense of observations of performer movement needs (Collins, Carson, and Collins 2016). Experience suggests that planning only enables more intuitive thinking when clear intentions for impact (Martindale and Collins 2005) have been carefully considered

at all levels from the big picture to the here and now (Ashford and Taylor 2022). The case study Nested Planning for Long-Term Success offers an example of nested plan function at multiple levels and time points, where a coach engages in forward and backward thinking.

Another way in which these planning principles can operate is through the curriculum design and application, which offer a structure for development across a group or cohort (cf. Moran, Craig, and Collins 2024). More specifically, recent work has suggested that experts are especially proficient at applying curriculum knowledge, which is an understanding of the desired experience for individual performers (cf. Taylor, Ashford, and Jefferson 2023). Importantly, successful application of curriculum knowledge depends on mental projection forward to and backward from desired intentions, something that depends on a conceptualization of a performer's current status. This process can be nicely captured by asking some simple questions.

CASE STUDY

NESTED PLANNING FOR LONG-TERM SUCCESS

Nested planning offers an excellent means of integration between process and outcome goals. For example, consider a gymnastics coach who has entered the first year of a quadrennial cycle and is supporting an athlete who is aspiring to qualify for the Olympic Games, with a specific focus on their uneven bar routine. The new difficulty and execution guidelines and rules for the discipline mean that some key movement patterns, such as repeated consecutive releases from the bars, will require the gymnast to engage in significant skill refinement and, in some cases, acquisition. To achieve this, a macro timescale will be required. The coach logically prioritizes these new movement patterns over a meso eight-week block. However, ongoing testing and monitoring of progress leads the coach to realize that the athlete is not yet physically equipped to string repeated consecutive releases from the bar together, due seemingly to a reduction in power output under fatigue. As a consequence, the meso cycle is modified to place a greater emphasis on task-specific conditioning, with evaluations of specific strength built into the program. In turn, the performance director should then address the nature of support (and by whom) that is needed and the extended amount of time this will take against the need to support progress in other areas of performance. Subsequent mesocycles (cascading down to the week-to-week microcycle) are planned or revised against progress, even though the macro goals remain unchanged.

This example captures the careful balance between forward and backward thinking that is being mentally projected toward macro-associated desired intentions for impact (see chapter 6), especially where skill learning is concerned (Collins et al. 2022). Also consider this with respect to the aspects of skill refinement covered in chapter 7.

1. What does the performer need and want by this point in time and why?
2. What needs and wants are the priorities and why?
3. How long will the acquisition and refinement of these needs and wants take?
4. Who is best placed to support this process?
5. What is likely to go wrong or need changing?
6. What is important now (WIN)?

The deliberative nature of thinking through the ifs, buts, and maybes of answers to questions 1 through 5 will shape and influence WIN decisions when supporting a performer's skill learning at any distinct moment in time. WIN decisions are largely captured by the notion that what we know determines what we see. This is summarized nicely by Kirschner and Hendrick (2020): "How people categorise a problem depends on previous experiences with similar problems which shapes how they determine what the problem is and the quality of their solutions" (p. 6). Thus, nested planning appears to be an essential component in the effective support of performers' skill learning over time, but a question remains regarding who makes the final decisions.

COMPONENTS OF LEADERSHIP

Once suitable plans have been made, they need to be effectively applied. The key operational factor is how leadership can influence the focus, activity, and experience of the performer (see chapter 6). In simple terms, what leadership style, and the actions that flow from it, will encourage the performer to focus on the development and execution of certain skills rather than others? Accordingly, and reflecting research that explores these links (e.g., Collins and Cruickshank 2015), we now look at different aspects and methods that work in performance environments, whatever the level, so long as the performers are concerned with the outcome.

Taking the mechanisms of skill acquisition and execution as a focus, coaches and practitioners need to consider the following factors:

- Are we choosing the right skills to develop at the right time?
- Are we developing them in the optimal way over that phase of time?

- Are we providing and leading an environment that encourages these skills at the right place and time?
- Does the **social milieu** encourage or discourage these skills or this style of performance or play?

All these elements should be developed, encouraged, and facilitated through multiple methods (e.g., the team or group culture). Check out the parallels presented in chapter 12.

Multilingual Leadership

This brief consideration of the challenges faced by performers, framed against the agenda shown as the components in the previous section, should have demonstrated the need for an adaptable style of leadership—in other words, an *it depends* variation resulting in well-informed decision making aimed at generating an optimal environment based on intended outcomes. This variation against context idea is, once again, not original in this domain. In 1978 Chelladurai had already developed a model that, drawing on extant theory in other domains, generated a multidimensional model for leadership in sport contests (figure 10.1).

Offering a simple and elegant overview, the multidimensional leadership model highlights how the optimal leader behavior for a setting will depend on a subtle blend of context (the left-hand column) and a balance between needs and preferences. The aim is decision making toward an optimal style that will satisfy the (hopefully) reconcilable aspects of performance outcome and please group members. We see this as one of the earliest models to acknowledge the need for conditional knowledge and the use of professional judgment and decision making (PJDM) to make decisions on how to lead.

Since then, other authors have expanded the range of leadership preference—for example, linking it to the performer's personality (e.g., Horn et al. 2011). Of interest, and in contrast to views stressing *one* style of relationship as *the* best approach, this study suggested a set of expressed preferences that related to levels of personal motivation (high = democratic and socially supportive, low = autocratic and using punishment-orientated feedback). Other personal characteristics affecting

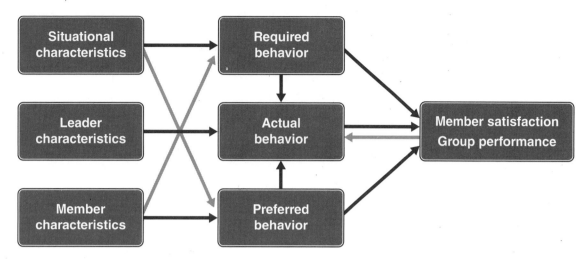

Figure 10.1 The multidimensional model of leadership.
Adapted from Chelladurai and Carron (1981).

preferences for leadership style included levels of cognitive anxiety, which, when high, was associated with an unsurprising need for more regular feedback.

More recently, our own work has extended this further, demonstrating how optimal leadership not only varies across context and recipient characteristics but likely requires a number of integrated routes and methods (e.g., Cruickshank and Collins 2016). Notably, the optimal leadership style and method for each particular circumstance may involve what the literature terms *dark leadership* as well—that is, the use of negative methods as well as positive and a contrast to the positivity stressed by much contemporary literature with a basis in positive psychology. Cruickshank and Collins (2016) offered a variety of examples. But for the present, consider that "dark" should surely relate to the intentions for impact. In short, a coach might do apparently wrong things for very right reasons. Once again, it depends.

Reflecting this increasing variation in what might work best and where, we have increasingly used the term **multilingual leadership** as the best way to consider and evolve leadership skills. For the moment, and for the present purpose of promoting learning and execution of skills, this stresses *the it depends* nature of optimizing progress. In other words, coaches and other users of skill-learning principles must take the time to assess performers and design the best combination approach over time, with different approaches, often better for short- or longer-term agendas (cf. nested ideas in the previous section). Furthermore, this involves keeping an eye on progress and being prepared to modify the approach as the context changes, an inevitability as the athlete matures in skill, age, and experience. As one example, young performers may well react best to clear leadership, while the more mature and experienced may be better led through a consultative style. As with any stereotype, this does not apply in a simple either-or fashion (cf. Collins, Abraham, and Collins 2012). Many performers of all ages, stages, and sports like the autocratic "I know best" attitude of an often charismatic and successful coach, at least as measured by their successes, even if these have been achieved as much by recruitment as by positive influence.

Role Clarity

Whatever the style selected and applied, one key component for any group, whether a squad of individuals or a team, is **role clarity**. One of ten key Psychological Characteristics for Developing Excellence (PCDE) across a wide variety of domains (e.g., MacNamara, Button, and Collins 2010a, 2010b; see also chapter 8), role clarity is essential if the performer is to know where they are going and how to get there.

As highlighted earlier in the book, understanding plays a big part in learning and execution of skills. From motivating by showing how important a skill can be, to being able to adapt it to meet different challenges, the effective leader, coach, or

The effective coach will always make sure that learners understand what they are doing and why.
Joos Mind/The Image Bank/Getty Images

teacher will always take pains to make sure that learners understand what they are doing and why. Formal methods such as questioning in tandem with less formal problem-solving practices are common methods. Indeed, successful leadership models, whether team, group, or class, can be built effectively through a combination of off-field meetings (away from the practice setting, including videos and chalkboard sessions) and structured practices, what Richards and colleagues termed "thinking slow to think fast" (Richards, Collins, and Mascarenhas 2017). (This is discussed more in the section on shared mental models.) For the moment, note that one big aim of these strategies is to ensure clarity on what each individual has to do, or perhaps better expressed as trying to achieve, in any given context.

Two other important aspects of this clarity must be discussed.

- *Role acceptance.* The first factor, **role acceptance**, relates to how well the individual accepts the role. The coaches may be utterly convinced that Ellie should play in a certain way, but, if she disagrees, things are likely to go wrong. This is especially likely in the pressures of competition and even more so if the team or squad is not doing well. It is at this point when fault lines are more likely to emerge. Consequently, effective coaching of a role (including playing style and decision making) must include selling the details to the individual, who is the target of the coaching. This is yet another important aspect of developing understanding.

- *Role reinforcement.* The second factor, **role reinforcement**, looks to exploit the social pressures that can encourage or discourage acceptance and execution of the required role. Individuals are far more likely to persist in a role if peers, teammates, or fellow performers encourage it. This can even extend to the performer's family or, in professional environments, what the fans and media expect. So the selling job mentioned in the previous paragraph needs to target more than just the performer. For example, Dave needs to know what he should be trying to do in any given context, Dave needs to accept that, and the rest of the team needs to encourage him in those behaviors. This is just one of the many benefits of shared mental models, which is examined in later sections of this chapter and others throughout the book.

Putting this together shows why setting behavior, even when focused on an individual, is both a top-down and bottom-up job. The leader or coach does the top down, explaining the why and convincing the performer. They also set up

Chapter 10 Planning and Leadership Systems **149**

and then facilitate the bottom-up stuff whereby the social pressures and associated reinforcement keep it going. The clever practitioner will attend to these psychosocial aspects as much as the details of the learning approach. The case study Role Clarity, Acceptance, and Reinforcement presents an example where role clarity, acceptance, and reinforcement make up a golden thread of top-down and bottom-up group dynamics within a rugby union context.

GROUP DYNAMICS

Extending the psychosocial nature of skill learning, the social interactions that exist between the top-down and bottom-up dynamics will have a direct or indirect impact on skill learning. The cohesiveness between individuals can form an adaptive or maladaptive mechanism that could help or hinder skill learning. For instance, in an Olympic swim team, there may be three athletes within the same squad who are in the top 10 recorded times in the world for the season, meaning they are all competing for medals at the Olympic Games. Their individual success may rest on the orchestration of top-down (coach or practitioner to athlete) *and* bottom-up (athlete to coach or practitioner *or* between athletes) social dynamics, all of which will contribute to ensuring a healthy rivalry, which benefits individual and collective performance. Without due care and attention, however, an unhealthy rivalry may develop, leading to intentional sabotage of one another. Therefore, while seemingly removed from the field of skill learning, psychosocial considerations of group dynamics are an essential feature that correlates to success in this domain.

CASE STUDY

ROLE CLARITY, ACCEPTANCE, AND REINFORCEMENT

Andy is a senior professional player in rugby union. He has achieved four international caps but is now nearing the end of his career. However, he was under consideration for selection to a prestigious select team, an achievement that would top off his career. Through the grapevine, Andy learned that the selectors were impressed with his ball carrying around the pitch. In Andy's position, however, he also had primary roles in the set pieces that restart the game. As a second row, he had a crucial job to do in scrum and maul as a primary provider of the grunt to push against the opposition forward and win the ball. In lineouts (when the ball goes over the sidelines), Andy had a primary role as one of three designated jumpers who were targeted by the player throwing in.

Unfortunately, because of his desire to show the selectors what he thought they wanted, Andy was saving energy by shirking on his set piece efforts to enhance his ball carrying. As a result, team performance in scrums, maul, and lineout—essential parts of the game—suffered. Furthermore, other key players in these elements of play started to express their views over Andy's lack of commitment to the team.

Solving this problem involved the coach using the three components of role: clarity, acceptance, and recognition. Initially, structured team meets were used to develop job descriptions (JDs) for the major positions, with a weighting scale attached to clarify how important each stage was for that position's total performance. Once agreed, these JDs were used in the team's program notes and highlight clips published on the club's social media used to promote the unseen work and so that spectators were educated on what to look for (cf. culture change ideas in chapter 12). In a friendly chat the head coach had a beer with the selectors of the special team to inform them of their concerns that Andy return to his previous level as a complete player. The head coach encouraged the selectors to mention these primary job roles in the media. Once clarified, the coach stressed that team members remain focused on the JD items when praising each other; this ensured both clarity and reinforcement. Finally, psychology and coach inputs to Andy talked through his feelings on the JD for his position, pushing role acceptance.

Recent research exploring group dynamics has considered the ideas of care (Cronin and Armour 2018), supportive coach and athlete relationships (Jowett 2017), and psychological safety (Vella et al. 2022) as features of successful sporting environments. These ideas have stressed the importance of positive group dynamics between coaches and athletes and between athletes, whereby comfort, having a voice, and feeling safe are promoted. While we feel the practical implications that flow from this body of work are useful conditionally (cf. Taylor, Ashford, and Collins 2022a), we also suggest that effective group dynamics rely on a much wider consideration of key mechanisms, perhaps one based on psychological honesty or even dark leadership when used appropriately and with the right intentions (cf. Cruickshank and Collins 2016). Finally, while we do not delve deeper into each of these features, we suggest that interested readers expand their search through the articles cited to add to the narrative within this chapter.

One big splitting variable (do we do this *or* that) in deciding on the optimal style relates to the performers' perceptions of what is being done. Taylor, Ashford, and Collins (2022b) compared rugby union players' perceptions of coaches' practice between a group who had progressed through a talent system to international level, against those who had gained a professional contract but had since lost it. A key finding was that when players found their coaches to be overly positive in their feedback, players struggled to make sense of this when compared to their actions in not selecting them. In Taylor and colleagues' findings, these coaches were often seen by players as people pleasers who desired to keep relationships positive and not upset the status quo. What the players actually wanted was honest, critical feedback of what improvements could be made. This misalignment created a lack of trust of the coach as well as demotivation and limited opportunity to engage in skill learning and development.

Instead, there is one body of work suggests that effective group dynamics are achieved through a careful application of push and pull factors through challenge applied in a conditional manner at the right time for individuals (Taylor, Ashford, and Jefferson 2023; Collins and MacNamara 2017). Push factors capture the decision of a coach to drive behavior through challenge, pressure, and critical feedback, while pull factors refer to more supportive strategies designed to pull the performer along to their destination. We will share examples that draw on both of these factors, used conditionally and even concurrently.

Unfortunately, some authors and social media experts have misinterpreted this call for balance, seeing challenge as inferring a constantly negative pressured environment. Within the literature, for example, challenge has often been misinterpreted to mean the application of difficult or traumatic experiences without a level of support for the performer to overcome this. Instead, we offer it as a mechanism that is nearly always used with and through performer support. For example, the roster size for a National Football League (NFL) team is 53 players, many of whom will not play much throughout a competitive season, and an additional practice squad of 16 who are not eligible to play. A later-round draft pick who has just been promoted to the active roster may only get a few special team snaps. For these individuals, it is essential to consider their attitude, how this is affected by open communication, and how they may influence the group dynamic. For example, how early are these individuals made aware that this is where they are (e.g., role clarity)? When and how have they been given an honest judgment by coaches on the gap between them and another player in their position, or have they even been told (e.g., understanding)? Finally, when, how, and why are they being supported and pulled along to cope with this, identify limitations, and pushed to develop skills to be selected in the future (e.g., skill learning and buy-in)? Without these challenges being presented to the performer, the likelihood of negative corridor talk, trust issues, and demotivation is likely within this system, all of which will hinder skill learning.

Consequently, at times, performers need pulling through methods often compared to "an arm around the shoulder" when initiating skill learning, offering heightened support and encouragement. In contrast, however, sometimes they will need pushing, through challenges higher than their prior capabilities. This can be done in various ways—for example, setting higher expectations or demanding more from them where skill learning is concerned (Collins, MacNamara, and McCarthy 2016; Hodges and Lohse 2022). Both styles demonstrate care toward the athlete to support them in their aspirational wants and needs (Taylor, Ashford, and Collins 2022b). However,

Involving performers in the creation of perceived role acceptance, role reinforcement, and role clarity are essential starting points to create effective group dynamics.
Cavan Images/Getty Images

involving performers in the creation of perceived role acceptance, role reinforcement, and role clarity are essential starting points to create effective group dynamics, because they create the feeling of things being done *with* them rather than *to* them (Carson and Collins 2016). Working in this way promotes two key outcomes: (1) the gradual improvement and subsequent development of understanding throughout the group, inclusive of coaches, practitioners, and athletes (Taylor, Collins, and Cruickshank 2021) and (2) where and how the standards, actions, and behaviors of the group are then accepted and driven by all, not just a few, leaders. The latter can be aligned to the following phrase: *the standards we walk past are the standards we accept.*

Shared Mental Models (SMMs)

Throughout this chapter, links have been made between models of performance, top-down ways of working, bottom-up group dynamics, and subsequent athlete buy-in and behavior toward skill learning. We strongly suggest that these links are largely underpinned by a well-constructed **shared mental model (SMM)** between coaches, practitioners, and performers within each system (Richards, Collins, and Mascarenhas 2012). Unfortunately, SMMs have often been misinterpreted to capture fixed game models and styles of play in team sports (cf. Mckay et al. 2021), whereas a significant body of evidence suggests that SMMs also capture ways of working together and the varied overlapping knowledge base required by individuals to be successful (Lines et al. 2022). Our focus in this chapter is to consider how SMMs may adjoin long-term desired intentions for impact to coach, practitioner, and performer behavior. Furthermore, the previous mechanisms explored (e.g., nested planning; multilingual leadership; role clarity, acceptance, and reinforcement; and push and pull factors) are carefully orchestrated to support the development of a SMM over time.

Consider a professional 1,500 m runner who has demonstrated potential to compete on the world stage in recent competitions. Yet in high-level competition, their tactical positioning leads to excessive energy expenditure. For the following season, the head coach has projected three specific focus areas: continued aerobic base improvement, a small increase in top-end speed through enhanced running mechanics, and a significant improvement in tactical understanding. According to Richards, Collins, and Mascarenhas (2017) the coach has developed an alpha version of the performance plan, but this needs to be subjected to a process of coconstruction and constructive conflict to promote multilingual leadership.

If we return to the mechanisms discussed throughout this chapter, these desired intentions cover several disciplines including physiology, biomechanics, and psychology, alongside technical and tactical factors. Before the nested plan is created, the head coach needs to consider the validity of available multidisciplinary knowledge, which may include physiology, psychology, biomechanics, and other coaches. This group should aim for honest group discussion and constructive conflict through what has been referred to as a *zone of uncomfortable debate* (Burke 2011) regarding what is best for the athlete.

The process of coconstruction and constructive conflict should not end with the coaches and practitioners. If role clarity, acceptance, and reinforcement of athletes are essential mechanisms feeding effective group dynamics, the desired alpha version of the plan should be subject to critique by the athlete and potentially the wider athlete group. Does this work for them? Do they understand the purpose of desired intentions? What it will take (time, effort, impact on performance), and are they okay with that? Are other athletes within the group aware of the reasons why their training stimulus looks different? This promotes varying levels of supportive autonomy that promotes ongoing significant and demonstrable athlete input, buy-in, and contribution throughout the process (Ashford et al. 2023). At this point the vision of performance has shifted from alpha to beta, and the basis of a SMM is constructed.

If we now focus on the second desired intention in our example, changing running mechanics, there is a need to bridge a gap between the athlete's increased awareness of the change required and transfer knowledge into action and performance. The work of Richards, Collins, and Mascarenhas (2012, 2017) suggests that employing cyclical methods of using slower and more deliberate coaching methods away from the track, court, or pitch is useful. Such methods require buy-in from athletes, through thinking and understanding. Then, following this, coaches can employ faster, on-track (or -court or -pitch) activities that require action and reflection. This cyclical process of of thinking, understanding,

acting, and reflecting regarding technical changes has demonstrated long-lasting skill refinement, learning, and transfer within complex movements (cf. Carson and Collins 2016). For the performer, as discussed in chapter 7, this promotes juxtaposing the old movement against the new movement pattern, aiming to gradually phase out the old and embedding the new (Hanin et al. 2002).

Perceived Equity and Who Knows What

Two other elements that will affect group dynamics relate to the balance of reward and the freedom of information. The first relates to a group effect called **perceived equity**. This idea acknowledges that, in almost any social setting, some individuals will receive more acknowledgment than others. This might be in financial reward (e.g., linemen are typically paid less than quarterbacks), coach attention (top and bottom performers might receive more coach attention than the larger group in the middle), or youngsters receiving more attention than older performers (or sometimes vice versa). Although some differences are understandable, even perhaps inevitable, it is the *degree* of difference that counts. In short, is it perceived as a fair or a disproportionate difference? This is the idea of perceived equity—how *much* difference is seen as fair before it becomes perceived as favoritism or an "anti-me" attitude.

This is a very psychosocial idea. Perceived equity will generally vary between individuals, but also, over time and as the group members chat, social pressures will kick in to influence these perceptions toward a more consistent cross-group perception. Sensible coaches, leaders, and managers will be aware of what performers are thinking through what is said, how they act, and their (often very telling) nonverbal behavior. For example, do group members exchange knowing looks or roll their eyes when the golden child in the group receives attention? Ways to manipulate this include balancing out attention; for example, when giving questions or instructions, the coach's gaze as should usually be split across the group. Another example is to develop an SMM on values, who might require more attention and when, and what that performer's role is in the team or group. If it is a central role, allocating more attention to them might be well received based on group benefit. The bottom line is that, when not monitored and managed carefully, perceived inequity can eat away at group identity and damage important dynamics.

The second and related idea is who knows what or, framed another way, who does (and does not) need to be informed about what is happening. The **need-to-know basis** of any item of knowledge is worth thinking about, especially when "Why do they know and I do not?" gossip is another source of perceived inequity. Everyone does not need to know everything. Big factors are the impact and time course of the decisions being taken. Is this something that the team has the time to share and debate? Is this so important that the team needs to allow some time for consultation and discussion?

Given the speed of gossip and miscommunication through a group, especially when everyone is very committed to the outcomes, the sensible leader will be aware of what is and is not communicated, in what detail, and to what effect. Ensuring effective communication and managing involvement is vital. As one of many scenarios, the increasing use of senior performer groups as a means for representative debate needs care, especially when performer members may vary in their sense of responsibility for confidentiality. This also applies to management meetings. As shown by Collins and colleagues (1999), levels of confidentiality across disciplines and individuals within a group may be highly variable. Ultimately,

carefully control who knows what. It might come back and bite the coach, and the team or group, in the back side.

Role Modeling

A final method for influencing the group dynamic is **role modeling**. In simple terms, this is the extent to which people who might be emulated (e.g., leader, peer, or parent) may hold up a target for behavior that the performer should acquire, albeit critically. This often happens spontaneously, whereby a developing performer picks a hero, individual, or team that they aspire to be like. It will also happen subconsciously where individuals copy the behavior and social norms of a peer group.

A key element here is criticality. Rarely, if ever, will all elements of the model's behavior be appropriate for adoption. This is especially true if a developing performer is basing their aspirations on an already established elite. Differences in ideal behavior, style, and attitude are likely to be more appropriate in specific scenarios than others. To counter this and encourage the critically informed *it depends* approach that is espoused throughout this book, performers should be encouraged to consider the reasons and logic underpinning the role model's actions—in short, why *might* they have done that and what bits might or might not be useful for you, and when, and why.

CHAPTER SUMMARY

Throughout this chapter we have aimed to critically explore key psychosocial interactions across and between key people within sporting systems (e.g., performers, coaches, practitioners, and, perhaps most significantly, leaders), which directly support skill learning. In summary, we referenced a number of individual concepts that are interlinked and mostly complementary of one another at different levels of hierarchy.

This chapter has drawn connections between a wide range of features, which adjoin top-down and bottom-up factors. From the top-down, planning, multilingual leadership, push and pull factors, shared mental models, and a deep consideration of perceived equity provide clarity on the desired destination. They ideally create buy-in on the skill acquisition required and support a performer to feel like coach interactions are being done with them or for them, not *to* them. From the bottom up, developing clear expectations and standards for performers will support role clarity, acceptance, and reinforcement, where group dynamics mutually reinforce roles and support healthy competition and more optimal skill learning. Furthermore, from the bottom up, this involves a careful consideration of role models, where normal day-to-day practices contribute to rather than hinder skill learning throughout an athlete group.

Previous chapters stressed the point that skill acquisition is biopsychosocial, yet much of the literature has more frequently focused on either the bio or psycho. This chapter has presented a deeper consideration of the psychosocial influence on skill acquisition.

REVIEW AND PRACTICAL QUESTIONS

1. What are the two types of thinking a coach can use to consider athlete needs?
2. State the key mechanisms discussed in the group dynamics section of this chapter.
3. What are three situational components that may influence the choice of multilingual leadership style?
4. Why might a coach or teacher encourage a performer to consider the pros *and* cons of a role model's behavior?

KEY TERMS

multilingual leadership

need-to-know basis

nested planning

perceived equity

role clarity, acceptance, and reinforcement

role modeling

shared mental model (SMM)

social milieu

PART IV

Team Movement

CHAPTER 11

PSYCHOSOCIAL DIMENSIONS: INTEGRATING MOVEMENT AND PSYCHOLOGICAL CONSIDERATIONS TO OPTIMIZE TEAM PERFORMANCE

Urvi Khasnis and Amy Price

Chapter Objectives

After studying this chapter, you should be able to do the following:

- Appreciate that psychological and social factors are just as important for performance as biological factors
- Understand three theoretical approaches underpinning the notion of getting on the same page
- Understand the importance of metacognition for team performance
- Have an understanding of methods for developing shared mental models (SMMs)
- Be able to apply tactical periodization (TP) to get on the same page

As has been suggested throughout this book, the biopsychosocial approach emphasizes that skill acquisition is not a mere biological preparation. Rather, it exists within us as sentient beings in a causally significant psychological and social milieu (McLaren 1998; see also chapter 9). As outlined in previous chapters, the focus within this approach is consequently on the interaction between and impact of biological, psychological, and social factors. For example, a county cricket bowler has had a series of matches in which they have not managed to take any wickets. The result is a decrease in confidence. While overtly this example might mainly draw our attention to the psychological side (i.e., decreased confidence), humans are biopsychosocial beings and will experience a complex interaction of all three factors. Specifically, because one of the major reasons for the decreased self-efficacy is not taking any wickets, the performer will need to focus on technique, thus taking a biological perspective. For instance, after careful consideration, it becomes evident that they need to modify the wrist action to get a greater spin, which would contribute to better bowling. Therefore, the biological approach would focus on making necessary technical modifications by exploring the wrist action (i.e., what currently is happening, how that is affecting the bowling, and what can be done to improve it).

In parallel to this, however, and from a psychological perspective, the focus would be on building the bowler's confidence (i.e., belief in their ability to succeed as a bowler). Finally, with decreased self-efficacy, it is highly possible that the team dynamics have also changed; for example, the performer now either self-isolates or perhaps the team perceives it that way. Consequently, from a psychosocial perspective, systems to provide support to the performer can be implemented, such as teammates encouraging the bowler if they do not get any wickets or the captain choosing not to give the over to the bowler at crucial points in the match until the bowler regains confidence. In short, performance of the bowler will improve by working on a combination of the biological (the performer's wrist action for greater spin), the psychological (increasing confidence), and the social (encouragement from teammates and support during crucial times until the performer's confidence increases).

Despite this interaction between the three factors, however, coaches, at least traditionally, would primarily focus on the biological components (i.e., motoric and technical) (Carson and Collins 2017). However, the focus on and expectations from the physical (or biological) components could significantly affect psychosocial components such as an overt pressure to win at all costs or a "more is better" mentality (Brown et al. 2022). Furthermore, the journey to the highest level is nonlinear, with multiple challenges throughout the pathway. Therefore, to overcome these challenges, the deployment of key psychosocial skills is essential (MacNamara, Button, and Collins 2010a, 2010b). In other words, achieving success comes down to a lot more than technical mastery, which is exactly what the current chapter focuses on: the impact of psychosocial dimensions on performance.

IMPORTANCE OF PSYCHOSOCIAL CONSIDERATIONS IN TEAM PERFORMANCE

Throughout a performer's pathway, they are very likely to face numerous challenges. Some individuals might stop making progress if they are deterred by setbacks, such as losing a game, sustaining an injury, or failing to achieve selections. In contrast, some individuals might consider these same experiences as opportunities to improve their skills while also strengthening their commitment. Whether a performer is demotivated or inspired depends on their psychobehavioral (e.g., coping) and psychosocial (e.g., seeking and using social support) skills. As noted by MacNamara and colleagues (2010b , 87), "the extent to which these micro stages and transitions were experienced as facilitators or debilitators varied considerably and was dependent on how they were interpreted by the individual". Consequently, whether a performer continues to progress to elite performance is highly dependent on the interaction between the context (environmental aspects of the performance domain) and the characteristics of the individual (e.g., age, cognitive maturity, personality). Therefore, equipping performers with a range of positive psychosocial assets such as coping with pressure, realistic performance

Injury presents a significant psychosocial and emotional risk for roller derby players.
David Sacks/The Image Bank/Getty Images

evaluation would assist both their performance and personal development (Toner et al. 2018). Thus, conducting ongoing and formalized assessments to monitor performers' psychological and social characteristics, and the consequent outcomes, is as important as assessing the biological factors (Evans et al. 2017).

Because individuals are in constant interaction with their environment right from the moment of conception (e.g., the womb, home, school, society), the social contexts within which performers have to perform are specifically important (Subotnik, Olszewski-Kubilius, and Worrell 2019). These environmental factors do have an impact on an individual's ability to participate and succeed in sport. For example, financial support from family could affect one's ability to participate as well as progress in some sports. Furthermore, society also could play a significant role; for instance, performers of color often encounter a range of unique psychosocial challenges due to their race, sex, and athletic status. Unfortunately, these challenges could lead to enhanced feelings of social isolation (Brown et al. 2022). Even the specific composition of each sport could have an impact on performers involved in that sport. For instance, roller derby, known for being an aggressive and macho sport (Finley 2010), is an often nonprofessional sport mainly played by women beyond college age who are remarkably diverse in body type, sexuality, gender identity, and socioeconomic status (Stockbridge, Keser, and Newman 2022). The specific composition of roller derby therefore makes the sport rather complex. Specifically, the psychological impact of this complex social environment seems very different from other similar contact team sports. Stockbridge and colleagues (2022) concluded that, unlike comparable rugby players, roller derby players were more likely to feel isolated, restless, and cheated after injury. With roller derby presenting a feeling of sisterhood, players generally perceived injuries more negatively because it seemed to present a threat to continued membership within the team. Because injury presents a significant psychosocial and emotional risk, roller derby players are more likely to return to play before they are fully healed, thereby contributing to more severe, compounded injuries. This example highlights the impact of the interaction between the biological, psychological, and social components on performers' performance. Consequently, within each sporting context, the social and cultural milieu as much as the body must be acknowledged and understood. Without considerations for these components, it will be almost impossible to produce a coherent and comprehensive strategy (Bailey et al. 2010).

CASE STUDY

UNDERSTANDING THE BIOPSYCHOSOCIAL DIMENSIONS

This case study focuses on a 14-year-old elite-level soccer player, Jim. Jim is technically proficient, works very hard, and has a good understanding of the game. Furthermore, he is mature for his age; his attitude is extremely serious and intense, and he almost seems to be like a mini adult. It seems likely that he is high on perfectionistic tendencies, as evident from observations during training and games, which include (but are not limited to) a dislike for making any mistakes, setting high standards, always wanting to score goals or at least wanting to assist, and, unfortunately, using this as a measure of his performance. Moreover, from a team interaction perspective, he is disconnected from his teammates, does not like to socialize with them, and keeps to himself. This is not only limited to training but has transferred to game situations. During the game two weeks ago, the team scored a goal, but he did not contribute to it or assist the goal. After the goal, the whole team celebrated, but he did not celebrate with his teammates; he was the only boy on the pitch who did not celebrate. The other players took Jim not celebrating as a personal attack on them, resulting in them developing negative feelings toward Jim.

Evidently, the relationship between Jim and his teammates has had an impact on team dynamics. In fact, in training, players start to exclude Jim from game plans. Eventually, this also translates to on-field complications (e.g., players have stopped passing the ball to Jim since the incident). In training coaches are mainly focused on developing the technical and tactical outcome. However, there is a lack of focus for the context, specifically, the individual differences between Jim and his teammates. With the players not passing the ball to Jim, the quality of Jim's training and thereby game is rapidly reducing (biological). Jim now notices he is not getting the ball and starts getting frustrated with it (psychological). With no consistent passes to Jim, the number of goals he scores reduces, thereby affecting his confidence. Furthermore, with continued tensions between Jim and other players, the overall success of the team is affected, thereby affecting the overall team morale (social).

With the environment having such an impact on performers, intricacies and interactions between the psychological and social factors need specific considerations. Whether performing as an individual (e.g., boxing) or as part of a team (e.g., hockey), performers must understand and cooperate not only with teammates but also with the team around the team. This includes the people who support athletes to prepare most optimally for performance, such as coaches, analysts, psychologists, or training partners. Indeed, the coaching team that surrounds the performers has been publicly attributed as a key part of successful performance by a range of high-profile performers, such as Harry Kane (Bayern Munich and England soccer player) and Serena Williams (former professional tennis player). Therefore, successful performers, whether competing in a team or individual sport, are part of a wider team that could extend to more than 20 staff, plus up to 50 other performers in teams such as American football.

That is apart from the performer's own personal support team, which will hopefully include positive inputs from family and friends. Considering this, it is important that everyone—staff, athletes, and support network—are on the same page in all situations, with clarity on what they are working toward and how their individual role will support the achievement of these goals (cf. chapter 10). Without this coherence, people will push and pull in different directions, which can result in suboptimal performance. For example, in sport, there will be high-challenge situations that require role clarity and planning on the field (or whatever surface), such as building play from a goal kick in soccer, defending in basketball during the last 20 seconds of the game, or returning a serve in doubles tennis to gain advantage on set point. In parallel, off the field, more coherent planning and enhanced role clarity can result in more optimal preparation and practice conditions, in addition to more effective feedback mechanisms and evaluations against goals (Taylor, Collins, and Cruickshank 2021).

A SHARED UNDERSTANDING: GETTING PERFORMERS AND COACHES ON THE SAME PAGE

As emphasized throughout the book, three major approaches to motor control exist, which will offer different explanations and advice on how athletes can work effectively and efficiently as a team. In these next sections, we introduce ideas from each perspective, highlighting strengths and weaknesses of each.

Shared Mental Models (SMMs): A Cognitive Psychology Perspective

Getting on the same page is not just something that is crucial off field in situations such as planning meetings and team analysis, but also on field during training sessions and competition. If an athlete thinks back to their experiences in sport, either as an athlete or as a coach, it is likely they can recall a moment when a teammate did not anticipate their pass or when the coach gave an instruction that was in conflict to an instruction provided by the analyst. The concept of getting on the same page is known in cognitive psychology as shared mental models (SMMs), where overlapping mental representations of tasks and knowledge guide coordinated decision making, resulting in enhanced team effectiveness (Van den Bossche et al. 2011). These overlapping mental representations can include knowledge that is task specific (e.g., how to score a try in rugby), knowledge that is task related (e.g., clarity of roles when attempting to score a try), knowledge about teammates (e.g., what are teammates' strengths and weaknesses in this situation), and knowledge about attitudes (e.g., what motivates and demotivates teammates in this situation) (Cannon-Bowers, Salas, and Converse 1993).

Underpinning these shared mental representations are cues and patterns that athletes indirectly perceive and use to compute probabilities. For example, the Manchester City player John Stones talks about knowing where his teammates would be positioned without having to look (TNT Sports 2021). He explains it was possible to play passes into areas of the pitch, which he knew would be occupied by teammates, because the team had practiced these situations and built a strong shared understanding. As a result, he saves mental resources because there is no need to weigh up options because he knows where his teammates will be with subconscious thinking, known as recognition primed decision making (RPDM). This RPDM style of decision making is considered fast and intuitive and has been evidenced as a prominent cognitive mechanism for professional (rugby) players during verbalization of decision making, where players perceived both discrete and global information to guide decisions (Ashford, Abraham, and Poolton 2021). Using the account from John Stones, even when he was being pressed in a different way by the opponent and therefore faced with a more complex or unfamiliar situation, Stones recognized which spaces his teammates would be moving into. By quickly assessing the situation (how is the opponent pressing) and applying cognitive strategies (what are the best options), Manchester City players were able to coordinate their actions, with application of rapid decision making. Later in this chapter, we will explore *how* to build coherent SMMs, including individual considerations for coordinating team decision making.

Shared Affordances: An Ecological Dynamics Perspective

Another line of reasoning behind the notion of getting on the same page originates from the idea known as **shared affordances** from ecological psychology, which was first discussed in the introduction. As explained there, ecological psychology suggests that individuals directly perceive information of the environment, and this information constrains behavior. As a result, constraints in the environment present affordances (opportunities to act) without reference to internalized memory representations—a process described in earlier chapters as perception-action coupling. The information being perceived is considered knowledge *of* the environment, which promotes adaptive behavior and is different from knowledge *about* the environment, which implies that intentions are predicted prior to competition through perception of language, video, and other information sources (Araújo and Davids 2011; Gibson 1966). This means that shared affordances occur when individuals are in sync with sensing opportunities for action, and this synergy results from perceiving relevant information (Silva et al. 2013) such as spatial relations (e.g., trajectory of the ball, distance between defender and attacker) in a similar (shared) fashion. Going back to the example of John Stones of Manchester City, he was able to sense where his teammates are positioned, based on ongoing individual and collective interactions between players. The distance between Stones, his teammates, and the defenders is relevant information to perceive. By perceiving spatial relations, Stones's behavioral possibilities for decision making are constrained, which results in shared affordances between Stones and his teammate who is receiving the pass.

The shared affordances approach describes, to some extent, how players coordinate their actions based on shared perceptions of the same or similar *relevant* information. However, what if Stones perceives different information from his teammates? What if Stones's perception of space was different from his teammates? Or what if Stones and his teammate perceived similar spatial information, but this constrained their behavior differently? According to Silva and colleagues (2013), more coordinated player-to-player interactions is more likely to be achieved through training methods that promote exploration of solutions between teammates, such as small-sided and conditioned games. However, despite what coaching methods might develop coordinated actions, it is important to appreciate how shared affordances work. For example, Stones is capable of playing a precise punch pass under pressure from an opponent. However, his teammate is not confident to receive a punched soccer ball cleanly against pressure, so he moves closer to Stones (to escape pressure) and opens up to receive a softer pass. This results in a miscommunication (or at least different understanding or perception) between players, and the defender intercepts. In this example, there are affordances *for* others (what an performer can provide) and affordances *of* others (what an performer's actions afford a perceiver). Both types of affordances contribute to shared affordances and help coordinate and control behavior, as explained in Passos and colleagues (2012), who aimed to establish what is affordable to the ball carrier in a 2v1 situation.

Predictive Processing: Getting on the Same Page (or Not)

As introduced in chapter 1, something of a compromise can be struck between SMMs (cognitive psychology) and shared affordances (ecological dynamics). When seeking to get on the same page, predictive processing (PP) is a feasible approach for individual perception and decision making in sport but has yet to explain how groups of people coordinate themselves or get on the same page. Essentially, PP is based on individual predictive mental models, which are built over time, based on the brain functioning within a specific task. Therefore, in the context of sport performance, the theory of PP does not explain how the brain makes predictions that are aligned to the predictions of others. Rather, one key premise of PP explains how predictive models can be tested by surprise behaviors (Mills et al. 2021), such as in soccer when a teammate decides to dribble rather than pass, or when an athlete uses an unexpected variation of skill execution. In other words, this involves something that is different from their already established movement patterns they have learned over time (O'Brien, Kennedy, and O'Keefe 2023). In sum, surprise behaviors are a mechanism to explore and adapt individual mental models, which can help account for surprise behavior in the future. Therefore, coming back to the example of John Stones and Manchester City, he knows where his teammates are without looking because he has built up a sophisticated model of predictive errors (mismatches) and portions (matches). If his teammate decided to execute a surprise behavior (e.g., position himself somewhere differently), Stones would generate an adapted mental model so that if this surprise behavior happened again, it would be somewhat predicted. Over time, Stones generates elaborate mental models and makes decisions based on predicting the most probable positioning of his teammate. Overall, PP does not provide a comprehensive account for how teams of people can get on the same page but does present a line of reasoning for how individuals can make decisions based on probabilities alone.

THE ESSENTIAL ROLE OF METACOGNITION FOR TEAM PERFORMANCE

The three theoretical ideas offered earlier in this chapter provide a basis for understanding the mechanisms that underpin how teams of people can get on the same page. This was presented in the context of team performance (performers and coaches), and its relevance was highlighted for both team and individual sports. The next section of this chapter will build on the concept of SMMs for team performance.

First, building SMMs is not easy given there can be a high volume of team members, all of whom have differing personal goals and motivations, with a wide range of experiences and expertise. In particular, sport occurs in real-world environments that often are highly pressurized. In the real world of sport performance, people (performers and coaches) must make decisions where information is uncertain and shifting, where goals are competing, under time constraints, and sometimes where decisions are high stakes (Klein et al. 1993). For example, the netball coach who coaches a group of young recreational players must cope with multiple situational changes, such as players arriving late (or not showing up at all). On the flip side, a swim coach who coaches an Olympic performer must be equipped to respond to changes in the performer's mental and physical readiness. Consequently, performers and coaches must be able to make coordinated decisions, even when time is limited to think through their options and when situations often are highly complex and difficult to navigate.

To get on the same page in real-world sporting situations, both on and off the field, metacognition can be seen as a key ingredient. Put simply, **metacognition** is described as thinking about thinking and can be broken down into **metacognitive knowledge** and **metacognitive skills** (Paris and Jacobs 1984). The former is related to **declarative knowledge**, or knowing what to do (McPherson 1994) and, importantly, why (and why not). Declarative knowledge, therefore, can be considered knowledge about the task and environment (as outlined previously). For example, in golf, what knowledge does the performer have about the sport itself (e.g., which club to use and why),

the course and weather conditions (e.g., what obstacles and opportunities exist), and their own capabilities and affective state (e.g., what shots can they play well and not so well, and how will their emotions impact performance)? The latter, metacognitive skill, refers to a strategic use of **procedural knowledge**, which McPherson (1994) has described as "doing it". Procedural knowledge is applied to solve problems and manage cognitive processes and can be considered knowledge of the task and environment. For example, a golfer will need to make strategic decisions about planning and executing their approach to the hole by avoiding bunkers and water. In doing so, they will need to monitor the effectiveness of their problem solving against their performance goals (Did the plan work? What needs tweaking and why? How can I execute better next time?). Overall, the use of metacognitive knowledge *and* skill has the potential to facilitate a deeper understanding of the situation, which perhaps could lead to greater success in real-world performance environments.

Team members who possess a deep understanding of their domain (or who use metacognition) are therefore better able to build more sophisticated and coherent SMMs. One clear benefit of metacognition, when getting on the same page, is the ability to forecast or anticipate what will happen next, largely because they have clarity on the why. For example, going back to the example of John Stones and the Manchester City players, his metacognitive knowledge is likely to include a rich array of mental models with high-quality option diversity. Put simply, before Stones receives the soccer ball, he perceives a number of options (e.g., pass backward, pass forward, dribble) and therefore will have generated (quickly) an optimal plan of how to connect with his teammate. In doing so, Stones is using task-specific contextual information known as *contextual priors* (cf. Gredin et al. 2018), which can include both static and dynamic priori. Static priori includes information that does not change in-competition, such as a badminton player's speed capabilities, while dynamic priori is information that changes in-competition, such as a boxer experiencing fatigue in the 10th round.

Returning to the Stones example, should the situation change, such as the opponent pressing with more intensity, he can quickly decide on the next most optimal plan, based on the updated information he has recognized about the opponent. For example, his plan B might decide to break the pressure using a one-touch pass (rather than using two touches). Similarly, his teammates will also replan based on what they have recognized about the opposition. Thus, using their knowledge of the task (more intensity on the press usually means that teammate needs closer support) and knowledge of their teammate (Stones is capable of disguising his intentions, and using body feints to break pressure using one touch), both players anticipate the situation and subsequently make a passing connection. Their coordinated decision in this situation may not have been perfectly executed (e.g., their timing may have been slightly off); however, if both players are thinking metacognitively, the next time they encounter a similar situation, they will tweak their timing to improve passing execution.

METHODS FOR DEVELOPING SMMs

There is no quick win or magic bullet for getting on the same page, and similarly, building coherent SMMs is not something that coaches can tick off or complete in short order. Rather, the development of SMMs is ongoing—something for coaches and performers to explicitly and deliberately work toward on a frequent basis. An example of this point was evidenced in a recent case study in professional rugby where two coaches explained the processes, challenges, and methods applied as they aimed to implement and develop SMMs (Ashford et al. 2023). Findings from this study underscored the need for coaches with flexible and conditional knowledge, where they can adapt to ongoing challenges in day-to-day practice.

Vision of Performance

A recommended starting point for building SMMs is to have a vision of performance, which, simply put, is knowing how the performer ideally wishes to perform on field. This has also been referred to as an *alpha vision of performance* (Richards, Collins, and Mascarenhas 2017). Commonly in sport, the head or lead coach will be ultimately responsible for having an alpha vision (figure 11.1). In soccer, for example, Jürgen Klopp, most recently of Liverpool, is identified as a coach who encourages high-intensity pressing and quick attacks. This is their ideal way of performing, which, depending on the action capabilities of performers and the level of the opponent and competition demands, may or may not be achievable in the short or even longer term. Part of an alpha vision might be for defenders to control possession in build-up play.

However, an ideal or alpha vision is probably unhelpful for building SMMs, unless it is reshaped to become more achievable for the performers and coaches involved, what Richards, Collins, and Mascarenhas (2017) term the *beta version*. For example, we have probably all witnessed the soccer coach who wants their team to play lots of passes before scoring, but the players are not capable. Consequently, they make lots of mistakes, and some players, if not equipped with mental skills (see chapter 6), can lose confidence and engagement in the learning process. To underline the significance of considering performers' action capabilities to guide a performance vision, Launder and Piltz (2013, p. 59) stated, "What is tactically desirable must be technically possible." Therefore, through a top-down (coach-performer) *and* bottom-up (performer-coach) approach, the alpha vision is reshaped to generate a beta version. This beta version accounts for performers' current and potential action capabilities (what coaches and performers believe is possible) and the current and future demands of the opposition (challenges caused by competitors). Using the previous alpha example of defenders controlling possession in soccer, a beta version will consider defenders' soccer specific skills (biological), mental skills required for turning over possession (psychological), within the context of individual and wider team relations (social).

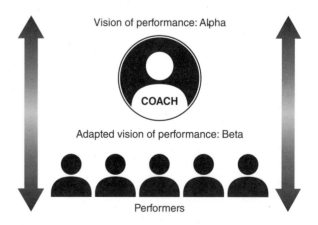

Figure 11.1 Applying alpha and beta versions of SMMs, evolving models in collaboration.

In both netball and hockey settings, Richards, Collins, and Mascarenhas (2012, 2017) explored the development of SMMs linked to a performance vision. In building more coherent SMMs of a beta vision, findings suggested the importance of using multiple methods to include a blend of slow and deliberate (off-field) learning and fast and dynamic (on-field) learning. In other words, building SMMs required explicit opportunities for coaches and performers to discuss and share knowledge and mental representations in situations where people could engage with more deliberate thinking (weighing options with time to think through ideas). In practice, this included activities such as video analysis and collaborative tasks that elicited declarative knowledge. These off-field examples of learning were not isolated from on-field learning, which exposed players to game situations where they had to make more intuitive, coordinated, and quick decisions under guidance from coaches. Ongoing game-specific and more explicit learning (fast and slow) were mechanisms to establish which parts of the performance vision were (and were not) underpinned by coherent SMMs and, over time, equipped both performers and coaches with enhanced knowledge and overlapping mental representations.

The real-world examples from Richards, Collins, and Mascarenhas (2012, 2017) are not alone in the literature, and a range of additional literature has pointed to the coherent development of SMMs benefitting from a multimethods approach that deploys slow to fast thinking processes (Ashford et al. 2023; Bourbousson et al. 2011; Gershgoren et al. 2013; Price and Collins 2022). There is clearly no best way to approach the development of SMMs, and the *conditionality* of any method (where it is best used or avoided) is a fundamental and critical consideration for coaches. In high-performance settings, where performers and coaches may be full-time professionals competing to win, there is likely (but not guaranteed) to be sufficient resources (including available time) to aid the development of SMMs. In contrast, many recreational settings with volunteer coaches are comparatively both time and resource poor. Nevertheless, the benefits of working on these components are still substantial, often outweighing the more common foci at this level on technique or physical fitness. This is especially so because SMMs often make the team more enjoyable to play for as you feel more affiliation (cf. the social aspects described earlier). Either way, the integration of doing (playing the sport), combined with coaching (instructional techniques, such as demonstrations and questioning to guide learning) are crucial for players and coaches to get on the same page.

Applying Tactical Periodization to Get on the Same Page

Another method for getting on the same page is the application of **tactical periodization** (TP), which has been a popular approach of many high-profile professional sport teams and personalities, such as José Mourinho and Emma Hayes of Chelsea FC Men and Women, respectively, and has been applied more recently in tennis and rugby union. However, despite the popularity of TP across professional sport, empirical evidence is so far limited to test its effectiveness (see Tee et al. [2020], who tested the effects of TP in rugby sevens). In its simplest form, TP, developed in the 1990s by Portuguese educator and soccer coach Victor Frade, is a training methodology that is applicable to both team and individual games. This training methodology is underpinned by the tactical development of performers and teams, ensuring that physical and psychological training is attached to a performance vision. It has recently been defined as "the systematic planning and execution of training activities that emphasise the tactical principles the players should adopt within each moment of the game" (Tee, Ashford, and Piggott 2018, p. 2). Essentially, this means that all physical and technical actions have a tactical intention, resulting in training activities that integrate the physical, technical, *and* tactical demands of competition. In rugby, for example, under the influence of TP, players would not perform isolated conditioning exercises (e.g., sprints) unless they were integrated within a tactical scenario, such as running forward and supporting play to break the defensive line. This type of practice requires the full support team (strength and conditioning, technical staff, sport psychologists) to plan collaboratively to ensure activities are designed to elicit multiple outcomes. Therefore, TP is considered an integrated approach to coaching and learning, connecting tactical and physical development during on-field training activities.

Importantly, and a critical point to stress, TP is a methodology that uses generic principles based on both sport science and psychological considerations. Specifically, in soccer for a session focused on speed, these generic principles can be based on high velocities of movement and exaggerated speeds of decision making (e.g., 3v2 scenarios). In practice, for a speed session in soccer, TP follows a recipe-like approach and would use a medium-sized playing area, with short (uninterrupted) playing intervals and frequent rest periods. In very simple terms, the physical and psychological demands put on performers are tapered to create gradual overload leading up to competition so that they are able to perform optimally during competition. This requires coordinated short- and longer-term planning from the coaching team (nested planning; see chapter 5), with clarity on which training activities to use, when, and why, based on their predicted physical and cognitive demands. In doing so, tactical objectives are operationalized through repetition and gradual progression, which considers both the short term (game to game) and longer term (season to season). This type of coach decision making, which is considered more deliberative when there is time to think through rationale, is critical for applying TP.

Clearly, however, having a well-thought-out plan for gradual overload and then enacting this plan cannot be the only solution for performance. Crucially, the generic principles that underpin TP are not specific to individual needs and the real-world environment where things change quickly and unexpectedly. Therefore, TP can sometimes miss opportunities to account for individual differences or contextual information that can affect performance—or, in other words, the full biopsychosocial development of performers. For example, this might apply to performers returning from injury who not only may require a scaled-back physical and cognitive load but also may be struggling mentally to integrate themselves back within the team context, or to a female performer whose menstrual cycle is causing uncomfortable symptoms that affect energy levels and mood. Consequently, a TP methodology, indeed any single methodology, cannot guarantee optimal performance, and impact would potentially be maximized when applied in combination with methods that encourage performers to engage with slow to fast thinking to build understanding. This would result in a coaching approach that is responsive to the psychosocial needs of performers (e.g., stopping an interval to make a coaching point, reducing individual load and increasing their rest, adapting on-field activities to focus predominantly on teamwork, or doing extras with individual performers on their technical execution). Accordingly, coaches would engage with *ongoing* planning rather than following the initial plan without any diversion. However, although TP may lack specificity and conditionality within the coaching context, it does have potential to help prepare performers to get on the same page and gain further clarity of their performance vision. With a tactical development underpinning, the gradual overloading of integrated sport-specific actions provides performers with repetition of physical, technical, and tactical competition demands.

The start point for TP is to appreciate the sport's tactical complexity, which can be simplified by identifying key moments. For invasion sports, five key moments must be considered: attack, defense, transition to attack, transition to defend, and in contest (figure 11.2).

Through generating a beta vision linked to these key moments, teams use bespoke team tactical principles, which form part of an overall game model that guides on-field coordinated decision making, and these principles act as an information filter for players and coaches to make optimal decisions under pressure. For example, in a transition to an attack moment, the first team principle to consider might be "go forward or secure possession," and a subprinciple attached to go forward might be "play in behind the defense" (figure 11.3). Because what is tactically desirable must be technically possible, the critical skills required to execute these principles include quality of first touch, weight of pass, and awareness of pressure.

By exposing players frequently to tactical scenarios, they experience opportunities to apply tactical principles under appropriate physical demands. Consequently, they begin to build a wider library of more sophisticated mental representations for tactical solutions and thus develop their SMMs. However, simply exposing perform-

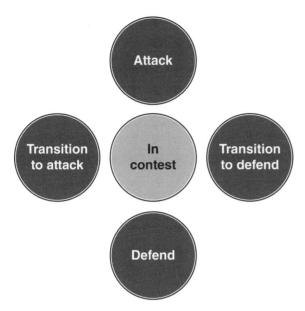

Figure 11.2 Elements of play in junior soccer: building from the beta version.

Figure 11.3 A sample beta version: the final working product.

CASE STUDY

SMMs IN ACTION: INTERACTION OF THE BIOLOGICAL, PSYCHOLOGICAL, AND SOCIAL COMPONENTS

In their preseason training, a roller derby team coach wants to work on getting the players to adopt the braced wall strategy. For this alpha vision, however, players would need a set of skills such as skate control, single-footed plow stop, quick lateral movement, proper bracing technique, and an ability to anticipate the jammer. Once the alpha vision has been reshaped into a beta version and linked to specific skills or movements (players would need to execute the braced wall strategy), a bespoke game plan will be developed. With each player aware of the game plan, they will be able to make coordinated decisions during games. However, because everything human is biopsychosocial, TP would need to accommodate for the interaction between these three factors. For instance, with roller derby inherently considered to be an aggressive sport (social), when blockers are working on their quick lateral movements, some of them might be displaying more aggressive behavior than others. If two blockers are more aggressive in their defense, they might perceive other blockers' efforts as unsatisfactory and vice versa or even lead to injuries (another common occurrence within roller derby). This might ultimately lead to uncoordinated efforts when executing the braced wall. Therefore, TP targeting the beta version of braced wall would (1) need to be practiced during TP for coordinated decision making to occur and for the players to form those SMMs (i.e., know what to do in different scenarios), and (2) need to collectively consider development of coordinated quick lateral movements (bio) while addressing deployment of mental skills (psycho; e.g., quality practice) to account for the aggressive nature (social and cultural milieu) of the sport.

ers to tactical scenarios does not guarantee learning, and the coach will likely need to engage with a broader range of approaches to support transfer (see chapter 4). Significantly in TP, the emphasis on learning occurs in fast and dynamic contexts (on field) rather than slow and deliberate (off field). This is different from the examples provided earlier in this chapter for developing SMMs (Richards, Collins, and Mascarenhas 2012, 2017), where performers and coaches enhanced their shared understanding and declarative knowledge using video footage and collaborative tasks away from the field (as well as building knowledge and mental models on the field). Thus, as is the emphasis in other chapters in this book, simply adopting a TP approach alone is unlikely to maximize skill development. It is necessary to draw on a range of methods that support tactical understanding and managing social factors that can affect performance.

In review of how TP can affect team performance, including the psychosocial development of performers, combined with building more coherent SMMs of performance, we find a mixture of pros and cons (just like any coaching approach). A strength of TP is that it is based on tactical development, and thus performers get exposure to gradual progression in cognitive and physical demands during the lead-up to competition and in the longer term across the season. This gradual overload approach that integrates physical and tactical demands means that players are repeatedly exposed to rapid on-field decision making, which is shaped by team tactical principles that aim to simplify the complexity of the sport and guide coordinated actions (for performers and even coaches). The drawbacks, however, have more to do with the conditionality of any coaching setting, which inherently is influenced by nuanced biopsychosocial differences between individuals. If a TP approach is applied in the same way all the time, little room remains for coaching expertise that recognizes and acts on the biopsychosocial needs of performers, by adapting plans to elicit individualized outcomes in the short and longer term.

CHAPTER SUMMARY

Traditionally, coaches primarily focus on the biological factors (i.e., motoric and technical components). However, as evident from this chapter, there is a lot more than just biological preparation that helps optimize team performance. Specifically, it is the psychological and social milieu that also has a significant impact on performance. Ultimately, no one factor can be considered in isolation. Because humans are biopsychosocial beings, everything about us is biopsychosocial.

Having established that, like the biological factors, the environment also has a significant impact on performance, this chapter specifically focused on the intricacies and interactions between the psychological and social factors. This need to understand and cooperate effort is necessary regardless of whether it is an individual (e.g., golf) or team sport (e.g., rugby). Importantly, it is not only about coordinating effort with teammates, but even the wider support team around the performer (i.e., those who help prepare performers optimally for performance, such as coaches, psychologists, and strength and conditioning coaches). Not being on the same page or not having the required coherence is likely to cause a push and pull in different directions, resulting in suboptimal performances. Consequently, it is important for everyone involved to be on the same page, with specific clarity around things they are working toward and how would their role contributes to achievement of shared goals. As highlighted throughout this chapter, having a shared understanding is important not just on the field but off it; specifically, having role clarity will contribute to optimal preparation and practice and competition conditions.

With getting on the same page being a key component for optimal performance, the chapter explored methods to develop this shared understanding. One of the important pieces of the puzzle that helps get people on the same page is having the ability to forecast or anticipate what will happen next, which is mostly underpinned by a clarity on the why. This is achieved by a deep understanding of the situation (i.e., both the knowledge *about* and *of* the environment).

Together, the knowledge about and of the environment forms a key ingredient for getting people on the same page: metacognition or thinking about thinking. The use of metacognitive knowledge (about the environment) and skill (of the environment) contributes to a deeper understanding of the situation, which could help build more sophisticated and coherent SMMs and thereby facilitate optimal performance.

Building coherent SMMs, however, is not an easy process, especially given the high volume of team members. As a starting point, an alpha vision of performance—essentially, a vision of the ideal performance—is created. To achieve this ideal performance, a training methodology or tactical periodization (TP) is implemented. TP is the systematic planning and execution of training activities that emphasize the tactical principles the players should adopt within each moment of the game. However, to build SMMs, just an alpha vision may not be helpful unless reshaped to a more achievable vision for the performers. A combination of a top-down (coach-performer) and bottom-up (performer-coach) approach is incorporated to reshape the alpha vision into a reshaped beta vision to ensure that what is tactically desirable is also technically possible. Once this beta vision is generated by linking it to specific skills or movement, a bespoke team tactical strategy that forms part of an overall game model is implemented. Each player being aware of the game model, therefore, would guide such coordinated decision making on the field with the strategy acting as an information filter for players to make optimal decisions under pressure. However, for this coordinated decision making to occur, the tactical solutions need to be practiced during TP for the players to form those SMMs (i.e., know what to do in different scenarios). It is also important to note that TP is just one piece of a complex puzzle when preparing performers for competition. In fact, it requires additional methods for supporting tactical understanding and managing social factors that can affect performance.

This links back to an important point discussed early on in the chapter: each sporting environment is unique. Therefore, application of any of the components discussed in this chapter would require a genuine acknowledgment of the interaction between the biopsychosocial factors. Furthermore, with each sport, each team, and each scenario not just being unique but dynamic and hence ever-changing, there is no one size fits all. No two netball teams, doubles tennis pairs, or groups of performers can use the same SMMs. It truly depends on the context of that particular environment.

REVIEW AND PRACTICAL QUESTIONS

1. What are the theoretical ideas underpinning the notion of getting on the same page?
2. What is the role of metacognition in performance?
3. What is tactical periodization (TP), and how does it contribute to SMMs?
4. Why are the biopsychosocial factors important within TP?

KEY TERMS

declarative knowledge

metacognition

metacognitive knowledge

metacognitive skills

procedural knowledge

shared affordances

tactical periodization (TP)

CHAPTER 12

TEAM MANAGEMENT

Andrew Cruickshank

Chapter Objectives

After studying this chapter, you should be able to do the following:

- Describe the relevance of culture and how it applies to the management of teams and squads
- Understand why reward and value are key components in shaping team or squad culture
- Explain how selection and performance management processes contribute to team or squad culture
- Explain how social identity contributes to team or squad culture
- Explain how support staff members and their operations contribute to team or squad culture
- Explain how the management of external stakeholders contributes to team or squad culture

As stressed throughout this book, the development, preparation, and performance of movement all rely on an interaction of biopsychosocial elements, meaning that optimal coaching invariably requires a biopsychosocial lens. Given the focus on team movement in this section, emphasis has been weighted toward the social or, more specifically, the biosocial (i.e., how group factors interact with an athlete's physical components) and psychosocial (i.e., how group factors interact with an athlete's mental components). In this chapter, the social emphasis continues but with a specific focus on culture and how coaches (or other leaders) can shape this to support a team or squad's movement goals. As two early qualifications, it is important to note that there is no single gold standard or correct culture that any performance environment should strive to establish and sustain. Certainly, major variations in factors such as history, goals, expectations, geography, and resources mean that each sport or activity—and each team or squad within that sport or activity—must constantly pursue and evolve their own gold standard or correct culture. Also, while much of this chapter is presented through the lens of a team or squad's coach or other leader, it is also important to note that culture is shaped to varying degrees by every member of a group (more on this shortly). With these caveats in mind, and following the theme of the book, this chapter will focus on some important guiding principles and practices rather than universal recommendations. First, the overall relevance of culture and its management will be discussed. Second, attention will be placed on reward and value as key drivers of culture, followed by a discussion of how these can be proactively shaped by team or squad leaders.

THE RELEVANCE OF TEAM OR SQUAD CULTURE AND ITS MANAGEMENT

Across most contexts, **culture** is often identified as one of the key contributors to the progress and success or stagnation and failure. This is particularly so for those operating at higher levels of performance, when groups usually spend more time developing, preparing, and performing together. Indeed, groups that do well often refer to the strength of their culture and groups that do not do often refer to shortcomings in their culture, or, in both cases, culture has been identified as a key factor by others (e.g., team management, funding bodies, broadcast and social media, parents, fans). However, references to culture in and around team and squad settings are often liberally applied, with culture often provided as a catchall reason for group outcomes or a catchall focus for coaches to address.

To bring some precision to this chapter, therefore, one of the first points to emphasize is that, as intuitive as it may seem, culture is a *group*-level construct. So while the rate and quality of development, preparation, and performance of movement in *one* individual, or even a handful of individuals, might tell us a lot about the culture in which they operate (i.e., if it is a representative sample), it might also tell us little (i.e., if it is an unrepresentative sample). Reflecting this, references to culture require us to focus on how the social functions of a team or squad affect the rate and quality of movement outcomes across the *whole* team or squad (or, for larger teams or squads, larger subgroups within them; e.g., the forwards or backs in a rugby union squad or offense versus defense in American football). In addition to an emphasis on the *group*, a focus on culture also requires us to consider how the group functions *normally*, plus the *normal* rate and quality of movement outcomes. Finally, a focus on culture requires us to recognize that group functions are never permanently fixed, given that the individuals who make up groups are often in regular flux (e.g., through selection or deselection processes) and that the biopsychosocial states of these individuals are also in regular flux, par-

ticularly so for younger athletes going through significant maturational transitions. For the purposes of this chapter, team or squad culture will be defined as "the normal way that a team or squad understands, develops, prepares, and performs movement in a specific moment or phase." This description aligns with the sentiments of many dictionary definitions, such as culture being "the way of life, especially the general customs and beliefs, of a particular group of people at a particular time" (Cambridge Dictionary 2023). An important point to stress is that this infers that *everyone* in the group follows or conveys the same customs and beliefs. In contrast, culture more accurately reflects the customs and beliefs held to a sufficient degree by a sufficient number of team or squad members to characterize the group's general way of life.

While space precludes a full exploration of this chapter's definition of culture—and comparison with the many other, often elaborate definitions that exist in academic literature—it is important to clarify a couple of additional aspects. First, normal should be read in both a generic and specific sense. More specifically, and in the context of this chapter, culture is evidenced by the normal way that a group understands, develops, prepares, and performs movement overall (i.e., the general sense). It is also evidenced by the normal way that a group understands, develops, prepares, and performs movement in certain moments or situations (i.e., the specific sense; e.g., during the off-season, leading up to a performance, for those just starting in the sport). Second, it is important to keep in mind that most, if not all, teams or squads operate within wider social networks, with a number of stakeholders (e.g., other coaches, sport science and medicine staff, management, parents, social media, sponsors, spectators) involved in shaping the normal way to understand, develop, prepare, and perform movement.

As an aside, the presence and role of **multidirectional influences** can be seen in many models of culture or group functioning (e.g., Cruickshank, Collins, and Minten 2014, 2015; Henriksen, Stambulova, and Roessler 2010). Ultimately, however, the main message here is that (1) the greater the coherence between stakeholders, in both general and specific situations, the more robust the culture will be, and (2) the less coherence between stakeholders, in both general

To help a diver push their limits, they could use imagery guided by the PETLEPP framework to master tougher dives.

JADE GAO/AFP via Getty Images

and specific situations, the less robust the culture will be (cf. chapter 10). In a practical sense, the bottom line is that coaches and leaders would do well to work toward a situation where the desired approach to a team or squad's movement challenge is the team or squad's normal approach. Indeed, the odds of a performer understanding, engaging with, and sticking to a particular approach invariably increase when they see this approach as the normal one (especially in younger cohorts).

As the first in a series of examples, and mirroring some of those provided across other chapters in this section, consider a soccer team who needs to expand their options for breaking down a highly structured, low-block defense. Success could be shaped by the coach helping players to normalize, or share, their understanding of different models of movement to destabilize the opposition and create space and numerical advantage. Similarly, take a netball team who is looking to improve their levels of execution in the final plays of close games. Success could be shaped by the coach helping players to normalize, or share, a functional perception of pressure and confidence in their ability to deliver in these moments (cf. chapter 10). Or consider a cricket team who needs to improve their ability to stem the tide when their batting opponents are in the ascendency. Success could be shaped by the coach helping players to normalize, or share, an understanding of the cues that trigger a quicker shift to their trusted go-to fielding tactics.

Alternatively, consider a 100 m relay team who is aiming to refine the changeover between the third and anchor leg. Success could be shaped by the coach helping the runners to normalize, or share, an appreciation of the need to first analyze and increase awareness of the current suboptimal movements before moving on to make the technical adjustments (cf. chapter 7). Or think about members of a young diving squad who are all aiming to increase the degree of difficulty of their hardest dives before attending the next squad camp in three months. Success could be shaped by the coach helping the divers to normalize, or share, the value of PETLEPP imagery as a core approach to priming and embedding their new or refined skills (cf. chapter 8). Finally, take the case of a powerlifting squad who is aspiring to return to established levels of performance after a disappointing last event. Success could be shaped by the coach helping athletes to normalize, or share, a belief that prior limitations have been addressed as well as a goal to prove a point.

Overall, these examples demonstrate some of the many areas that benefit from establishing a *normal* way to understand, develop, prepare, and perform movement in a specific moment or phase. More specifically, these examples can be placed in two broad categories:

1. *Optimizing understanding.* This first category relates to the work that coaches do to make a desired approach the normal one by optimizing athletes' knowledge or awareness of the movement outcome and the process to achieve this. Examples of this work are reflected in previous examples (i.e., those referring to soccer, netball, and cricket).

2. *Optimizing value.* The second category relates to the work that coaches do to make a desired approach the normal one by optimizing the importance, usefulness, or benefits of the movement outcome and the process to achieve this. This was reflected in the 100 m relay, diving, and powerlifting examples.

For those who are reading this chapter in isolation or not reading the chapters of this book in chronological order, an exploration of the ways coaches might optimize athlete understanding is provided in earlier chapters. As such, the rest of this chapter will build on points introduced in chapter 10 and emphasize the ways coaches might optimize the *value* of specific outcomes (i.e., moving like *this* or *that*), as well as the processes by which these movements can be developed, prepared, and performed. By means of illustration, attention also will be given to some ways by which coaches can promote an environment that operates as closely as possible to the concentric circles on the left-hand side of figure 12.1 as opposed to the concentric circles on the right-hand side. For clarity, this example relates to an environment where parents, support staff, and peers are three of the main influences on most team members' approaches to developing, preparing, and performing movement.

OPTIMIZING THE VALUE OF SPECIFIC MOVEMENT OUTCOMES AND PROCESSES

Before considering some principles and practices to optimize the value of specific movement outcomes and processes, it is worth considering why value plays such a significant role in group functioning. In simple terms, the job of our brain is to help us use our energy in the most efficient and rewarding way (Barrett 2021). In other words, it could be suggested that we are hardwired to engage in activities that lead to sufficient reward for the energy invested in attaining them, whether that reward represents some form of gain or the avoidance of some form of threat (see the predic-

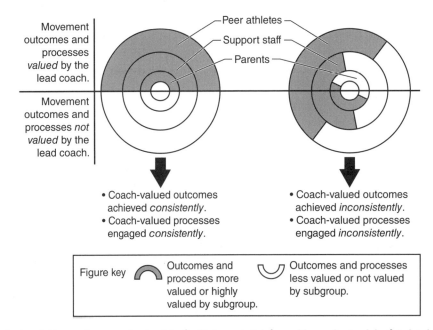

Figure 12.1 A depiction of more desirable (left-hand side) and less desirable (right-hand side) value alignment

tive processing notion of surprise reduction in chapter 1). Reflecting this, theories consistently highlight that the maintenance or modification of a behavior (e.g., athletic movement) relies on this behavior leading to returns (perceived or actual) that benefit the individual in some way. As one particularly well-established perspective, **self-determination theory (SDT)** is built on the idea that health, growth, and positive change is driven by three basic psychological needs: the need for autonomy, the need for competence, and the need for relatedness (Deci and Ryan 2012). In this regard, behaviors are more likely to be maintained or modified when they lead to these three needs being met (i.e., when these rewards are obtained). More specifically, research in SDT has shown that when these three needs are supported, individuals typically experience greater intrinsic motivation (i.e., engaging in activities for their own sake or that are internally regulated) and more internalized forms of extrinsic motivation (i.e., engaging in activities that are regulated by external reward but also a degree of internal reward; Ryan and Deci 2020). Importantly, and as a note of explanation about this psychosocial construct in a book on skill, a greater balance of rewards sought toward the internal is generally more influential, in simple terms, because the needs the athlete is trying to satisfy are more within their own control, or at least are perceived as such.

From the perspective of a culture-focused sport coach, the implication is that the value of specific movement outcomes and processes can be effectively promoted when they support the autonomy, competence, or relatedness of team or squad members (cf. Ashford et al. 2023) or, more accurately, from a team or squad perspective, when a sufficient number of members buy in to a sufficient degree. Indeed, and returning to the definition provided earlier, culture reflects a group's general way of life, not necessarily everyone's way of life. Of course, it is inevitable that some team or squad members will experience peaks and troughs in the extent to which their needs are being met or thwarted at any given moment. However, a balance of *perceived* equity (cf. chapter 10) often helps to smooth out some of these bumps.

Of course, in particular contexts, the thwarting of some needs may in fact be a deliberate strategy of the coach. For example, a coach may design activities in which some individuals are likely to fail in order to promote a consideration of new approaches (cf. Taylor, Ashford, and Collins 2022) or to lessen the credibility of a problematic subgroup (Cruickshank and Collins 2015). Regarding the latter, it is not unusual to hear (at least privately) about cases of high-status professionals being encouraged to adopt new playing styles by carefully designed drills that expose their weaknesses in front of their teammates—in other words, an exploitation of peer pressure. In this regard, coaches hold much influence when it comes to the needs of team or squad members being supported or thwarted, with a fine line clearly existing between appropriate and inappropriate application of this influence. To ensure that coaching behavior is appropriately intentioned and delivered, once again the requirement for strong professional judgment and decision-making skills comes to the fore (Cruickshank and Collins 2016).

Accepting that not *everyone* in a team or squad will see value in specific movement outcomes and processes, but that part of the coach's job is to ensure that a critical mass value these outcomes and processes, focus now turns to routes by which this might be achieved. One of these, as described in chapter 10, is leadership. In particular, the chapter highlighted the importance of a clear direction of travel or, more precisely, a nested map of the skills to be initiated, prepared for, developed, and performed at the best time (primarily supporting athlete competence). Coverage was also provided on the importance of role clarity, which can, with the right design, support autonomy (e.g., "I can act with autonomy as I know what role I play"), competence (e.g., "When I know my role, I can focus on doing it well"), and relatedness (e.g., "I know how my role fits in with and helps the team"). Similarly, the impact of role modeling, which broadly can work to support competence (e.g., "That's what good looks like, so I'll work toward that") and relatedness (e.g., "This person is important to have a connection with") in the observer. Perceived equity, as further noted in chapter 10, is also a key driver of culture, with a particular impact on relatedness (e.g., "I feel like I belong because I'm recognized and rewarded in a proportionate manner to my peers").

MANIPULATING VALUE: COACHING TOOLS

Building on the constructs covered in chapter 10, consideration will now be given to a further set of ideas that can optimize the value of specific movement outcomes and processes. More specifically, the following sections will focus on how coaches can shape value through

- selection and review processes,
- team or squad identity,
- support staff and their operations, and
- managing external stakeholders.

Shaping Value Through Selection and Review Processes

Bearing in mind that the normalization of approaches is tightly linked to reward and reinforcement structures, one of the most influential factors in team or squad culture relates to the ways in which athletes achieve or retain their place in that team or squad. Indeed, given that the basic needs of most athletes are supported by opportunities to perform, team selection therefore remains one of the most potent tools at a coach's disposal for promoting the value of specific approaches to developing, preparing, and performing movement. In short, if moving in a certain way results in selection for the team or squad—or moving in a certain way results in deselection from the team or squad—greater value will generally be placed on that way of moving. Of course, selection and deselection typically operate on multiple levels in higher-level sport. As well as selection or deselection for the next game or competition, for example, athletes are also often focused on selection or deselection over a season or year (e.g., securing a new contract for a professional sport team or a funded place in Olympic or Paralympic programs). In this regard, the value of specific movements can be significantly elevated by managing their links to selection and deselection.

In addition to shaping selection principles or policies, another significant source of reward and reinforcement can arrive via performance review processes. In particular, the feedback provided in formal and informal reviews can do much to recognize or promote change in a group's approach to developing, preparing, and performing movement, especially when this is timed with emotionally significant moments (e.g., notable success or underperformance). Shifting from a post- to a preperformance process, individual athlete plans are also now commonplace in elite sport; essentially, these are tools that lay out a team or squad member's goals for a defined period and the ways in which these will be achieved. In contrast to the feedback emphasis of performance reviews, individual athlete plans enable a feed forward emphasis and can therefore place value on specific future movement.

Shaping Value Through Team or Squad Identity

Supported by a long history of research, albeit less so in the context of sport teams or squads, social identity is one of the most significant factors in understanding and shaping how a group behaves. More specifically, **social identity** refers to the idea that individuals in a group behave relative to the characteristics of the group that they belong to (their ingroup) and, crucially, the characteristics of others (their outgroups) (Haslam 2004). In other words, a significant portion of individual behavior can be explained by the extent to which that individual positively identifies with the team or squad of which they are part, as well as the extent to which they do *not* identify with *other* teams or squads. Providing a way to reduce the complexity of social environments, social identity theory also suggests that the differentiation of "we're like *this* and they're like *that*" helps to promote the self-esteem of group members by placing emphasis on what "we" do differently or better (Tajfel and Turner 1979), at least as perceived (see Ashford et al. [2023] for some ways in which these shared identities can be created).

From the perspective of this chapter, the initial headline for coaches is that the value of certain approaches to developing, preparing, or performing movement can be promoted by demonstrating or selling how these approaches enable "us" to be different from or better than "them." Indeed, this is a core principle of coaching practice in the lead-up to a team or squad performance, with coaches building game plans around movements that play to the team or squad's identity (e.g., speed in attacking transitions) and exploit some of

Social identity theory explains that people's behavior is influenced by their identification with their own team and differentiation from others, boosting self-esteem through group identity.
Cameron Spencer/Getty Images

the weaknesses in their opponent's identity (e.g., reliance on defensive structure), an approach that taps into the effects of stereotype boost and stereotype lift (Martiny et al. 2011; Shih, Pittinsky, and Ho 2012). Similarly, the postperformance review process will also sensibly keep this principle at the forefront, with coaches working to show how the team's desired movements delivered success and how better commitment to or execution of desired movements would have limited or prevented their opposition's success. A key point here is that the team or squad's identity needs to be consistently revisited and reinforced, both explicitly and implicitly, if it is to be best consolidated (Cruickshank, Collins, and Minten 2014, 2015).

However, it is important to note that positive self-esteem and positive perceptions of an ingroup are clearly not a guarantee of being in a team or squad. More specifically, social identity theory argues that these outcomes depend on the extent to which

1. an individual incorporates the team's identity within their own self-identity or self-concept,
2. comparison with other teams or squads is meaningful, and
3. the consequences of comparison are contestable.

In team or squad sport, comparison and contest with external teams or squads is, of course, inherent. However, it is important to note that these components also operate on an internal basis (i.e., meaningful comparison and contest *within* the team or squad). In this sense, the effective coach will be aware of and consciously shape competition for places as a key driver of movement behavior. Indeed, when the boundaries between groups are seen to be permeable, those belonging to perceived lower-status groups (e.g., occasional or potential starters) will typically engage in social mobility efforts to join a perceived higher-status group (e.g., regular starters).

Considering the third driver of positive self-esteem and ingroup favoritism (i.e., the integration of self-identity and group identity), the effective coach will also need to ensure that valued movements are those that the team or squad members can relate to, especially for those who exert significant influence on group dynamics. For example, consider the approach that a coach might need to adopt with a maverick athlete. To achieve this, it is important to recognize that the formation and evolution of identity is not a linear process. So it is not just a question of helping individuals to integrate team identity within their personal identity but also how individual identity can be integrated within the team's identity. In this respect, the importance of understanding the individual comes to the fore once again. More specifically, coaches would do well to recognize and cater to the identity of the members of their team or squad—or key members of their team or squad—to develop a way of life that taps into the movements that they inherently value. This becomes particularly relevant in situations where the team or squad members will remain stable over time (e.g., if individuals with less compatible identities cannot be readily replaced by others). Coaches also would do well to consider whether the degree of athlete involvement in planning, execution, and review processes is enough to support a strong integration of individual and group identities. Indeed, if insufficient opportunities are given for athletes to have their say on what movements are valuable, the integration of team and self-identity is likely to be limited (or reliant on a particularly high level of coach understanding). This may be evidenced, for example, by the common challenge of team or squad members playing for themselves when they identify with a type of performing that is not the team or squad's intended style of performing.

Shaping Value Through Support Staff and Their Operations

Somewhat linked to the importance of social identity is the role played by a team or squad's support staff. Indeed, who a coach has working alongside them and how they operate will indicate a lot about what is valued with regard to team or squad movement. Of course, coaches operating at lower levels of performance invariably have much fewer, if any, people supporting their work. Many of the points that follow therefore are more relevant to those coaching at higher levels of performance, where resources allow for greater numbers of staff. However, the principles discussed should still provide a source of reflection for all. It is also important to note that having more coaching and support staff is not always better. In fact, it could be argued that many elite environments now have a surplus of staff, made up of more and more specialties (e.g., the throw-in coach in soccer). Some of these specialties offer important additions— namely, when these perspectives are particularly important for the sport in question (cf. Burns and Collins 2023). Others, however, contribute

to a detrimental separation of goals, plans, and methods, typically driven by the efforts of each specialty to demonstrate independent value rather than integration with others. As such, much coordination is required to ensure that the agendas of multipersonnel and multidisciplinary teams are complementary rather than contradictory (Alfano and Collins 2023; Ekstrand et al. 2019).

Against this backdrop, and returning to the ways in which certain outcomes and processes can have value placed on them, who a coach has working alongside them is a particularly significant lever. Indeed, the chosen members of a team and how often they are involved (e.g., on a part-time to full-time basis) can say a lot about what is considered important when it comes to developing, preparing, and performing movement. For example, inclusion of performance analysts typically will indicate the extent to which systematic recording, monitoring, and evaluation of movement—internally and of the opposition—is valued. Similarly, the inclusion of a biomechanist will demonstrate value in understanding the specific movement signatures of individual team or squad members, digging into aspects such as force, torque, aerodynamics, ergonomics for purposes of performance enhancement, and injury prevention. Additionally, the involvement of a psychologist also can place value on the mental aspects of developing, preparing, and performing movement or, more specifically, particular mental aspects. In this regard, it is fair to state that psychologists vary significantly in terms of their competence or expertise across the biopsychosocial continuum, with many more skilled in psycho and psychosocial matters than biopsycho or biosocial (i.e., the interface of cognition and motor control). As such, the type of psychologist used will place value on a certain type of psychological consideration; generally speaking, this means a narrower consideration if the practitioner is more of a specialist in one or two domains (i.e., in the psychological, psychosocial, or psychobiological) or a broader consideration if the practitioner has more of a balanced specialism across all three.

In addition to disciplines that have a focus on movement execution in the moment (i.e., during the performance event or episode), other disciplines can play a key role in preparation and recovery phases, particularly strength and conditioning, physiology, and nutrition. Again, the inclusion or exclusion of these disciplines offers a

CASE STUDY

USING MULTIPLE IDENTITIES TO SOLVE TEAM TRANSITION CHALLENGES

In some contexts, a particular challenge for coaches is finding a way to integrate athletes who train and compete together relatively infrequently, with the rest of their time spent training and competing with other teams or squads. For example, transitions between being a member of a domestic team to being a member of an international team often are tricky given that most athletes will to identify with one style of play more than the other, whether because this style offers a closer match to their current abilities or because it represents something that they aspire to achieve in the future. In this situation, the solution often requires the ability to generate and sustain multiple appealing identities. As an example, consider the approach taken by Steve Clarke, head coach of the Scotland men's soccer team, when trying to accommodate two influential players with similar identities at their respective clubs:

> *Between November and March I was thinking about what we were good at. Defensively we weren't great and needed a change. I phoned my coaches and said, "We can't go with a back four [formation in defense]; I want to go with a back three." I had never coached a back three in my life, so it was a challenge for me and my coaches. . . . We [also] had two of the best left-backs in [club] world football, [Kieran] Tierney and [Andy] Robertson, and had to figure out how to get them in the [national] team [where the new formation appeared to suit playing one of them only]. . . . My idea was that Tierney could play center-back [instead of left-back]. . . . I had a really good conversation with Tierney to tell him he was going to be the best left-sided center-back that Scotland had ever had. . . . I think he always felt that he was a better left-back than Andy Robertson. Every player thinks they're better than the immediate competition, and if you compare them, there isn't a cigarette paper between them. . . . I had to persuade Kieran that he was better than Andy and that's why I trusted him to play left center-back and not Andy. Now, that's probably not strictly true, but that's how I had to sell it to Kieran. Now we've got the best overlapping center-back in world football. It works. Selling that position to Kieran was important, and it was a really good conversation; he asked a lot of really good questions. (Humphrey and Hughes 2022)*

Based on this excerpt, a new way of performing, and therefore moving, for the player in question seemed to be driven (in part, presumably) by their perceived value of this additional or extended identity rather than focusing on the partial loss of their established domestic club identity.

---

statement of their value in optimizing movement performance. As a more recent evolution, some elite sport organizations are now appointing skill-acquisition specialists to work alongside coaches, staff, and athletes. Like the previous point on different types of sport psychologists, the lens applied by this individual will place greater value on certain types of outcomes and processes over others. One core recommendation of this book is that teams and squads will be best served by individuals who are not just specialists in skill acquisition, but also in skill refinement and execu-

tion, plus performance psychology if ideas are to be optimally developed and applied. Indeed, there is a strong argument for performance psychology assuming the role of parent discipline given the overlaps in required knowledge. More fundamentally, the advice is that optimal, long-term impact also will arrive from approaching movement goals and tasks through multiple theoretical lenses rather than strict adherence to perspective alone.

Moving on from what practitioners are included in a team, promoting the value of certain approaches to developing, preparing, and performing movement is arguably most affected by how these practitioners are required to work. More specifically, two important factors here are integration and timing. Regarding **integration**, the extent to which different disciplines evaluate, plan, and deliver as a collective or in silos will shape perceptions on how the development, preparation, and performance of movement is best approached—in general terms, whether it is to be seen as something more biopsychosocial or more biological, more psychological, or more social. To achieve this, it is clearly important that these inputs are coordinated by an individual with a strong understanding of movement science and, mirroring points by the authors of chapter 10, the ability to facilitate honest, critical debate so that optimal approaches can be identified (Bradley et al. 2015). An understanding of which perspectives are more important than others for different outcome and processes and how these perspectives need to be blended is therefore key to promoting the value of a biopsychosocial approach. Integration also can relate to the extent to which discipline specialists, or a multi- or interdisciplinary team of specialists, interact directly with athletes and coaches. In this respect, the importance of one message comes to the fore for building athlete confidence in the advice provided.

In terms of timing, the use of specialists, or a multi- or interdisciplinary team, in certain phases or moments and less so at others can do much to shape perceptions of value. Indeed, promoting access to certain specialists at certain times of the week, month, block, year, or quadrennial can reinforce views on what is normal and valued in specific moments. For example, some sports will benefit from providing or promoting greater use of biomechanists further away from a performance event or episode, or by making performance analysts less visible in the lead-up to a performance event or episode, to promote a more external focus of attention in the performance event or episode. Similarly, sport psychologists will sensibly be tasked with working to remind, reassure, and reinforce in these same late epochs, principles discussed in chapters 7 and 8 as the moment of performance nears. Ultimately, different disciplines will logically play different roles at different times, depending on the phase and intended outcomes.

Shaping Value Through External Stakeholder Management

Having outlined the role of selection and review processes, identity, and support staff, the final component considered relates to external stakeholders. Indeed, while a team or squad's culture is shaped by what happens internally, it is also shaped, at times dramatically, by peripheral or outside influences. In other words, these are stakeholders who are not part of the regular functions of the team or squad, such as other coaches, parents, athlete and staff peers, committees, boards, funders, coaching and sport science bodies, research institutes, fans, the public, broadcast media, and social media. In this respect, it is important to recognize that the micro environment of any team or squad operates within broader meso and macro contexts (Sotiriadou and de Bosscher 2018). As such, reward and reinforcement structures are not neatly contained within the team or squad; normality is typically driven by what the team or squad believes to important but also what those surrounding them believe to be important (Cruickshank, Collins and Minten 2014, 2015). From the perspective of this book, much can be done to promote specific movement outcomes and processes through internal inputs; however, efforts also need to be made to consider and, wherever possible, promote alignment and consistency in external inputs. In other words, this means striving for a situation where influential people and groups promote the value of similar outcomes and approaches or, more accurately, enough of the right people and groups in the eyes of the team or squad (as per earlier comments on critical mass). Given that all external stakeholders have their own basic psychological needs when it comes to involvement with a team or squad (i.e., most want to achieve a degree of autonomy, competence, or relatedness through their interactions, some a lot more than others), this is clearly no easy task. To manage this challenge, coaches can take three general approaches:

1. They can seek to proactively shape the perceptions of external stakeholders.

2. They can seek to buffer the team or squad from confusing or contradictory external perceptions.

3. They can seek to upskill staff and athletes on how to engage with, filter, and challenge external perceptions.

In keeping with a major theme of this book, optimal approaches typically involve a balance and blend of all three.

Regarding the first approach, shaping external stakeholder views relies on the coach's ability to communicate and sell the value of specific approaches to developing, preparing, or performing movement. As well as delivering this in one-on-one conversations or arranged meetings, coaches may also take advantage of other channels, such as newsletters, blogs, broadcast media, or social media. Where circumstances allow, proactive messaging also can be delivered through coach education and development programs, or parent education or integration programs (Dorsch et al. 2019; Santos, Gould, and Strachan 2019). As a brief aside, this reference to integration is intentional and important in that many organizations assume that parent knowledge is the limiting factor for system alignment (leading to a focus on education). In reality, parents are invariably the experts on their children and so can do much to educate or inform coaches on which approaches might work best (cf. Pankhurst, Collins, and Mac-Namara 2013). As such, providing opportunities for parents to share information, suggestions, and advice relating to the coaching of their child can provide an important foundation for effective sporting programs.

In terms of the second approach, the value of certain methods to developing, preparing, and performing movement may also require the coach or other team or squad leader to actively manage or block the contributions of certain individuals (e.g., specialists promoted by top management who are not that specialist in the eyes of those on the ground). Another function of the coach or leader in this area is acting as a translator or sensemaker (cf. Hansen and Andersen 2014)—in other words, providing an interpretation of approaches promoted by external stakeholders, such as the latest trends (or the fads). Once again, the focus is to try to maintain value on the outcomes and processes seen to be most desirable for the team or squad in question.

Finally, the third approach recognizes that leaders of teams or squads can only influence so much at one time and that influencing every value-shaping factor is, in realistic terms, impossible. In this respect, leaders can instead supplement their efforts in the two preceding areas by helping athletes and staff in the team or squad to interpret, sift, and, where relevant, push back against the perceptions of others. Indeed, research has highlighted the importance of feedback literacy in athletes to help them best manage multiple, and often misaligned or contradictory, sources of information (Taylor, Collins, and Cruickshank 2021). Similarly, efforts will sensibly be placed on helping coaches and staff develop their skills in critical thinking and baloney detection (Stoszkowski et al. 2021). In sum, if the source of information cannot be changed or managed, the alternative to is change or manage the lens through which it is viewed or, ideally, a combination of both.

CHAPTER SUMMARY

Against a focus on team movement, this chapter has considered culture as a particularly influential aspect in the behavior of teams or squads. More specifically, the opening section identified some of the specific reasons that make culture and its management relevant for coaches and other leaders of teams or squads. Attention was then placed on the key components of reward and value, followed by discussion on how reward and value can be driven through the management of selection and review processes, team or squad identity, support staff members and their operations, and finally, through the management of external stakeholders. Ultimately, this chapter has shed some light on a key social cog in developing, preparing, and performing movement and therefore some key considerations for biopsychosocial coaching.

REVIEW AND PRACTICAL QUESTIONS

1. Why is culture and its management an important focus for coaches or leaders of teams and squads?
2. Why do rewards play a significant role in shaping team or squad culture?
3. According to social identity theory, what three factors drive positive self-esteem and positive ingroup perceptions when part of a team or squad?
4. Which three general approaches can be taken by coaches or leaders to manage the inputs of external stakeholders?

KEY TERMS

culture

integration

multidirenctional influences

self-determination theory (SDT)

social identity

EPILOGUE

UNDERPINNING YOUR FUTURE DEVELOPMENT: NEXT STEPS, HOW TO TAKE THEM, AND WHAT TO LOOK OUT FOR

Jamie Taylor and Dave Collins

Chapter Objectives

After studying this chapter, you should be able to do the following;

- Understand the basis of professional development in your role as a consumer and user of skill-development principles
- Be aware of the different approaches available for professional development
- Be aware of and able to check for behavioral consequences of an effective self- or other-provided development program

As suggested throughout the book, underpinning future development will involve employing a skeptical approach to all aspects of practice. Practitioners must be critical with their coaching and practice, taking regular (but not constant, to avoid paralysis by analysis) pains to examine what, how, and why they are doing. They will engage in research, either formally to generate new ideas or testing emerging ones or less formally to examine and experiment with their own practice. They will engage in regular interactions with peers, asking them to watch or discuss elements of their work and reciprocating in an open and honest, rather than point-scoring, manner. In short, they will be driven to get better—for themselves (taking pride in what and how well they do it) and for the performers with whom they work. In this chapter, as a conclusion to the different perspectives and ideas presented in the book, we offer some practical ideas for next and subsequent steps on the coach or practitioner journey.

WHAT TO FOCUS ON

In the current body of evidence in skill-acquisition science there is a long way to go before we have a single grand unified theory (GUT) that has the potential to guide all practice. Some attempts at a GUT have already been published, but they should be viewed with caution. Indeed, as has been suggested, attempts to pigeonhole theory, placing ideas in neat but discrete boxes, may well be stunting progress in the field (Ranganathan and Driska 2023).

In fact, this critique could be leveled at us, most particularly in our use of the three approaches. We hope not, for a few reasons. First, we aimed to be scrupulous in maintaining a balance of relative strengths and weaknesses across the ideas both theoretically and more importantly, practically. As stated up front, good practice should be based on explicit statements of what theories can *and cannot* do. As is shown throughout the book, none of the three perspectives presents a wholly clear and consistent approach that a practitioner can simply pick up and apply, nor necessarily should they. Indeed, having used the term *approaches* throughout, we might suggest that the degree of overlap, the issues with the evidence base, and the emerging "growing together" between these ideas might make the term *perspectives* a more accurate and useful way to think about things. To reiterate points made throughout the book, "everything works somewhere but nothing works everywhere" (Wiliam 2013, p. 19), and *all* these perspectives have something to offer.

It is also worth noting that while we have presented three broader theoretical perspectives, all with a lot to offer skill-acquisition practice, these are far from the only ones that could be used. It just so happens that the cognitive perspective and, more recently, the ecological dynamics (EcoD) perspective have been used to underpin much of the sport literature and typically been directly pitted against each other (somewhat erroneously as several chapters have stressed). In contrast, the predictive processing (PP) or active inference approach has grown in mainstream research and has only recently started being considered in the sport literature.

The question is whether skill-acquisition science or practice would be improved dramatically if coaches decided to label themselves by any particular theoretical perspective (e.g., McGann 2020) or a specific subset of our three. We think the answer is relatively self-evident. It is worth noting that this in no way suggests incoherent flip-flopping between positions (once again, something that the book has emphasized). What it *does* call for is carefully considered professional judgment and decision making (PJDM), which should use different theories and evidence to generate optimal solutions for each specific context and with reasoning that can be articulated to performers. In short, someone who holds a single theoretical viewpoint must be able to give a clear reason as to why and demonstrate an openness to critique of the theory and tolerance of those who take a different view or can see the value in multiple perspectives.

HOW TO DEVELOP YOURSELF

With this complexity in mind, there is a need for constant self-development. This may be as a pracademic (i.e., someone spanning both research and practice), a practitioner, or an academic whose purpose is researching skill-acquisition but not doing it. For all three, we hope that some of the messages on conditional knowledge, knowing why and considering mechanisms, and reading critically have offered some wider benefit. All three roles have an important place, but if practitioners want to evolve, we suggest the need for a genuinely open but ruthlessly skeptical approach to evidence-informed practice (see chapter 2). Here at the end of the book, we highlight some suggestions, starting with a pattern or system of examining one's own practice and later considerations for those working with others (e.g., skill-acquisition specialists, psychologists, and coaches).

A Systematic Way to Consider Decision Making: The Big Five

First, and for clarity, the big five we describe here has nothing to do with the big five psychological characteristics often referred to by the acronyms OCEAN or CANOE. Rather, this is a series of five questions that, when used systematically, can stimulate thoughts in a positive direction for the essential conditionality of knowledge. Table E.1 presents the principles of this approach.

Several points can be taken from this approach, which has been tried effectively in several professional coaching environments. First, the direction toward an analytic style of questioning (of oneself, or another) can tease out and test the logic of key decisions. Second, the more subtle and indirect questioning tests the depth of planning and decision making. Finally, it elicits consideration of how well the bigger-picture plan hangs together. In short, has the practitioner considered, evaluated, and acted to refine their actions against the nested planning they completed? It is also worth pointing out that the big five approach can work really as a proactive tool (i.e., using the same questions but before the session to support planning).

Other- and Self-Driven Development Strategies

This book has already stressed the need for a good knowledge of pedagogy, the science of how people learn and, consequently, implications for teaching. As stressed, such conditional knowledge is central to the approach we have presented. However, two other parallel approaches are worthy of consideration. The first, andragogy, is seen as the more specific study of how adults learn, though we would question the delimitation to adults alone, especially because the principles work just as well for those below the age of 18. This becomes important for coach developers and

is described next. The second, heutagogy, is then covered although in less detail.

Andragogic Approaches: How to Work Most Effectively With More Independent Learners

Although several earlier authors offered inputs that adult learning may be stylistically distinguished from children's, in several ways, the term *andragogy* has most commonly been credited to Malcom Knowles (1968, 1980, 1984). He developed six principles, which we paraphrase in figure E.1, applying them to a coach-development setting. Note that the principles are said to apply to any adult learning, whether someone is learning new skills (being coached) or learning to coach themselves.

Importantly, some elements of this approach have been criticized as too simplistic (e.g., the extent to which all adults are intrinsically motivated; Misch 2002). Reflecting such concerns, the structure has also been effectively applied to younger, more independent learners across several environments, including in coaching. Accordingly, figure E.1 should offer heuristic guidance for the design and operation of an effective coach-development course. Reflecting this, aspirant coaches should seek out such characteristics, while coach developers should ensure that they are accounted for.

Based on our own research and experience, we would add in one other factor, that coaching

Table E.1 The Big Five Approach to Session Review

Question	Factors considered and addressed
1. What did you do in the session?	• Micro goals (as nested within meso and macro) • Tests for accurate recall (did they actually do what they intended?)
2. What were your goals?	• Tests for comprehension (micro decision making toward stated goals) • Procedural, episodic, semantic, conceptual (What made you choose the way you did?)
3. Provide up to three alternative ways you could have done the session.	• Encourages adaptive thinking from the get-go • Tests for reflection on relevant factors (e.g., weather, group characteristics, meso and macro goals, need and recognition of presession adjustments) • Situational awareness
4. What would have been different in the situation to make you choose one of these alternatives?	• Tests for presession reflection • Highlights what they consider important precursors
5. When and how will you test if you chose the right options?	• Encourages and requires an experimenter approach to coaching (cf. Schön 1983 and chapter 1) • Encourages an evaluate and reflect approach (cf. chapter 8)

Figure E.1   Knowles' six principles of andragogy, applied to a coaching setting.

1. *Self-concept.* Adult learners show up with a self-concept, of which coaching prowess can play an important part. They *want* to be good at it.

2. *Learning from experience.* Adults arrive with a lot of varied experiences, much of which will be relevant to working as a coach. For example, they are likely to have more and varied social interactions, equipping them to deal with the different needs of their performers.

3. *Readiness to learn.* If attending a coach development course, adults presumably want to be there because the content matters to them. In simple terms, they want to learn stuff so they can use it.

4. *Immediate applications.* By choosing to attend a coaching course, adults demonstrate their desire for knowledge that they can use. As such, the material needs to be applicable rather than too academic.

5. *Internally motivated.* Adults can choose to do stuff to a greater extent than children. Accordingly, they show up ready to learn and are internally driven

6. *Need to know.* Adult learners tend to seek out the what, how, *and* why for the material presented.

Adapted from Knowles (1986, 1980, 1984).

is a social game (Stoszkowski and Collins 2014), especially for adults. The idea here is, first, that committing time to coaching must be carrying some source of reward or reinforcement and that, unless we are talking about high ego drive for personal recognition, the social setting can offer this. As a consequence, encouraging and even facilitating social interactions will often benefit both development and criticality, leading to better performance.

Heutagogy Approaches: The Essence of Self-Driven Development

Presented as a natural extension to andragogy, a personal drive to learn, termed *heutagogy*, is another important consideration. A developing practitioner should be motivated by the ideas presented in chapter 3, applying a level of critical skepticism to knowledge sources while being driven to find out more. Indeed, such a personal determination will be a central feature of the conditional knowledge we espouse (see the introduction and Stoszkowski et al. [2020]). Interestingly, several unpublished social media studies have suggested that younger learners express a greater preference for self-directed learning than older knowledge consumers. So it might be that a self-directed approach could fit better with some younger age-group learners than others. In parallel, coach developers should consider

how their material is presented, using Knowles's principles to make it attractive but encouraging and facilitating an inquisitive, self-learning style in their learners.

Advantages of Teaching Explicit Conditionality

Finally, it is worth thinking about how the concept of conditionality might be best developed. Given that what we are talking about here is clearly a cognitive task, it is worth turning to the substantial literature that has examined this sort of question. Surprisingly, research has recently started to return to support for explicit approaches—for example, the relative merits of implicit versus explicit teaching of spelling rules (e.g., Burton, Nunes, and Evangelou 2021). (For what it is worth, explicit was more effective.) This reflects a strong groundswell of support from others (e.g., Kirschner, Sweller, and Clark 2006; Mayer 2004), which calls into question the trend toward implicit and discovery learning paradigms as being better (cf. de Jong et al. 2023).

Recognize that in making these assertions, we are talking about a predominantly cognitive expertise, an area that should not always be considered directly applicable to motor-skill development, which is the focus of this book. For this application, however, and based on our own experiences as coach and teacher developers, we strongly support the development of explicit thinking skills when it comes to the PJDM of how-to-coach decision making. Thus, in simple terms, coach development should be built around a series of principles that are then applied to increasingly complex situations, allowing for the development of a blend of tools as has been promoted across this text.

AND WHAT SHOULD HAPPEN?

Another aspect worth considering is the behavioral outcomes that should accrue from high-quality and well-focused training. Interestingly, our research has suggested that these outcomes will be driven, at least in part, by the attitude the coach brings to the development process. For example, in a paper that exploited the excellent ideas of Noel Entwistle, which he developed in higher-education settings (e.g., Entwistle and Peterson 2004), we were able to discern important subgroups of coaches through their attitude to the learning process. One group, whom we termed *vampires* (Collins, Abraham, and Collins 2012), were characterized by a hardwired certainty that they were right in their methods of coaching. This certainty was paralleled by a nonengagement with personal development (unless run by other vampires) but also generated a strong charisma that served to bind some performers to them. In contrast, whom we termed *wolves* were inquisitive, acquisitive, and highly social, interacting at every opportunity to check their ideas and seek new knowledge. As stated, both these "species" were reasonably successful. Importantly, however, it was the wolves who progressed and also served as the most effective mentors.

SO WHAT ARE WE SAYING?

In closing the text, we recognize that this is far from the last word on skill development. We hope that over the course of the chapters, we have been able to outline a broad view of the current state of play when it comes to the application of theory and evidence in practice.

As has been highlighted in several places, the habit of the field to present some differences between alternative perspectives as wholly contrasting has led to misunderstandings and drastic contrasts (e.g., the often-presented strawperson notion of traditional coaching; Taylor et al. 2023). As the field progresses, it may be the case that we start to see greater divergence *within* each perspective than *between* them. The differences may be greater in those seeking to generate and work with the output of various evidence bases (e.g., Chow et al. 2023) than more positivist attempts to build generalizable theory. Regardless of presumed future direction for the skill-development literature, everyone must be more cautious in the use of dichotomous thinking.

Finally, throughout the book we have emphasized the need to consider mechanisms if we are to influence practice. This, we emphasize, is not in a manner consistent with linear (albeit perhaps complicated) systems in which we can predict outcomes based on inputs (cf. Kuhlmann 2011). It instead uses a broader conception—one that enables us to think in terms of broad causality in dynamic complexity. In doing so, we hope to continue building our understanding of how to orchestrate the development of movement in all its biopsychosocial complexity.

GLOSSARY

action and emotion strategies—Practiced techniques that help an individual to (re)focus on performance-supporting actions and (re)establish a performance-supporting emotional state.

adaptive expertise—Broad construct that encompasses cognitive, motivational, and personality-related components and habits of mind; problem solvers will demonstrate adaptive expertise when they are able to solve novel tasks and generate new procedures through existing tools.

active inference—A process of removing unexpected responses by revising one's expected model following a prediction error or altering the situation to fit the expected reality.

active treatment—A control condition that replicates a known, usual, or best-practice approach.

activity design—A series of informed choices considering various elements related to learning such as content, structure and sequencing of activities, both in and out of practice.

affordance—A quality of the environment or object that affords opportunities for action. For example, a door handle affords up-and-down movement.

attentional control theory (ACT)—A perspective on the interaction between anxiety and a goal-driven and a stimulus-driven attentional system.

attribution—The reasons to which a person might credit or blame the outcome.

augmented feedback—Feedback that is provided by a source external to the body (e.g., video replay or a coach rating).

automaticity—The idea that well-learned skills become automatic in that no conscious thought is necessary. See chapter 8 on MESH for more detailed consideration of this idea.

blocked—Practice of a single skill for a block of time.

case conceptualization—A process of evaluating symptoms and causes used to design interventions. Originating in psychology, this process is increasingly employed in coaching domains, including strength and conditioning and sport coaching.

challenge point theory—A theory suggesting that too much or too little challenge hinders learning.

coaching intention—The rationale for selecting a specific coaching approach, action, or response in a specific context and moment.

coaching methods—The tools available to the coach in the form of activity design and coaching style to influence performer experience.

coaching structure and design—How coaching activities are organized and shaped to achieve specific intentions.

coaching style—The behaviors and interactions through which intentions are delivered by a coach.

cognitive approach—A theoretical perspective on coaching that emphasizes the importance of central, brain-led processes in acquiring and performing skills. Learning is seen as a process of building from a template or model.

cognitive load—In simple terms, how hard the brain and nervous system are working. Analogous to physical workload.

combination training—High-quality psychomotor and psychobehavioral training in which a high-demand technique is paired with physical fatigue—for example, pairing mountain bike laps with a motocross technical course on sand (e.g., Collins, Doherty, and Talbot 1993).

constraints-led approach (CLA)—A pedagogic approach informed by EcoD that uses constraints to direct and encourage the learner's search for effective solutions to each context. For example, the shape of the pitch could be changed to afford certain movement solutions.

contextual interference—A factor in learning where better retention and transfer can result from more challenging randomized practice; making it harder for the learner generates better-quality learning.

contextual priors—Information that is pertinent for the performer to consider. Contextual priors can be static (consistent throughout a performance) or dynamic (evolving with the performance).

critical thinking—The objective interpretation, analysis, and evaluation of information and knowledge in order to form a judgment.

culture—The normal way of life for a group, including how they perceive, develop, prepare for, and perform in their focal tasks.

decision making—The cognitive process of weighing options to fit the context.

declarative knowledge—The knowledge of facts and specific points of information. It can always be verbalized and stated as undisputable fact.

dependent variable—Factors measured within a study that reveal the impact resulting from manipulated variables (e.g., time, skill level, practice type). Examples of dependent variables include performance score, self-confidence ratings, or movement variability in the skill-acquisition context.

direct perception-action coupling—Action control without the need for any internal processing of external information or retrieval of movement from memory.

downregulation—The process of transitioning from a more effective to a less effective state during performance.

drilling—Repetitive practice of techniques, often in a low-fidelity situation (e.g., unopposed, with conditioned opposition or through mental rehearsal).

ecological dynamics approach (EcoD)—A theoretical perspective that deemphasizes central processes, exploring direct links between contextual stimuli and actions. Learning is seen as an individually focused process that sees the evolution of a personal technique.

effector—The set of instructions that is developed in cognitive models of control and then sent to the muscles for execution.

embodiment—Movement is understood as an immersive experience within an environment, with perception, cognition, and action all being interrelated (e.g., how one thinks and perceives the environment is a result of how one moves, but equally, how one moves alters how one thinks and perceives the environment).

emotional disturbance—The relative experience of positive or negative affective states that affect learning and performance.

epistemological chain—Based on the coach's personal views on the philosophy of optimal learning, which will drive a logical chain of reasoning so that all aspects of the learning process (e.g., programming, scheduling, practices, and feedback) are clearly in line.

especial skills—A factor in learning whereby certain skills become stronger because of more frequent practice, either due to game demands (e.g., basketball shooting from the free throw line) or preferences (e.g., having a favorite golf club).

evidence-informed practice—An approach to professional practice that draws on the best available evidence and theory along with the needs of the context and the personal experience of the coach to inform decisions.

expectation effects—The interaction of an individual or group's assumptions or predictions on a future event or situation.

explicit knowledge—Knowledge that is easy to articulate, write down, and share.

explicit motor learning—Learning with verbal understanding of the movement.

explore-exploit continuum—In PP, the relative weighting of behavior that exploits a familiar movement and exploration of unfamiliar options or environments.

external perspective—This relates to how the performer views the performance in imagery, such as watching themselves as another on TV.

external validity—The extent to which something (e.g., a manipulation or conclusion) is true in real life, outside of the research study.

fidelity—The extent to which practice activity conditions re-create the performance it is designed to replicate.

flow—The idea that when perceived ability and perceived challenge are matched, an optimal state of execution, characterized by enjoyment, effortless performance, and tight but relaxed focus, is achieved. It is a popular term, but more recent work has challenged how or why it occurs.

free energy principle—The principle suggesting that the prerogative of living organisms is to minimize surprise or entropy in the form of free energy.

generative model—The internal model used to generate predicted sensory input underpinning predictive processing.

implicit motor learning—Learning without conscious awareness of the movement.

integration—The process by which individual elements are combined and blended to deliver a joined-up rather than siloed approach to a goal, task, or challenge.

intentions for impact—A term that originated in counseling. Intentions for impact represent a summary of the outcome goals on which sessions are designed and run.

interdisciplinary—A system where disciplines work in an integrated manner, including regular meetings and other interactions to design and then monitor and refine support for performers.

internal validity—The extent to which observed changes result from an intended experimental manipulation.

internal visual perspective—This relates to how the performer views the performance in imagery through their own eyes (i.e., first person).

mechanistic—Pertaining to a theory or approach. Put simply, how does it work?

meshed control theory—A theory of motor control that sees expert performance as automatic but with cognitive activity shifted to higher-order functions (e.g., less movement, more tactical planning).

metacognition—Simply put, metacognition is thinking about thinking. The two components within this are metacognitive knowledge and metacognitive skills.

metacognitive knowledge—Metacognitive knowledge is related to declarative knowledge, i.e., people's understanding about the task and environment.

metacognitive skills—Metacognitive skills refer to procedural knowledge or knowledge of the environment, which is applied to solve problems and manage cognitive processes.

multi-action planning (MAP)—An action-focused, sport-specific, mixed-methods intervention model, characterized by four performance types.

multidirectional influences—Impact that emanates from top-down, bottom-up, and lateral stakeholders.

multilingual leadership—The ability to use a variety of leadership tools, first, to send the message through a variety of methods and, second, to be adaptable in the selection and use of leadership tools.

need-to-know basis—Leaders need to be aware of who needs to know about why decisions or actions have been made. Promoting an open environment is generally a good idea, but leaders and managers are in those roles for a reason. Everyone does not need to know everything.

nested planning—Designing a layered program, encompassing short-, medium- and longer-term goals, which helps the coach make decisions on what is important now, how to achieve it, and how to address these different levels of goals progressively.

nonlinear pedagogy (NLP)—The EcoD-informed framework that encourages practitioners to use five pedagogical principles: information-movement coupling, manipulation of constraints, attentional focus, representativeness, and functional variability.

pan-theoretical—An idea or approach that runs across (pan) theories.

perceived equity—The extent to which group or team members think the system is fair rather than equal. For example, one player might be more valued than another (and perhaps paid more) but how much more is seen as equitable.

perception—The process of detecting then interpreting a stimulus (cognitive) or affordance (EcoD) in the context.

perception-action coupling (P-A coupling)—The idea that perception and action are fundamentally entwined, highlighting the continuity of perceiving and responding to stimuli. In EcoD, learners become attuned to linking certain perceptions to an action, so developing a quick response. Furthermore, at least in EcoD, the process of the action is tightly linked (coupled) to the perception by how the action changes what is perceived and vice versa.

perceptual attunement—The process of learning which information sources to attend to, in which situations, and when to attend to these variables.

perceptual-motor landscape—The scope of tendencies an individual has in perceiving and moving.

performance safety—The relative perception of consequence for mistakes or poor performance.

performer centeredness—Methods used by the coach to ask the learner/performer to produce movement in a learning episode.

pracademic—A person or approach that is both an academic and practitioner in their field. One pertinent example is high-level coaches who are also researching and developing practice.

predictive processing approach—A more recent theoretical perspective that stresses the role of the brain as a prediction engine. Performers build expectations of what is more likely to occur or be required. Execution in these circumstances is more automatic and quick. Surprises, where less likely or unexpected things occur, result in slower and more detailed thinking to develop appropriate plans.

pressure proofed—When a skill is sufficiently resistant to the expected and spontaneous stresses of performance.

priors—The PP notion of the prior beliefs and expectations that influence the prediction of sense data based on prior knowledge and experience.

procedural knowledge—Doing it, or the knowledge applied in the performance of a task.

professional judgment and decision making (PJDM)—An approach to decision making used by various professions (including coaching) in which different options are generated to fit the context, then selected through a conscious evaluation of pros and cons.

psychological load—The volume, intensity, and frequency of demands placed on an individual's mental reserves.

representative design—A important principle of the EcoD approach that stresses that for learning and behavior change to be effective, the display must be realistic to the target activity. For example, learners should practice passing in a game-like situation, not in two lines between cones.

retention—The assessment of how well a motor skill can be performed following an interval without practice.

role clarity, acceptance, and reinforcement—The extent to which a performer accurately knows (clarity), accepts (acceptance), and is appropriately praised by their peers (reinforcement) for what they are expected to do, either as an individual or team member.

role modeling—Using others (e.g., coach, peers, stakeholder) as an example of positive behaviors for the performer to consider and use. This is best done when both the strengths and weaknesses of the model are considered, thus encouraging reflection on the appropriateness of following rather than blindly copying.

routine expertise—A mindset oriented toward solving routine problems through the application of procedural knowledge.

satisficing—The very common and often functional human trait of taking the first-option solution to meet a challenge—literally, one that satisfies the needs, even if this is less than optimal.

self-control—The internal regulation of thoughts, emotions, and behaviors.

self-determination theory (SDT)—A perspective that views health, growth, and positive change as products of individuals meeting their need for autonomy, competence, and relatedness.

self-organization—The idea that a move can emerge directly from the environment without any input or contribution from a central representation or executive system.

shared affordances—When perceiving relevant information results in a synergy of individuals being in sync with sensing opportunities for action.

shared mental model (SMM)—The extent to which performers, coaches, and other stakeholders hold a common understanding of what they need to do.

situational awareness—The understanding of an environment, its elements, and how it changes with respect to time or other factors.

situational comprehension—Understanding the factors in the environment and their causes, demands, and impact on the decision maker.

situational demands—The understanding of the demands created by the environment, the people being coached, and the coaching process.

skill refinement—The process of modifying an already learned and embedded technique.

social identity—How we view and define ourselves based on the groups to which we do and do not belong.

social milieu—Related to the culture of an organization or group setting—in simple terms, "what things are like around here."

source of information—A stimulus for performing a skill that offers a total movement reminder, rather than cues that often are one element of the technique. This can lead to an overemphasis on that element to the detriment of the whole skill.

tacit knowledge—Sometimes also known as *implicit knowledge*, this knowledge is often difficult to express or articulate, unlike explicit knowledge, and is therefore more complex to transfer to other skills or domains via formal means.

tactical periodization (TP)—The systematic planning and execution of training activities that emphasize the tactical principles the players should adopt within each moment of the game.

upregulation—The process of transitioning from a less effective to a more effective state during performance.

variable—The extent of variation in movement problems at they are performed.

REFERENCES

Preface

Anderson, David, Keith Lohse, Thiago Videira-Lopes, and A. Mark Williams. 2021. "Individual Differences in Motor Skill Learning: Past, Present and Future." *Human Movement Science*, 78, 102818.

Brackley, Victoria, Sian Barris, Elaine Tor, and Damian Farrow. 2020. "Coaches' Perspective Towards Skill Acquisition in Swimming: What Practice Approaches Are Typically Applied in Training?" *Journal of Sports Sciences* 38 (22): 2532-2542. https://doi.org/10.1080/02640414.2020.1792703.

Collins, Dave, Jamie Taylor, Mike Ashford, and Loel Collins. 2022. "It Depends Coaching—The Most Fundamental, Simple and Complex Principle or a Mere Copout?" *Sports Coaching Review*, 1-21. https://doi.org/10.1080/21640629.2022.2154189.

de Jong, Ton, Ard Lazonder, Clark Chinn, Frank Fischer, Janice Gobert, Cindy Hmelo-Silver, Ken Koedinger, Joseph Krajcik, Elni Kyza, Marcia Linn, Margus Pedaste, Katharina Scheiter, and Zacharas Zacharia. 2023. "Let's Talk Evidence—The Case for Combining Inquiry-Based and Direct Instruction." *Educational Research Review*, 39, 100536. https://doi.org/10.1016/j.edurev.2023.100536.

Moran, David, Jamie Taylor, and Áine MacNamara. 2024. "Understanding the Pedagogic Underpinning and Knowledge Sources of Game Form Coaching in High-Level Team Sport Coaches." *Sports Coaching Review*, 1-32. https://doi.org/10.1080/21640629.2024.2335450.

Robson, David. 2019. *The Intelligence Trap*. London: Hodder & Stoughton.

Sagan, Carl. 1995. *The Demon-Haunted World: Science as a Candle in the Dark*. New York: Random House.

Stoszkowski, Jon, Áine MacNamara, Dave Collins, and Alun Hodgkinson. 2020. "Opinion and Fact, Perspective and Truth: Seeking Truthfulness and Integrity in Coaching and Coach Education." *International Sport Coaching Journal* 8 (2): 263-269. https://doi.org/10.1123/iscj.2020-0023.

Wiliam, Dylan. 2013. "Assessment: The Bridge Between Teaching and Learning." *Voices from the Middle* 21 (2): 15-20.

Introduction

Abraham, Andrew, Bob Muir, and Gareth Morgan. 2013. *UK Centre for Coaching Excellence Scoping Project Report: National and International Best Practice in Level 4 Coach Development*. Leeds: Sports Coach UK.

Ashford, Michael. 2021. "A Theoretical Examination of the Role and Development of Decision Making in Rugby Union Through Applied Settings." PhD thesis, Leeds Beckett University.

Bakker, Arthur. 2018. "Discovery Learning: Zombie, Phoenix, or Elephant?" *Instructional Science*, 46, 169-183. https://doi.org/10.1007/s11251-018-9450-8.

Bernstein, Nickolai A. 1996. Dexterity and Its Development, edited by M.L. Latash, M.L. Latash, & M.T. Turvey. New York: Psychology Press. https://doi.org/10.4324/9781410603357.

Berry, Paul. 2021. "An Alternative Conceptualisation of Coach Expertise." *Coaching: An International Journal of Theory, Research and Practice* 14 (2): 202-213. https://doi.org/10.1080/17521882.2020.1853189

Bjork, Robert, and Elizabeth Bjork. 2020. "Desirable Difficulties in Theory and Practice." *Journal of Applied Research in Memory and Cognition*, 9, 475-479.

Bobrownicki, Ray, Dave Collins, Howie Carson, and Alan MacPherson. 2021. "Unloading the Dice: Selection and Design of Comparison and Control Groups in Controlled Trials to Enhance Translational Impact Within Motor Learning and Control Research." *International Journal of Sport and Exercise Psychology* 20 (5). https://doi.org/10.1080/1612197X.2021.1956567.

Bobrownicki, Ray, Howie Carson, Alan MacPherson, and Dave Collins. 2023. "An Explicit Look at Implicit Learning: An Interrogative Review for Sport Coaching Research and Practice." *Sports Coaching Review*, 1-22. https://doi.org/10.1080/21640629.2023.2179300.

Bruton, Adam, Steve Mellalieu, and David Shearer. 2016. "Observation as a Method to Enhance Collective Efficacy: An Integrative Review." *Psychology of Sport and Exercise*, 24, 1-8. https://doi.org/10.1016/j.psychsport.2016.01.002.

Button, Chris, Ludovic Seifert, Jia Li Chow, Keith Davids, and Duarte Araujo. 2020. *Dynamics of Skill Acquisition: An Ecological Dynamics Approach*. Champaign, IL: Human Kinetics.

Carson, Howie, and Dave Collins. 2011. "Refining and Regaining Skills in Fixation/Diversification Stage Performers: The Five-A Model." *International Review of Sport and Exercise Psychology* 4 (2): 146-167.

Carson, Howie, and Dave Collins. 2015. "The Fourth Dimension: A Motoric Perspective on the Anxiety–Performance Relationship." *International Review of Sport and Exercise Psychology* 9 (1): 1-21. http://dx.doi.org/10.1080/1750984X.2015.1072231.

Collins, Dave, Calvin Morriss, and John Trower. 1999. "Getting It Back: A Case Study of Skill Recovery in an Elite Athlete." *The Sport Psychologist* 13 (3): 288-298.

Collins, Dave, Tom Willmott, and Loel Collins. 2016. "Over Egging the Pudding? Comments on Ojala and Thorpe." *International Sport Coaching Journal* 3, 90-93. https://doi.org/10.1123/iscj.2015-0068.

Crowther, Matt, Dave Collins, Loel Collins, David Grecic, and Howie Carson. 2022. "Investigating Academy Coaches' Epistemological Beliefs in Red and White Ball Cricket." Sports Coaching Review, 1-23. https://doi.org/10.10 80/21640629.2022.2101912.

de Jong, Ton, Ard Lazonder, Clark A. Chinn, Frank Fischer, Janice Gobert, Cindy E. Hmelo-Silver, Ken R. Koedinger, Joseph S. Krajcik, Eleni A. Kyza, Marcia C. Linn, Margus Pedaste, Katharina Scheiter, and Zacharias C. Zacharia. 2023. "Let's Talk Evidence—The Case for Combining Inquiry-Based and Direct Instruction." Educational Research Review, 39, 100536. https://doi.org/10.1016/j.edurev.2023.100536.

Engel, George. 1977. "The Need for a New Medical Model: A Challenge for Biomedicine." Science 196 (4286): 129-136.

Francesconi, Denis, and Shaun Gallagher. 2019. "Embodied Cognition and Sport Pedagogy." In Handbook of Embodied Cognition and Sport Psychology, edited Massimiliano Cappuccio, 249-272. Cambridge: MIT Press.

Gallagher, Shaun. 2023. Embodied and Enactive Approaches to Cognition. Cambridge: Cambridge University Press.

Gibbs, Benjamin, Jonathan Jarvis, and Mikaela Dufur. 2012. "The Rise of the Underdog? The Relative Age Effect Reversal Among Canadian-Born NHL Hockey Players: A Reply to Nolan and Howell." International Review for the Sociology of Sport 47 (5): 644-649. https://doi.org/10.1177/1012690211414343.

Grecic, David, Aine MacNamara, and David Collins. 2013. "The Epistemological Chain in Action: Coaching in High Level Golf." Journal of Qualitative Research in Sports Studies 7 (1): 103-126.

Hanin, Yuri, Tapio Korjus, Petteri Ouste, and Paul Baxter. 2013. "Rapid Technique Correction Using Old Way/New Way: Two Case Studies with Olympic Athletes." The Sport Psychologist 16 (1):79-99. https://doi.org/10.1123/tsp.16.1.79.

Hauck, Anne Logan and Finch Jr. (1993). The effect of relative age on achievement in middle school. Psychology in the Schools, 30(1), 74-79. https://doi.org/10.1002/1520-6807(199301)30:1<74::AID-PITS2310300112>3.0.CO;2-E

Lindberg, Kolbjørn, Thomas Bjørnsen, Fredrik T. Vårvik, Gøran Paulsen, Malene Joensen, Morten Kristoffersen, Ole Sveen, Hilde Gundersen, Gunnar Slettaløkken, Robert Brankovic, and Paul Solberg. 2023. "The Effects of Being Told You Are in the Intervention Group on Training Results: A Pilot Study." Scientific Reports 13 (1): Article 1. https://doi.org/10.1038/s41598-023-29141-7.

Luft, Caroline, Ioanna Zioga, Michael Banissy, and Joydeep Bhattacharya. 2017. "Relaxing Learned Constraints Through Cathodal tDCS on the Left Dorsolateral Prefrontal Cortex." Scientific Reports 7 (1): 2916. https://doi.org/10.1038/s41598-017-03022-2

Martindale, Amanda, and Dave Collins. 2013. "The Development of Professional Judgment and Decision Making Expertise in Applied Sport Psychology." The Sport Psychologist, no. 27, 390-398.

Masters, Rich, Tina van Duijn, and Liis Uliga. 2019. Advances in Implicit Motor Learning. London: Routledge.

McCarthy, Neil, Jamie Taylor, Andrew Cruickshank, and Dave Collins. 2022. "Happy Birthday? Relative Age Benefits and Decrements on the Rocky Road." Sports, no. 10, 82. https://doi.org/ 10.3390/sports10060082.

McKay, Brad, Abbey E. Corson, Jeswende Seedu, Jeswende, Celeste S. De Faveri, Hasan Hasan, Kristen Arnold, Faith C. Adams, and Michael J. Carter. In press. "Reporting Bias, Not External Focus: A Robust Bayesian Meta-Analysis and Systematic Review of the Attentional Focus Literature." Psychological Bulletin.

Mees, Alice, Sid Sinfield, Dave Collins, and Loel Collins. 2020. "Adaptive Expertise—A Characteristic of Expertise in Outdoor Instructors?" Physical Education and Sport Pedagogy 25 (4): 423-438. https://doi.org/10.1080/17408 989.2020.1727870.

Meijer, O.G., and K. Roth. 1988. Complex Movement Behaviour: "The" Motor-Action Controversy. Amsterdam: Elsevier.

Mosston, Muska, (1992). Tug-O-War, No More: Meeting Teaching-Learning Objectives Using the Spectrum of Teaching Styles. Journal of Physical Education, Recreation & Dance, January, 27-56.

Mosston, Muska, and Sara Ashworth. 2008. Teaching Physical Education. 1st online edition. New York: Spectrum Institute for Teaching and Learning. https://spectrumofteachingstyles.org/index.php?id=16

Niklasson, Erik, Oliver Lindholm, Marlene Rietz, John Lind, David Johnson, and Tommy R. Lundberg. 2024. "Who Reaches the NHL? A 20-Year Retrospective Analysis of Junior and Adult Ice Hockey Success in Relation to Biological Maturation in Male Swedish Players." Sports Medicine, no. 54, 1317-1326. https://doi.org/10.1007/s40279-023-01985-z.

Ojala, Anna-Liisa, and Holly Thorpe. 2015. "The Role of the Coach in Action Sports: Using a Problem-Based Learning Approach." International Sport Coaching Journal 2 (1), 64-71. https://doi.org/10.1123/iscj.2014-0096.

Price, Amy, Dave Collins, Jon Stoszkowski, and Shane Pill. 2020. "Strategic Understandings: An Investigation of Professional Academy Youth Soccer Coaches' Interpretation, Knowledge and Application of Game Strategies." International Coaching Science Journal 7 (2): 151-162. https://doi.org/10.1123/iscj.2019-0022.

Price, Amy, Dave Collins, Jon Stoszkowski, and Shane Pill. 2021. "How Do High-Level Youth Soccer Players Approach and Solve Game Problems? The Role of Strategic Understanding." Physical Education and Sport Pedagogy 28 (3): 229-243. https://doi.org/10.1080/17408989.202 1.1967307.

Raab, Markus, and Duarte Araújo. 2019. "Embodied Cognition With and Without Mental Representations: The Case of Embodied Choices in Sports." Frontiers in Psychology 7 (10): 1825. https://doi.org/10.3389/fpsyg.2019.01825.

Schmidt, Richard, Timothy Lee, Carolee Winstein, Gabrielle Wulf, and Howard Zelaznik. 2018. *Motor Control and Learning*. Champaign, IL: Human Kinetics.

Seifert Ludovic, Keith Davids, Denis Hauw, and Marek McGann. 2020. "Editorial: Radical Embodied Cognitive Science of Human Behavior: Skill Acquisition, Expertise and Talent Development." *Frontiers in Psychology*, no. 11, 1376. https://doi.org/10.3389/fpsyg.2020.01376.

Shearer, David, Paul Holmes, and Steve Mellalieu. 2009. "Collective Efficacy in Sport: The Future From a Social Neuroscience Perspective." *International Review of Sport and Exercise Psychology* 2 (1): 38-53.

Smaldino, Paul, David Pietraszewski, and Annie Wertz. 2023. "On the Problems Solved by Cognitive Processes. *Cognitive Science*, no. 47, e13297. https://doi.org/10.1111/cogs.13297.

Stone, Mike, Meg Stone, and William Sands. 2007. The Concept of Periodization. *Principles and Practice of Resistance Training*, pp. 259-286). Champaign, IL: Human Kinetics.

SueSee, Brendan, Mitch Hewitt, and Shane Pill. 2020. *The Spectrum of Teaching Styles in Physical Education*. London: Routledge.

Taylor, Robin, Jamie Taylor, Mike Ashford, and Rosie Collins. 2023. "Contemporary Pedagogy? The Use of Theory in Practice: An Evidence-Informed Perspective." *Frontiers in Sports and Active Living*, no. 5. https://doi.org/10.3389/fspor.2023.1113564.

Thon, Bernard. 2015. "Cognition and Motor Skill Learning." *Annals of Physical and Rehabilitation Medicine* 58 (S1): e25. https://doi.org/10.1016/j.rehab.2015.07.062.

Wattie, Nick, **Jörg** Schorer, and Joseph Baker. 2015. "The Relative Age Effect in Sport: A Development Model." *Sports Medicine* 45 (1): 83-94 https://doi.org/10.1007/s40279-014-0248-9.

Werner, Inge, and Peter Federolf. 2023. "Focus of Attention in Coach Instructions for Technique Training in Sports: A Scrutinized Review of Review Studies." *Journal of Functional Morphology and Kinesiology* 8 (1): 7. https://doi.org/10.3390/jfmk8010007.

Wilding, Melody. 2021. "How to Stop Overthinking Everything." *Harvard Business Review*. February 10, 2021. https://hbr.org/2021/02/how-to-stop-overthinking-everything.

Williams, A. Mark, and Keith Davids. 1998. "Visual Search Strategy, Selective Attention, and Expertise in Soccer." *Research Quarterly for Exercise and Sport*, 69 (2): 111-128. https://doi.org/10.1080/02701367.1998.10607677.

Wong, Sarah, and Stephen Wee Hun Lim. 2022. "Deliberate Errors Promote Meaningful Learning." *Journal of Educational Psychology* 114 (8): 1817-1831. https://doi.org/10.1037/edu0000720.

Wulf, Gabrielle. 2016. "An External Focus of Attention Is a Condition Sine Qua Non for Athletes: A response to

Carson, Collins, and Toner. *Journal of Sports Sciences* 34 (13): 1293-1295. https://doi.org/10.1080/02640414.2015.1136746.

Chapter 1

Adams, Jack. 1971. "A Closed-Loop Theory of Motor Learning." *Journal of Motor Behavior* 3 (2): 111-149.

Adams, Rick A., Stewart Shipp, and Karl Friston. 2013. "Predictions Not Commands: Active Inference in the Motor System." *Brain Structure and Function* 218 (3): 611-643. https://doi.org/10.1007/s00429-012-0475-5.

Adolph, Karen. 2019. "Ecological Approach to Learning in (Not and) Development." *Human Development*, 63, 180-201. https://doi.org/10.1159/000503823.

Ammar, Achraf, Khaled Trabelsi, Mohamed Ali Boujelbane, Omar Boukhris, Jordan M. Glenn, Hamdi Chtourou, and Wolfgang I. Schöllhorn. 2023. "The Myth of Contextual Interference Learning Benefit in Sports Practice: A Systematic Review and Meta-Analysis." *Educational Research Review*, 39, 100537. https://doi.org/10.1016/j.edurev.2023.100537.

Andersen, Marc Malmdorf, Julian Kiverstein, Mark Miller, and Andreas Roepstorff. 2023. "Play in Predictive Minds: A Cognitive Theory of Play." *Psychological Review* 130 (2): 462-479. https://doi.org/10.1037/rev0000369.

Ashford, Michael, Andrew Abraham, and Jamie Poolton. 2021. "Understanding a Player's Decision-Making Process in Team Sports: A Systematic Review of Empirical Evidence." *Sports* 9 (5): 65.

Atkinson, Richard, and Ernest Hilgard. 1953. *Introduction to Psychology*. Belmont, CA: Wadsworth Publishing.

Baggs, Edward, Vicente Raja, and Michael Anderson. 2009. "Extended Skill Learning." *Frontiers in Psychology*, 11, 1956. https://doi.org/10.3389/fpsyg.2020.01956.

Battig, William. 1972. Intratask interference as a source of facilitation in transfer and retention. In Thompson, R.F and Ross, J. (Eds)., *Topics in Learning and Performance*, 131-159.

Bernstein, Nikolai. 1967. *The Coordination and Regulation of Movement*. Oxford: Pergamon Press.

Bosco, Annalisa, Pablo Sanz Diez, Matteo Filippini, and Patrizia Fattori. 2023. "The Influence of Action on Perception Spans Different Effectors." *Frontiers in Systems Neuroscience*, 17. https://doi.org/10.3389/fnsys.2023.1145643.

Chow, Jia-Yi, Keith Davids, Robert Hristovski, Duarte Araújo, and Pedro Passos. 2011. "Nonlinear Pedagogy: Learning Design for Self-Organizing Neurobiological Systems." *New Ideas in Psychology*, 29, 189-200.

Clark, Andy. 2015. "Predicting Peace: The End of the Representation Wars—A Reply to Michael Madary. In *Open MIND: 7(R)*, edited by Thomas K. Metzinger and Jennifer M. Windt. Frankfurt am Main: MIND Group. https://doi.org/10.15502/9783958570979.

Clark, Andy. 2016. *Surfing Uncertainty: Prediction, Action and the Embodied Mind*. Oxford: Oxford University Press.

Clark, Andy. 2023. *The Experience Machine: How Our Minds Predict and Shape Reality*. New York: Random House.

Collins, Dave, and Howie Carson. 2017. "The Future for PETTLEP: A Modern Approach on an Effective and Established Tool." *Current Opinion in Psychology*, 16, 12-16.

Constant, Axel, Andy Clark, and Karl J. Friston. 2021. "Representation Wars: Enacting an Armistice Through Active Inference." *Frontiers in Psychology*, 11. https://doi.org/10.3389/fpsyg.2020.598733.

Constant, Axel, Maxwell J.D. Ramstead, Samuel P.L. Veissière, and Karl Friston. 2019. "Regimes of Expectations: An Active Inference Model of Social Conformity and Human Decision Making." *Frontiers in Psychology*, 10. https://doi.org/10.3389/fpsyg.2019.00679.

Cope, Ed, and Chris Cushion. 2020. "A Move Towards Reconceptualising Direct Instruction in Sport Coaching Pedagogy." The Chartered College of Teaching. September 14, 2020. https://my.chartered.college/impact_article/a-move-towards-reconceptualising-direct-instruction-in-sport-coaching-pedagogy/.

Davids, Keith, and Duarte Araújo. 2010. "The Concept of 'Organismic Asymmetry' in Sport Science." *Journal of Sports Sciences*, 13, 633-640.

Fitts, Paul, and Michael Posner, M. 1967. *Human Performance*. Belmont, CA: Brooks/Cole.

Friedman, Jason, and Maria Korman. 2019. "Observation of an Expert Model Induces a Skilled Movement Coordination Pattern in a Single Session of Intermittent Practice." *Scientific Reports*, 9, 4609. https://doi.org/10.1038/s41598-019-40924-9.

Friston, Karl. 2010. "The Free-Energy Principle: A Unified Brain Theory?" *Nature Reviews Neuroscience* 11 (2): 127-138. https://doi.org/10.1038/nrn2787.

Friston, Karl. 2018. "Does Predictive Coding Have a Future?" *Nature Neuroscience* 21 (8): 1019-1021. https://doi.org/10.1038/s41593-018-0200-7.

Ghorbani, Saeed, and Andreas Bund. 2016. "Observational Learning of a New Motor Skill: The Effect of Different Model Demonstrations." *International Journal of Sports Science and Coaching* 11 (4), 514-522. https://doi.org/10.1177/1747954116655049.

Gibson, James J. 1966. *The Senses Considered as Perceptual Systems*. Boston: Houghton Mifflin.

Gibson, James J. 1979. *The Ecological Approach to Visual Perception: Classic Edition*. New York: Psychology Press.

Gray, Rob. 2022. *Learning to Optimize Movement: Harnessing the Power of the Athlete-Environment Relationship*. Self-pub.

Harris, David, Sam Wilkinson, and Toby Ellmers. 2023. "From Fear of Falling to Choking Under Pressure: A Predictive Processing Approach of Disrupted Motor Control Under Anxiety." *Neuroscience & Biobehavioral Reviews* 148, 105115. https://doi.org/10.1016/j.neubiorev.2023.105115.

Hodges, Nicola, A. Mark Williams, Spencer Hayes, and Gavin Breslin. 2007. "What Is Modelled During Observational Learning?" *Journal of Sports Sciences* 25 (5): 531-545. https://doi.org/10.1080/02640410600946860.

Keetch, Katherine, Timothy Lee, and Richard Schmidt. 2009. "Especial Skills: Specificity Embedded Within Generality." *Journal of Sport and Exercise Psychology* 30 (6): 723-736. https://doi.org/10.1123/jsep.30.6.723.

Kiefer, Alex, and Jakob Hohwy. 2018. "Content and Misrepresentation in Hierarchical Generative Models." *Synthese* 195 (6): 2387-2415. https://doi.org/10.1007/s11229-017-1435-7.

Kirchhoff, Michael D., and Ian Robertson. 2018. "Enactivism and Predictive Processing: A Non-Representational View." *Philosophical Explorations* 21 (2): 264-281. https://doi.org/10.1080/13869795.2018.1477983.

Kiverstein, Julian, Mark Miller, and Erik Rietveld. 2019. "The Feeling of Grip: Novelty, Error Dynamics, and the Predictive Brain." *Synthese* 196 (7): 2847-2869. https://doi.org/10.1007/s11229-017-1583-9.

Linson, Adam, Andy Clark, Subramanian Ramamoorthy, and Karl Friston. 2018. "The Active Inference Approach to Ecological Perception: General Information Dynamics for Natural and Artificial Embodied Cognition." *Frontiers in Robotics and AI* 5 (March): 21. https://doi.org/10.3389/frobt.2018.00021.

Meijer, Onno, and Klaus Roth. 1988. *Complex Movement Behaviour: "The" Motor-Action Controversy*. Amsterdam: Elsevier.

Myszka, Shawn, Tyler Yearby, and Keith Davids. 2023. "(Re)conceptualizing Movement Behavior in Sport as a Problem-Solving Activity." *Frontiers in Sports and Active Living*, 5, 1130131. https://doi.org/10.3389/fspor.2023.113013.

Oliva, Damian, and Daniel Tomsic. 2014. "Computation of Object Approach by a System of Visual Motion-Sensitive Neurons in the Crab Neohelice." *Journal of Neurophysiology*, 112, 1477-1490. https://doi.org/10.1152/jn.00921.2013.

Orth, Dominic, Keith Davids, and Ludovic Seifert. 2018. "Constraints Representing a Meta-Stable Régime Facilitate Exploration During Practice and Transfer of Learning in a Complex Multi-Articular Task." *Human Movement Science*, 57, 291-302. https://doi.org/10.1016/j.humov.2017.09.007.

Parr, Thomas, Giovanni Pezzulo, and Karl Friston. 2022. *Active Inference: The Free Energy Principle in Mind, Brain, and Behavior*. Cambridge, MA: MIT Press.

Pinder, Ross, Ian Renshaw, and Keith Davids. 2009. "Information-Movement Coupling in Developing Cricketers Under Changing Ecological Practice Constraints." *Human Movement Science* 28 (4), 468-479. https://doi.org/10.1016/j.humov.2009.02.003

Ranganathan, Rajiv, and Karl M. Newell. 2010. "Motor Learning Through Induced Variability at the Task Goal and Execution Redundancy Levels." *Journal of Motor Behaviour* 42 (5): 307-316. https://doi.org/10.1080/00222895.2010.510542.

Ranganathan, Rajiv, Mei-Hua Lee, and Karl M. Newell. 2020. "Repetition Without Repetition: Challenges in Understanding Behavioral Flexibility in Motor Skill." *Frontiers in Psychology*, 11. https://doi.org/10.3389/fpsyg.2020.02018.

Ribeiro, João, Keith Davids, Pedro Silva, Patricia Coutinho, Daniel Barreira, and Julio Garganta. 2021. "Talent Development in Sport Requires Athlete Enrichment: Contemporary Insights from a Nonlinear Pedagogy and the Athletic Skills Model." Sports Medicine 51 (6): 1115-1122. https://doi.org/10.1007/s40279-021-01437-6.

Rorty, Richard. 1979. *Philosophy and the Mirror of Nature.* Princeton, NJ: Princeton University Press.

Schön, Donald. 1983. *The Reflective Practitioner: How Practitioners Think in action.* San Francisco: HarperCollins.

Schmidt, Richard. 1975. "A Schema Theory of Discrete Motor Skill Learning." *Psychological Review,* 82, 225-260.

Schmidt, Richard. 2003. "Motor Schema Theory After 27 Years: Reflections and Implications for a New Theory." *Research Quarterly for Exercise and Sport,* 74, 366-375.

Scott, Matthew, Greg Wood, Paul Holmes, Ben Marshall, Jacqueline Williams, and David Wright. 2023. "Combined Action Observation and Motor Imagery Improves Learning of Activities of Daily Living in Children With Developmental Coordination Disorder." *PLoS ONE* 18 (5): e0284086.

Seifert, Ludovic, and Keith Davids. 2017. "Ecological Dynamics: A Theoretical Framework for Understanding Sport Performance, Physical Education and Physical Activity." In *First Complex Systems Digital Campus World E-Conference 2015,* edited by P. Bourgine, P. Collet, and P. Parrend, 29-40. Cham, Switzerland: Springer.

Shamrock, Frank, and Charles Fleming. 2012. *Uncaged: My Life as a Champion MMA Fighter.* Chicago: Chicago Review Press.

Sims, Matt, and Giovanni Pezzulo. 2021. "Modelling Ourselves: What the Free Energy Principle Reveals About Our Implicit Notions of Representation." *Synthese* 199 (3): 7801-7833. https://doi.org/10.1007/s11229-021-03140-5.

Stanley, Jason, and John Krakauer. 2013. "Motor Skill Depends on Knowledge of Facts." *Frontiers in Human Neuroscience,* 7, 503. https://doi.org/10.3389/fnhum.2013.00503.

Stockard, Jean, Timothy Wood, and Caitlin Khoury. 2018. "The Effectiveness of Direct Instruction Curricula: A Meta-Analysis of a Half Century of Research." *Review of Educational Research* 88 (4): 479-507. https://doi.org/10.3102/0034654317751919.

Van der Weel, Fleur, and Adrian Van der Meer. 2009. "Seeing It Coming: Infants' Brain Responses to Looming Danger." *Naturwissenschaften,* 96, 1385-1391. https://doi.org/10.1007/s00114-009-0585-y.

Chapter 2

Abraham, Andrew, and Dave Collins. 2011. "Effective Skill Development—How Should Athletes' Skills Be Developed." In *Performance Psychology: A Practitioner's Guide,* edited by D. Collins, A. Button, and H. Richards, 207-230. Oxford: Elsevier.

Adams, Rick A., Stewart Shipp, and Karl Friston. 2013. "Predictions Not Commands: Active Inference in the Motor System." *Brain Structure and Function* 218 (3): 611-643. https://doi.org/10.1007/s00429-012-0475-5.

Alali, Norah N., Dave Collins, and Howie J. Carson. 2024. "A Pragmatic Approach to Skill Acquisition for Physical Education: Considering Cognitive and Ecological Perspectives." *Quest* 76 (2): 227-246. https://doi.org/10.1080/00336297.2023.2298931

Ammar, Achraf, Khaled Trabelsi, Mohamed Ali Boujelbane, Omar Boukhris, Jordan M. Glenn, Hamdi Chtourou, and Wolfgang I. Schöllhorn. 2023. "The Myth of Contextual Interference Learning Benefit in Sports Practice: A Systematic Review and Meta-Analysis." *Educational Research Review* 39 (May): 100537. https://doi.org/10.1016/j.edurev.2023.100537.

Araújo, Duarte, Robert Hristovski, Ludovic Seifert, João Carvalho, and Keith Davids. 2019. "Ecological Cognition: Expert Decision-Making Behaviour in Sport." *International Review of Sport and Exercise Psychology* 12 (1): 1-25. https://doi.org/10.1080/1750984x.2017.1349826.

Ashford, Michael, Andrew Abraham, and Jamie Poolton. 2021. "Understanding a Player's Decision-Making Process in Team Sports: A Systematic Review of Empirical Evidence". *Sports* 9 (5): 65. https://doi.org/10.3390/sports9050065.

Atkinson, Richard C., and Ernest Hilgard. 1953. *Introduction to Psychology.* Belmont, CA: Wadsworth Publishing.

Barreiros, João, Teresa Figueiredo, and Mário Godinho. 2007. "The Contextual Interference Effect in Applied Settings." *European Physical Education Review* 13 (2): 195-208. https://doi.org/10.1177/1356336X07076876.

Bobrownicki, Ray, Howie J. Carson, Alan C. MacPherson, and Dave Collins. 2022. "Unloading the Dice: Selection and Design of Comparison and Control Groups in Controlled Trials to Enhance Translational Impact within Motor Learning and Control Research." *International Journal of Sport and Exercise Psychology* 20 (5): 1330-1344. https://doi.org/10.1080/1612197X.2021.1956567.

Bobrownicki, Ray, Howie J. Carson, Alan C. MacPherson, and Dave Collins. 2023. "Constraints of the Constraints-Led Approach in American Football and Comments on Yearby et al. (2022)." *Sports Coaching Review*: Advance online publication. https://doi.org/10.1080/21640629.2022.2158579.

Bobrownicki, Ray, Alan MacPherson, Dave Collins, and Jon Sproule. 2019. "The Acute Effects of Analogy and Explicit Instruction on Movement and Performance." *Psychology of Sport and Exercise* 44 (September): 17-25. https://doi.org/10.1016/j.psychsport.2019.04.016.

Brady, Frank. 1998. "A Theoretical and Empirical Review of the Contextual Interference Effect and the Learning of Motor Skills." *Quest* 50 (3): 266-293. https://doi.org/10.1080/00336297.1998.10484285.

Carson, Howie J., and Dave Collins. 2017. "Refining Motor Skills in Golf: A Biopsychosocial Perspective." In *Routledge International Handbook of Golf Science*, edited by Martin Toms, 196-206. London: Routledge.

Chow, Jia Yi, Chris Button, Miriam Chang Yi Lee, Craig Morris, and Richard Shuttleworth. 2023. "Advice From 'Pracademics' of How to Apply Ecological Dynamics Theory to Practice Design." *Frontiers in Sports and Active Living* 5: 1192332. https://doi.org/10.3389/fspor.2023.1192332.

Christensen, Wayne, John Sutton, and Doris J.F. McIlwain. 2016. "Cognition in Skilled Action: Meshed Control and the Varieties of Skill Experience." *Mind & Language* 31 (1): 37-66. https://doi.org/10.1111/mila.12094.

Christina, Robert. W. 1987. "Motor Learning: Future Lines of Research." In *The Cutting Edge in Physical Education and Exercise Science Research*, by H.M. Eckert, edited by M.J. Safrit, 26-41. Champaign, IL: Human Kinetics.

Clark, Andy. 2015. "Predicting Peace: The End of the Representation Wars—A Reply to Michael Madary." In *Open MIND: 7(R)*, edited by Thomas K. Metzinger and Jennifer M. Windt. Frankfurt am Main: MIND Group. https://doi.org/10.15502/9783958570979.

Collins, Dave, and Sara Kamin. 2012. "The Performance Coach." In *Handbook of Sport and Performance Psychology*, edited by S. Murphy, 692-706. Oxford: Oxford University Press.

Collins, Loel, and Howie J. Carson. 2022. "Proposing a New Conceptualisation for Modern Sport Based on Environmental and Regulatory Constraints: Implications for Research, Coach Education and Professional Practice." *Journal of Adventure Education and Outdoor Learning* 22 (3): 228-238. https://doi.org/10.1080/14729679.2021.1902829.

Correia, Vanda, João Carvalho, Duarte Araújo, Elsa Pereira, and Keith Davids. 2019. "Principles of Nonlinear Pedagogy in Sport Practice." *Physical Education and Sport Pedagogy* 24 (2): 117-132. https://doi.org/10.1080/17408989.2018.1552673.

Firestone, Chaz, and Brian J. Scholl. 2016. "Cognition Does Not Affect Perception: Evaluating the Evidence for 'Top-Down' Effects." *Behavioral and Brain Sciences* 39 (January): e229. https://doi.org/10.1017/S0140525X15000965.

Frank, Cornelia, Sarah N. Kraeutner, Martina Rieger, and Shaun G. Boe. 2023. "Learning Motor Actions via Imagery—Perceptual or Motor Learning?" *Psychological Research*: Advance online publication. https://doi.org/10.1007/s00426-022-01787-4.

Friston, Karl, Jérémie Mattout, and James Kilner. 2011. "Action Understanding and Active Inference." *Biological Cybernetics* 104 (1-2): 137-160. https://doi.org/10.1007/s00422-011-0424-z.

Friston, Karl, Christopher Thornton, and Andy Clark. 2012. "Free-Energy Minimization and the Dark-Room Problem." *Frontiers in Psychology* 3 (May): 130. https://doi.org/10.3389/fpsyg.2012.00130.

Gibson, James J. 1966. "The Problem of Temporal Order in Stimulation and Perception." *The Journal of Psychology* 62 (2): 141-149. https://doi.org/10.1080/00223980.1966.10543777.

Gibson, James J. 1979. *The Ecological Approach to Visual Perception: Classic Edition*. New York: Psychology Press.

Goode, Sinah, and Richard McGill. 1986. "Contextual Interference Effects in Learning Three Badminton Serves." *Research Quarterly for Exercise and Sport* 57 (4): 308-314. https://doi.org/10.1080/02701367.1986.10608091

Handford, Craig, Keith Davids, Simon Bennett, and Chris Button. 1997. "Skill Acquisition in Sport: Some Applications of an Evolving Practice Ecology." *Journal of Sports Sciences* 15 (6): 621-640. https://doi.org/10.1080/026404197367056.

Harris, David J., Tom Arthur, David P. Broadbent, Mark R. Wilson, Samuel J. Vine, and Oliver R. Runswick. 2022. "An Active Inference Account of Skilled Anticipation in Sport: Using Computational Models to Formalise Theory and Generate New Hypotheses." *Sports Medicine* 52 (9): 2023-2038. https://doi.org/10.1007/s40279-022-01689-w

Hays, Kate, Ian Maynard, Owen Thomas, and Mark Bawden. 2007. "Sources and Types of Confidence Identified by World Class Sport Performers." *Journal of Applied Sport Psychology* 19 (4): 434-456. https://doi.org/10.1080/10413200701599173.

Khezri, Bijan. 2022. *Governing Continuous Transformation: Re-Framing the Strategy-Governance Conversation*. Contributions to Management Science. Cham, Switzerland: Springer.

Kiverstein, Julian, Mark Miller, and Erik Rietveld. 2019. "The Feeling of Grip: Novelty, Error Dynamics, and the Predictive Brain." *Synthese* 196 (7): 2847-2869. https://doi.org/10.1007/s11229-017-1583-9.

Kogo, Naoki, and Chris Trengove. 2015. "Is Predictive Coding Theory Articulated Enough to Be Testable?" *Frontiers in Computational Neuroscience* 9: 111.

Krein, Kevin, and Jesús Ilundáin-Agurruza. 2017. "High-Level Enactive and Embodied Cognition in Expert Sport Performance." *Sport, Ethics and Philosophy* 11 (3): 370-384. https://doi.org/10.1080/17511321.2017.1334004.

Landin, Dennis, and Edward P. Hebert. 1997. "A Comparison of Three Practice Schedules Along the Contextual Interference Continuum." *Research Quarterly for Exercise and Sport* 68 (4): 357-361. https://doi.org/10.1080/02701367.1997.10608017.

Lang, Peter J., Michael J. Kozak, Gregory A. Miller, Daniel N. Levin, and Alvin McLean Jr. 1980. "Emotional Imagery: Conceptual Structure and Pattern of Somato-Visceral Response." *Psychophysiology* 17 (2): 179-192. https://doi.org/10.1111/j.1469-8986.1980.tb00133.x.

Lee, Tim. 2012. "Contextual Interference: Generalizability and Limitations." In *Skill Acquisition in Sport: Research, Theory and Practice*, edited by N. J. Hodges and A. M. Williams, 2nd ed., 79-93. London: Routledge.

Lewin, Kurt. 1943. "Psychology and the Process of Group Living." *The Journal of Social Psychology* 17 (1): 113-131. https://doi.org/10.1080/00224545.1943.9712269.

Lindberg, Kolbjørn, Thomas Bjørnsen, Fredrik T. Vårvik, Gøran Paulsen, Malene Joensen, Morten Kristoffersen, Ole Sveen, et al. 2023. "The Effects of Being Told You Are in the Intervention Group on Training Results: A Pilot Study." *Scientific Reports* 13 (1): 1972. https://doi.org/10.1038/s41598-023-29141-7.

Linson, Adam, Andy Clark, Subramanian Ramamoorthy, and Karl Friston. 2018. "The Active Inference Approach to Ecological Perception: General Information Dynamics for Natural and Artificial Embodied Cognition." *Frontiers in Robotics and AI* 5 (March): 21. https://doi.org/10.3389/frobt.2018.00021.

Masters, Rich S. W. 1992. "Knowledge, Knerves and Know-How: The Role of Explicit Versus Implicit Knowledge in the Breakdown of a Complex Motor Skill Under Pressure." *British Journal of Psychology* 83 (3), 343–358. https://doi.org/10.1111/j.2044-8295.1992.tb02446.x

Masters, Rich, and Jon Maxwell. 2008. "The Theory of Reinvestment." *International Review of Sport and Exercise Psychology* 1 (2): 160-183. https://doi.org/10.1080/17509840802287218.

Maurer, Heiko, and Jörn Munzert. 2013. "Influence of Attentional Focus on Skilled Motor Performance: Performance Decrement Under Unfamiliar Focus Conditions." *Human Movement Science* 32 (4): 730-740. https://doi.org/10.1016/j.humov.2013.02.001.

Meier, Christopher, Cornelia Frank, Bernd Gröben, and Thomas Schack. 2020. "Verbal Instructions and Motor Learning: How Analogy and Explicit Instructions Influence the Development of Mental Representations and Tennis Serve Performance." *Frontiers in Psychology* 11: 2. https://doi.org/10.3389/fpsyg.2020.00002

Moffat, David, Dave Collins, and Howie J. Carson. 2017. "Target Versus Ball Focused Aiming When Putting: What Has Been Done and What Has Been Missed". *International Journal of Golf Science* 6 (1): 35-55. https://doi.org/10.1123/ijgs.2017-0002.

Orr, Steven, Andrew Cruickshank, and Howie J. Carson. 2021. "From the Lesson Tee to the Course: A Naturalistic Investigation of Attentional Focus in Elite Golf." *The Sport Psychologist* 35 (4): 305-319. https://doi.org/10.1123/tsp.2021-0003.

Parr, Thomas, Giovanni Pezzulo, and Karl Friston. 2022. *Active Inference: The Free Energy Principle in Mind, Brain, and Behavior.* Cambridge, MA: MIT Press.

Raab, Markus, and Duarte Araújo. 2019. "Embodied Cognition With and Without Mental Representations: The Case of Embodied Choices in Sports." *Frontiers in Psychology* 10, 1825. https://doi.org/10.3389/fpsyg.2019.01825

Richards, Pam, Dave Collins, & Duncan R.D. Mascarenhas. 2017. "Developing Team Decision-Making: A Holistic Framework Integrating Both On-Field and Off-Field Pedagogical Coaching Processes". *Sports Coaching Review* 6 (1): 57-75. https://doi.org/10.1080/21640629.2016.1200819

Salmoni, Alan, Richard Schmidt, and Charles Walter. 1984. "Knowledge of Results and Motor Learning: A Review and Critical Reappraisal." *Psychological Bulletin* 95 (3): 355-386. https://doi.org/10.1037/0033-2909.95.3.355.

Schempp, Paul, Bryan McCullick, Peter St. Pierre, Sophie Woorons, Jeongae You, and Betsy Clark. 2004. "Expert Golf Instructors' Student-Teacher Interaction Patterns." *Research Quarterly for Exercise and Sport* 75 (1): 60-70. https://doi.org/10.1080/02701367.2004.10609134.

Seifert, Ludovic, Duarte Araújo, John Komar, and Keith Davids. 2017. "Understanding Constraints on Sport Performance From the Complexity Sciences Paradigm: An Ecological Dynamics Framework." *Human Movement Science* 56 (December): 178-180. https://doi.org/10.1016/j.humov.2017.05.001.

Silva Pedro, Júlio Garganta, Duarte Araújo, Keith Davids, and Paulo Aguiar. 2013. "Shared Knowledge or Shared Affordances? Insights From an Ecological Dynamics Approach to Team Coordination in Sports." *Sports Medicine* 43 (9): 765-772. https://doi.org/10.1007/s40279-013-0070-9

Sun, Zekun, and Chaz Firestone. 2020. "The Dark Room Problem." *Trends in Cognitive Sciences* 24 (5): 346-348. https://doi.org/10.1016/j.tics.2020.02.006.

Taylor, Robin D., Jamie Taylor, Michael Ashford, and Rosie Collins. 2023. "Contemporary Pedagogy? The Use of Theory in Practice: An Evidence-Informed Perspective." *Frontiers in Sports and Active Living* 5: 1113564. https://doi.org/10.3389/fspor.2023.1113564.

Van den Bossche, Piet, Wim Gijselaers, Mien Segers, Geert Woltjer, and Paul Kirschner. 2011. "Team Learning: Building Shared Mental Models." *Instructional Science* 39 (3): 283-301. https://doi.org/10.1007/s11251-010-9128-3.

Walsh, Kevin S., David P. McGovern, Andy Clark, and Redmond G. O'Connell. 2020. "Evaluating the Neurophysiological Evidence for Predictive Processing as a Model of Perception." *Annals of the New York Academy of Sciences* 1464 (1): 242-268. https://doi.org/10.1111/nyas.14321.

Williams, Sarah E, Sam J. Cooley, Elliott Newell, Fredrik Weibull, and Jennifer Cumming. 2013. "Seeing the Difference: Developing Effective Imagery Scripts for Athletes". *Journal of Sport Psychology in Action* 4 (2): 109-121. https://doi.org/10.1080/21520704.2013.781560

References

Willingham, Daniel T. 2009. "Three Problems in the Marriage of Neuroscience and Education." *Cortex: A Journal Devoted to the Study of the Nervous System and Behavior* 45 (4): 544-545. https://doi.org/10.1016/j.cortex.2008.05.009.

Wrisberg, Craig A., and Zhan Liu. 1991. "The Effect of Contextual Variety on the Practice, Retention, and Transfer of an Applied Motor Skill." *Research Quarterly for Exercise and Sport* 62 (4): 406-412. https://doi.org/10.1080/02701367.1991.10607541.

Wulf, Gabriele, Nancy McNevin, and Charles H. Shea. 2001. "The Automaticity of Complex Motor Skill Learning as a Function of Attentional Focus." *The Quarterly Journal of Experimental Psychology Section A* 54 (4): 1143-1154. https://doi.org/10.1080/713756012.

Yearby, Tyler, Shawn Myszka, William M. Roberts, Carl T. Woods, & Keith Davids. 2022. "Applying an Ecological Approach to Practice Design in American Football: Some Case Examples on Best Practice." *Sports Coaching Review*: Advance online publication. https://doi.org/10.1080/21640629.2022.2057698

Chapter 3

Abraham, Andrew, and Dave Collins. 2011. "Effective Skill Development." In *Performance Psychology: A Practitioner's Guide*, edited by Dave Collins, Angela Button, and Hugh Richards, 207-229. Edinburgh: Elsevier.

Aguilar, Francis Joseph. 1967. *Scanning the Business Environment*. New York: MacMillan.

Argyris, Chris. 1996. Organizational learning II. *Theory, method, and practice.*

Bailin, S., Case, R., Coombs, J.R. and Daniels, L.B., 1999. Conceptualizing critical thinking. *Journal of curriculum studies*, 31(3), pp.285-302. https://doi.org/10.1080/002202799183133

Bailey, Catherine. 2011. "Working through the ZOUD." *Management Focus* 30 (Spring): 14-15.

Barry, Martin., Loel Collins, and Dave Grecic, 2023. Differences in epistemological beliefs in a group of high-level UK based caving, mountaineering and rock-climbing instructors. *Journal of Adventure Education and Outdoor Learning*, pp.1-21. http://doi.org.1080/14729679.2023.2220834

Becker, Andrea J. 2009. "It's Not What They Do, It's How They Do It: Athlete Experiences of Great Coaching." *International Journal of Sports Science & Coaching* 4 (1): 93-119. https:// doi.org/10.1260/1747-9541.4.1.93

Benzies, Karen M., Shahirose Premji, K. Alix Hayden, and Karen Serrett. 2006. "State-of-the-Evidence Reviews: Advantages and Challenges of Including Grey Literature." *Worldviews on Evidence-Based Nursing* 3 (2): 55-61. https://doi.org/10.1111/j.1741-6787.2006.00051.x.

Bobrownicki, Ray, and Stephanie Valentin. 2022. "Adding Experiential Layers to the Transnational-Athlete Concept: A Narrative Review of Real-World Heterogeneous Mobility Experiences." *Psychology of Sport and Exercise* 58: Article 102075. https://doi.org/10.1016/j.psychsport.2021.102075.

Bobrownicki, Ray, Howie J. Carson, Alan C. MacPherson, and Dave Collins. 2023. "Constraints of the Constraints-Led Approach in American Football and Comments on Yearby et Al. (2022)." *Sports Coaching Review*, 1-13. https://doi.org/10.1080/21640629.2022.2158579.

Carbonell, Katerina Bohle, Karen D. Könings, Mien Segers, and Jeroen J. G. van Merriënboer. 2016. "Measuring Adaptive Expertise: Development and Validation of an Instrument." *European Journal of Work and Organizational Psychology* 25 (2): 167-180. https://doi.org/10.1080/1359432X.2015.1036858.

Christian, Ed, Christopher I. Hodgson, Matt Berry, and Phil Kearney. 2020. "It's Not What, but Where: How the Accentuated Features of the Adventure Sports Coaching Environment Promote the Development of Sophisticated Epistemic Beliefs." *Journal of Adventure Education and Outdoor Learning* 20 (1): 68-80. https://doi.org/10.1080/14729679.2019.1598879.

Collins, Dave, Alan C. MacPherson, Ray Bobrownicki, and Howie J. Carson. 2023. "An Explicit Look at Implicit Learning: An Interrogative Review for Sport Coaching Research and Practice." *Sports Coaching Review*, 1-22. https://doi.org/10.1080/21640629.2023.2179300.

Collins, Dave, Jamie Taylor, Mike Ashford, and Loel Collins. 2022. "It Depends Coaching—The Most Fundamental, Simple and Complex Principle or a Mere Copout?" *Sports Coaching Review*, 1-21. https://doi.org/10.1080/21640629.2022.2154189.

Collins, Loel. and Chris Eastabrook, 2023. The importance of critical thinking in coaching: Separating the wheat from the chaff. In *Developing Sport Coaches* Edited by Christine Nash, 119-132. Routledge.

Collins, Loel, and Howie J. Carson. 2022. "Proposing a New Conceptualisation for Modern Sport Based on Environmental and Regulatory Constraints: Implications for Research, Coach Education and Professional Practice." *Journal of Adventure Education and Outdoor Learning* 22 (3): 228-238. https://doi.org/10.1080/14729679.2021.1902829.

Collins, Loel, and Dave Collins. 2015. "Integration of Professional Judgement and Decision-Making in High-Level Adventure Sports Coaching Practice." *Journal of Sports Sciences* 33 (6): 622-633. https://doi.org/10.1080/02640414.2014.953980.

Collins, Loel, and Dave Collins. 2016. "Professional Judgement and Decision-Making in Adventure Sports Coaching: The Role of Interaction." *Journal of Sports Sciences* 34 (13): 1231-1239. https://doi.org/10.1080/02640414.2015.1105379.

Collins, Loel. and Dave Collins, 2016. Professional judgement and decision-making in the planning process of high-level adventure sports coaching practice. *Journal of Adventure Education and Outdoor Learning*, 16(3), pp.256-268. http:// doi.org. 10.1080/14729679.2016.1162182

Collins, Loel. and Dave Collins, 2021. Managing the cognitive loads associated with judgment and decision-making in a group of adventure sports coaches: A mixed-method investigation. *Journal of Adventure Education and Outdoor Learning*, 21(1), pp.1-16.http://doi.org.10.10.80/14729679.2019.1686041

Collins, Dave., Tom Willmott, and Loel Collins, 2018. Periodization and self-regulation in action sports: coping with the emotional load. *Frontiers in psychology*, 9, 1652. *http:// doi.org. 10.3389/fpsyg.2018.01652*

Collins, Loel, Howie J. Carson, and Dave Collins. 2016. "Metacognition and Professional Judgment and Decision Making in Coaching: Importance, Application and Evaluation." *International Sport Coaching Journal* 3 (3): 355-361. https://doi.org/10.1123/iscj.2016-0037.

Collins, Loel, Dave Collins, and David Grecic. 2015. "The Epistemological Chain in High-Level Adventure Sports Coaches." *Journal of Adventure Education and Outdoor Learning* 15 (3): 224-238. https://doi.org/10.1080/14729679.2014.950592.

Crawford, Valerie M., Mark S. Schlager, Yukie Toyama, Margaret Mary Riel, and Phil Vahey. 2005. "Characterizing Adaptive Expertise in Science Teaching." In *American Educational Research Association Annual Conference, Montreal, Quebec, Canada* (pp. 1-26).

Culver, Diane M., Penny Werthner, and Pierre Trudel. 2019. "Coach Developers as 'Facilitators of Learning' in a Large-Scale Coach Education Programme: One Actor in a Complex System." *International Sport Coaching Journal* 6 (3): 296-306.

Dewey, J. 1938. *Experience and Education*. New York: Macmillan.

Eastabrook, C. and Collins, L., 2021. What do participants perceive as the attributes of a good adventure sports coach?. *Journal of Adventure Education and Outdoor Learning*, 21(2), pp.115-128. http:// doi.org.:10.1080/14729679.2020.1730207

Eaton, Sarah Elaine. 2018. "Educational Research Literature Reviews: Understanding the Hierarchy of Sources." *Journal of Educational Thought*, February, 22(3), 239-249.

Endsley, Mica R. 1995. "Toward a Theory of Situation Awareness in Dynamic Systems." *Human Factors* 37 (1): 32-64. https://doi.org/10.1518/001872095779049543.

Engel, George.L., 1977. The need for a new medical model: a challenge for biomedicine. *Science*, 196(4286), pp.129-136.

Ennis, R.H., 1962. A concept of critical thinking. *Harvard educational review*.

Ennis, R.H., 2015. Critical thinking: A streamlined conception. In *The Palgrave handbook of critical thinking in higher education* (pp. 31-47). New York: Palgrave Macmillan US.

Grecic, David, and Dave Collins. 2013. "The Epistemological Chain: Practical Applications in Sports." *Quest* 65 (2): 151-168. https://doi.org/10.1080/00336297.2013.773525.

Hatano, Giyoo, and Kayoko Inagaki. 1986. "Two Courses of Expertise." In *Child Development and Education in Japan*, edited by H.W. Stevenson, H. Azuma, and K. Hakuta, 262-272. New York: Freeman.

Hatano, Giyoo, and Yoko Oura. 2003. "Commentary: Reconceptualizing School Learning Using Insight From Expertise Research." *Educational Researcher* 32 (8): 26-29. https://doi.org/10.3102/0013189X032008026.

Hattie, John, Deb Masters, and Kate Birch. 2015. *Visible Learning Into Action: International Case Studies of Impact*. Abingdon, UK: Routledge.

Hoffman, Robert R., Paul Ward, Paul J. Feltovich, Lia DiBello, Stephen M. Fiore, and Dee H. Andrews. 2014. *Accelerated Expertise: Training for High Proficiency in a Complex World*. New York: Psychology Press.

Howard, Bruce C., Steven McGee, Neil Schwartz, and Steve Purcell. 2000. "The Experience of Constructivism: Transforming Teacher Epistemology." *Journal of Research on Computing in Education* 32 (4): 455-465. https://doi.org/10.1080/08886504.2000.10782291.

Jones, Robyn L., and Mike Wallace. 2006. "The Coach as 'Orchestrator': More Realistically Managing the Complex Coaching Context." In *The Sports Coach as Educator: Reconceptualising Sports Coaching*, edited by Robyn L. Jones, 51-64. Abingdon, UK: Routledge.

Jowett, Sophia, and Katelynn Slade. 2021. "Understanding the Coach-Athlete Relationship and the Role of Ability, Intentions and Integrity." In *Athletic Development: A Psychological Perspective*, edited by Caroline Heaney, Nichola Kentzer, and Ben Oakley, 1-25. London: Routledge.

Klein, Gary. 2007. "Flexecution as a Paradigm for Replanning, Part 1." *IEEE Intelligent Systems* 22 (5): 79-83. https://doi.org/10.1109/MIS.2007.4338498.

Lipman, Matthew. 1987. "Critical Thinking: What Can It Be?" *Analytic Teaching* 8 (1): 5-12.

Lyle, John. 2002. *Sports Coaching Concepts: A Framework for Coaches' Behaviour*. London: Routledge.

Martindale, Amanda, and Dave Collins. 2005. "Professional Judgement and Decision Making: The Role of Intention for Impact." *The Sport Psychologist* 19 (3): 303. https://doi.org/10.1123/tsp.19.3.303.

Mees, Alice, and Loel Collins. 2022. "Doing the Right Thing, in the Right Place, with the Right People, at the Right Time; a Study of the Development of Judgment and Decision Making in Mid-Career Outdoor Instructors." *Journal of Adventure Education and Outdoor Learning*, 1-17. https://doi.org/10.1080/14729679.2022.2100800.

Mees, Alice., Tynke Toering, and Loel Collins, 2022. Exploring the development of judgement and decision making in 'competent' outdoor instructors. *Journal of Adventure Education and Outdoor Learning*, 22(1), pp.77-91. http://doi.org.10/1080/14729679.2021.1884105

Mees, Alice, Dean Sinfield, Dave Collins, and Loel Collins. 2020. "Adaptive Expertise—A Characteristic of Expertise in Outdoor Instructors?" *Physical Education and Sport Pedagogy* 25 (4): 423-438. https://doi.org/10.1080/17408989.2020.1727870.

Nash, Christine, Alan C. MacPherson, and Dave Collins. 2022. "Reflections on Reflection: Clarifying and Promoting Use in Experienced Coaches." *Frontiers in Psychology*, 13, 867720. https://doi.org/10.3389/fpsyg.2022.867720.

Nelson, Lee J., Christopher J. Cushion, and Paul Potrac. 2006. "Formal, Nonformal and Informal Coach Learning: A Holistic Conceptualisation." *International Journal of Sports Science & Coaching* 1 (3): 247-259. https://doi.org/10.1260/174795406778604627.

Nonaka, Ikujiro, and Ryoko Toyama. 2003. "The Knowledge-Creating Theory Revisited: Knowledge Creation as a Synthesizing Process." *Knowledge Management Research & Practice* 1 (1): 2-10. https://doi.org/10.1057/palgrave.kmrp.8500001.

Perry, William.G., 2014. Cognitive and ethical growth: The making of meaning. In *College student development and academic life* (pp. 48-87). Routledge.

Schommer, Marlene. 1994. "Synthesizing Epistemological Belief Research: Tentative Understandings and Provocative Confusions." *Educational Psychology Review* 6 (4): 293-319. https://doi.org/10.1007/BF02213418.

Schön, Donald. 1983. *The Reflective Practitioner: How Professionals Think in Action*. Aldershot, UK: Ashgate.

Simon, Scott, Loel Collins, and Dave Collins. 2017. "Observational Heuristics in a Group of High Level Paddle Sports Coaches." *International Sport Coaching Journal* 4 (2): 23-245. https://doi.org/10.1123/iscj.2017-0012.

Stanovich, Keith E., and Paula J. Stanovich. 2010. "A Framework for Critical Thinking, Rational Thinking, and Intelligence." In *Innovations in Educational Psychology: Perspectives on Learning, Teaching, and Human Development*, edited by David D. Preiss and Robert J. Sternberg, 195-237. New York: Springer.

Stoszkowski, John, Áine MacNamara, Dave Collins, and Aran Hodgkinson. 2020. "'Opinion and Fact, Perspective and Truth': Seeking Truthfulness and Integrity in Coaching and Coach Education." *International Sport Coaching Journal* 8 (2): 263-269. https://doi.org/10.1123/iscj.2020-0023.

Tiller, Nicholas B., John P. Sullivan, and Panteleimon Ekkekakis. 2022. "Baseless Claims and Pseudoscience in Health and Wellness: A Call to Action for the Sports, Exercise, and Nutrition-Science Community." *Sports Medicine*, 53, 1-5. https://doi.org/10.1007/s40279-022-01702-2.

Trotter, Margaret J., Paul M. Salmon, Natassia Goode, and Michael G. Lenné. 2018. "Distributed Improvisation: A Systems Perspective of Improvisation 'Epics' by Led Outdoor Activity Leaders." *Ergonomics* 61 (2): 295-312. https://doi.org/10.1080/00140139.2017.1355071.

Chapter 4

Abdollahipour, Reza, Gabriele Wulf, Rudolf Psotta, and Miriam Palomo Nieto. 2015. "Performance of Gymnastics Skill Benefits From an External Focus of Attention." *Journal of Sports Sciences* 33 (17): 1807-1813. https://doi.org/ 10.1080/02640414.2015.1012102.

Al-Abood, Saleh A., Simon J. Bennett, Francisco Moreno Hernandez, Derek Ashford, and Keith Davids. 2002. "Effect of Verbal Instructions and Image Size on Visual Search Strategies in Basketball Free Throw Shooting." *Journal of Sports Sciences* 20 (3): 271-278. https://doi.org/10.1080/026404102317284817.

Araújo, Duarte, and Keith Davids. 2016. "Team Synergies in Sport: Theory and Measures." *Frontiers in Psychology*, 7, 1449. https://doi.org/10.3389/fpsyg.2016.01449.

Barker, Jamie B., Matthew J. Slater, Geoff Pugh, Stephen D. Mellalieu, Paul J. McCarthy, Marc V. Jones, and Aidan Moran. 2020. "The Effectiveness of Psychological Skills Training and Behavioral Interventions in Sport Using Single-Case Designs: A Meta Regression Analysis of the Peer-Reviewed Studies." *Psychology of Sport and Exercise*, 51 (November), 101746. https://doi.org/10.1016/j.psychsport.2020.101746.

Beilock, Sian L., and Thomas H. Carr. 2001. "On the Fragility of Skilled Performance: What Governs Choking Under Pressure?" *Journal of Experimental Psychology: General* 130 (4): 701-725. https://doi.org/10.1037/0096-3445.130.4.701.

Beilock, Sian L., Thomas H. Carr, Clare MacMahon, and Janet L. Starkes. 2002. "When Paying Attention Becomes Counterproductive: Impact of Divided Versus Skill-Focused Attention on Novice and Experienced Performance of Sensorimotor Skills." *Journal of Experimental Psychology: Applied* 8 (1): 6-16. https://doi.org/10.1037/1076-898x.8.1.6.

Bennett, Simon, Christopher Button, Damian Kingsbury, and Keith Davids. 1999. "Manipulating Visual Informational Constraints During Practice Enhances the Acquisition of Catching Skill in Children." *Research Quarterly for Exercise and Sport* 70 (3): 220-232. https://doi.org/10.1080/02701367.1999.10608042.

Bernier, Marjorie, Christiane Trottier, Emilie Thienot, and Jean Fournier. 2016. "An Investigation of Attentional Foci and Their Temporal Patterns: A Naturalistic Study in Expert Figure Skaters." *The Sport Psychologist* 30 (3): 256-266. https://doi.org/10.1123/tsp.2013-0076.

Bobrownicki, Ray, Howie J. Carson, and Dave Collins. 2022. "Conducting Systematic Reviews of Applied Interventions: A Comment on Cabral et al. (2022)." *Sport, Exercise, and Performance Psychology* 11 (3): 264-274. https://doi.org/10.1037/spy0000299.

Bobrownicki, Ray, Howie J. Carson, Alan C. MacPherson, and Dave Collins. 2022. "Unloading the Dice: Selection and Design of Comparison and Control Groups in Controlled Trials to Enhance Translational Impact Within

Motor Learning and Control Research." *International Journal of Sport and Exercise Psychology* 20 (5): 1330-1344. https://doi.org/10.1080/1612197X.2021.1956567.

Bobrownicki, Ray, Howie J. Carson, Alan C. MacPherson, and Dave Collins. 2023. "Constraints of the Constraints-Led Approach in American Football and Comments on Yearby et al. (2022)." *Sports Coaching Review*: Advance online publication. https://doi.org/10.1080/21640629.2022.2158579.

Bobrownicki, Ray, Dave Collins, John Sproule, and Alan C. MacPherson. 2018. "Redressing the Balance: Commentary on 'Examining Motor Learning in Older Adults Using Analogy Instruction' by Tse, Wong, and Masters (2017)." *Psychology of Sport & Exercise* 38 (1): 211-214. https://doi.org/10.1016/j.psychsport.2018.05.014.

Bobrownicki, Ray, Alan C. MacPherson, Simon G.S. Coleman, Dave Collins, and John Sproule. 2015. "Re-Examining the Effects of Verbal Instructional Type on Early Stage Motor Learning." *Human Movement Science*, 44 (December), 168-181. https://doi.org/10.1016/j.humov.2015.08.023.

Button, Chris, Keith Davids, Simon J. Bennett, and Geert J.P. Savelsbergh. 2002. "Anticipatory Responses to Perturbation of Co-Ordination in One-Handed Catching." *Acta Psychologica* 109 (1): 75-93. https://doi.org/10.1016/S0001-6918(01)00052-X.

Carson, Howie J., and Dave Collins. 2011. "Refining and Regaining Skills in Fixation/Diversification Stage Performers: The Five-A Model." *International Review of Sport and Exercise Psychology* 4 (2): 146-167. https://doi.org/10.1080/1750984x.2011.613682.

Christensen, Wayne, John Sutton, and Doris J.F. McIlwain. 2016. "Cognition in Skilled Action: Meshed Control and the Varieties of Skill Experience." *Mind and Language* 31 (1): 37-66. https://doi.org/10.1111/mila.12094.

Christina, Robert W. 1987. "Motor Learning: Future Lines of Research." In *The Cutting Edge in Physical Education and Exercise Science Research*, edited by M.J. Safrit and H.M. Eckert, 26-41. Champaign, IL: Human Kinetics.

Christina, Robert W. 2017. "Motor Control and Learning in the North American Society for the Psychology of Sport and Physical Activity (NASPSPA): The First 40 Years." *Kinesiology Review*, 6 (3), 221-231. https://doi.org/10.1123/kr.2017-0018.

Claxton, Guy. 2002. *Building Learning Power: Helping Young People Become Better Learners*. Bristol, UK: TLO Limited.

Collins, Dave, Howie J. Carson, and John Toner. 2016. "Letter to the Editor Concerning the Article 'Performance of Gymnastics Skill Benefits From an External Focus of Attention' by Abdollahipour, Wulf, Psotta & Nieto (2015)." *Journal of Sports Sciences* 34 (13): 1288-1292. https://doi.org/10.1080/02640414.2015.1098782.

Collins, Dave, and Sara Kamin. 2012. "The Performance Coach." In *The Oxford Handbook of Sport and Performance Psychology*, edited by S.M. Murphy, 692-706. New York: Oxford University Press.

Collins, Dave, Alan C. MacPherson, Ray Bobrownicki, and Howie J. Carson. 2023. "An Explicit Look at Implicit Learning: An Interrogative Review for Sport Coaching Research and Practice." *Sports Coaching Review*: Advance online publication. https://doi.org/10.1080/21640629.2023.2179300.

Collins, Loel, and Dave Collins. 2019. "The Role of 'Pracademics' in Education and Development of Adventure Sport Professionals." *Journal of Adventure Education and Outdoor Learning* 19 (1): 1-11. https://doi.org/10.1080/14729679.2018.1483253.

Collins, Rosie, Dave Collins, and Howie J. Carson. 2022. "Muscular Collision Chess: A Qualitative Exploration of the Role and Development of Cognition, Understanding and Knowledge in Elite-Level Decision Making." *International Journal of Sport and Exercise Psychology* 20 (3): 828-848. https://doi.org/10.1080/1612197X.2021.1907768.

Collins, Rosie, David Moffat, Howie J. Carson, and Dave Collins. 2023. "Where You Look During Golf Putting Makes No Difference to Skilled Golfers (but What You Look at Might!): An Examination of Occipital EEG α-Power During Target and Ball Focused Aiming." *International Journal of Sport and Exercise Psychology* 21 (3): 456-472. https://doi.org/10.1080/1612197X.2022.2066706.

Deuker, Albert, Bjoern Braunstein, Jia Yi Chow, Maximilian Fichtl, Hyoek Kim, Swen Körner, and Robert Rein. 2023. "'Train as You Play': Improving Effectiveness of Training in Youth Soccer Players." *International Journal of Sports Science & Coaching* 19 (2): 677-868. https://doi.org/10.1177/17479541231172702.

di Fronso, Selenia, Claudio Robazza, Edson Filho, Laura Bortoli, Silvia Comani, and Maurizio Bertollo. 2016. "Neural Markers of Performance States in an Olympic Athlete: An EEG Case Study in Air-Pistol Shooting." *Journal of Sports Science and Medicine* 15 (2): 214-222.

di Fronso, Selenia, Gabriella Tamburro, Claudio Robazza, Laura Bortoli, Silvia Comani, and Maurizio Bertollo. 2018. "Focusing Attention on Muscle Exertion Increases EEG Coherence in an Endurance Cycling Task." *Frontiers in Psychology*, 9, 1249. https://doi.org/10.3389/fpsyg.2018.01249.

English, Horace B. 1942. "How Psychology Can Facilitate Military Training—A Concrete Example." *Journal of Applied Psychology* 26 (1): 3-7. https://doi.org/10.1037/h0060298.

Fitts, Paul M., and Michael I. Posner. 1967. *Human Performance*. Belmont, CA: Brooks/Cole.

Fitts, Paul M., and Barbara K. Radford. 1966. "Information Capacity of Discrete Motor Responses Under Different Cognitive Sets." *Journal of Experimental Psychology* 71 (4): 475-482. https://doi.org/10.1037/h0022970.

Fitzpatrick, Anna, Keith Davids, and Joseph Antony Stone. 2017. "Effects of Lawn Tennis Association Mini Tennis as Task Constraints on Children's Match-Play Characteristics." *Journal of Sports Sciences* 35 (22): 2204-2210. https://doi.org/10.1080/02640414.2016.1261179.

Frank, Cornelia, Sarah N. Kraeutner, Martina Rieger, and Shaun G. Boe. 2023. "Learning Motor Actions via Imagery—Perceptual or Motor Learning?" *Psychological Research*: Advance online publicationhttps://doi.org/10.1007/s00426-022-01787-4.

Gallicchio, Germano, Andrew Cooke, and Christopher Ring. 2016. "Lower Left Temporal-Frontal Connectivity Characterizes Expert and Accurate Performance: High-Alpha T7-Fz Connectivity as a Marker of Conscious Processing During Movement." *Sport, Exercise, and Performance Psychology* 5 (1): 14-24. https://doi.org10.1037/spy0000055.

Giblin, Georgia, Damian Farrow, Machar Reid, Kevin Ball, and Bruce Abernethy. 2015. "Exploring the Kinaesthetic Sensitivity of Skilled Performers for Implementing Movement Instructions." *Human Movement Science*, 41 (June), 76-91. https://doi.org/10.1016/j.humov.2015.02.006.

Goginsky, Alesia M., and Dave Collins. 1996. "Research Design and Mental Practice." *Journal of Sports Sciences* 14 (5): 381-392. https://doi.org/10.1080/02640419608727725.

Gray, Rob. 2018. "Comparing Cueing and Constraints Interventions for Increasing Launch Angle in Baseball Batting." *Sport, Exercise, and Performance Psychology* 7 (3):318-332. https://doi.org/10.1037/spy0000131.

Gray, Rob. 2020. "Comparing the Constraints Led Approach, Differential Learning and Prescriptive Instruction for Training Opposite-Field Hitting in Baseball." *Psychology of Sport and Exercise* 51 (November): 101797. https://doi.org/10.1016/j.psychsport.2020.101797.

Handford, Craig, Keith Davids, Simon Bennett, and Chris Button. 1997. "Skill Acquisition in Sport: Some Applications of an Evolving Practice Ecology." *Journal of Sports Sciences* 15 (6): 621-640. https://doi.org/10.1080/026404197367056.

Herrebrøden, Henrik. 2023. "Motor Performers Need Task-Relevant Information: Proposing an Alternative Mechanism for the Attentional Focus Effect." *Journal of Motor Behavior* 55 (1): 125-134. https://doi.org/10.1080/00222895.2022.2122920.

Higgins, Joseph R., and Ronald W. Angle. 1970. "Correction of Tracking Errors Without Sensory Feedback." *Journal of Experimental Psychology* 84 (3): 412-416. https://doi.org/10.1037/h0029275.

Hristovski, Robert, Keith Davids, Duarte Araújo, and Chris Button. 2006. "How Boxers Decide to Punch a Target: Emergent Behaviour in Nonlinear Dynamical Systems." *Journal of Sports Science and Medicine*, 5, 60-73.

Jackson, Robin C., and Julien S. Baker. 2001. "Routines, Rituals, and Rugby: Case Study of a World Class Goal Kicker." *The Sport Psychologist* 15 (1): 48-65. https://doi.org/10.1123/tsp.15.1.48.

Lam, Wing Kai, Jon P. Maxwell, and Richard Masters. 2009. "Analogy Learning and the Performance of Motor Skills Under Pressure." *Journal of Sport & Exercise Psychology* 31 (3): 337-357. https://doi.org/10.1123/jsep.31.3.337.

Leavitt, Harold J., and Harold Schlosberg. 1944. "The Retention of Verbal and of Motor Skills." *Journal of Experimental Psychology* 34 (5): 404-417. https://doi.org/10.1037/h0057218.

Lee, Miriam Chang Yi, Jia Yi Chow, John Komar, Clara Wee Keat Tan, and Chris Button. 2014. "Nonlinear Pedagogy: An Effective Approach to Cater for Individual Differences in Learning a Sports Skill." *PLoS ONE* 9 (8): e104744. https://doi.org/10.1371/journal.pone.0104744.

Li, Shiyang, Howie J. Carson, and Dave Collins. 2023. "The Nature of Sports Coach Development in China: What Are We Trying to Achieve?" *International Sport Coaching Journal*: Advance online publication. https://doi.org/10.1123/iscj.2022-0096.

Lindsay, Riki S., John Komar, Jia Yi Chow, Paul Larkin, and Michael Spittle. 2023. "Is Prescription of Specific Movement Form Necessary for Optimal Skill Development? A Nonlinear Pedagogy Approach." *Research Quarterly for Exercise and Sport* 94 (3): 793-801. https://doi.org/10.1080/02701367.2022.2054925.

Loze, Gavin M., Dave Collins, and Paul S. Holmes. 2001. "Pre-Shot EEG Alpha-Power Reactivity During Expert Air-Pistol Shooting: A Comparison of Best and Worst Shots." *Journal of Sports Sciences* 19 (9): 727-733. https://doi.org/10.1080/02640410152475856.

Masters, Rich, and Jon Maxwell. 2008. "The Theory of Reinvestment." *International Review of Sport and Exercise Psychology* 1 (2): 160-183. https://doi.org/10.1080/17509840802287218.

Orangi, Behzad Mohammadi, Rasoul Yaali, Abbas Bahram, John van der Kamp, and Mohammad Taghi Aghdasi. 2021. "The Effects of Linear, Nonlinear, and Differential Motor Learning Methods on the Emergence of Creative Action in Individual Soccer Players." *Psychology of Sport and Exercise* 56 (September): 102009. https://doi.org/10.1016/j.psychsport.2021.102009.

Orr, Steven, Andrew Cruickshank, and Howie J. Carson. 2021. "From the Lesson Tee to the Course: A Naturalistic Investigation of Attentional Focus in Elite Golf." *The Sport Psychologist* 35 (4): 305-319. https://doi.org/10.1123/tsp.2021-0003.

Pinder, Ross A., Ian Renshaw, and Keith Davids. 2009. "Information–Movement Coupling in Developing Cricketers Under Changing Ecological Practice Constraints." *Human Movement Science*, 28 (August), 468-479. https://doi.org/10.1016/j.humov.2009.02.003.

Schempp, Paul, Bryan McCullick, Peter St. Pierre, Sophie Woorons, JeongAe You, and Betsy Clark. 2004. "Expert Golf Instructors' Student-Teacher Interaction Patterns." *Research Quarterly for Exercise and Sport* 75 (1): 60-70. https://doi.org/10.1080/02701367.2004.10609134.

Seifert, Ludovic, Léo Wattebled, Romain Herault, Germain Poizat, David Adé, Nathalie Gal-Petitfaux, and Keith Davids. 2014. "Neurobiological Degeneracy and Affordance Perception Support Functional Intra-Individual

Variability of Inter-Limb Coordination During Ice Climbing." *PLoS ONE* 9 (2): e89865. https://doi.org/10.1371/journal.pone.0089865.

Souissi, Mohamed Abdelkader, Achraf Ammar, Omar Trabelsi, Jordan M. Glenn, Omar Boukhris, Khaled Trabelsi, Bassem Bouaziz, et al. 2021. "Distance Motor Learning During the COVID-19 Induced Confinement: Video Feedback With a Pedagogical Activity Improves the Snatch Technique in Young Athletes."" *International Journal of Environmental Research and Public Health* 18 (6): 3069. https://doi.org/10.3390/ijerph18063069.

Steel, Kylie A., Ben Harris, David Baxter, Mike King, and Eathan Ellam. 2014. "Coaches, Athletes, Skill Acquisition Specialists: A Case of Misrecognition." *International Journal of Sports Science & Coaching* 9 (2): 367-378. https://doi.org/10.1260/1747-9541.9.2.367.

Summers, Jeffery J. 2004. "A Historical Perspective on Skill Acquisition." In *Skill Acquisition in Sport: Research, Theory and Practice*, edited by Andrew Mark Williams and Nicola J. Hodges, 1-26. London: Routledge.

Swann, Christian, Richard Keegan, Lee Crust, and David Piggott. 2016. "Psychological States Underlying Excellent Performance in Professional Golfers: 'Letting It Happen' vs. 'Making It Happen.'" *Psychology of Sport and Exercise,* 23 (March), 101-113. https://doi.org/10.1016/j.psychsport.2015.10.008.

Toner, John, and Aidan Moran. 2014. "In Praise of Conscious Awareness: A New Framework for the Investigation of 'Continuous Improvement' in Expert Athletes." *Frontiers in Psychology,* 5, 769. https://doi.org/10.3389/fpsyg.2014.00769.

Warren-Westgate, Laurence S., Robin C. Jackson, Glen M. Blenkinsop, and Michael J. Hiley. 2021. "Earlier Detection Facilitates Skilled Responses to Deceptive Actions." *Human Movement Science* 80 (December): 102885. https://doi.org/10.1016/j.humov.2021.102885.

Williams, Andrew Mark, and Keith Davids. 1998. "Visual Search Strategy, Selective Attention, and Expertise in Soccer." *Research Quarterly for Exercise and Sport* 69 (2): 111-128. https://doi.org/10.1080/02701367.1998.10607677.

Williams, Andrew Mark, and Paul R. Ford. 2009. "Promoting a Skills-Based Agenda in Olympic Sports: The Role of Skill acquisition Specialists." *Journal of Sports Sciences* 27 (13): 1381-1392.

Woodward, Patricia. 1943. "An Experimental Study of Transfer of Training in Motor Learning." *Journal of Applied Psychology* 27 (1): 12-32. https://doi.org/10.1037/h0059610.

Wulf, Gabriele. 2013. "Attentional Focus and Motor Learning: A Review of 15 Years." *International Review of Sport and Exercise Psychology* 6 (1): 77-104. https://doi.org/10.1080/1750984x.2012.723728.

Wulf, Gabriele. 2016. "An External Focus of Attention Is a Conditio Sine Qua Non for Athletes: A Response to Carson, Collins, and Toner (2015)." *Journal of Sports Sciences* 34 (14): 1293-1295. https://doi.org/10.1080/02640414.2015.1136746.

Chapter 5

Abraham, Andrew, and Dave Collins. 1998. "Examining and Extending Research in Coach Development." *Quest,* 50, 59-79.

Abraham, Andrew, and Dave Collins. 2011a. "Effective Skill Development: How Should Athletes' Skills Be Developed?" In *Performance Psychology: A Practitioner's Guide,* edited by Dave Collins, Hugh Richards, and Angela Button, 207-229. London: Churchill Livingstone.

Abraham, Andrew, and Dave Collins. 2011b. "Taking the Next Step: Ways Forward for Coaching Science." *Quest* 63 (4): 366-384. https://doi.org/10.1080/00336297.2011.10483687.

Abraham, Andrew, Dave Collins, Gareth Morgan, and Bob Muir. 2009. "Developing Expert Coaches Requires Expert Coach Development: Replacing Serendipity With Orchestration." In *Aportaciones Teóricas y Prácticas Para el Baloncesto del Futuro,* edited by A. Lorenzo, S.J. Ibáñez, and E. Ortega, 183-205. Sevilla: Wanceulen Editorial Deportiva.

Araújo, Duarte, Hristovski, Robert Hristovski, Ludovic Seifert, João Carvalho, and Keith Davids. 2019. "Ecological Cognition: Expert Decision-Making Behaviour in Sport." *International Review of Sport and Exercise Psychology* 12 (1): 1-25.

Ashford, Michael, Jamie Taylor, Jared Payne, Dom Waldouck, and Dave Collins. 2023. "Getting on the same page" enhancing team performance with shared mental models—case studies of evidence informed practice in elite sport." *Frontiers in Sports and Active Living* 5 (2023): 1057143. https://doi.org/10.3389/fspor.2023.1057143

Ashford, Michael, Ed Cope, Andrew Abraham, and Jamie Poolton. 2022. "Coaching Player Decision Making in Rugby Union: Exploring Coaches Espoused Theories and Theories in Use as an Indicator of Effective Coaching Practice." *Physical Education and Sport Pedagogy,* 1-22. https://doi.org/10.1080/17408989.2022.2153822.

Bergmann, Fynn, Rob Gray, Svenja Wachsmuth, and Oliver Höner. "Perceptual-motor and perceptual-cognitive skill acquisition in soccer: a systematic review on the influence of practice design and coaching behavior." *Frontiers in psychology* 12 (2021): 772201. https://doi.org/10.3389/fpsyg.2021.772201

Bjork, Elizabeth L., and Robert A. Bjork. 2011. 'Making Things Hard on Yourself, but in a Good Way: Creating Desirable Difficulties to Enhance Learning'. In *Psychology and the Real World: Essays Illustrating Fundamental Contributions to Society,* by M. A. Gernsbacher, R. W. Pew, L. M. Hough, and J. R. Pomerantz, 56–64. New York, NY, US: Worth Publishers.

Bobrownicki, Ray, Howie J. Carson, Alan C. MacPherson, and Dave Collins. 2022. "Unloading the Dice: Selection and Design of Comparison and Control Groups in Controlled Trials to Enhance Translational Impact Within Motor Learning and Control Research." *International Journal of Sport and Exercise Psychology* 20 (5): 1330-1344. https://doi.org/10.1080/1612197X.2021.1956567.

Breslin, Gavin, Nicola J. Hodges, Andrew Steenson, and A. Mark Williams (2012). "Constant or Variable Practice: Recreating the Especial Skill Effect." *Acta Psychologica* 140 (2): 154-157.

Carson, Howie J., and Dave Collins. 2015 "Tracking Technical Refinement in Elite Performers: The Good, the Better, and the Ugly." *International Journal of Golf Science* 4 (1): 67-87.

Carson, Howie J., and Dave Collins. 2016. "Implementing the Five-A Model of Technical Refinement: Key Roles of the Sport Psychologist." *Journal of Applied Sport Psychology* 28 (4): 392-409. https://doi.org/10.1080/10413200.2016.1162224.

Carson, Howie J., and Dave Collins. 2017. "Refining Motor Skills in Golf: A Biopsychosocial Perspective." In *Routledge International Handbook of Golf Science*, edited by Martin Toms, 196-206. London: Routledge.

Chen, Ouhao, Endah Retnowati, Juan Cristobal Castro-Alonso, Fred Paas, and John Sweller. 2023. "The Relationship between Interleaving and Variability Effects: A Cognitive Load Theory Perspective" *Education Sciences* 13, no. 11: 1138. https://doi.org/10.3390/educsci13111138

Chow, Jia Yi. 2013. "Nonlinear Learning Underpinning Pedagogy: Evidence, Challenges, and Implications." *Quest* 65 (4): 469-484. https://doi.org/10.1080/00336297.2013.807746.

Collins, Loel, and Dave Collins. 2015. "Integration of Professional Judgement and Decision-Making in High-Level Adventure Sports Coaching Practice." *Journal of Sports Sciences* 33 (6): 622-633.

Collins, Dave, Richard Bailey, Paul A. Ford, Áine MacNamara, Martin Toms, and Gemma Pearce. 2012. "Three Worlds: New Directions in Participant Development in Sport and Physical Activity." *Sport, Education and Society* 17 (2): 225-243. https://doi.org/10.1080/13573322.2011.607951.

Collins, Dave, Alan C. MacPherson, Ray Bobrownicki, and Howie J. Carson. 2023. "An Explicit Look at Implicit Learning: An Interrogative Review for Sport Coaching Research and Practice." *Sports Coaching Review*, 1-22. https://doi.org/10.1080/21640629.2023.2179300.

Collins, Dave, Jamie Taylor, Mike Ashford, and Loel Collins. 2022. "It Depends Coaching—The Most Fundamental, Simple and Complex Principle or a Mere Copout?" *Sports Coaching Review*, 1-21. https://doi.org/10.1080/21640629.2022.2154189.

Cope, Ed, Mark Partington, and Stephen Harvey. 2017. "A Review of the Use of a Systematic Observation Method in Coaching Research Between 1997 and 2016." *Journal of Sports Sciences* 35 (20): 2042-2050. https://doi.org/10.1080/02640414.2016.1252463.

Cope, Ed, Christopher J. Cushion, Stephen Harvey, and Mark Partington. 2022. "Re-visiting Systematic Observation: A Pedagogical Tool to Support Coach Learning and Development." *Frontiers in Sports and Active Living*, 4, 962690. https://doi.org/10.3389/fspor.2022.962690.

Correia, Vanda, Duarte Araújo, Ricardo Duarte, Bruno Travassos, Pedro Passos, and Keith Davids. "Changes in practice task constraints shape decision-making behaviours of team games players." *Journal of Science and Medicine in Sport* 15, no. 3 (2012): 244-249. https://doi.org/10.1016/j.jsams.2011.10.004

Correia, Vanda, João Carvalho, Duarte Araújo, Elsa Pereira, and Keith Davids. 2019. "Principles of Nonlinear Pedagogy in Sport Practice." *Physical Education and Sport Pedagogy* 24 (2): 117-132. https://doi.org/10.1080/17408989.2018.1552673.

Cushion, Christopher. 2010. "Coach Behavior." In *Sports Coaching Professionalization and Practice*, edited by J. Lyle and C.J. Cushion, 43-62. London: Elsevier.

Cushion, Christopher, Stephen Harvey, Bob Muir, and Lee Nelson. 2012. "Developing the Coach Analysis and Intervention System (CAIS): Establishing Validity and Reliability of a Computerised Systematic Observation Instrument." *Journal of Sports Sciences* 30 (2): 201-216. https://doi.org/10.1080/02640414.2011.635310.

Davids, Keith, Paul Glazier, Duarte Araujo, and Roger Bartlett. 2003. 'Movement Systems as Dynamical Systems: The Functional Role of Variability and Its Implications for Sports Medicine'. *Sports Medicine* 33 (4): 245–60. https://doi.org/10.2165/00007256-200333040-00001.

de Jong, Ton, Ard W. Lazonder, Clark A. Chinn, Frank Fischer, Janice Gobert, Cindy E. Hmelo-Silver, Ken R. Koedinger, et al. 2023. "Let's Talk Evidence—The Case for Combining Inquiry-Based and Direct Instruction." *Educational Research Review* 39 (1): 100536. https://doi.org/10.1016/j.edurev.2023.100536.

Deuker, Albert, Bjoern Braunstein, Jia Yi Chow, Maximilian Fichtl, Hyoek Kim, Swen Körner, and Robert Rein. 2023. "Train as You Play": Improving Effectiveness of Training in Youth Soccer Players." *International Journal of Sports Science & Coaching* 19 (2): 677-686. https://doi.org/10.1177/17479541231172702.

dos Santos, Fernando Garbeloto, Matheus Maia Pacheco, Luciano Basso, and Go Tani. 2016. "A Comparative Study of the Mastery of Fundamental Movement Skills Between Different Cultures." *Motricidade* 12 (2): 116-126.

Ferguson, Callum, Howie J. Carson, and Dave Collins. 2023. 'Skill Execution Errors: An "It Depends" Perspective on Their Role, Type and Use When Coaching for Player Development in Sport'. *Sports Coaching Review*, 1–18. https://doi.org/10.1080/21640629.2023.2263268.

Giacobbi, Peter R., Jr., Artur Poczwardowski, and Peter Hager. 2005. "A Pragmatic Research Philosophy for Sport and Exercise Psychology." *The Sport Psychologist* 19 (1): 18-31. https://doi.org/10.1123/tsp.19.1.18.

Gibson, James J. 1960. "Pictures, Perspective, and Perception." *Daedalus* 89(1): 216–27. http://www.jstor.org/stable/20026561.

Gray, Rob. 2018. "Comparing Cueing and Constraints Interventions for Increasing Launch Angle in Baseball Batting." *Sport, Exercise, and Performance Psychology* 7 (3): 318-332. https://doi.org/10.1037/spy0000131.

Gray, Rob. 2020. "Changes in Movement Coordination Associated With Skill Acquisition in Baseball Batting: Freezing/Freeing Degrees of Freedom and Functional Variability." *Frontiers in Psychology* 11 (1295). https://doi.org/10.3389/fpsyg.2020.01295.

Green, Andrew, Jason Tee, and Warrick McKinon. 2019. "A Review of the Biomechanical Determinants of Rugby Scrummaging Performance." *South African Journal of Sports Medicine* 31 (1): 1-8. http://dx.doi.org/10.17159/2078-516X/2019/v31i1a7521.

Hodges, Nicola J., and Keith R. Lohse. 2020. 'Difficulty Is a Real Challenge: A Perspective on the Role of Cognitive Effort in Motor Skill Learning.' *Journal of Applied Research in Memory and Cognition* 9 (4): 455–60. https://doi.org/10.1016/j.jarmac.2020.08.006.Klein, Gary. 2008. "Naturalistic Decision Making." *Human Factors* 50 (3): 456-460. https://doi.org/10.1518/001872008X288385.

Lee, Miriam Chang Yi, Jia Yi Chow, John Komar, Clara Wee Keat Tan, and Chris Button. 2014. "Nonlinear Pedagogy: An Effective Approach to Cater for Individual Differences in Learning a Sports Skill." *PLOS ONE* 9 (8): e104744. https://doi.org/10.1371/journal.pone.0104744.

Li, Yuhua, and David L. Wright. 2000. "An Assessment of the Attention Demands During Random-and Blocked-Practice Schedules." *The Quarterly Journal of Experimental Psychology Section A*, 53 (2): 591-606. https://doi.org/10.1080/713755890.

Lindsay, Riki, John Komar, Jia Yi Chow, Paul Larkin, and Michael Spittle. 2022. "Influence of a Nonlinear Pedagogy Approach on Individual Routes of Learning When Acquiring a Complex Weightlifting Skill." *Journal of Science and Medicine in Sport* 25 (Suppl. 2): S16. https://doi.org/10.1016/j.jsams.2022.09.145.

Magill, Richard A. 2011. *Memory and Control of Action.* London: Elsevier.

Magill, Richard A., and Kellie G. Hall. 1990. "A Review of the Contextual Interference Effect in Motor Skill Acquisition. *Human Movement Science* 9 (3-5): 241-289. https://doi.org/10.1016/0167-9457(90)90005-X.

Martindale, Amanda, and Dave Collins. 2005. "Professional Judgment and Decision Making: The Role of Intention for Impact." *The Sport Psychologist* 19 (3): 303-317. https://doi.org/10.1123/tsp.19.3.303.

McMorris, Terry. *Acquisition and performance of sports skills.* John Wiley & Sons, 2014.

Mosston, Muska. 1966. *Teaching Physical Education.* Columbus, OH: Merrill.

Mosston, Muska, and Sara Ashworth (1994). Teaching physical education (5th ed.). New York: Macmillan.

Muir, Bob, and Julian North. 2023. "Supporting Coaches to Learn Through and From Their Everyday Experiences: A 1:1 Coach Development Workflow for Performance Sport." *International Sport Coaching Journal* 11 (2): 288-297. https://doi.org/10.1123/iscj.2022-0101.

Myszka, Shawn, Tyler Yearby, and Keith Davids. 2023. '(Re)Conceptualizing Movement Behavior in Sport as a Problem-Solving Activity'. *Frontiers in Sports and Active Living* 5. https://www.frontiersin.org/articles/10.3389/fspor.2023.1130131.

O'Connor, Donna, Paul Larkin, and A. Mark Williams. 2017. "What Learning Environments Help Improve Decision-Making?" *Physical Education and Sport Pedagogy* 22 (6): 647-660. https://doi.org/10.1080/17408989.2017.1294678.

Orangi, Behzad M., Rasoul Yaali, Abbas Bahram, John van der Kamp, and Mohammad Taghi Aghdasi. 2021. "The Effects of Linear, Nonlinear, and Differential Motor Learning Methods on the Emergence of Creative Action in Individual Soccer Players." *Psychology of Sport and Exercise* 56 (102009). https://doi.org/10.1016/j.psychsport.2021.102009.

Parr, Thomas, Giovanni Pezzulo, and Karl J. Friston. 2022. *Active Inference: The Free Energy Principle in Mind, Brain, and Behavior.* Cambridge, MA: MIT Press.

Penney, Dawn, & Kidman, Lynn. 2014. "Opening Call for Discourse: Athlete Centered Coaching—A Time for Reflection on Meanings, Values and Practice." *Journal of Athlete Centered Coaching* 1 (1): 1-5.

Pill, Shane, Brendan SueSee, Joss Rankin, and Mitch Hewitt. 2021. *The Spectrum of Sport Coaching Styles.* London: Routledge.

Portus, Marc R., and Damian Farrow. 2011. "Enhancing Cricket Batting Skill: Implications for Biomechanics and Skill Acquisition Research and Practice." *Sports Biomechanics* 10 (4): 294-305.

Powell, Daniel, Greg Wood, Philip Kearney, and Carl Payton. 2021. "Skill Acquisition Practices of Coaches on the British Para Swimming World Class Programme." *International Journal of Sports Science & Coaching* 16 (5): 1097-1110. https://doi.org/10.1177/1747954121026248.

Renshaw, Ian, Keith Davids, Daniel Newcombe, and Will Roberts. 2019. *The Constraints-Led Approach: Principles for Sports Coaching and Practice Design.* London: Routledge.

Renshaw, Ian, Jonathon Headrick, Michael Maloney, Brendan Moy, and Ross Pinder. 2019. "Constraints-Led Learning in Practice: Designing Effective Learning Environments." In *Skill Acquisition in Sport*, edited by Nicola J. Hodges and A. Mark Williams, 163-182. London: Routledge.

Richards, Pam, Dave Collins, and Duncan R. D. Mascarenhas. 2017. 'Developing Team Decision-Making: A Holistic Framework Integrating Both on-Field and off-Field Pedagogical Coaching Processes'. *Sports Coaching Review* 6 (1): 57–75. https://doi.org/10.1080/21640629.2016.1200819.

Rymarz, Richard. 2012. "Constructivist Instruction: Success or Failure? – Edited by Sigmund Tobias and Thomas Duffy." *Teaching Theology & Religion* 15 (2): 186-187. https://doi.org/10.1111/j.1467-9647.2012.00787.x.

Schmidt, Richard A. 1975. 'A Schema Theory of Discrete Motor Skill Learning.' *Psychological Review* 82 (4): 225–60. https://doi.org/10.1037/h0076770.

Schunk, Dale. 2012. *Learning Theories: An Educational Perspective*. 6th ed. London: Pearson.

Shea, John B., and Robyn L. Morgan. 1979. 'Contextual Interference Effects on the Acquisition, Retention, and Transfer of a Motor Skill.' *Journal of Experimental Psychology: Human Learning and Memory* 5 (2): 179–87. https://doi.org/10.1037/0278-7393.5.2.179.

Shier, David. 2017. "Beyond 'Crude Pragmatism' in Sports Coaching: Insights From C.S. Peirce, William James, and John Dewey: A Commentary." *International Journal of Sports Science & Coaching* 12 (1): 20-22. https://doi.org/10.1177/1747954116684029.

Silva, Pedro, Júlio Garganta, Duarte Araújo, Keith Davids, and Paulo Aguiar. "Shared knowledge or shared affordances? Insights from an ecological dynamics approach to team coordination in sports." *Sports medicine* 43 (2013): 765-772. https://doi.og/ 10.1007/s40279-013-0070-9

Simon, Scott, Loel Collins, and Dave Collins. 2017. "Observational Heuristics in a Group of High-Level Paddle Sports Coaches." *International Sport Coaching Journal* 4 (2): 235-245.

Tan, Clara Wee Keat, Jia Yi Chow, and Keith Davids. 2012. "'How Does TGfU Work?': Examining the Relationship Between Learning Design in TGfU and a Nonlinear Pedagogy." *Physical Education and Sport Pedagogy* 17 (4): 331-348. https://doi.org/10.1080/17408989.2011.582486.

Taylor, Jamie, Michael Ashford, and Dave Collins. 2022. 'Tough Love: Impactful, Caring Coaching in Psychologically Unsafe Environments'. *MDPI Sports* 10 (6): 83. https://doi.org/10.3390/sports10060083.

Taylor, Robin D., Jamie Taylor, Michael Ashford, and Rosie Collins. 2023. "Contemporary Pedagogy? The Use of Theory in Practice: An Evidence-Informed Perspective." *Frontiers in Sports and Active Living*, 5, 81. https://doi.org/10.3389/fspor.2023.1113564.

Till, Kevin, Bob Muir, Andrew Abraham, David Piggott, and Jason Tee. 2019. "A Framework for Decision-Making Within Strength and Conditioning Coaching." *Strength & Conditioning Journal* 41 (1): 14-26. https://doi.org/10.1519/ssc.0000000000000408.

Tomkins, Leah, and Alexandra Bristow. 2023. 'Evidence-Based Practice and the Ethics of Care: "What Works" or "What Matters"?' *Human Relations* 76 (1): 118–43. https://doi.org/10.1177/00187267211044143.

Wade, Allen. (1967). The F.A. Guide to Training and Coaching. Football Association.

Wiliam, Dylan. *Principled curriculum design*. London, UK: SSAT (The Schools Network) Limited, 2013.

Williams, A. Mark, and Nicola J. Hodges. 2005. "Practice, Instruction and Skill Acquisition in Soccer: Challenging Tradition." *Journal of Sports Sciences* 23 (6): 637-650. https://doi.org/10.1080/02640410400021328.

Williams, A. Mark, and Robin C. Jackson. 2019. "Anticipation in Sport: Fifty Years on, What Have We Learned and What Research Still Needs to Be Undertaken?" *Psychology of Sport and Exercise* 42 (1): 16-24. https://doi.org/10.1016/j.psychsport.2018.11.014.

Wilson, Ricky, Matt Dicks, Gemma Milligan, Jamie Poolton, and David Alder. 2018. "An Examination of Action Capabilities and Movement Time During a Soccer Anticipation Task." *Movement & Sport Sciences—Science & Motricité*, 102, 61-70. https://doi.org/10.1051/sm/2019001.

Wittenberg, Ellen, Jessica Thompson, Chang S. Nam, and Jason R. Franz. 2017. "Neuroimaging of Human Balance Control: A Systematic Review." *Frontiers in Human Neuroscience*, 11, 170. https://doi.org/10.3389/fnhum.2017.00170.

Woods, Carl T., Ian McKeown, Martyn Rothwell, Duarte Araújo, Sam Robertson, and Keith Davids. "Sport practitioners as sport ecology designers: how ecological dynamics has progressively changed perceptions of skill "acquisition" in the sporting habitat." *Frontiers in psychology* 11 (2020): 654. https://doi.org/10.3389/fpsyg.2020.00654

Yan, Veronica X., Mark A. Guadagnoli, and Neeil Haycocks. 2019. "Appropriate Failure to Create Effective Learning: Optimizing Challenge." In *Skill Acquisition in Sport*, edited by Nicola J. Hodges and A. Mark Williams, 313-329. London: Routledge.

Chapter 6

Abraham, Andy, and Dave Collins. 2011a. "Effective Skill Development—How Should Athletes' Skills Be Developed." In *Performance Psychology: A Practitioner's Guide*, edited by Dave Collins, Angela Button, and Hugh Richards, 207-230. Oxford: Elsevier.

Abraham, Andy, and Dave Collins. 2011b. "Taking the Next Step: Ways Forward for Coaching Science." *Quest* 63 (4): 366-384. https://doi.org/10.1080/00336297.2011.10483687.

Abraham, Andy, Dave Collins, Gareth Morgan, and Bob Muir. 2009. "Developing Expert Coaches Requires Expert Coach Development: Replacing Serendipity With Orchestration." In *Aportaciones Teoricas y Practicas Para el*

Baloncesto del Futuro, edited by Alberto Lorenzo, Sergio J. Ibañez, and Enrique Ortega, 183-205. Sevilla, Spain: Wanceulen Editorial Deportiva.

Abraham, Andy, Sergio L.J. Saiz, Steve McKeown, Gareth Morgan, Bob Muir, Julian North, and Kevin Till. 2022. "Planning Your Coaching: A Focus on Youth Participant Development." In *Practical Sports Coaching*, edited by Christine Nash, 2nd ed., 18-44. Oxon, UK: Routledge.

Agarwal, Pooja K., Ludmila D. Nunes, and Janell R. Blunt. 2021. "Retrieval Practice Consistently Benefits Student Learning: A Systematic Review of Applied Research in Schools and Classrooms." *Educational Psychology Review* 33 (4): 1409-1453. https://doi.org/10.1007/s10648-021-09595-9.

Anyadike-Danes, Kechi, Lars Donath, and John Kiely. 2023. "Coaches' Perceptions of Factors Driving Training Adaptation: An International Survey." *Sports Medicine*, 53, 2505-2512. https://doi.org/10.1007/s40279-023-01894-1.

Ashford, Michael, Andrew Abraham, and Jamie Poolton. 2021. "Understanding a Player's Decision-Making Process in Team Sports: A Systematic Review of Empirical Evidence." *Sports* 9 (5): 65.

Ashford, Michael, Jamie Taylor, Danny Newcombe, Áine MacNamara, Stephen Behan, Simon Phelan, and Scott McNeill. 2024. 'Coaching Adaptive Skill and Expertise in Premier League Football Academies—Paving a Way Forward for Research and Practice'. *Frontiers in Sports and Active Living* 6 (April):1386380. https://doi.org/10.3389/fspor.2024.1386380.

Bjork, Elizabeth L., and Robert A. Bjork. 2011. "Making Things Hard on Yourself, but in a Good Way: Creating Desirable Difficulties to Enhance Learning." In *Psychology and the Real World: Essays Illustrating Fundamental Contributions to Society*, edited by Morton Ann Gernsbacher, Richard W. Pew, Leaetta M. Hough, and James R. Pomerantz, 56-64. New York: Worth Publishers.

Clemmons, Alexa W., Deborah A. Donovan, Elli J. Theobald, and Alison J. Crowe. 2022. "Using the Intended–Enacted–Experienced Curriculum Model to Map the Vision and Change Core Competencies in Undergraduate Biology Programs and Courses". *CBE—Life Sciences Education* 21 (1): ar6. https://doi.org/10.1187/cbe.21-02-0054.

Collins, Dave, Tom Willmott, and Loel Collins. 2018. "Periodization and Self-Regulation in Action Sports: Coping With the Emotional Load." *Frontiers in Psychology*, 9, 1652. https://doi.org/10.3389/fpsyg.2018.01652.

Cushion, Christopher J., and Robyn L. Jones. 2014. 'A Bourdieusian Analysis of Cultural Reproduction: Socialisation and the "Hidden Curriculum" in Professional Football'. *Sport, Education and Society* 19 (3): 276–98. https://doi.org/10.1080/13573322.2012.666966.

Dewey, John. 1938. *Experience and Education*. New York: Macmillan.

Edmondson, Amy C. 1999. "Psychological Safety and Learning Behavior in Work Teams." *Administrative Science Quarterly* 44 (2): 350-383. https://doi.org/10.2307/2666999.

Edmondson, Amy C. 2018. *The Fearless Organization: Creating Psychological Safety in the Workplace for Learning, Innovation, and Growth*. Hoboken, NJ: Wiley.

Edmondson, Amy C. 2023. *Right Kind of Wrong: The Science of Failing Well*. New York: Simon and Schuster.

Edmondson, Amy C., and Derrick P. Bransby. 2023. "Psychological Safety Comes of Age: Observed Themes in an Established Literature." *Annual Review of Organizational Psychology and Organizational Behavior* 10 (1): 55-78. https://doi.org/10.1146/annurev-orgpsych-120920-055217.

Ericsson, K. Anders. 2020. "Towards a Science of the Acquisition of Expert Performance in Sports: Clarifying the Differences Between Deliberate Practice and Other Types of Practice." *Journal of Sports Sciences* 38 (2): 159-176. https://doi.org/10.1080/02640414.2019.1688618.

Ericsson, K. Anders, Ralf T. Krampe, and Clemens Tesch-Römer. 1993. "The Role of Deliberate Practice in the Acquisition of Expert Performance." *Psychological Review* 100 (3): 363-406. https://doi.org/10.1037/0033-295X.100.3.363.

Fitts, Paul M., and Michael I. Posner. 1967. *Human Performance*. Oxford: Brooks/Cole.

Friston, Karl, Francesco Rigoli, Dimitri Ognibene, Christoph Mathys, Thomas Fitzgerald, and Giovanni Pezzulo. 2015. "Active Inference and Epistemic Value." *Cognitive Neuroscience* 6 (4): 187-214. https://doi.org/10.1080/17588928.2015.1020053.

Gray, Rob. 2019. "Virtual Environments and Their Role in Developing Perceptual-Cognitive Skills in Sports." In *Anticipation and Decision Making in Sport*, edited by A. Mark Williams and Robin Jackson. London: Routledge. https://doi.org/10.4324/9781315146270.

Gray, Rob, and Randy Sullivan. 2023. *A Constraints-Led Approach to Baseball Coaching*. New York: Routledge. https://doi.org/10.4324/9781003274490.

Gréhaigne, Jean-Francis, and Paul Godbout. 1995. "Tactical Knowledge in Team Sports From a Constructivist and Cognitivist Perspective." *Quest* 47 (4): 490-505. https://doi.org/10.1080/00336297.1995.10484171.

Gréhaigne, Jean-Francis, Nathalie Wallian, and Paul Godbout. 2005. "Tactical-Decision Learning Model and Students' Practices." *Physical Education and Sport Pedagogy* 10 (3): 255-269. https://doi.org/10.1080/17408980500340869.

Guadagnoli, Mark A., and Timothy D. Lee. 2004. "Challenge Point: A Framework for Conceptualizing the Effects of Various Practice Conditions in Motor Learning." *Journal of Motor Behavior* 36 (2): 212-224. https://doi.org/10.3200/JMBR.36.2.212-224.

Hamstra, Stanley J., Ryan Brydges, Rose Hatala, Benjamin Zendejas, and David A. Cook. 2014. "Reconsidering Fidelity in Simulation-Based Training." *Academic Medicine* 89 (3): 387-392. https://journals.lww.com/academicmedicine/fulltext/2014/03000/reconsidering_fidelity_in_simulation_based.11.aspx.

Harris, David J., Jonathan M. Bird, Philip A. Smart, Mark R. Wilson, and Samuel J. Vine. 2020. "A Framework for the Testing and Validation of Simulated Environments in Experimentation and Training." *Frontiers in Psychology* 11. https://doi.org/10.3389/fpsyg.2020.00605.

Headrick, Jonathon, Ian Renshaw, Keith Davids, Ross A. Pinder, and Duarte Araújo. 2015. "The Dynamics of Expertise Acquisition in Sport: The Role of Affective Learning Design." *The Development of Expertise and Excellence in Sport Psychology* 16 (January): 83-90. https://doi.org/10.1016/j.psychsport.2014.08.006.

Hendrick, Carl, and Jim Heal. 2020. "Just Because They're Engaged, It Doesn't Mean They're Learning." *Impact Chartered College of Teaching.* https://my.chartered.college/impact_article/just-because-theyre-engaged-it-doesnt-mean-theyre-learning/.

Henry, Franklin M., and Leon E. Smith. 1961. "Simultaneous vs. Separate Bilateral Muscular Contractions in Relation to Neural Overflow Theory and Neuromotor Specificity." *Research Quarterly. American Association for Health, Physical Education and Recreation* 32 (1): 42-46. https://doi.org/10.1080/10671188.1961.10762069.

Hodges, Nicola J., and Keith R. Lohse. 2022. "An Extended Challenge-Based Framework for Practice Design in Sports Coaching." *Journal of Sports Sciences* 40 (7): 754-768. https://doi.org/10.1080/02640414.2021.2015917.

Kahneman, Daniel, and Gary Klein. 2009. "Conditions for Intuitive Expertise: A Failure to Disagree." *American Psychologist* 64 (6): 515-526. https://doi.org/10.1037/a0016755.

Kegelaers, Jolan, and Raôul R.D. Oudejans. 2022. "Pressure Makes Diamonds? A Narrative Review on the Application of Pressure Training in High-Performance Sports." *International Journal of Sport and Exercise Psychology* 22 (1): 141-159. https://doi.org/10.1080/1612197X.2022.2134436.

Kelly, Albert V. 2009. *The Curriculum: Theory and Practice.* 6th ed. London: Sage.

Klein, Gary. 2007. "Flexecution as a Paradigm for Replanning, Part 1". *IEEE Intelligent Systems* 22 (5): 79-83. https://doi.org/10.1109/MIS.2007.4338498.

Lohse, Keith, Matthew Miller, Mariane Bacelar, and Olav Krigolson. 2019. "Errors, Rewards, and Reinforcement in Motor Skill Learning." In *Skill Acquisition in Sport: Research, Theory and Practice*, edited by Nicola J. Hodges and A. Mark Williams, 3rd ed., 39-60. London: Routledge.

Lövdén, Martin, Benjamín Garzón, and Ulman Lindenberger. 2020. "Human Skill Learning: Expansion, Exploration, Selection, and Refinement." *Sensitive and Critical Periods* 36 (December): 163-168. https://doi.org/10.1016/j.cobeha.2020.11.002.

Low, William R., Mike Stoker, Joanne Butt, and Ian Maynard. 2023. "Pressure Training: From Research to Applied Practice"." *Journal of Sport Psychology in Action* 15 (1): 3-18. https://doi.org/10.1080/21520704.2022.2164098.

Mariani, Luciano. 1997. "Teacher Support and Teacher Challenge in Promoting Learner Autonomy." *Perspectives* 23 (2): 5-19.

Martindale, Amanda, and Dave Collins. 2005. "Professional Judgment and Decision Making: The Role of Intention for Impact." *The Sport Psychologist* 19 (3): 303-317. https://doi.org/10.1123/tsp.19.3.303.

McEwen, Bruce S. 2019. "The Good Side of 'Stress.'" *Stress* 22 (5): 524-525. https://doi.org/10.1080/10253890.2019.1631794.

Moodie, Graham, Jamie Taylor, and Dave Collins. 2023. "Developing Psycho-Behavioural Skills: The Talent Development Coach Perspective." *Psych* 5 (2): 427-446. https://doi.org/10.3390/psych5020029.

Moran, Jack J., Murray P. Craig, and Dave Collins. 2024. "How Might We Do It Better? Applying Educational Curriculum Theory and Practice in Talent Development Environments." *Sports Coaching Review*, February, 1-22. https://doi.org/10.1080/21640629.2024.2321047.

Muir, Bob, Gareth Morgan, Andy Abraham, and David Morley. 2011. "Developmentally Appropriate Approaches to Coaching Children." In *Coaching Children in Sport*, edited by Ian Stafford, 17-37. Oxon, UK: Routledge.

Newell, Karl M. 1985. "Coordination, Control and Skill." In *Advances in Psychology*, edited by David Goodman, Robert B. Wilberg, and Ian M. Franks, 27:295-317. Amsterdam: Elsevier. https://doi.org/10.1016/S0166-4115(08)62541-8.

Paige, Jane B., and Karen H. Morin. 2013. "Simulation Fidelity and Cueing: A Systematic Review of the Literature." *Clinical Simulation in Nursing* 9 (11): e481-489. https://doi.org/10.1016/j.ecns.2013.01.001.

Pinder, Ross A., Keith Davids, Ian Renshaw, and Duarte Araújo. 2011. "Representative Learning Design and Functionality of Research and Practice in Sport." *Journal of Sport and Exercise Psychology* 33 (1): 146-155. https://doi.org/10.1123/jsep.33.1.146.

Proteau, Luc. 1992. "On the Specificity of Learning and the Role of Visual Information for Movement Control." In *Advances in Psychology*, edited by Luc Proteau and Digby Elliott, 85:67-103. Amsterdam: Elsevier. https://doi.org/10.1016/S0166-4115(08)62011-7.

Renshaw, Ian, Keith Davids, Danny Newcombe, and Will Roberts. 2019. *The Constraints-Led Approach: Principles for Sports Coaching and Practice Design.* London: Routledge.

Riccio, Gary E. 1995. "Coordination of Postural Control and Vehicular Control: Implications for Multimodal Perception and Simulation of Self-Motion." In *Local Applications of the Ecological Approach to Human–Machine Systems*, vol. 2., edited by Peter Hancock, John M. Flach, Jeff Caird, and Kim Vincente, 122-181. Boca Raton, FL: CRC Press. https://doi.org/10.1201/9780203748749.

Richards, Pam, Dave Collins, and Duncan R.D. Mascarenhas. 2017. "Developing Team Decision-Making: A Holistic Framework Integrating Both On-Field and Off-Field Pedagogical Coaching Processes." *Sports Coaching Review* 6 (1): 57-75. https://doi.org/10.1080/21640629.2016.1200819.

Savage, Jennifer, Dave Collins, and Andrew Cruickshank. 2017. "Exploring Traumas in the Development of Talent: What Are They, What Do They Do, and What Do They Require?" *Journal of Applied Sport Psychology* 29 (1): 101-117. https://doi.org/10.1080/10413200.2016.1194910.

Schmidt, Richard, and Timothy D. Lee. 2019. *Motor Learning and Performance: From Principles to Application.* 6th ed. Champaign, IL: Human Kinetics.

Schunk, D. H. 2012. *Learning Theories: An Educational Perspective.* 6th ed. Pearson.

Schwartenbeck, Philipp, Thomas FitzGerald, Ray Dolan, and Karl Friston. 2013. "Exploration, Novelty, Surprise, and Free Energy Minimization." *Frontiers in Psychology*, 4. https://doi.org/10.3389/fpsyg.2013.00710.

Shamrock, Frank, and Charles Fleming. 2012. *Uncaged: My Life as a Champion MMA Fighter.* Chicago: Chicago Review Press.

Stoker, Mike, Pete Lindsay, Joanne Butt, Mark Bawden, and Ian W. Maynard. 2016. "Elite Coaches' Experiences of Creating Pressure Training Environments." *International Journal of Sport Psychology*, 47, 262-281.

Sweeney, Liam, Jamie Taylor, and Aine MacNamara. In Press. "Riding the wave: A prospective exploration of the temporal impact of perceived challenges on the development of relatively early high performing national-level youth soccer players." European Journal for Sport and Society.

Taylor, Jamie, and Dave Collins. 2020. "The Highs and the Lows—Exploring the Nature of Optimally Impactful Development Experiences on the Talent Pathway." *The Sport Psychologist* 34 (4): 319-328. https://doi.org/10.1123/tsp.2020-0034.

Taylor, Jamie, and Dave Collins. 2021. "Navigating the Winds of Change on the Smooth Sea—The Interaction of Feedback and Emotional Disruption on the Talent Pathway." *Journal of Applied Sport Psychology* 34 (4): 886-912. https://doi.org/10.1080/10413200.2021.1894505.

Taylor, Jamie, and Dave Collins. 2022. "The Talent Development Curriculum." In *Practical Sport Coaching*, edited by Christine Nash, 2nd ed., 77-91. Oxon, UK: Routledge. https://doi.org/10.4324/9781003179733-7.

Taylor, Jamie, Michael Ashford, and Dave Collins. 2022. "Tough Love: Impactful, Caring Coaching in Psychologically Unsafe Environments." *MDPI Sports* 10 (6): 83. https://doi.org/10.3390/sports10060083.

Taylor, Jamie, Dave Collins, and Michael Ashford. 2022. "Psychological Safety in High Performance Sport: Contextually Applicable?" *Frontiers in Sports and Active Living*, 4. https://doi.org/10.3389/fspor.2022.823488.

Till, Kevin, Bob Muir, Andrew Abraham, Dave Piggott, and Jason Tee. 2019. "A Framework for Decision-Making Within Strength and Conditioning Coaching." *Strength and Conditioning Journal* 41 (1): 14-26. https://doi.org/10.1519/ssc.0000000000000408.

Vella, Stewart A., Elizabeth Mayland, Matthew J. Schweickle, Jordan T. Sutcliffe, Desmond McEwan, and Christian Swann. 2022. "Psychological Safety in Sport: A Systematic Review and Concept Analysis." *International Review of Sport and Exercise Psychology*, 17 (1): 516-539. https://doi.org/10.1080/1750984X.2022.2028306.

Wade, Alan. 1967. *The FA Guide to Training and Coaching.* London: Heinemann.

Walton, Courtney C., Rosemary Purcell, Vita Pilkington, Kate Hall, Göran Kenttä, Stewart Vella, and Simon M. Rice. 2023. "Psychological Safety for Mental Health in Elite Sport: A Theoretically Informed Model." *Sports Medicine*, 54, 557-564. https://doi.org/10.1007/s40279-023-01912-2.

Williams, Graham, and A. MacNamara. 2023. "Making Sense of the Challenge: Forecasting and Reflecting on Challenging Experiences on the Talent Pathway." *Journal of Expertise* 6 (2): 207-233.

Williams, A. Mark, and Nicola J. Hodges. 2023. 'Effective Practice and Instruction: A Skill Acquisition Framework for Excellence'. *Journal of Sports Sciences* 41 (9): 833–49. https://doi.org/10.1080/02640414.2023.2240630.

Wilson, Robert C., Amitai Shenhav, Mark Straccia, and Jonathan D. Cohen. 2019. "The Eighty Five Percent Rule for Optimal Learning." *Nature Communications* 10 (1): 4646. https://doi.org/10.1038/s41467-019-12552-4.

Chapter 7

Alessi, Stephen M. 1988. "Fidelity in the Design of Instructional Simulations." *Journal of Computer-Based Instruction* 15 (2): 40-47.

Alfano, Helen, and Dave Collins. 2020. "Good Practice Delivery in Sport Science and Medicine Support: Perceptions of Experienced Sport Leaders and Practitioners." *Managing Sport and Leisure* 26 (3): 145-160. doi.org/10.1080/23750472.2020.1727768.

Alfano, Helen, and Dave Collins. 2021. "Good Practice in Sport Science and Medicine Support: Practitioners' Perspectives on Quality, Pressure and Support." *Managing Sport and Leisure*, 38, 1-39.

Blasi, Damian, Joseph Henrich, Evangelina Adamou, and David Kemmerer. 2022. "Over Reliance on English Hinders Cognitive Science." *Trends in Cognitive Sciences* 26 (12): 1153-1170. doi.org/10.1016/j.tics.2022.09.015.

Bortoli, Laura, Maurizio Bertollo, Yuri Hanin, and Claudio Robazza. 2012. "Striving for Excellence: A Multi-Action Plan Intervention Model for Shooters." *Psychology of Sport and Exercise*, 13, 693-701.

Brunswik, Egon (1956). Perception and the representative design of psychological experiments. Berkeley: University of California Press

Burns, Andrew, and Dave Collins. 2023. "Interdisciplinary Practice in Performance Sport: A Scoping Review of Evidence of Collaboration." *European Journal of Sport Science* 23 (9): 1877-1891. https://doi.org/10.1080/17461391.2023.2201812.

Carson, Howie, and Dave Collins. 2011. "Refining and Regaining Skills in Fixation/Diversification Stage Performers: The Five-A Model." *International Review of Sport and Exercise Psychology* 4 (2): 146-167.

Carson, Howie, and Dave Collins. 2015. "The Fourth Dimension: A Motoric Perspective on the Anxiety–Performance Relationship." *International Review of Sport and Exercise Psychology* 9 (1): 1-21. doi.org/10.1080/1750984X.2015.1072231.

Carson, Howie, and Dave Collins. 2016. "Implementing the Five-A Model of Technical Change: Key Roles for the Sport Psychologist." *Journal of Applied Sport Psychology* 28 (4): 392-409.

Carson, Howie, and Dave Collins. 2020. "Training for Success Under Stress: Appropriately Embedding Motor Skills in Sport." In *Feelings in Sport: Theory, Research, and Practical Implications for Performance and Well-Being*, edited by Montse Ruiz and Claudio Robazza, 168-177. London: Routledge.

Carson, Howie, Dave Collins, and Bryan Jones. 2014. "A Case Study of Technical Change and Rehabilitation: Intervention Design and Interdisciplinary Team Interaction." *International Journal of Sport Psychology* 45 (1): 57-78. https://doi.org/10.7352/IJSP 2014.45.057.

Christensen, Wayne, and Kath Bicknell. 2022. "Cognitive Control, Intentions, and Problem Solving in Skill Learning." *Synthese*, 200, 439-460. https://doi.org/10.1007/s11229-022-03920-7.

Christensen, Wayne, John Sutton, and Doris McIlwain. 2016. "Cognition in Skilled Action: Meshed Control and the Varieties of Skill Experience." *Mind and Language* 31 (1): 37-66. doi.org/10.1111/mila.12094.

Collins, Dave, Mike Doherty, and Steve Talbot. 1993. "Performance Enhancement in Moto Cross: A Case Study of the Sport Science Team in Action." *The Sport Psychologist*, 7, 290-297.

Collins, Dave, Calvin Morriss, and John Trower. 1999. "Getting It Back: A Case Study of Skill Recovery in an Elite Athlete." *The Sport Psychologist* 13 (3): 288-298.

Collins, Dave, Tom Willmott, and Loel Collins. 2018. "Periodisation and Self-Regulation in Action Sports: Coping With the Emotional Load." *Frontiers in Psychology*, 9. https://doi.org/10.3389/fpsyg.2018.01652.

Dhami, Mandeep, Ralph Hertwig, and Ulrich Hoffrage. 2004. "The Role of Representative Design in an Ecological Approach to Cognition." *Psychological Bulletin* 130 (6): 959-988. https://doi.org/10.1037/0033-2909.130.6.95.

Hancock, Peter, Denis Vincenzi, John Wise, and Mustapha Mouloua. 2019. *Human Factors in Simulation and Training*. Boca Raton, FL: CRC Press.

Hanin, Yuri, Tapio Korjus, Petteri Jouste, and Paul Baxter. 2013. "Rapid Technique Correction Using Old Way/New Way: Two Case Studies With Olympic Athletes." *The Sport Psychologist* 16 (1): 79-99. https://doi.org/10.1123/tsp.16.1.79.

Hodges, Nicola, and Kenneth Lohse. 2022. "An Extended Challenge-Based Framework for Practice Design in Sports Coaching." *Journal of Sports Sciences* 40 (7): 754-768. https://doi.org/10.1080/02640414.2021.2015917.

Kearney, Phil, Howie Carson, and Dave Collins. 2018. "Implementing Technical Refinement in High-Level Athletics: Exploring the Knowledge Schemas of Coaches." *Journal of Sports Sciences* 36 (10): 1118-1126.

Kellerman, Bernadette, Dave Collins, Alan MacPherson, and Maurizio Bertollo. 2024. "Exploring Characteristics of and Transitions Between Mental States Within the Multi-Action Plan Model in High-Level Judo." *European Journal of Sports Sciences* 24 (7): 907-917. https://doi.org/10.1002/ejsc.12117.

Krause, Lyndon, Damian Farrow, Ross Pinder, Tim Buszard, Stephanie Kovalchik, and Machar Reid. 2019. "Enhancing Skill Transfer in Tennis Using Representative Learning Design." *Journal of Sports Sciences* 37 (22): 2560-2568. https://doi.org/10.1080/02640414.2019.1647739.

MacNamara, Áine, and Dave Collins. 2015. "Twitterati and Paperati—Evidence Versus Popular Opinion in Science Communication." *British Journal of Sports Medicine*, 49, 1227-1228. https://doi.org/10.1136/bjsports-2015-094884.

Martindale, Amanda, and Dave Collins. 2007. "Enhancing the Evaluation of Effectiveness With Professional Judgement and Decision Making." *The Sport Psychologist*, 21, 458-474.

Massoth, Christina, Hannah Röder, Hendrik Ohlenburg, Michael Hessler, Alexander Zarbock, Daniel M. Pöpping, and Manuel Wenk. 2019. "High-Fidelity Is Not Superior to Low-Fidelity Simulation but Leads to Overconfidence in Medical Students." *BMC Medical Education*, 19, 29. https://doi.org/10.1186/s12909-019-1464-7.

McAuley, Alexander B.T., Joseph Baker, Adam L. Kelly. 2022. "Defining 'Elite' Status in Sport: From Chaos to Clarity." *German Journal of Exercise and Sport Research* 52 (1): 193-197. https://doi.org/10.1007/s12662-021-00737-3.

Pinder, Ross, Keith Davids, Ian Renshaw, and Duarte Araújo. 2011. "Representative Learning Design and Functionality of Research and Practice in Sport." *Journal of Sport and Exercise Psychology* 33 (1): 146-155.

Richardson, Stephen, Alistair McRobert, Don Vinson, Colum Cronin, Chris Lee, and Simon Roberts. 2023. "Systematic Review of Sport Coaches' and Teachers' Perceptions and Application of Game-Based and Constraints-Led Pedagogy: A Qualitative Meta-Study." *Quest* 76 (1): 113-134. https://doi.org/10.1080/00336297.2023.2257343.

Ruch, Simon, Michael Valiadis, and Alireza Gharabaghi. 2023. "Sleep to Learn." *Sleep* 44 (8): zsab160. https://doi.org/10.1093/sleep/zsab160.

Schmidt, Richard, and Craig Wrisberg. 2008. *Motor Learning and Performance: A Situation-Based Learning Approach.* Champaign, IL: Human Kinetics.

Simonsmeier, Bianca, Melina Andronie, Susanne Buecker, and Cornelia Frank. 2021. "The Effects of Imagery Interventions in Sports: A Meta-Analysis." *International Review of Sport and Exercise Psychology* 14 (1): 186-207. https://doi.org/10.1080/1750984X.2020.1780627.

Taylor, Jamie, Andrew Cruickshank, and Dave Collins. 2021. "Too Many Cooks, Not Enough Gourmets: Examining Provision and Use of Feedback for the Developing Athlete." *The Sport Psychologist* 36 (2): 89-100. https://doi.org/10.1123/tsp.2021-0037.

Toner, Jon, Howie Carson, Dave Collins, and Adam Nicholls. 2020. "The Prevalence and Influence of Psychosocial Factors on Technical Refinement Amongst Highly Skilled Tennis Players." *International Journal of Sport and Exercise Psychology* 18 (2): 201-217.

Chapter 8

Araújo, Duarte, Robert Hristovski, Ludovic Seifert, João Carvalho, and Keith Davids. 2019. "Ecological Cognition: Expert Decision-Making Behaviour in Sport." *International Review of Sport and Exercise Psychology* 12 (1): 1-25. https://doi.org/10.1080/1750984X.2017.1349826.

Ashford, Michael, Andrew Abraham, and Jamie Poolton. 2021. "What Cognitive Mechanism, When, Where and Why? Exploring the Decision Making of University and Professional Rugby Union Players." *Frontiers in Psychology*, 12. https://doi.org/10.3389/fpsyg.2021.609127.

Benz, Adam, Nick Winkelman, Jared Porter, and Sophia Nimphius. 2016. "Coaching Instructions and Cues for Enhancing Sprint Performance." *Strength and Conditioning Journal* 38 (1): 1-11. https://doi.org/10.1519/SSC.0000000000000185.

Bortoli, Laura, Maurizio Bertollo, Yuri Hanin, and Claudio Robazza. 2012. "Striving for Excellence: A Multiaction Plan Intervention Model for Shooters." *Psychology of Sport and Exercise* 13 (5): 693-701. https://doi.org/10.1016/j.psychsport.2012.04.006.

Bruning, Alison, Meghan M. Mallya, and Jarrod A. Lewis-Peacock. 2023. "Rumination Burdens the Updating of Working Memory." *Attention, Perception, & Psychophysics*, 85, 1452-1460. https://doi.org/10.3758/s13414-022-02649-2.

Carpenter, William. 1984. *Principles of Mental Physiology.* New York: Appleton.

Carson, Howie J., and Dave Collins. 2011. "Refining and Regaining Skills in Fixation/Diversification Stage Performers: The Five-A Model." *International Review of Sport and Exercise Psychology* 4 (2): 146-167. https://doi.org/10.1080/1750984x.2011.613682.

Christensen, Wayne, John Sutton, and Doris McIlwain. 2016. Cognition in skilled action: Meshed control and the varieties of skill experience. *Mind and Language*, 31(1), 37–66. https://doi.org/10.1111/mila.12094

Collins, Dave. 2011. "Practical Dimensions of Realising Your Peak Performance." In *Performance Psychology: A Practitioner's Guide*, edited by Dave Collins, Angela Button, and Hugh Richards, 381-391. London: Churchill Livingstone.

Collins, Dave, and Judy Collins. 2011. "Putting Them Together: Skills Packages to Optimize Team/Group Performance." In *Performance Psychology: A Practitioner's Guide*, edited by Dave Collins, Angela Button, and Hugh Richards, 361-381. London: Churchill Livingstone.

Collins, Dave, and Andrew Cruickshank. 2022. *Sport Psychology Essentials.* Champaign, IL: Human Kinetics.

Collins, Dave, and Sara Kamin. 2012. "The Performance Coach." In *Handbook of Sport and Performance Psychology*, edited by Shane M. Murphy, 692-706. Oxford: Oxford University Press.

Collins, Rosie, Dave Collins, and Howie J. Carson. 2022. "Muscular Collision Chess: A Qualitative Exploration of the Role and Development of Cognition, Understanding and Knowledge in Elite-Level Decision Making." *International Journal of Sport and Exercise Psychology* 20 (3): 828-848. https://doi.org/10.1080/1612197X.2021.1907768.

Collins, Dave, Mike Doherty, and Steve Talbot. 1993. "Performance Enhancement in Moto Cross: A Case Study of the Sport Science Team in Action." *The Sport Psychologist*, 7, 290-297.

Collins, Dave, Áine MacNamara, and Andrew Cruickshank. 2018. "Research and Practice in Talent Identification and Development: Some Thoughts on the State of Play." *Journal of Applied Sport Psychology* 31 (3): 340-351. https://doi.org/10.1080/10413200.2018.1475430.

Collins, Rosie, David Moffat, Howie J. Carson, and Dave Collins. 2023. "Where You Look During Golf Putting Makes No Difference to Skilled Golfers (but What You Look at Might!): An Examination of Occipital EEG α-Power During Target and Ball Focused Aiming." *International Journal of Sport and Exercise Psychology* 21 (3): 456-472. https://doi.org/10.1080/1612197X.2022.2066706.

Csikszentmihalyi, Mihaly. 1990. "Flow: The Psychology of Optimal Experience." *Journal of Leisure Research* 24 (1): 93-94. https://doi.org/10.1080/00222216.1992.11969876.

Decety, Jean, and Marc Jeannerod. 1995. "Mentally Simulated Movements in Virtual Reality: Does Fitts' Law Hold in Motor Imagery?" *Behavioral Brain Research*, 72, 127-134.

Doran, George. 1981. "There's a S.M.A.R.T. Way to Write Management's Goals and Objectives." *Management Review*, 70, 35-36.

Duckworth, Angela L., Christopher Peterson, Michael D. Matthews, and Dennis R. Kelly. 2007. "Grit: Perseverance and Passion for Long-Term Goals." *Journal of Personality and Social Psychology* 92 (6): 1087-1101.

Franks, Benjamin, William R. Roberts, and John Jakeman. 2019. "Representing Reality: Investigating the Perception-Action Couplings of Expert Soccer Goal Keepers Under Representative Constraints Studies." In *Studies in Perception and Action XV*, edited by R. Withagan and L. Dijk, 84-86. London: Routledge.

Gibbs, Graham. 1988. Learning by Doing: A guide to teaching and learning methods. Further Education Unit. Oxford Polytechnic: Oxford.

Gibson, James. 1979. *The Ecological Approach to Visual Perception*. New York: Houghton Mifflin.

Hanin, Yuri L. 2000. "Individual Zone of Optimal Functioning (IZOF) Model: Emotion-Performance Relationships in Sport." In *Emotions in Sport*, edited by Yuri L. Hanin, 65-89. Champaign, IL: Human Kinetics.

Hardy, Lew. 1990. "A Catastrophe Model of Performance in Sport." In *Stress and Performance in Sport*, edited by J. Graham Jones and Lew Hardy, 81-106. Chichester, UK: Wiley.

Herrebrøden, Henrik. 2023. "Motor Performers Need Task-Relevant Information: Proposing an Alternative Mechanism for the Attentional Focus Effect." *Journal of Motor Behavior* 55 (1): 125-134. https://doi.org/10.1080/00222895.2022.2122920.

Holmes, Paul S., and Dave Collins. 2001. "The PETTLEP Approach to Motor Imagery: A Functional Equivalence Model for Sport Psychologists." *Journal of Applied Sport Psychology* 13 (1): 60-83. https://doi.org/10.1080/10413200109339004.

Jacobsen, Eric. 1931. "Electrical Measurement of Neuromuscular States During Mental Activities." *American Journal of Physiology*, 96, 115-121.

Jeannerod, Marc. 1994. "The Representing Brain: Neural Correlates of Motor Intention and Imagery." *Behavioral and Brain Sciences*, 17, 187-245.

Keegan, Richard. 2016. *Being a Sport Psychologist*. London: Bloomsbury Academic.

Kolb, David A. 1984. *Experiential Learning: Experience as the Source of Learning and Development*. Englewood Cliffs, NJ: Prentice Hall.

Lang, Peter J. 1977. "Imagery in Therapy: An Information Processing Analysis of Fear." *Behavior Therapy* 8 (5): 862-886.

Lang, Peter J. 1979. "A Bio-Informational Theory of Emotional Imagery." *Psychophysiology* 16 (6): 495-512.

Levi, Hannah R., and Robin C. Jackson. 2018. "Contextual Factors Influencing Decision Making: Perceptions of Professional Soccer Players." *Psychology of Sport and Exercise*, 37, 19-25. https://doi.org/10.1016/j.psychsport.2018.04.001.

Lipshitz, Raanan, and Orna Strauss. 1997. "Coping with Uncertainty: A Naturalistic Decision-Making Analysis." *Organizational Behavior and Human Decision Processes* 69 (2): 149-163. https://doi.org/10.1006/obhd.1997.2679.

MacNamara, Áine, Angela Button, and Dave Collins. 2010a. "The Role of Psychological Characteristics in Facilitating the Pathway to Elite Performance Part 1: Identifying Mental Skills and Behaviors." *The Sport Psychologist*, 24, 52-73. https://doi.org/10.1123/TSP.24.1.74.

MacNamara, Áine, Angela Button, and Dave Collins. 2010b. "The Role of Psychological Characteristics in Facilitating the Pathway to Elite Performance Part 2: Examining Environmental and Stage-Related Differences in Skills and Behaviors." *The Sport Psychologist*, 24, 74-96. https://doi.org/10.1123/TSP.24.1.74.

MacPherson, Alan, Dave Collins, and Sukhvinder Obhi. 2009. "The Importance of Temporal Structure and Rhythm for the Optimum Performance of Motor Skills: A New Focus for Practitioners of Sport Psychology." *Journal of Applied Sport Psychology* 21 (S1): S48-S61.

Maurer, Heiko, and Jörn Munzert. 2013. "Influence of Attentional Focus on Skilled Motor Performance: Performance Decrement Under Unfamiliar Focus Conditions." *Human Movement Science* 32 (4): 730-740. https://doi.org/10.1016/j.humov.2013.02.001.

Moodie, Graham, Jamie Taylor, and Dave Collins. 2023. "Developing Psycho-Behavioural Skills: The Talent Development Coach Perspective." *Psych* 5 (2): 427-446. https://doi.org/10.3390/psych5020029.

Morris, Tony, Michael Spittle, and Anthony P. Watt. 2005. *Imagery in Sport*. Champaign, IL: Human Kinetics.

Paivio, A. 1985. Cognitive and motivational functions of imagery in human performance. *Canadian Journal of Applied Sport Sciences*, 10, 22-28.

Pezzulo, Giovanni. 2008. "Coordinating With the Future: The Anticipatory Nature of Representation." *Minds and Machines*, 18, 179-225. https://doi.org/10.1007/s11023-008-9095-5.

Proietti, Riccardo, Giovanni Pezzulo, and Alessia Tessari. 2023. "An Active Inference Model of Hierarchical Action Understanding, Learning and Imitation." *Physics of Life Reviews*, 46, 92-118. https://doi.org/10.1016/j.plrev.2023.05.012.

Ridderinkhof, K. Richard, and Marcel Brass. 2015. "How Kinesthetic Motor Imagery Works: A Predictive-Processing Theory of Visualization in Sports and Motor Expertise." *Journal of Physiology-Paris*, 109, 1-3. https://doi.org/10.1016/j.jphysparis.2015.02.003.

Robazza, Claudio, Maurizio Bertollo, Edson Filho, Yuri Hanin, and Laura Bortoli. 2016. "Perceived Control and Hedonic Tone Dynamics During Performance in Elite Shooters." *Research Quarterly for Exercise and Sport* 87 (3): 284-294. https://doi.org/10.1080/02701367.2016.1185081.

Sackett, R.S. 1934. "The Influences of Symbolic Rehearsal Upon the Retention of Maze Habit." *The Journal of General Psychology*, 10, 376-395.

Schack, Thomas, and Franz Mechsner. 2006. "Representation of Motor Skills in Human Long-Term Memory." *Neuroscience Letters* 391 (3): 77-81. https://doi.org/10.1016/j.neulet.2005.10.009.

Schoenfeld, Brad. 2016. "Attentional Focus for Maximizing Muscle Development: The Mind-Muscle Connection." *Strength and Conditioning Journal* 38 (1): 27-29. https://doi.org/10.1519/SSC.0000000000000190.

Schön, Donald. 1983. *The Reflective Practitioner: How Professionals Think in Action*. New York: Basic Books.

Stephens, Andreas, and Trond A. Tjøstheim. 2022. "The Cognitive Philosophy of Reflection." *Erkenntnis*, 87, 2219-2242. https://doi.org/10.1007/s10670-020-00299-0.

Sims, Matthew. 2020. "Coupling to Variant Information: An Ecological Account of Comparative Mental Imagery Generation." *Review of Philosophy and Psychology*, 11, 899-916. https://doi.org/10.1007/s13164-019-00454-9.

Swann, Christian, Richard Keegan, Lee Crust, and David Piggott. 2016. "Psychological States Underlying Excellent Performance in Professional Golfers: 'Letting It Happen' vs. 'Making It Happen.'" *Psychology of Sport and Exercise*, 23, 101-113. https://doi.org/10.1016/j.psychsport.2015.10.008.

Swann, Christian, Patricia C. Jackman, Alex Lawrence, Rebecca M. Hawkins, Scott G. Goddard, Ollie Williamson, Matthew J. Schweickle, Stewart A. Vella, Simon Rosenbaum, and Panteleimon Ekkekakis. 2022. "The (Over) use of SMART Goals for Physical Activity Promotion: A Narrative Review and Critique." Health Psychology Review 17 (2): 211-226. https://doi.org/10.1080/17437199.2021.2023608.

Vickers, J.N. 1996. "Visual Control When Aiming at a Far Target." *Journal of Experimental Psychology: Human Perception and Performance 22* (342): 342-354.

Weiner, Bernard. 1985. "Drive Theory." In *Human Motivation*, 85-139. New York: Springer.

Winkelman, Nick C., Kenneth P. Clark, and Larry J. Ryan. 2017. "Experience Level Influences the Effect of Attentional Focus on Sprint Performance." *Human Movement Science*, 52, 84-95. https://doi.org/10.1016/j.humove.2017.01.012.

Winter, Stacy and Dave Collins. 2015. Why do we do, what we do? Journal of Applied Sport Psychology, 27(1), 35–51. https://doi.org/10.1080/10413200.2014.941511

Wulf, Gabriele. 2016. "An External Focus of Attention Is a Conditio Sine Qua Non for Athletes: A Response to Carson, Collins, and Toner (2015)." *Journal of Sports Sciences* 34 (13): 1293-1295. https://doi.org/10.1080/02640414.2015.1136746.

Wulf, Gabriele, Nancy McNevin, and Charles H. Shea. 2001. "The Automaticity of Complex Motor Skill Learning as a Function of Attentional Focus." *The Quarterly Journal of Experimental Psychology* 54A (4): 1143-1154. https://doi.org/10.1080/02724980143000118.

Chapter 9

Abraham, Andrew, and Dave Collins. 2011. "Taking The Next Step: Ways Forward For Coaching Science." *Quest* 11 (4): 366-384. https://doi.org/10.1080/00336297.2011.10483687.

Bortoli, Laura, Maurizio Bertollo, Yuri Hanin, and Caludio Robazza. 2012. "Striving for Excellence: A Multi-Action Plan Intervention Model for Shooters." *Psychology of Sport and Exercise* 13 (5): 693-701. https://doi.org/10.1016/j.psychsport.2012.04.006.

Carson, Howie J., and Dave Collins. 2016. "The Fourth Dimension: A Motoric Perspective on the Anxiety–Performance Relationship." *International Review of Sport and Exercise Psychology 9 (1)*: 1-21. https://doi.org/10.1080/1750984X.2015.1072231.

Dorris, Derek C., David A. Power, and Emily Kenefick. 2012. "Investigating the Effects of Ego Depletion on Physical Exercise Routines of Athletes." *Psychology of Sport and Exercise* 13 (2): 118-125. https://doi.org/10.1016/j.psychsport.2011.10.004.

Eysenck, Michael W., Nazanin Derakshan, Rita Santos, and Maniel G. Calvo. 2007. "Anxiety and Cognitive Performance: Attentional Control Theory." *Emotion* 7 (2): 336-353. https://doi.org/10.1037/1528-3542.7.2.336.

Jones, Marc, Carla Meijen, Paul J. McCarthy, and David Sheffield. 2009. "A Theory of Challenge and Threat States in Athletes." *International Review of Sport and Exercise Psychology* 2 (2): 161-180. https://doi.org/10.1080/17509840902829331.

Hagger, Martin S., Chantelle Wood, Chris Stiff, and Nikos L.D. Chatzisarantis. 2010. "Ego Depletion and the Strength Model of Self-Control: A Meta-Analysis." *Psychological Bulletin* 136 (4): 495-525. https://doi.org/10.1037/a0019486.

Kellermann, Bernadette, Alan MacPherson, Dave Collins, and Maurizio Bertollo. 2022. "Reading the MAP: A Pracademic Perspective on the Current State of Play of the Multi-Action Plan Model With Regard to Transitions Between Mental States." *International Journal of Environmental Research and Public Health* 19 (23): 15520. https://doi.org/10.3390/ijerph192315520.

Kreiner-Phillips, Kathy, and Terry Orlick. 1993. "Winning After Winning: The Psychology of Ongoing Excellence." *The Sport Psychologist* 7 (1): 31-48. https://doi.org/10.1123/tsp.7.1.31.

Lovden, Martin, Benjami Garzon, and Ulman Lindenberger. 2020. "Human Skill Learning: Expansion, Exploration, Selection, and Refinement." *Current Opinion in Behavioral Sciences*, 36, 163-168. https://doi.org/10.1016/j.cobeha.2020.11.002.

Low, William R., Paul Freeman, Joanne Butt, Mike Stoker, and Ian Maynard. 2022. "The Role and Creation of Pressure in Training: Perspectives of Athletes and Sport Psychologists." *Journal of Applied Sport Psychology* 35 (4): 710-730. https://doi.org/10.1080/10413200.2022.2061637.

Mason, Robert J., Damian Farrow, and John A.C. Hattie. 2020. "Sports Coaches' Knowledge and Beliefs About the Provision, Reception, and Evaluation of Verbal Feedback." *Frontiers in Psychology*, 11, 571552. https://doi.org/10.3389/fpsyg.2020.571552.

Mellalieu, Stephen, Christopher Jones, Christopher Wagstaff, Simon Kemp, Matthew J. Cross. 2021. "Measuring Psychological Load." *International Journal of Sports Medicine* 42 (9): 782-788. https://doi.org/10.1055/a-1446-9642.

Mosston, Muska, and Sara Ashworth. 2008. *Teaching Physical Education*. 1st online edition. New York: The Spectrum Institute for Teaching and Learning.

Pill, Shane, Brendan SueSee, Joss Rankin, and Mitch Hewitt. 2021. *The Spectrum of Sport Coaching Styles*. New York: Routledge.

Rejeski, W. Jack, and Lawrence R. Brawley. 1983. "Attribution Theory in Sport: Current Status and New Perspectives." *Journal of Sport Psychology 5* (1): 77-99.

Taylor, Jamie, Dave Collins, and Andrew Cruickshank. 2021. "Too Many Cooks, Not Enough Gourmets: Examining Provision and Use of Feedback for the Developing Athlete." *The Sport Psychologist* 36 (2): 89-100. https://doi.org/10.1123/tsp.2021-0037.

Thom, Christiana B., Frédéric Guay, and Christiane Trottier. 2020. "Mental Toughness in Sport: The Goal-Expectancy-Self-Control (GES) Model." *Journal of Applied Sport Psychology* 33 (6): 627-643. https://doi.org/10.1080/10413200.2020.1808736.

Timler, Amanda, Fluer McIntyre, Elizabeth Rose, and Beth Hands. 2019. "Exploring the Influence of Self-Perceptions on the Relationship Between Motor Competence and Identity in Adolescents." *PLoS ONE 14* (11): e0224653. https://doi.org/10.1371/journal.pone.0224653.

Török, Lilla, Zsolt P. Szabo, and Gábor Orosz. 2022. "Elite Athletes' Perfectionistic Striving vs. Concerns as Opposing Predictors of Self-Handicapping With the Mediating Role of Attributional Style." *Frontiers in Psychology*, 13, 862122. https://doi.org/10.3389/fpsyg.2022.862122.

Chapter 10

Abraham, Andrew, and Dave Collins. 2011. "Taking the Next Step: Ways Forward for Coaching Science." *Quest* 63 (4): 366-384. https://doi.org/10.1080/00336297.2011 10483687.

Ashford, Michael, and Jamie Taylor. 2022. "Planning Your Coaching for Young Rugby Players." In *The Young Rugby Player: Science and Application*, edited by Kevin Till, Jonathon Weakley, Sarah Whitehead, and Ben Jones, 331-346. New York: Routledge.

Ashford, Michael, Ed Cope, Andrew Abraham, and Jamie Poolton. 2022. "Coaching Player Decision Making in Rugby Union: Exploring Coaches Espoused Theories and Theories in Use as an Indicator of Effective Coaching Practice." *Physical Education and Sport Pedagogy*, 1-22. https://doi.org/10.1080/17408989.2022.2153822.

Ashford, Michael, Jamie Taylor, Jared Payne, Dom Waldouck, and Dave Collins 2023. "'Getting on the Same Page' Enhancing Team Performance With Shared Mental Models—Case Studies of Evidence Informed Practice in Elite Sport." *Frontiers in Sports and Active Living*, 5, 1057143. https://doi.org/10.3389/fspor.2023.1057143.

Burke, V. (2011). Organizing for excellence. In Collins, Dave, Angela Button, and Hugh Richards (Eds.),. *Performance Psychology: A Practitioner's Guide*. pp., 99-120. Oxford: Elsevier. Carson, Howie J., and Dave Collins. 2016. "Implementing the Five-A Model of Technical Refinement: Key Roles of the Sport Psychologist." *Journal of Applied Sport Psychology* 28 (4): 392-409. https://doi.org/10.1080/10413200.2016.1162224.

Chelladurai, P. (1978). *A contingency model of leadership in athletics*. Unpublished doctoral dissertation, Department of Management Sciences, University of Waterloo, Waterloo, ON, Canada.

Collins, Dave, and Andrew Cruickshank. 2015. "Take a Walk on the Wild Side: Exploring, Identifying, and Developing Consultancy Expertise With Elite Performance Team Leaders." *Psychology of Sport and Exercise*, 16, 74-82.

Collins, Dave, and Áine MacNamara, 2017. "Making Champs and Super-Champs—Current Views, Contradictions, and Future Directions." *Frontiers in Psychology*, 8. https://doi.org/10.3389/fpsyg.2017.00823.

Collins, Dave, and Áine MacNamara. 2022. *Talent Development: A Practitioner and Parents Guide*, 2nd ed. London: Routledge.

Collins, Dave, Andrew Abraham, and Rosie Collins. 2012. "On Vampires and Wolves—Exploring and Countering Reasons for the Differential Impact of Coach Education." *International Journal of Sport Psychology*, 43, 255-271.

Collins, Loel, Howie J. Carson, and Dave Collins. 2016. "Metacognition and Professional Judgment and Decision Making in Coaching: Importance, Application and Evaluation." *International Sport Coaching Journal* 3 (3): 355-361. https://doi.org/10.1123/iscj.2016-0037.

Collins, Dave, Loel Collins, and Howie Carson. 2016. "'If It Feels Right, Do It': Intuitive Decision Making in a Sample of High-Level Sport Coaches." *Frontiers in Psychology*, 7, 504. https://doi.org/10.3389/fpsyg.2016.00504.

Collins, R., Collins, D. & Carson, H. (2022). Show me, tell me: An investigation into learning processes within skateboarding as an informal coaching environment. *Frontiers in Psychology: Movement Science and Sport Psychology*, 13, doi.org/10.3389/fpsyg.2022.812068

Collins, Dave, Áine MacNamara, and Neil McCarthy. 2016. "Super Champions, Champions, and Almosts: Important Differences and Commonalities on the Rocky Road." *Frontiers in Psychology*, 6. https://doi.org/10.3389/fpsyg.2015.02009.

Collins, Dave, Phil Moore, David Mitchell, and Faith Alpress, 1999. "Role Conflict and Confidentiality in Multidisciplinary Athlete Support Programmes. *British Journal of Sports Medicine*, 33, 208-211.

Cronin, Colum, and Kathleen Armour. 2018. *Care in Sport Coaching: Pedagogical Cases*. London: Routledge.

Cruickshank, Andrew, and Dave Collins. 2016. "Advancing Leadership in Sport: Time to Take Off the Blinkers?" *Sports Medicine* 46 (9):1199-204. https://doi.org/10.1007/s40279-016-0513-1.

Fiske, Donald. W. (1949). Consistency of the factorial structures of personality ratings from different sources. *The Journal of Abnormal and Social Psychology*, 44 (3), 329–344

Hanin, Yuri, Tapio Korjus, Petteri Jouste, and Paul Baxter. 2002. "Rapid Technique Correction Using Old Way/New Way: Two Case Studies With Olympic Athletes." *The Sport Psychologist* 16 (1): 79-99. https://doi.org/10.1123/tsp.16.1.79.

Harvey, Stephen, John William Baird Lyle, and Bob Muir. 2015. "Naturalistic Decision Making in High Performance Team Sport Coaching." *International Sport Coaching Journal* 2 (2): 152-168.

Hodges, Nicola J., and Keith R. Lohse. 2022. "An Extended Challenge-Based Framework for Practice Design in Sports Coaching." *Journal of Sports Sciences* 40 (7): 754-768. https://doi.org/10.1080/02640414.2021.2015917.

Horn, Thelma, Patrick Bloom, Katie Berglund, and Stacie Packard. 2011. "Relationship Between Collegiate Athletes' Psychological Characteristics and Their Preferences for Different Types of Coaching Behavior." *The Sport Psychologist* 25 (2): 190-211. https://doi.org/10.1123/tsp.25.2.190.

Hunter, Emily M., Mitchell, J. Neubert, Sara Jensen Perry, L.A. Witt, Lisa M. Penney, and Evan Weinberger. 2012. "Servant Leaders Inspire Servant Followers: Antecedents and Outcomes Employees and the Organization." *The Leadership Quarterly* 24 (2): 316-331. https://doi.org/10.1016/j.leaqua.2012.12.001.

Jones, Dennis Floyd, Lynn Dale Housner, and Alan Seth Kornspan. 1995. "Interactive Decision Making and Behavior of Experienced and Inexperienced Basketball Coaches During Practice." *Journal of Teaching in Physical Education* 16 (4): 454-468. https://doi.org/10.1123/jtpe.16.4.454.

Jowett, Sophia. 2017. "Coaching Effectiveness: The Coach-Athlete Relationship at its Heart." *Current Opinion in Psychology* 16 (1): 154-158. https://doi.org/10.1016/j.copsyc.2017.05.006.

Jowett, Sophia, and Artur Pocwardowski. 2007. "Understanding the Coach-Athlete Relationship." In *Social Psychol-*

ogy of Sport, edited by Sophia Jowett and David Lavallee, 3-14. Champaign, IL: Human Kinetics.

Judge, Timothy A., Joyce Bono, Remus Ilies, and Megan W. Gerhardt. 2002. *Journal of Applied Psychology* 87 (4): 765-780

Kirschner, Paul A., and Carl Hendrick. 2020. "How Learning Happens: Seminal Works in Educational Psychology and What They Mean in Practice." London: Routledge.

Klein, Gary. 2007. "Flexecution as a Paradigm for Replanning, Part 1." *IEEE Intelligent Systems* 22 (1): 79-83.

Lines, Robin L.J., Benjamin L. Hoggan, Sasha Nahleen, Philip Temby, Monique Crane, and Daniel F. Gucciardi. 2022. "Enhancing Shared Mental Models: A Systematic Review and Meta-Analysis of Randomized Controlled Trials." *Sport, Exercise, and Performance Psychology* 11 (4): 524-549. https://doi.org/10.1037/spy0000288.

López de Subijana, Christina, Luc J. Martin, Javier Ramos, and Jean Côté. 2021. "How Coach Leadership Is Related to the Coach-Athlete Relationship in Elite Sport." *International Journal of Sports Science and Coaching* 16 (6): 1239-1246. https://doi.org/10.1177/17479541211021523.

Lyle, John. 2002. *Sport Coaching Concepts: A Framework for Coaching Practice*. Milton Park, UK: Taylor and Francis.

Lyle, John. 2010. "Coaches' Decision Making: A Naturalistic Decision Making Analysis." In *Sports Coaching: Professionalisation and Practice*, edited by John Lyle and Chris Cushion, 27-41. Edinburgh: Churchill Livingstone.

MacNamara, Áine, Angela Button, and Dave Collins. 2010a. "The Role of Psychological Characteristics in Facilitating the Pathway to Elite Performance. Part 1: Identifying Mental Skills and Behaviours." *The Sport Psychologist*, 24, 52-73.

MacNamara, Áine, Angela Button, and Dave Collins, 2010b. "The Role of Psychological Characteristics in Facilitating the Pathway to Elite Performance. Part 2: Examining Environmental and Stage-Related Differences in Skills and Behaviours." *The Sport Psychologist*, 24, 74-96.

Martindale, Amanda, and Dave Collins. 2005. "Professional Judgment and Decision Making: The Role of Intention for Impact." *The Sport Psychologist* 19 (3): 303-317.

McKay, Jim, Keith Davids, Sam Robertson, and Carl T. Woods. "An ecological insight into the design and integration of attacking principles of play in professional rugby union: a case example." *International Sport Coaching Journal* 8, no. 3 (2021): 394-399. https://doi.org/10.1123/iscj.2020-0065

Moran, Jack, Murray Craig, and Dave Collins. 2024. "How Might We Do It Better? Applying Educational Curriculum Theory and Practice in Talent Development Environments." *Sports Coaching Review*. https://doi.org/10.1080/21640629.2024.2321047.

Richards, Pam, Dave Collins, and Duncan R.D. Mascarenhas. 2012. "Developing Rapid High-Pressure Team Decision-Making Skills. The Integration of Slow Deliberate Reflective Learning Within the Competitive Performance Environment: A Case Study of Elite Netball." *Reflective Practice* 13 (3): 407-424. https://doi.org/10.1080/14623943.2012.670111.

Richards, Pam, Dave Collins, and Duncan R.D. Mascarenhas. 2017. "Developing Team Decision-Making: A Holistic Framework Integrating Both On-Field and Off-Field Pedagogical Coaching Processes." *Sports Coaching Review* 6 (1): 57-75. https://doi.org/10.1080/21640629.2016.1200819.

Sloman, Stephen. 1996. "The Empirical Case for Two Systems of Reasoning." *Psychological Bulletin* 119 (1): 3-22.

Taylor, Jamie, Michael Ashford, and Dave Collins. 2022a. "The Role of Challenge in Talent Development: Understanding Impact in Response to Emotional Disturbance." *Psych* 4 (4): 668-694. https://doi.org/10.3390/psych4040050.

Taylor, Jamie, Michael Ashford, and Dave Collins. 2022b. "Tough Love—Impactful, Caring Coaching in Psychologically Unsafe Environments." *Sports* 10 (6): 83. https://doi.org/10.3390/sports10060083.

Taylor, Jamie, Michael Ashford, and Matt Jefferson. 2023. "High Performance Coach Cognition in the Wild: Using Applied Cognitive Task Analysis for Practical Insights—Cognitive Challenges and Curriculum Knowledge." *Frontiers in Psychology* 14 (1154168). https://doi.org/10.3389/fpsyg.2023.1154168.

Taylor, Jamie, Dave Collins, and Andrew Cruickshank. 2021. "Too Many Cooks, Not Enough Gourmets: Examining Provision and Use of Feedback for the Developing Athlete." *The Sport Psychologist* 36 (2): 89-100.

Vella, Stewart A., Elizabeth Mayland, Matthew J. Schweickle, Jordan T. Sutcliffe, Desmond McEwan, and Christian Swann. 2022. "Psychological Safety in Sport: A Systematic Review and Concept Analysis." *International Review of Sport and Exercise Psychology* (2022): 1-24. https://doi.org/10.1080/1750984X.2022.2028306.

Chapter 11

Araújo, Duarte., and Davids, Keith. 2011. "What Exactly is Acquired During Skill Acquisition?" *Journal of Consciousness Studies* 18 (3-4): 7-23.

Ashford, Michael, Andrew Abraham, and Jamie Poolton. 2021. "What Cognitive Mechanism, When, Where, and Why? Exploring the Decision Making of University and Professional Rugby Union Players During Competitive Matches." *Frontiers in Psychology*, 12, 1608. https://doi.org/10.3389/fpsyg.2021.609127.

Ashford, Michael, Jamie Taylor, Jared Payne, Dom Waldouck, and Dave Collins 2023. "'Getting on the Same Page' Enhancing Team Performance With Shared Mental Models—Case Studies of Evidence Informed Practice in Elite Sport." *Frontiers in Sports and Active Living*, 5, 1057143. https://doi.org/10.3389/fspor.2023.1057143.

Bailey, Richard, Dave Collins, Paul Ford, Áine MacNamara, Gemma Pearce, and Martin Toms. 2010. *Participant Development in Sport: An Academic Review*. Leeds, UK: Sports Coach UK.

Bourbousson, Jérôme, Germain Poizat, Jacques Saury, and Carole Sève. 2011. "Description of Dynamic Shared Knowledge: An Exploratory Study During a Competitive Team Sports Interaction." *Ergonomics* 54 (2): 120-138. https://doi.org/10.1080/00140139.2010.544763

Brown, Braden J., Ty B. Aller, Logan K. Lyons, Jakob F. Jensen, and Jennifer L. Hodgson. 2022. "NCAA Student-Athlete Mental Health and Wellness: A Biopsychosocial Examination." *Journal of Student Affairs Research and Practice* 59 (3): 252-267. https://doi.org/10.1080/19496591.2021.1902820

Cannon-Bowers, Janis A., Eduardo Salas, and Sharolyn Converse. 1993. "Shared Mental Models in Expert Team Decision Making." In *Individual and Group Decision Making: Current Issues*, edited by N.J. Castellan Jr., 221-246. Mahwah, NJ: Lawrence Erlbaum Associates, Inc. https://doi.org/10.4324/9780203772744

Carson, Howie J., and Dave Collins. 2017. "Refining Motor Skills in Golf: A Biopsychosocial Perspective." In *Routledge International Handbook of Golf Science*, edited by Martin Toms, 196-206. Oxon, UK: Routledge.

Evans, M. Blair, Veronica Allan, Karl Erickson, Luc J. Martin, Ross Budziszewski, and Jean Côté. 2017. "Are All Sport Activities Equal? A Systematic Review of How Youth Psychosocial Experiences Vary Across Differing Sport Activities." *British Journal of Sports Medicine* 51 (3): 169-176. https://doi.org/10.1136/bjsports-2016-096725

Finley, Nancy J. 2010. "Skating Femininity: Gender Manoeuvring in Women's Roller Derby." *Journal of Contemporary Ethnography* 39 (4): 359-387. https://doi.org/10.1177/0891241610364230

Gershgoren, Lael, Edson Medeiros Filho, Gershon Tenenbaum, and Robert J. Schinke. 2013. "Coaching Shared Mental Models in Soccer: A Longitudinal Case Study." *Journal of Clinical Sport Psychology* 7 (4): 293-312. https://doi.org/10.1123/jcsp.7.4.293

Gibson, James Jerome. 1966. *The Senses Considered as Perceptual Systems*. Westport, CT: Praeger.

Gredin, N. Viktor, Daniel T. Bishop, David P. Broadbent, Allan Tucker, and A. Mark Williams. 2018. "Experts Integrate Explicit Contextual Priors and Environmental Information to Improve Anticipation Efficiency." *Journal of Experimental Psychology: Applied* 24 (4): 509. https://doi.org/10.1037/xap0000174

Humphrey, Jake, and Damian Hughes, hosts. 2022. "Steve Clarke: Playing With the Expectation of Success and Not the Fear of Failure." *The High Performance Podcast*, episode 104, February 20, 2022. www.thehighperformancepodcast.com/podcast/steveclarke

Klein, Gary A., Orasanu, Judith, Roberta Calderwood, and Caroline E. Zsambok. 1993. *Decision Making in Action: Models and Methods*. Vol. 3. Norwood, NJ: Ablex.

Launder, Alan G., and Wendy Piltz. 2013. *Play Practice: Engaging and Developing Skilled Players From Beginner to Elite*. Champaign, IL: Human Kinetics. https://doi.org/10.5040/9781718209060

MacNamara, Áine, Angela Button, and Dave Collins. 2010a. "The Role of Psychological Characteristics in Facilitating the Pathway to Elite Performance Part 1: Identifying Mental Skills and Behaviors." *The Sport Psychologist* 24 (1): 52-73. https://doi.org/10.1123/tsp.24.1.52

MacNamara, Áine, Angela Button, and Dave Collins. 2010b. "The Role of Psychological Characteristics in Facilitating the Pathway to Elite Performance Part 2: Examining Environmental and Stage-Related Differences in Skills and Behaviors." *The Sport Psychologist* 24 (1): 74-96. https://doi.org/10.1123/tsp.24.1.74

McPherson, Sue L. 1994. "The Development of Sport Expertise: Mapping the Tactical Domain." *Quest* 46 (2): 223-240. https://doi.org/10.1080/00336297.1994.10484123

McLaren, Niall. 1998. "A Critical Review of the Biopsychosocial Model." *Australian & New Zealand Journal of Psychiatry* 32 (1): 86-92. https://doi.org/10.1046/j.1440-1614.1998.00343.x

Mills, Caitlin, Andre Zamani, Rebecca White, and Kalina Christoff. 2021. "Out of the Blue: Understanding Abrupt and Wayward Transitions in Thought Using Probability and Predictive Processing." *Philosophical Transactions of the Royal Society B* 376 (1817): 0190692. https://doi.org/10.1098/rstb.2019.0692

O'Brien, Katherine A., Andrew Kennedy, and Michael J. O'Keeffe. 2023. "The Element of Surprise: How Predictive Processing Can Help Coach Practitioners Understand and Develop Skilled Movement in Sport Settings." *International Sport Coaching Journal* 11 (2): 298-307. https://doi.org/10.1123/iscj.2023-0012

Paris, Scott G., and Janis E. Jacobs. 1984. "The Benefits of Informed Instruction for Children's Reading Awareness and Comprehension Skills." *Child Development* 55 (6): 2083-2093. https://doi.org/10.2307/1129781

Passos, Pedro, Rita Cordovil, Orlando Fernandes, and João Barreiros. 2012. "Perceiving Affordances in Rugby Union." *Journal of Sports Sciences* 30 (11): 1175-1182. https://doi.org/10.1080/02640414.2012.695082

Price, Amy, and Dave Collins. 2022. "Contributing to a Coaching Team's Shared Mental Model of Player Game Understanding: An Intervention Within High-Level Youth Soccer." *Journal of Sport Psychology in Action* 14 (1): 25-39. https://doi.org/10.1080/21520704.2022.2103224

Richards, Pam, Dave Collins, and Duncan R.D. Mascarenhas. 2012. "Developing Rapid High-Pressure Team Decision-Making Skills. The Integration of Slow Deliberate reflective Learning Within the Competitive Performance Environment: A Case Study of Elite Netball." *Reflective Practice* 13 (3): 407-424. https://doi.org/10.1080/14623943.2012.670111

Richards, Pam, Dave Collins, and Duncan R.D. Mascarenhas. 2017. "Developing Team Decision-Making: A Holistic Framework Integrating Both On-Field and Off-Field Pedagogical Coaching Processes." *Sports Coaching Review* 6 (1): 57-75. https://doi.org/10.1080/21640629.2016.1200819

Silva, Pedro, Júlio Garganta, Duarte Araújo, Keith Davids, and Paulo Aguiar. 2013. "Shared Knowledge or Shared Affordances? Insights From an Ecological Dynamics Approach to Team Coordination in Sports." *Sports Medicine*, 43, 765-772. https://doi.org/10.1007/s40279-013-0070-9

Stockbridge, Melissa D., Zafer Keser, and Rochelle S. Newman. 2022. "Concussion in Women's Flat-Track Roller Derby." *Frontiers in Neurology*, 13, 809939. https://doi.org/10.3389/fneur.2022.809939

Subotnik, Rena Faye, Paula Olszewski-Kubilius, and Frank C. Worrell. 2019. "Environmental Factors and Personal Characteristics Interact to Yield High Performance in Domains." *Frontiers in Psychology*, 10, 2804. https://doi.org/10.3389/fpsyg.2019.02804

Taylor, Jamie, Dave Collins, and Andrew Cruickshank. 2021. "Too Many Cooks, Not Enough Gourmets: Examining Provision and Use of Feedback for the Developing Athlete." *The Sport Psychologist* 36 (2): 89-100. https://doi.org/10.1123/tsp.2021-0037

Tee, Jason C., Michael Ashford, and David Piggott. 2018. "A Tactical Periodization Approach for Rugby Union." *Strength and Conditioning Journal* 40 (5): 1-13. https://doi.org/10.1519/ssc.0000000000000390

Tee, Jason, Bradley Diamandis, Andy Vilk, and Cameron Owen. 2020. "Utilising a Tactical Periodization Framework to Simulate Match Demands During Rugby Sevens Training." *Journal of Science in Sport and Exercise* 5 (5): 321-338. https://doi.org/10.31236/osf.io/d4jpm

TNT Sports. 2021. "Rio Meets John Stones | City's CB on personal rejuvenation, UCL hopes, and Phil Foden 2023." YouTube video, 8:54, February 5, 2021. www.youtube.com/watch?v=9YEW3TVN8qA&t=21s.

Toner John, Carson Howie J., Collins Dave & Nicholls Adam (2020) The prevalence and influence of psychosocial factors on technical refinement amongst highly-skilled tennis players, International Journal of Sport and Exercise Psychology, 18:2, 201-217. https://doi.org/10.1080/1612197X.2018.1511621

Van den Bossche, Piet, Wim Gijselaers, Mien Segers, Geert Woltjer, and Paul Kirschner. 2011. "Team Learning: Building Shared Mental Models." *Instructional Science*, 39, 283-301. https://doi.org/10.1007/s11251-010-9128-3

Chapter 12

Alfano, Helen, and Dave Collins. 2023. "Good Practice in Sport Science and Medicine Support: Practitioners' Perspectives on Quality, Pressure and Support." *Managing Sport and Leisure* 28 (4): 396-411. https://doi.org/10.1080/23750472.2021.1918019.

Ashford, Mike, Jamie Taylor, Jared Payne, Dom Waldouck, and Dave Collins. 2023. "'Getting on the Same Page': Enhancing Team Performance With Shared Mental Models—Case Studies of Evidence Informed Practice in Elite Sport." *Frontiers in Sports and Active Living*, 5, 1057143. https://doi.org/10.3389/fspor.2023.1057143.

References

Barrett, Lisa F. 2021. *Seven and a Half Lessons About the Brain*. London: Picador.

Bradley, Bret H., H.J. Anderson, J.E. Baur, and A.C. Klotz. 2015. "When Conflict Helps: Integrating Evidence for Beneficial Conflict in Groups and Teams Under Three Perspectives." *Group Dynamics: Theory, Research, and Practice* 19 (4): 243-272. http://dx.doi.org/10.1037/gdn0000033.

Burns, Andrew, and Dave Collins. 2023. "Interdisciplinary Practice in Performance Sport: A Scoping Review of Evidence of Collaboration." *European Journal of Sports Science* 23 (9): 1877-1891. https://doi.org/10.1080/17461391.2023.2201812.

Cambridge Dictionary. 2024. https://dictionary.cambridge.org/dictionary/english/culture

Cruickshank, Andrew, and Dave Collins. 2016. "Advancing Leadership in Sport: Time to Take Off the Blinkers?" *Sports Medicine* 46 (9): 1199-1204. http://doi.org/10.1007/s40279-016-0513-1.

Cruickshank, Andrew, and Dave Collins. 2015. "Illuminating and Applying 'The Dark Side': Insights from Elite Team Leaders." *Journal of Applied Sport Psychology* 27 (3): 249-267. http://doi.org/10.1080/10413200.2014.982771

Cruickshank, Andrew, Dave Collins, and Sue Minten. 2013. "Culture Change in a Professional Sports Team: Shaping Environmental Contexts and Regulating Power." *International Journal of Sports Science and Coaching* 8 (2): 271-290. https://doi.org/10.1260/1747-9541.8.2.271.

Cruickshank, Andrew, Dave Collins, and Sue Minten. 2014. "Driving and Sustaining Culture Change in Olympic Sport Performance Teams: A First Exploration and Grounded Theory." *Journal of Sport & Exercise Psychology* 36 (1): 107-120. https://doi.org/10.1123/jsep.2013-0133.

Cruickshank, Andrew, Dave Collins, and Sue Minten. 2015. "Driving and Sustaining Culture Change in Professional Sport Performance Teams: A Grounded Theory." *Psychology of Sport & Exercise*, 20, 40-50. https://doi.org/10.1016/j.psychsport.2015.04.007.

Deci, Edward L., and Richard M. Ryan. 2012. "Self-Determination Theory." In *Handbook of Theories of Social Psychology*, edited by Paul A.M. Van Lange, Arie W. Kruglanski, and E. Tory Higgins, 416-437. London: Sage.

Dorsch, Travis E., Michael Q. King, Sarah Tulane, Keith V. Osai, C. Ryan Dunn, and Chalyce P. Carlsen. 2019. "Parent Education in Youth Sport: A Community Case Study of Parents, Coaches, and Administrators". *Journal of Applied Sport Psychology* 31 (4): 427-450. https://doi.org/10.1080/10413200.2018.1510438.

Ekstrand, Jan, Daniel Lundqvist, Michael Davison, Michel D'Hooghe, and Anne Marte Pensgaard. 2019. "Communication Quality Between the Medical Team and the Head Coach/Manager Is Associated With Injury Burden and Player Availability in Elite Football Clubs." *British Journal of Sports Medicine* 53 (5): 304-308. https://doi:10.1136/bjsports-2018-099411.

Hansen, Per Øystein, and Svein S. Andersen. 2014. "Coaching Elite Athletes: How Coaches Stimulate Elite Athletes' Reflection." *Sports Coaching Review* 3 (1): 17-32.

https://doi.org/10.1080/21640629.2014.901712.

Haslam, S. Alexander. 2004. *Psychology in Organizations: The Social Identity Approach*. 2nd ed. Thousand Oaks, CA: Sage.

Henriksen, Kristoffer, Natalia Stambulova, and Kirsten Kaya Roessler. 2010. "Holistic Approach to Athletic Talent Development Environments: A Successful Sailing Milieu." *Psychology of Sport and Exercise* 11 (3): 212-222. https://doi.org/10.1016/j.psychsport.2009.10.005.

Martiny, Sarah E., Jenny Roth, Petra Jelenec, Melanie C. Steffens, and Jean-Claude Croizet. 2011. "When a New Group Identity Does Harm on the Spot: Stereotype Threat in Newly Created Groups." *European Journal of Social Psychology* 42 (1): 65-71. https://doi.org/10.1002/ejsp.840.

Pankhurst, Anne, Dave Collins, and Áine MacNamara. 2013. "Talent Development: Linking the Stakeholders to the Process." *Journal of Sports Sciences* 31 (4): 370-80. https://doi.org/10.1080/02640414.2012.733821.

Ryan, Richard M., and Edward L. Deci. 2020. "Intrinsic and Extrinsic Motivation From a Self-Determination Theory Perspective: Definitions, Theory, Practices, and Future Directions." *Contemporary Educational Psychology*, 61, 101860. https://doi.org/10.1016/j.cedpsych.2020.101860.

Santos, Fernando, Dan Gould, and Leisha Strachan. 2019. "Research on Positive Youth Development-Focused Coach Education Programs: Future Pathways and Applications." *International Sport Coaching Journal* 6 (1): 132-138. https://doi.org/10.1123/iscj.2018-0013.

Shih, Margaret J., Todd L. Pittinsky, and Geoffrey C. Ho. 2012. "Stereotype Boost: Positive Outcomes From the Activation of Positive Stereotypes." In *Stereotype Threat: Theory, Process, and Application, edited by* Michael Inzlicht and Toni Schmader, 141-156. Oxford: Oxford University Press.

Sotiriadou, Popi, and Veerle de Bosscher. 2018. "Managing High-Performance Sport: Introduction to Past, Present and Future Considerations." *European Sport Management Quarterly* 18 (1): 1-7. https://doi.org/10.1080/16184742.2017.1400225.

Stoszkowski, John, Áine MacNamara, Dave Collins, and Aran Hodgkinson. 2021. "'Opinion and Fact, Perspective and Truth': Seeking Truthfulness and Integrity in Coaching and Coach Education." *International Sport Coaching Journal* 8 (2): 263-269. https://doi.org/10.1123/iscj.2020-0023.

Taylor, Jamie, Dave Collins, and Mike Ashford. 2022. "Psychological Safety in High-Performance Sport: Contextually Applicable?" *Frontiers in Sports and Active Living* 4, 823488. https://doi: 10.3389/fspor.2022.823488

Taylor, Jamie, Dave Collins, and Andrew Cruickshank. 2021. "Too Many Cooks, Not Enough Gourmets: Examining Provision and Use of Feedback for the Developing Athlete." *The Sport Psychologist* 36 (2): 89-100. https://doi: 10.1123/tsp.2021-0037

Tajfel Henri, and John Turner. 1979. "An integrative theory of intergroup conflict." In: *The social psychology of intergroup relations*, edited by William G. Austin, and Stephen Worchel, 33-47. Monterey: Brooks-Cole.

Epilogue

Burton, Lauren, Terezinha Nunes, and Maria Evangelou. 2021. "Do Children Use Logic to Spell Logician? Implicit Versus Explicit Teaching of Morphological Spelling Rules." *British Journal of Educational Psychology* 91 (4): e12414. https://doi.org/10.1111/bjep.12414.

Chow, Jia Yi, Chris Button, Miriam Chang Yi Lee, Craig Morris, and Richard Shuttleworth. 2023. "Advice From 'Pracademics' of How to Apply Ecological Dynamics Theory to Practice Design." *Frontiers in Sports and Active Living* 5: 1192332. https://doi.org/10.3389/fspor.2023.1192332.

Collins, Dave, Andy Abraham, and Rosie Collins. 2012. "On Vampires and Wolves—Exposing and Exploring Reasons for the Differential Impact of Coach Education." *International Journal of Sport Psychology* 43 (3): 255-271.

de Jong, Ton de, Ard W. Lazonder, Clark A. Chinn, Frank Fischer, Janice Gobert, Cindy E. Hmelo-Silver, Ken R. Koedinger, et al. 2023. "Let's Talk Evidence—The Case for Combining Inquiry-Based and Direct Instruction." *Educational Research Review* 39 (May): 100536. https://doi.org/10.1016/j.edurev.2023.100536.

Entwistle, Noel J., and Elizabeth R. Peterson. 2004. "Conceptions of Learning and Knowledge in Higher Education: Relationships with Study Behaviour and Influences of Learning Environments." *International Journal of Educational Research* 41 (6): 407-428. https://doi.org/10.1016/j.ijer.2005.08.009.

Kirschner, Paul A., John Sweller, and Richard E. Clark. 2006. "Why Minimal Guidance During Instruction Does Not Work: An Analysis of the Failure of Constructivist, Discovery, Problem-Based, Experiential, and Inquiry-Based Teaching." *Educational Psychologist* 41 (2): 75-86. https://doi.org/10.1207/s15326985ep4102_1.

Knowles, Malcom S. 1968. "Andragogy—Not Pedagogy." *Adult Learning* 16 (10): 350-352.

Knowles, Malcom S. 1980. *The Modern Practice of Adult Education: From Pedagogy to Andragogy: Revised and Updates.* New York: Association Press.

Knowles, Malcom S. 1984. *Andragogy in Action: Applying Modern Principles of Adult Learning.* San Francisco: Jossey-Bass.

Kuhlmann, Meinard. 2011. "Mechanisms in Dynamically Complex Systems." In *Causality in the Sciences*, edited by Phyllis McKay Illari, Federica Russo, and Jon Williamson, 880-906. Oxford: Oxford University Press.

Mayer, Richard E. 2004. "Should There Be a Three-Strikes Rule Against Pure Discovery Learning?" *American Psychologist* 59 (1): 14-19. https://doi.org/10.1037/0003-066X.59.1.14.

McGann, Marek. 2020. "Convergently Emergent: Ecological and Enactive Approaches to the Texture of Agency." *Frontiers in Psychology*, 11. https://doi.org/10.3389/fpsyg.2020.01982.

Misch, Donald A. 2002. "Andragogy and Medical Education: Are Medical Students Internally Motivated to Learn?" *Advances in Health Sciences Education* 7 (2): 153-160. https://doi.org/10.1023/A:1015790318032.

Ranganathan, Rajiv, and Andrew Driska. 2023. "Is Premature Theorizing Hurting Skill Acquisition Research?" *Frontiers in Sports and Active Living*, 5. https://doi.org/10.3389/fspor.2023.1185734.

Schön, D. A. 1983. *The Reflective Practitioner: How Practitioners Think in Action.* San Francisco: Harper Collins.

Stoszkowski, John, and Dave Collins. 2014. "Communities of Practice, Social Learning and Networks: Exploiting the Social Side of Coach Development." *Sport, Education and Society* 19 (6): 773-788. https://doi.org/10.1080/13573322.2012.692671.

Stoszkowski, John, Àine MacNamara, Dave Collins, and Aran Hodgkinson. 2020. "'Opinion and Fact, Perspective and Truth': Seeking Truthfulness and Integrity in Coaching and Coach Education." *International Sport Coaching Journal* 8 (2): 263-269. https://doi.org/10.1123/iscj.2020-0023.

Taylor, Robin D., Jamie Taylor, Michael Ashford, and Rosie Collins. 2023. "Contemporary Pedagogy? The Use of Theory in Practice: An Evidence-Informed Perspective." *Frontiers in Sports and Active Living* 5: 1113564. https://doi.org/10.3389/fspor.2023.1113564.

Wiliam, Dylan. 2013. "Assessment: The Bridge Between Teaching and Learning." *Voices From the Middle* 21 (January): 15-20.

INDEX

Note: The italicized *f* and *t* following page numbers refer to figures and tables, respectively.

A

Abraham, A. 144
ACT (attentional control theory) 132, 132*f*
action. *See also* perception-action coupling
  beliefs and 49
  efficiency of 28
  types of 28
action and emotion strategies 131
active inference 25, 28
active treatment 63
activity design
  blending of concepts across theories 77*t*
  case study 97
  focus of activity 79-80
  intentions for impact and 78*f*
  nature of activity 80
  task constraints 79
Adams, J. 18
adaptability 24
adaptive expertise 2, 46-47, 48
affective learning design 83, 95
affordances 23, 79, 161-162
age of learner 1, 8
Aguilar, F. 45
alpha performance plan 151-152, 164, 164*f*
andragogy 185, 186*f*
anticipatory coding 124
anxiety 124-125, 132
arousal levels 124-125
associative stage 20
assurance stage 104
athlete management 129-130. *See also* preperformance phase
athletes. *See also* performer experience
  action and emotion strategies 131
  benefits of MAP for 131
  buy-in from 4, 152
  care toward 150
  confidence 75, 77, 106, 134, 137, 158
  curriculum 88, 88*t*, 90
  emotional investment 131, 133
  individual differences 74, 125, 160, 166
  meaningful goals of 131, 135
  perceptions of consequence 131-133, 134
  personal characteristics of 146-147
  pressure proofing 134
  self-efficacy 75, 77, 158

  self-identity 177
  understanding, optimizing 174
  wants and needs 75, 80-81, 150
Atkinson, R. 16
attention. *See* focus
attentional control theory (ACT) 132, 132*f*
attributions 131
augmented cues 103
augmented feedback 67, 138
automaticity 19, 65, 91, 108
autonomous stage 20
autonomy 175

B

backward and forward thinking 88-89
backward planning 88-90, 144
Bakker, A. 8
baseball study 64
basketball 47, 68*t*
BPS. *See* biopsychosocial (BPS) model
behavioral analysis tools 81-82
behavioral outcomes 187
beliefs 48-49
beta versions of performance 164-165, 164*f*, 166, 167*f*
bias
  coach beliefs and 49
  examples 50*t*
  study design and 62-63
  theoretical approaches and 62-63, 73
big five approach to decision making 184-185, 185*t*
big five trait characteristics 143
bio-informational theory 118
biomechanists 61, 178
biopsychosocial (BPS) model
  applications of 8-10
  case study 160
  components of 45*f*
  examples 8*f*, 158
  performance environment and 44
  support staff considerations and 178, 180
Bjork, Bob 10
Bjork, Elizabeth 10
Black, Neil 110
blocked practice 33, 33*f*, 66*f*, 76, 77
Bobrownicki, R. 55
Bortoli, L. 130

bottom-up perspective 26, 34-35, 53, 54, 149
boxing 68
BPS. *See* biopsychosocial model
Burke, V. 152

C

CAIS (Coach Analysis Intervention System) 81
case conceptualization 4, 108, 117
catastrophe theory 125
causality 144
CDM (classical decision making) 54, 75, 144
challenge
  desirable difficulties and 10-11, 80, 92
  error rate and 92
  meso level 94-95
  micro level 92-93
  role for performers 92
challenge point theory 92, 95
Chelladurai, P. 146
child development 8-9
Chow, J. 40
Christensen, W. 127
CLA. *See* constraints-led approach (CLA)
Clarke, Steve 179
classical decision making (CDM) 54, 75, 144
closed-loop control 18
Coach Analysis Intervention System (CAIS) 81
coaches. *See also* professional development for practitioners
  attitude to learning 187
  behaviors 81-83
  evaluation of 109
  expertise 45-47
  self-driven development 183, 185-186
  theoretical focus of 184
  types of thinking 75
coaching practice. *See also* activity design; coaching sessions; coaching styles
  application of theories 43-44
  conditionality of 4, 75-76, 186-187
  criticality 47-52
  curiosity in 51
  directionality of 144
  evidence-informed 40, 40*f*, 75, 102, 184

(continued)

223

224 Index

coaching practice. *(continued)*
    feedback, giving 138-140
    grand unifying theory of 184
    intentions 129, 133-134, 137, 140
    learning styles and 7-8
    methods 76, 76f
    pedagogic agility 44
    principles of andragogy for 186f
    reflection on experiences 49, 51, 54
    skeptical approach to 183, 184
    sport challenges in 41
    stakeholder communications 181
    supporting high-level performers 108-111

coaching sessions. *See also* practices
    big five approach to reviewing 184-185, 185t
    content 135
    format 91
    framing of sessions 134-135
    goals of 135
    intensity 135
    intention 78
    purpose 135
    sequencing 136
    social dynamics and 136
    structure and design 129, 134-136
    traditional format 91
    volume of 136

coaching styles
    canopies of 82-83
    case study 97
    changing over time 84
    clusters of 80, 82t
    coach behavior and 81-83
    concept of 80
    descriptions of 82t
    key considerations 81f
    performer needs and 80-81
    in preperformance phase 136-138
    problem setting and solving 81
    spectrum theory 3-4, 3f

coconstruction process 152
cocreation of curriculum 88
cognitive approach
    application 69
    case study 70
    computer metaphor for 17-18, 19
    description of 5
    information processing *versus* interactive, bottom-up perspective 34-35
    lack of unified explanation in 32
    learning in 19-20
    open- and closed-loop control 18
    versus other approaches 4-5, 39-40
    schema theory in 10-19
    theory *versus* practical application 32-34, 60

cognitive load 20, 67
cognitive load theory 75
cognitive stage of learning 19-20
collective efficacy 9
combination training 104, 128
command canopy 83
communication management 153
communities of practice (CoP) 51-52
comparison studies 61-62, 63-64
computer metaphor 17-18, 19
conditionality
    of coaching approach 4, 75-76, 78, 79
    coaching style and 81
    consequential consideration and 3
    explicit approach to teaching 186-187
    of knowledge application 52
    professional judgment and decision making and 2-3, 54
    risk and 137
    SMM development method 165

confidentiality 153
constrained action hypothesis 32
constrain to afford 78, 79
constraints-led approach (CLA) 23, 24, 60, 64, 64t, 78-79
constraints triangle model 5f
constructive conflict 152
contextual factors 144
contextual interference 19, 33-34, 76, 78
contextual priors 123, 124, 126, 163
CoP (communities of practice) 51-52
coping models 20
coping skills 158
cricket 84, 158
criticality
    adaptive expertise and 48, 49
    in appraisal of practice sessions 51
    case for 2, 43-44
    concept of 47-48
    developing 31, 51
    practical implications 52-55
    role modeling and 153

critical thinking 47-48, 51
Csikszentmihalyi, M. 125
cues 103, 126, 161
culture 172. *See also* team culture
curriculum 88, 88t, 90
curriculum knowledge 145

D

dark leadership 147, 150
dark room problem 37
decision making. *See also* professional judgment and decision making
    big five approach to 184-185, 185t
    classical 54, 75, 144
    dual systems theory of 144

    leadership and 146
    naturalistic 54, 144, 145
    performance environment and 44
    recognition primed 161
    speed of 148, 161, 165, 166

decision-making stage 18
declarative knowledge 44, 75, 163
deliberate practice 91, 92
deliberative actions 28
deliberative planning 97f
deliberative thinking 75, 89, 90, 145, 146
demonstrations 20
demotivation 150, 158, 161
dependent variables 64
derring effect 11
desirable difficulties 10-11, 80, 92
developmental stage 1
Dhami, M. 105
difficulty levels 10-11, 80, 92, 95
direct instruction 5, 7-8, 20
directionality 144
direct perception-action coupling 60
discovery learning 7-8, 74
distraction control 117, 124, 126, 127
domain-specific skills 46-47
downregulation 131
drills 24, 104
drive theory 124
dry drilling 106
dual systems theory 144
dynamic contextual priors 124
dynamic priori 163

E

Eastabrook, C. 48
ecological dynamics (EcoD) approach
    application 69
    case study 70
    components of 21-24
    conceptual clarity 36
    constraints triangle model 5f
    description 5
    existence of internal representations in 36-37
    frameworks in 78
    learning in 24
    limitations for coaching 35-36
    versus other approaches 4-5, 39-40
    performers' knowledge and 75-76
    shared affordances in 161-162
    skill level and 91
    summary of 24

ecological psychology 21
effector (output stage) 18
either-or problem
    application of approaches 69
    case study 69-71

lack of comparison studies 61-62
origins of 60-61
research bias and 62-69
solution to 61
elite performers 102. *See also* high-level performers
embedded skills 104
embodied cognition 7*t*
embodiment 34
emotional consequences 131, 133
emotional disturbance 94
emotional investment 131
emotional periodization 107
emotional profile 130*t*
emotional regulation 108
emotion-based strategies 137
enacted curriculum 88, 90
Entwistle, Noel 187
environment
complexity 52, 53
knowledge of 23
multisensory 22-23
novel 29
performance 44-45
predictability 28
psychosocial factors in 159
representativeness 22, 105
epistemic foraging 25
epistemological chain 3, 48-49
equity 152-153
errors
challenge level and 92
consequences 94
deliberately making and correcting 11
performance safety and 94
in prediction 26-27
types of 93-94, 93*f*
especial skills 19
evaluations
of coaches 109
of performance 121-124
performance safety and 94
for skill-acquisition support 109
team performance reviews 176
evidence-based information 12, 75
evidence-informed practice 40, 40*f*, 75, 102, 184
execution stage 91
expansion 90
expectation effects 134
experienced performers. *See* high-level performers
experimentation 16, 24
expertise
adaptable nature of 2, 46-47, 48
generative models and 26
routine 45, 46, 47

explicit knowledge 52
explicit motor learning 68*t*
exploitation 90
exploration 90, 91, 92, 93
exploratory learning 90, 94
explore-exploit continuum 29
explore-test continuum 90-92
external focus 10, 64, 64*t*, 126
external perspective 120
external stakeholders 180-181
external validity 67

F
fatigue 104, 136
feedback
augmented 67, 138
delivery of 139
from learner 51
loops 18
negative *versus* positive perception of 138-139
overly positive 150
in preperformance phase 138-140
relevance of 140
sources of 139, 140
video 103
fencing 122
Feynman, Richard 16
fidelity 98, 98*t*, 106-107
financial factors 159
Fitts, P. 19, 91
Fitts's law 119
five A model 103-104, 103*t*
flow 125
focus
case study in motorsports 127
creation of 125-126
cues and 126
distraction control and 117, 124, 126, 127
experimental manipulations 64, 64*t*
internal *versus* external 10, 32, 64, 64*t*, 126
optimal levels 124-125
prediction error and 27
priming and 126
football, American 41, 54, 150
four Es paradigm 6, 7*t*
Frade, Victor 165
framing 134-135
free energy principle 25, 37
functional equivalence theory 118
functional task difficulty 95
functional variability 78, 79-80

G
Gallicchio, G. 64
generalized motor programs 5, 18

generative model 26, 26*f*
Gibbs' cycle 121, 122*f*
Gibson, James 21
goals 116, 131, 135
golf 64-65, 70-71, 135
gossip 153
Gray, R. 64
group dynamics
performer perception and 150
push and pull factors in 150
research on 150
role clarity, acceptance, and reinforcement in 149, 151, 152
role modeling and 153
shared mental models and 151-152
standards and 151
top-down and bottom-up dynamics 149
guide discovery canopy 83

H
habitual actions 28
Hamilton, Bruce 110
heutagogy 186
high-level performers
case studies of 104, 105
embedding skills in 104
execution under pressure 107-108
fidelity and 106-107
optimizing support for 108-111
representative design needs 105-106
skill refinement for 103-104, 103*t*
skill shaping 105
skill switching 104
as special case 101-102
high-risk sports 107
Hodges, N. 95
Holmes, P. 119
human needs 175
hybrid model 127

I
if-then plans 97
imagery
case study 122
defined 118
functions of 106, 119, 120*t*
instruction giving and 68
models 119-121
terminology for 32
theoretical approaches alignment with 119, 120-121
theoretical explanations for 118-119
use of 20
implicit motor learning 67, 68*t*
in-action reflection 49, 54
individual differences 74, 125, 160, 166
individualized instruction 34

226 Index

individual zone of optimal functioning (IZOF) 125
inequity 152-153
information
confidentiality 153
hierarchy of source credibility 50*t*
need-to-know basis 153
sources 126, 181
information-processing approach. *See* cognitive approach
injuries
perception of 159
role clarity in 110, 110*f*
innovation skills 47
inquiry-based instruction 7-8
instruction
demonstrations 20
direct 5, 7-8, 20
imagery and 68
individualized approach to 34
of study participants 66-68
verbal 67, 68
integration 180
intention 126
intentions for impact 76, 76*f*, 78*f*, 81*f*, 88, 89, 96-97
interdisciplinary teams 109-111, 110*f*
internal constraints 5, 24, 119
internal focus 10, 64, 64*t*, 126
internal motivation 186
internal representations 6, 19, 20, 25-26, 36-37, 106, 120
internal validity 63
internal visual perspective 120
interpersonal factors 143
intuitive thinking 75, 97, 145, 161
inverted-U theory 125
it depends approach
debates about 11
evidence for 12
examples 3-4, 7-8, 10
explanation for why 2-3
overview 1-2
practical implications of 52-55
IZOF (individual zone of optimal functioning) 125

J
javelin 104
Jong, T. 7

K
Kellerman, B. 130
Kirschner, P. 146
knowledge
adaptive application of 2
cognitive load and 75

conditional 2-3
curriculum 145
declarative 44, 75, 163
diversity of 52
explicit 52
metacognitive 163
need-to-know basis 153
prior experience as 75, 76
procedural 75, 79, 163
reproducing 137
sharing 51, 52, 52*f*
source credibility 49, 50*t*
tacit 52, 75
Knowles approach 185, 186*f*
Kolb's reflective cycle 121*f*

L
Lang, P. 32
layered stimulus and response training 32
leadership
big five trait characteristics and 143-144
components of 146
dark leadership 147, 150
factors affecting 144, 146
multidimensional model of 147*f*
multilingual 146-147
performer characteristics and 146-147
role clarity and 147-149
servant type 144
value of movement outcomes and processes and 175
learners. *See also* performer experience
at center of process 9-10, 74, 87-88
feedback from 51
principles of andragogy for 186*f*
self-confidence 9, 75
skill level 9, 65, 91, 137
learning. *See also* motor learning
affective 83, 95
coaching style and 7-8
in cognitive approach 19
contexts 44
contextual interference and 33-34
in ecological dynamics approach 24
from experience 186
explicit *versus* implicit 67, 68*t*
exploratory 90, 94
golden rules for 88
immediate application of 186
objectives 89
on- and off-field 165
personal drive for 186
in predictive processing approach 28-29
readiness 186
retention 33, 66, 77, 78, 89, 91

stages of 19-20
transfer 19, 33, 33*f*, 77, 95
legal factors 45*t*
long-term planning 92
long-term retention 33, 77, 78, 89, 91
looming 21

M
MacNamara, A. 158
macro level 52, 53, 55
management meetings 153
Manchester City rugby 161, 162, 163
MAP. *See* multi-action planning
Mariani, L. 92
measurement variables 65-66
mechanistic approach 16
meetings 153
mental imagery. *See* imagery
mental representations. *See* internal representations
mental resources 130*t*
mental skills. *See also* focus; imagery; reflection
application of 117-118
case conceptualization and 117
combining 126-128
evolution of 115-117
intention for impact for 117
PCDE framework of 116, 117*f*, 147
meshed control theory 108, 127
meso level challenge 94-95
meso level planning 52, 53, 55
metacognition 10, 47, 163-164
metacognitive knowledge 163
metacognitive skills 47, 163
micro level challenge 92-93
micro level planning 52, 53, 55
mindless state 34
miscommunication 153
mistakes. *See* errors
modeling movement 20
modern sport, conceptualization 46*f*
Mosston, M. 3, 80, 137
motivation 138, 175, 186
motor-action controversy 12
motor commands 28, 38
motor control 28
motor learning. *See also* learning
explicit 62, 67
implicit 67
motor predictions 28, 38
motor programs 5, 18
motorsport 106, 107, 127
movement
awareness 103
control 130*t*
execution 91, 107-108, 130-131

quality 130t
selection 91
moving walkway example 22
multi-action planning
attentional control theory and 132, 132f
optimal performance in 125
overview 130t
performance types in 130-131, 130t
thinking types 108, 144
multidirectional influences 173
multilingual leadership 146-147
multi-theoretical perspective 6, 40-41
mushin (Japanese state) 34

N

National Football League 150
naturalistic decision making (NDM) 54, 144, 145
need-to-know basis 153
negative emotional states 94
nested planning
case studies 53, 145
curriculum knowledge and 145
decision making types 144-145
levels in 52-53
WIN decisions and 146
neural activity 74, 90-91
neuronal organization 37
neuroscience 16, 25, 38
Newell. K. 91
Nonaka, I. 51
nonlinear pedagogy (NLP) 23, 24, 78
novelty seeking 90

O

off-field meetings 148
Olympic level athletes 149. *See also* high-level performers
on-action reflection 49, 54
open-loop control 18
optimal skill templates 20, 62, 80, 118

P

Paivio, A. 119
pan-theoretical process 61
parent influences 181
PCDE (Psychological Characteristics of Developing Excellence) 116, 117f, 147
pedagogic applications 7-11
peer pressure 175
perceived equity 152-153, 175
perceived threats 131, 132
perception
in cognitive approach 18
direct *versus* indirect 21f
in ecological approach 21-22
in predictive processing approach 25

perception-action coupling 22, 60, 161
perceptual attunement 37, 124
perceptual-motor landscape 69
performance
anxiety and 124-125, 132
athlete management 129-130
conscious control 130
debriefs 123
environment 44-45
evaluations 121-124
inverted-U theory of arousal 125
movement execution during 130-131
perceptions of consequence and 131-133
plans 151-152
reviews 176
types 130-131, 130t, 132-133, 132f
vision of 164-165, 164f
performance analysts 178
performance psychology 179
performance safety 94
performer experience
backward planning and 88-90
case study 96-97
centeredness 74-75
challenge level and 92-94
for coach decision making 89f, 90f, 96f
curriculum levels and 88, 88t
desired interaction with activity 90-91, 91t
fidelity of practice and 95-98, 98t
intentions for impact and 88, 96-97
overview of 87-88
support 44
performers. *See* athletes
periodization
emotional 107
psychological 107
tactical 165, 169
personality characteristics 143-144
PESTLE model 45, 45t
PETTLEP model 119, 121f, 173
physical fatigue 104
Pill, S. 80, 137
Pinder, R. 105
PJDM. *See* professional judgment and decision making (PJDM)
placebo effect 27
planning
backward and forward 88-90
case study in 53
coaching methods and 76, 76f
deliberative 89, 97f
nested 52-53, 144-146
ongoing 166
process 52
usefulness of 145

play 29
post-performance reviews 132
PP approach. *See* predictive processing (PP) approach
pracademic approach 16, 60-61
practices. *See also* activity design; coaching sessions
blocked 33, 33f, 66f, 76, 77
drills 24, 104
dry drilling 106
fidelity of 95, 98, 98t
part-progressive 78
random 33, 33f, 66f, 78
representative design and 22, 35, 95, 98
retention after delays in 66f
schedules 33-34
session format 91
specificity 95
unopposed 106
variability in 19, 76
whole and part 98
prediction error 26-27, 28, 37
predictive coding 25
predictive processing (PP) approach
approach overview 25
basic schema 27f
case study 71
free energy principle and 25
generative models and 26-27
importance of motor predictions 28
learning in 28-29
neurophysiological evidence 37-38
versus other approaches 39-40
philosophical challenge 37
practical application 38, 69, 71
shared understandings in 162
simplified picture in action 26f
team coordination implications 39, 162
preperformance phase
athletes management challenges in 131-133
case study of 140
coaching feedback in 138-140
coaching intentions in 133-134
coaching structure and design 134-136
coaching style in 136-138
description of 129-130, 133
time factor in 137
preservative actions 28
pressure proofed 134
pressure training 91, 94
priming 126
priors 26, 76, 81, 92, 123
problem solving 81
procedural knowledge 75, 79, 163
professional conversations 52

228 Index

professional development for practitioners
andragogic approaches 185, 186f
attitude to learning 187
big five approach, adopting 184-185, 185t
communities of practice and 51
development of conditionality 186-187
focus areas 184
heutagogy approaches 186
overview 183-184
SECI knowledge-sharing model and 51-52, 52f
professional judgment and decision making (PJDM)
description 2-3
intentions for impact and 89
nested planning and 53-55
versus theoretically based paradigm 39, 184
types of decision making 54
why question in 11
psychobehavioral skills 158
Psychological Characteristics of Developing Excellence (PCDEs) 116, 117f, 147
psychological load 136
psychological needs 175, 180
psychological periodization 107
psychological safety 94, 150
psychologists 178
psychology
in BPM model 8-9
definition 16
for sport 116
of sport 116
through sport 116
psychoneuromuscular theory 118
psychosocial domain. *See also* biopsychosocial model; shared mental models
case study 160
interactions in 158
metacognition in 10, 47, 163-164
support staff considerations 160
team performance and 158-161
psychosocial skills 158
push and pull factors 150
push-drill-play enabled variation 107
psychological factors 8

Q
quiet eye (QE) 125

R
RAE (relative age effect) 8
random practice 33, 33f, 66f, 78
realistic performance evaluations 121-124

real-world settings
conditionality and 55f
fidelity and 98
making sense of 49, 51
shared mental models and 163, 165
theory *versus* application 32-33, 34, 39, 43
recall schema 18
recognition primed decision making (RPDM) 161
recognition schema 18-19
reflection
for action 123-124
on action 49, 54, 121, 123
challenge level and 95
Gibbs' cycle 122f
in-action 49, 54, 124
Kolb's cycle 121f
tools for 123
regulation
dimension of sport 45
emotional 108
self-regulatory skills 108, 116-117
reinvestment theory 32
relatedness 175
relative age effect (RAE) 8
repetition 6, 24, 104
repetition without repetition 78
representation wars 40
representative design
conditionality and 78, 98
fidelity of practice and 95, 98, 98t
high-level performer need for 105-106
as limitation to EcoD approach 35, 95
of practice environment 6, 9, 22, 24, 35
research. *See* skill-acquisition research; study designs
retention 33, 66, 66f, 77, 78, 89, 91
retrieval process 91
review-then-apply cycle 35
rewards 174, 175, 176, 180
Richards, P. 148, 164
risk management 138
role acceptance 148, 149, 151, 152
role clarity 110-111, 110f, 147-149, 175
role modeling 153, 175
role reinforcement 148, 149, 151, 152
roller derby 159, 167
routine expertise 45, 46, 47
RPDM (recognition primed decision making) 161
rugby 150, 161

S
safety 94, 150
satisficing 117

scaffold canopy 83
schema theory 18-19
Schmidt, R. 18, 108
SDT(self-determination theory) 175
sea kayaking 53
SECI knowledge-sharing model 51-52, 52f
selection of movement pattern 91
selection pressure 94
self-concept 186
self-control 136
self-determination theory (SDT) 175
self-efficacy 75, 77, 106, 158
self-esteem 176, 177
self-organization 22, 24, 25, 37, 65
self-regulatory skills 108, 116-117
sensemaking 145
sensory inputs 18
servant leadership 144
Shamrock, Frank 28
shared affordances 161-162
shared mental models (SMMs)
case study 167
desired intentions and 151-152
development methods 164
knowledge areas in 161
metacognition and 163-164
predictive processing and 162
recognition primed decision making and 161
soccer examples 167f
tactical periodization and 165-168, 167f
for team performance 9, 163
vision of performance and 164-165, 164f
short-term adaptation 89
simulations 98, 106
situational awareness 47
situational comprehension 47
situational demands 47
skiing 46f
skill-acquisition research. *See also* study designs
bias in 49, 50t, 62-63, 73
comparison studies, lack of 61-62
external validity 67
fallibility of findings 74
future directions 187
gap between practice and 74
history of 60-61
pragmatic view on 74
skill-acquisition specialists
for high-level performers 108
interdisciplinary teams and 109-111, 110f

Index **229**

need for 109
social context of 61
value of 179-180
skill analysis 103
skill level 9, 65, 91, 137
skills
in adaptive expertise 46-47
adjustment stage 103
awareness stage 103
changing 103
embedding 104
metacognitive 163
reautomation 103-104
refinement 91, 103-104, 103t, 126
retention 33, 77, 78, 89, 91
shaping 103, 105
stabilization 90, 91
switching 103, 104
templates for 20, 62, 80, 118
transfer of 92
types 1
sleep learning 107
SMART goals 116
SMMs. *See* shared mental models (SMMs)
soccer 166, 167f
social context 61, 159
social dynamics 136
social identity 176
social isolation 159
social milieu 146, 159
social pressures 152
social systems 39
socioeconomic status 159
sociological factors 8, 9, 144
source credibility 50t
source of information 126, 181
specificity 95
spectrum theory 3-4, 3f
sport
high-risk 107
oppositional types 92
participation challenges 159
two-axes conceptualization 45, 46f
sport psychology 109, 115, 116
squads. *See* teams
stakeholders 172, 180-181
static priori 163
stereotypes 177
stimulus and response training 32
structured practices 148
study designs
attentional focus manipulations in 64, 64t
constraints-led conditions in 64, 64t
control or comparison group 63-64

measures in 65-66
methodological components within 63t
outcome bias 62-63
participant instructions and 66-69
tasks in 64-65
subroutines 18, 20, 21
Suesee, B. 3
support staff
for high-level performers 108-111
integration 180
interdisciplinary teams 109-111, 110f
psychosocial interactions with 160
role clarity 110-111, 110f, 160
shaping value through 178-180
timing of use 180
surprises 25, 26, 37, 108, 162
symbolic learning theory 118

T
tacit knowledge 52
tactical periodization (TP) 165-168, 167f
tactical thinking 108
task constraints 79, 95
task variables 64-65
teaching styles 3f, 137. *See also* coaching styles
team culture
athlete understanding and 174
correctness 171
defined 172
ingroup perceptions 177
multidirectional influences on 172
multiple identities usage 179
normality in 172-174
relevance of 172-174
rewards and 174, 175, 176, 180
selection and review processes and 176
self-esteem and 176, 177
social identity and 176-178
stakeholder management and 180-181
support staff role and 178-180
value optimization and 174-176
team games 35
team management. *See also* support staff; team culture
performance reviews 176
role of value in groups 174-175
selection process 176
shaping value 176
stakeholder communications 180-181
team identity and 176-178, 179
team performance. *See also* shared mental models (SMMs)
case study 160
coordination and 39, 162

metacognition, role of 163-164
psychosocial considerations in 158-161
reviews 176
shared understanding for 161-162
teams. *See also* group dynamics
collective efficacy in 9
identity 176-178, 179
selection for 176
theoretical approaches to skill acquisition. *See also* cognitive approach; ecological dynamics approach; either-or problem; predictive processing approach
applying single approaches 69-71, 184
basis for multi-theoretical perspective 6, 40-41
bias and 62-63, 73
blending of 74, 75-76, 184
case study 41
comparison studies, lack of 61-62
criteria for goodness 16-17
differences among 39-40
evaluation of 31-32
factors affecting relevance 33
functionality 16
historical evolution 16-17
mental skills alignment to 118
practical application 6, 33, 38, 70-71
pragmatic integration in planning 55, 55f
pragmatic view of 74
simplicity in explanation 16
study design and 63-69
thinking
backward and forward 88-89
cycles 152
types 108, 144-145
thinking slow to think fast 148
top-down processes 26, 53, 54, 132, 149
TP (tactical periodization) 165-168, 167f
traditional approach. *See* cognitive approach
transfer of learning 19, 33, 33f, 77, 95

U
upregulation 131

V
validity 63
values
actions and 49
alignment 174f
coaching tools for shaping 176-181
continuum of 48
optimization 174-175
variable practice 18, 76, 77, 84
verbal instructions 67, 68

video analysis 123, 165
video feedback 103
virtual reality 98
vision of performance 164-165, 164*f*

W
weightlifting 105
why question 2-3
WIN decisions 146

Y
young athletes 8-9, 137, 160
Z
zone of uncomfortable debate 52, 152

ABOUT THE EDITORS

Dave Collins, PhD, earned a doctorate in psychology from the University of Surrey in 1990. He is currently the director of Grey Matters UK, a performance-focused company that offers applied consultancy services in sports, business, performing arts, and more. He is also a professor at the University of Edinburgh, an institution ranked in the world's top 20 by QS World University Rankings. Collins has written over 450 peer-reviewed publications and has authored or contributed to 90 books. His research interests include performer and coach development, expertise, and peak performance. As a practitioner, Collins has worked with more than 90 world-class athletes or Olympic medalists as well as professional athletic teams and performers. He is the director of the Rugby Coaches Association, a fellow of the Society of Martial Arts, a fellow of the British Association of Sport and Exercise Sciences (BASES), and an associate fellow of the British Psychological Society. Collins is a former Royal Marine and a fifth dan in karate.

Jamie Taylor, PhD, earned a doctorate in psychology from the University of Edinburgh in 2020. He is currently an assistant professor and lecturer in coaching and elite performance at Dublin City University. As a senior coach developer at Grey Matters UK, Taylor offers ongoing contributions to the development of coaches and coach supporters in athletics, netball, rugby union, football, adventure sports, and the Special Olympics. He has worked with over 150 coaches in a developmental capacity and consulted across a wide range of sports and contexts, including Olympic and Paralympic programs. While working with the English Institute of Sport, Taylor supported the creation of the Coach Developer CIMSPA standards. His research focus spans across performance enhancement in sport, specifically in coaching, coach development, high performance, and talent development.

ABOUT THE CONTRIBUTORS

Michael Ashford, PhD, is a coach developer and postdoctoral researcher working across a number of sport-based contexts. His current work includes supporting the development of England Rugby's international coaches throughout their performance pathway, leading coach development at Aviron Bayonnais Rugby in France, and conducting a two-year independent postdoctoral research position exploring coaching expertise in Premier League Category 1 football academies. Previously, through Grey Matters Performance, Ashford also worked within Olympic sports, supporting coaches working in individual and team sports. He has also worked as an academic within the sports coaching discipline, at the University of Edinburgh, Coventry University, and Leeds Beckett University.

Ray Bobrownicki is a lecturer in sport psychology, a chartered psychologist, and a licensed coach (jumping events). He is an associate fellow of the British Psychological Society and a fellow of the Higher Education Academy. He joined the Institute for Sport, Physical Education, and Health Sciences at the University of Edinburgh in November 2021 and is currently program codirector for their BSc applied sport science program. Before this, he worked at the University of the West of Scotland (2016-2021), where he was program leader for the BSc sport coaching degree. Alongside his academic roles, Bobrownicki has been actively involved in real-world sports in a number of capacities, including as an athlete (e.g., high jumper and Commonwealth Games finalist), a coach (e.g., to Scottish record holder in the women's high jump), a referee (e.g., basketball), and a consultant (e.g., Glasgow Athletics Association). Bobrownicki's interests relate to interdisciplinary research and practice, linking sport psychology, coaching instruction, and motor learning and performance. His recent research has focused on exploring the impact of coaching instruction (e.g., traditional verbal instructions or analogies) on performance, movement, and psychological factors (e.g., understanding, confidence, and motivation) in both learning and competition environments.

Howie J. Carson, PhD, received his doctorate in 2014 from the University of Central Lancashire for his study on motor skill refinement in elite-level performers. This research incorporated the fields of motor behavior, sport coaching, sport psychology, and biomechanics. Between 2014 and 2019, Carson was employed as a research fellow in motor skill development and coaching at the University of Central Lancashire, and he is currently a senior lecturer in motor learning and control at the University of Edinburgh. Within this role, he leads the Human Performance Science Research Group and is program codirector of the BSc applied sport science degree. Across a range of applied topics—including skill acquisition and refinement, coach decision making, performance under pressure, and talent development—he has published over 65 peer-reviewed journal articles and book chapters. Professionally, Carson is a BASES-accredited sport and exercise scientist within the interdisciplinary subject area for both support and research. He is a chartered scientist and is a fellow of the Professional Golfers' Association of GB&I. Reflecting these roles, he has worked with performers and organizations across a variety of performance contexts, including golf, archery, motor sport, dance, cricket, and rugby.

Loel Collins, DProf, works at the University of Edinburgh in the Moray House School for Education and Sport. He has an applied research focus and a particular interest in the field of coaching and decision making in hyperdynamic environments such as adventure sports and emergency response. Collins' earlier career was as an outdoor instructor, adventure sports coach, sea kayaking and canoe guide, and emergency response trainer. He holds a wide range of U.K. coaching and guiding qualifications, notably in canoeing and kayaking, free-heel skiing, mountaineering, and rescue and emergency care. He has taught outdoor education for over 35 years. He is a prolific author with over 100 books, book chapters, magazine articles, and academic peer-reviewed papers in his fields of interest. He has explored some of the deepest and most remote gorges in the world by kayak. He has also competed in international competitions in both canoe and kayak. He currently divides his time between the university and sea kayak guiding in the Arctic and Antarctica.

Rosie Collins, PhD, CPsychol, is a chartered sport psychologist with extensive experience across a diverse range of performance domains. Having started her training in motorsport, supporting drivers' development from Karting to GP2 level, Collins has since supported international-level athletes at Commonwealth Games, Olympic Games, and world championships in golf, modern pentathlon, and rugby sevens. Collins completed her PhD at the University of Edinburgh and has since published in the domains of skill execution, talent development, and decision making. At present, she splits her time between academia and professional practice, holding an assistant professor post with Dublin City University and supporting the English Football Association Women's Pathway teams.

FA/Evaldas Semiotas

Andrew Cruickshank, PhD, CPsychol, HCPC Registered, is a senior psychologist at Grey Matters Performance Ltd, with a primary responsibility of leading the delivery of integrated psychology services across Olympic, Paralympic, and professional sport performance programs. As part of this work—and the priority focus in other consultancies and projects—Cruickshank also provides coach education and development inputs for those operating in senior elite and talent pathway environments, spanning biological, psychological, and social aspects of athlete development and performance. From an academic perspective, Cruickshank holds a position at Dublin City University, supporting coaches, leaders, and support personnel in the institution's professional masters and doctorate courses. Cruickshank has also published over 30 peer-reviewed papers on coaching, leadership, culture, talent development, and other psychology-related topics, and he has contributed to various books on psychology and elite performance through written chapters and invited editorial roles.

Urvi Khasnis, PhD, completed her doctorate from the University of Edinburgh in 2022; her work focused on exploring impactful factors and alternative ways to facilitate sporting success in India. This research specifically looked at policies implemented by Indian sport as well as the quality of coaching and the broader coaching system within the country. Khasnis is currently a teaching fellow in sport psychology at the University of Edinburgh. Within this role, she is the director of the MSc performance psychology program and also contributes on the BSc applied sport science degree program. Professionally, Khasnis is a chartered psychologist, having completed her QSEP qualification in 2022. She is currently also employed as a performance psychologist at Grey Matters Performance Ltd. Within her applied experience, she has worked with a diverse range of individuals, groups, and organizations (in basketball, rugby, golf, and canoeing) to facilitate performance enhancement and development-related goals.

Amy Price works as a coach developer with Grey Matters Performance Ltd and as a national coach developer with the English Football Association (FA). In Price's role with the English FA, she develops and educates coaches in the women's senior professional game. Previous to Price's coach development role, she had a career in academia at St. Mary's University in Twickenham, London. A UEFA A Licence coach who started coaching in 2003 while playing for AFC Wimbledon Ladies, Price has experience in coaching both male and female teams at various levels. Most notably, Price coached England's U15 women's team and is currently coaching at Fulham FC Academy. Price's applied experience complemented her doctoral studies, where she investigated the role of game understanding for high-level youth soccer players. Price's PhD was under the supervision of Professor Dave Collins at the University of Edinburgh.